The Cavapoo Handbook

BY

LINDA WHITWAM

ISBN: 978-1090854810

Copyright

Acknowledgements

My sincere thanks to the dedicated Cavapoo breeders, owners and canine experts who have generously contributed their invaluable expertise. This is the 14th book in the Canine Handbook series and never have I experienced such an outpouring of love as shown by owners and breeders for their beloved Cavapoos in the pages of this book.

Specialist Contributors:

PETIT JEAN PUPPIES

LOTTIES CAVAPOOS

CALLA LILY CAVAPOO

DENISE KNIGHTLEY

Contributors:

Special thanks to: Laura Koch of Petit Jean Puppies, Charlotte Purkiss of Lotties Cavapoos, Brent and Windie of Calla Lily Cavapoo, Laura Lambert, Denise Knightley, Beverley Burlison, Claire Cornes, Dayna Rosindale, Gina Desmond, Hilary Morphy, June Hicks, Karen Howe, Kit Lam, Lindsey McDonald and Alex Kostiw, Rebecca Seabrook, Trevor and Tracey Nott, Val Boshart, Dr Sara Skiwski, Pets As Therapy and The Doodle Trust.

(Full details appear at the back of the book)

TABLE OF CONTENTS

1. Meet The Cavapoo

The Cavapoo is one of the most in-demand crossbreed dogs on the planet. Originally thought to have developed either in the USA or Australia, where it is known as the Cavoodle, this adaptable medium-sized canine with the big heart has shot vertically through the canine ranks to become a firm family favourite.

Cavapoos are highly affectionate, honest, handsome and good-natured. They get on well with other dogs, but most of all they love their humans. Sometimes described as a "Velcro dogs," these little Love Machines have boundless affection for their owners and love nothing more than snuggling up with them - preferably after a good walk.

When it comes to exercise, they can hike for hours once they have built up to it, but won't be bouncing around the house if they miss a walk.

Because they have sporting ancestry from both sides - the Poodle and the Cavalier King Charles Spaniel - some retain a certain amount of "drive", which means their active minds need exercising as well as their bodies. Many live quite happily with a cat at home, but think that chasing birds and small furry animals is a great game when outdoors, so teaching the recall from an early age is very important.

Our photo shows an adult Cavapoo with a five-week-old puppy.

All Cavapoos are playful and love toys and games. One breeder commented that Cavapoo puppies would even rather play than eat. You'll find they have their favourite toy or toys and devise their own games or special hiding places for them.

Like the Poodle, the Cavapoo can be quirky, and some will develop personal little rituals, such as doing the same things at the same time, guarding a precious toy or playing a game in a certain way - much to their owner's amusement. Your Cavapoo will not only make you laugh, but also warm your heart. As you will read, many owners are surprised at just how deeply they love their Cavapoos - and the feeling is reciprocated.

Cavapoos' eagerness to please and love of a challenge mean they can be relatively easily trained. As well as family pets, some go on to become certified therapy dogs that "read" with children, visit the sick in hospital and the elderly in nursing homes, and bring companionship and happiness to autistic children. They also love being given a chance to use their brains and burn off energy in agility and other canine competitions.

Cavapoos tick all the boxes for a family dog and are an excellent choice for first-time owners, as:

- ❧ They are medium-sized; not too big for a family home and not too small and delicate to get easily injured
- ❧ Many are "hypoallergenic" or low shedding
- ❧ They are adaptable when it comes to exercise

- They love children - provided both the kids and the puppy are taught to respect each other
- They are non-aggressive with other dogs
- They generally do not have dominance traits
- They are biddable, i.e. easy to train, if time is spent training early on, as they are quick learners and eager to please their owners
- They are easy-going and able to adapt to fit in well with family life
- They are friendly with everyone

For a detailed list of all the main Cavapoo traits, visit **Chapter 8. Cavapoo Behaviour.** If you are considering a Cavapoo but haven't yet got one, here are two points to consider:

1. The Cavapoo's life revolves around his or her people. This is not a dog that is happy being left alone for long periods. Separation anxiety is not uncommon if the dog has not got used to being alone at all when young. If you are out at work all day, consider a breed less reliant on humans for happiness.

2. The Cavapoo's beautiful coat is high maintenance and you'll need to factor in the expense of trips to the groomer every few weeks (unless you learn to clip the dog yourself) as well as regular home maintenance in between.

Pictured enjoying the high life in his private jet is Rondo, F1 Toy Cavapoo bred by Petit Jean Puppies. Photo courtesy of owner Jimmy Lee Hook.

Now you know a couple of the downsides, read on to learn just why Cavapoos have become so popular right across the world and what makes them tick.

History of The Poodle Cross

Like all of the oodles of Doodles and piles of Poos around today, the Cavapoo's success follows the creation and popularity of the Labradoodle, the first "designer crossbreed". The man credited with creating the first officially-recognised Labradoodles in 1989 was Wally Conron, Royal Guide Dog Association of Australia's breeding manager in Melbourne.

Wally received a request from Pat Blum, a visually-impaired woman living in Hawaii. She had never applied for a guide dog before because of her husband's allergy to dogs, and wrote to Wally in the hope that he might be able to help. Wally at first optimistically described her request as a "piece of cake." He had the novel idea of breeding the Labrador with the Standard Poodle. His goal was to combine the low-shedding coat of the Poodle with the gentleness and trainability of the Labrador. He hoped this would ultimately produce a service/guide dog suitable for people with allergies to fur and dander.

It took Wally several years and 33 disappointing trials, but, to cut a long story short, he achieved his goal. He produced three puppies, Sultan, Sheik and Simon. Coat and saliva samples were flown to Hawaii, but Pat's husband was allergic to two of the dogs. However, he had no reaction to Sultan, who went on become Pat's guide dog for 10 years. Sheik and Simon also had happy lives, one as a therapy dog and the other as a guide dog.

....

Breeders on Cavapoos

Three breeders have shared their in-depth knowledge and many years of experience with Cavapoos in this book. All three carry out extensive health testing on their dogs to ensure (as far as is scientifically possible) that their Cavapoo puppies are free from genetic disease. Unscreened dogs can pass on inherited diseases to their puppies.

If you haven't got your puppy yet or are thinking of getting a second Cavapoo, our advice is to choose a breeder who FULLY health tests his or her breeding dogs and ask to see the relevant certificates.

We asked our breeders what first attracted them to the Cavapoo and how they would describe the typical temperament, and this is what they said, starting with Laura Koch, of Petit Jean Puppies, Arkansas, USA, who has bred Cavapoos for 10 years: "I love both breeds; Cavaliers are so gentle-hearted and loving, but I have allergies so can't really handle a shedding breed in my home. Poodles are so intelligent and have great attachment to humans, so with the non-shed, it's just a win-win!"

Photo of these Petit Jean Puppies courtesy of Monique Pedersen, Pedersen Photography.

"The personalities of the Mini and Toy are different. We find that Miniature Poodles are more accepting of strangers and better with children and other dogs. That's not to say Toys are bad dogs; they are great, just different and are really more suited to older adult homes. It's always better to use a Poodle with heavier bone structure than a fine-boned Poodle so the Cavapoo retains the beautiful head and chest of the Cavalier.

"Cavapoos can look like little Teddy bears, even fully grown, and everyone wants to know what breed they are. We have people call us after seeing one of our Cavapoos in Central Park in New York and want to add one of these amazing dogs to their family. This happens all over the US! The typical temperament is comical, tender-hearted, playful, smart, monkey-like by using their paws to grab and cat-like by enjoying the back of the sofa. I've yet to see a Cavapoo with an Alpha-type personality; it's just not them. They are prissy, loyal and very bonded to their family.

"We find that Cavapoos are perfect for the first-time owner as well as a family with well-behaved young children. They are an easy breed for a first-time owner and are easily trained and don't challenge their owner much. They want to please and that makes training easy; the perfect family dog. If anything surprises people, it's how intelligent they are right off and how loving and cuddly they are."

Windie, hobby breeder of Calla Lily Cavapoo, Oklahoma, USA, has bred Cavapoos since 2006 and says: "Cavaliers make you smile; Cavapoos make you laugh out loud! I grew up with a Toy Poodle, while my grandmother had two Mini Poodles. Poodles are brilliant, and the combination of Poodle and Cavalier is "the cat's meow!" I am an Oncology RN (Registered Nurse) and dog therapy is special to my heart. Whether professionally or simply in their new family's homes, Cavapoos, in my opinion, are therapy to their humans' souls. They are smart, quick to train and please, playful yet laid back and they keep that puppy/Teddy bear-look into adulthood. A Cavapoo is happiest when around his or her people most of the time. I love them!"

Photo courtesy of Brent and Windie, Calla Lily Cavapoo.

Charlotte Purkiss, of Lotties Cavapoos, Hampshire, UK, has bred Cavapoos since 2012 and says: "I think what first attracted me to the Cavalier was the Teddy bear look, and then I soon realised that the Cavalier and Poodle mix created fantastic personalities. It's unreal how much love a Cavapoo has to give. They will become a best friend for all of their canine life, which can be up to 14 years.

"Cavapoos are really unique and special. They are cuddly and affectionate with an intelligent mind and SOOO much love to give you. They love a warm lap and follow you everywhere - even to the toilet! They get on with all animals if introduced slowly and each given their own space, and I have never had any problems homing my Cavapoos with families who already have other animals. They love lots of company, whether it be human or animal. Cavapoos are clever and thrive in the right conditions with the right family, although I personally do not place my puppies in families with children under five years of age.

"They love to please anyone and have different traits from the Cavalier and Poodle sides – they both have quirks too. Most Cavaliers like to cuddle up around your neck when called; this is called Cavalier Cuddles! The Poodle loves to jump up high into your arms and this trait is often passed on to Cavapoos.

....

Owners on Cavapoos

Experienced dog owner June Hicks: "Six months before we had to have our Westie put to sleep we decided to consider another dog and got Archie. I chose a Cavapoo for their temperament, nature, look, size and they are easy to train. It was a decision we have never regretted as it really helped us at the end.

"When we went to see Archie for the first time, we took Daisy with us and when we brought him home he loved having another dog to snuggle up with and they slept together. When we let Daisy out in the garden, Archie would follow and knew what to do. To this day I don't think we had any accidents, except when he was on his own in the kitchen and we had a few puddles - more as a telling off for us leaving him! Cavapoos certainly know how to get your attention. Archie is the most intelligent of all the dogs I have had and he's not two yet.

"Cavapoos are also extremely agile! Prepare for a puppy that loves to climb and reach heights, for example along the narrow back of the sofa. Archie also seems to be able to walk on his hind legs - meaning you do need to keep food well back on kitchen surfaces!"

Laura Lambert, founder of the UK Facebook Group All About Poos: "Dolly prefers humans to other dogs. She is more excited to see humans that to run round with other dogs, and she is brilliant with children. She is also very wimpy! Our vet has a note on Dolly's records that she has the lowest pain threshold of any dog. She will cry like she has been shot at the slightest discomfort. After spaying, she was crying and we took her back to the vet, but she was absolutely fine and stopped crying when we got there!"

Trevor and Tracey Nott: "We were searching for a dog that was fairly small, hypoallergenic, good with children and affectionate, and we got Ethel who's now five. She is very loving and affectionate, no trouble, easily trained and keen to please. She does, however, have a tendency to be nervous, a bit vocal and suffer from separation anxiety. She is very good with children; playful but will remove herself if she doesn't want to be involved if things get too noisy and boisterous. She is a good house dog, very vocal when anyone passes or comes to our house and she becomes very attached to those she likes. She settled in very quickly. Initially she slept in a crate in the bedroom, now she sleeps wherever she likes in the bedroom!"

Claire Cornes got Bob and Boris from the same litter two and a half years ago: "The first few months were very hard, especially with two; you need eyes in the back of your head! Please ensure you do your research before getting a puppy; it's hard work. You need a lot of time, patience and lots of love. Mine have never had any signs of "littermate syndrome." They both have their own little character and are very different.

"They are an affectionate, loving and loyal breed - and they are super gorgeous! They love humans and other Doodles and are brilliant around children. My two love being around my niece and godchildren, and I would definitely recommend Cavapoos to a family with children."

Gina Desmond: "Living in New York City, we wanted a dog that was small enough to enjoy the coziness of a city apartment, while still getting the exercise that he needs. Cavapoos are known to be friendly, loving, and caring companions and it was important to us that the breed we chose was well-behaved around young children. Cavapoos also have a reputation for being extremely intelligent and easy to train. When we found out about this breed it seemed too good to be true.

"Our Cavapoo, Duncan, is sweet, loving, calm and intelligent. He has the sweetest heart and loves cuddling. He always wants to hang out with us and go wherever we go. Fortunately, New York City is very dog-friendly. My husband and I bring him with us to many places. We call ourselves "The Three Musketeers" because we do so much together!

"I think Cavapoos are a great family dog. We introduced Duncan to children early on and we try to bring him around children as much as we can. When we babysit for family members, Duncan always tags along and he is never anything but playful and gentle. He instinctively knows not to jump on a small child who is running, which I found interesting. He understands that if he jumps on a little child they would likely fall or get hurt. He can safely play with them and run around, able to adapt to his audience. I think that says a lot about his intelligence.

"Duncan likes other dogs, but I consider him more of a "people dog". I think this is probably because he is our only pet and we do most activities with him. He loves hanging out with smaller dogs of similar weight, but definitely gets assertive and nervous around dogs that are more muscular than him (Bulldogs, Pugs). He loves larger Poodles and Golden/Labradoodles."

Dayna Rosindale: "I was attracted to their stunning looks and wonderful temperament. The Cavapoo temperament is absolutely perfect! Harper can be very affectionate, but also likes her own space at times. She's so sweet and highly intelligent. She's very loyal to me, but loves to socialise too. She's also very playful at times and a little cheeky! Harper is so sweet and calm around children; very caring and patient. She is obsessed with my pregnant sister's baby bump. Every time Harper sees my sister, she cuddles up to her baby bump; it's like she knows there is a baby in there and wants to be as close to her as possible. It's so loving to see."

Hilary Morphy: "I wanted a small dog with a good temperament. I saw a Cockapoo in our park and found the breeder, but she had stopped breeding them and gone onto Cavapoos. Once I saw the picture of Teddy, that was it! Plus, the breeder said Cavapoos are less wilful than Cockapoos, which I felt was better for me. Teddy is friendly with other dogs and loves people, but he hates cats. I don't like the local cats who use my garden as a toilet; I shoo them away and so he barks at them – it's my fault! When he meets a puppy or a dog who jumps up at him, he's a bit wimpy! Cavapoos just want to please. I took him to all kinds of classes and he mixed very well with the other puppies and then dogs. I think it's essential. Even if you've owned other dogs before and think you can train a puppy yourself, going to classes really is the best way."

Karen Howe: "I was originally planning to get a Cavalier King Charles Spaniel and, whilst researching the breed, I joined some Facebook groups to learn more about them. One day a photo of a Cavapoo puppy came up and I immediately fell in love with their cute Teddy bear looks. I then started to research Cavapoos and found that they too ticked the boxes of being great family dogs, good with children and had the added bonus of potentially being non-moulting. My decision was made.

"Rodney and Mabel *(pictured)* love children and I would highly recommend Cavapoos for families with small children. They are well-loved at the school gates and sit quite calmly whilst the children stroke them. They also love getting involved with games with my nephews and I never feel I have to worry about their interaction at all. One tip for new owners is to keep on top of the brushing as their coats can matt so easily. If you do it regularly from the start, they will get used to it and make life so much easier in the future."

Val Boshart: "We met a Cavapoo at the airport over the holidays and were absolutely smitten. We had never met such a sweet, social, well-behaved dog, and we loved the size and temperament. Cavapoos are sweet, silly, playful, snuggly, smart and loving. They adore people, children and other dogs. Our Cavapoo, Millie, adores children. She greets them with excitement, giving them gentle kisses. We have noticed that around babies, she is extra gentle. She is quite honestly obsessed with infants - she will not leave their side and wants to be right there with them constantly.

"We have been surprised at how sensitive she is. When Millie does something wrong and is reprimanded, she will jump up onto our laps and snuggle to apologize. She wants to follow us everywhere, and at first was very sad to be left alone - even just in the kitchen if I was in another part of the house. As she has grown, she has become more independent and confident, but she still likes to keep tabs on where her humans are and stay close!"

Beverley Burlison: "We were attracted by the temperament, size and no hair shedding and researched for a year online before finding the breeder. If Max is a typical Cavapoo then I would say he is inquisitive, stubborn and quite lazy! He likes to sleep in a morning, but likes to be active in an afternoon and early evening. He takes himself off to bed in an evening.

"He loves to be petted and fussed over. Max also likes his own space. He is good around children, but doesn't like his face being touched. Once he sees a bird or a rabbit he will chase and it is difficult to recall him. Max socializes with other breeds of dogs at weekly day care, but can get jealous if I fuss over other dogs."

Lindsey McDonald and Alex Kostiw: "We were first attracted to this breed after looking at various Poodle crosses due to allergies. We were drawn to the calmer nature, compared with the Cockapoo, though with just as much personality. The Cavapoo temperament is mischievous, stubborn, loving, attention-demanding and playful. Cavapoos are extremely clever. Winston is very much food-orientated, but only when he wants to be. A ball is the highest in the pecking order, though. He has been very easy to train, and we find that if we don't keep his mind active throughout the day then he can become very mischievous. Consistency is key, and all members of the household need to be on the same page."

Rebecca Seabrook adopted Max through the Doodle Trust after her beloved Bichon Frise died: "Max has so much love to give. Because he was kept in a house for his first nine months without being taken out, he has issues. We will keep on working with him until he no longer has his insecurity issues. He has settled into our family life so well and our other dog, Amble, and Max are now the best of friends and spend a lot of time playing together. Max has healed Amble and brought laughter back into our house."

Denise Knightley: "Cavapoos are friendly, outgoing, confident and happiest when with their humans. Both of our Cavapoos are very comfortable around children and enjoy their company. Carmen Rose is a registered Pets As Therapy (PAT) dog and works almost exclusively in primary schools under the Kennel Club/PAT Read2Dogs scheme. She works with children to give them confidence in reading out loud. We visit mainstream schools and help children with a range of issues, such as ADHD/autism/Asperger's/dyslexia/phobias etc., including some children who have a fear of dogs.

"Cavapoos are relatively easy to housetrain as long as you are consistent in taking them outside at very regular intervals in the first four to six weeks. One thing that surprises me about my Cavapoos is their ability to swim very well and quite fast!"

Kit Lam: "I chose a Cavapoo as I had heard they were non-moulting and supposedly calmer than Cockapoo. Cookie is calm, intelligent, gentle and happy-go-lucky. She was housetrained in two weeks, using a bell hanging by the door. I've been surprised by her calmness and how much they attach to one person if allowed to. My advice to new owners is to take time out to train your dog and that will make things easier in the long run."

We also asked owners to sum up their Cavaliers in a few words:

- ❧ Playful, Loyal, Cuddly, Intelligent
- ❧ Calm, Friendly, Playful Loyal
- ❧ Loving, Playful, Personality, Beautiful
- ❧ Affectionate, Soft-Hearted, Adored, Cuddly
- ❧ Gentle, Loving, Intelligent
- ❧ Loyal, Loved by my Friends, Beautiful, Patient.
- ❧ Cuddly, Lapdogs, Cheeky, Clever
- ❧ Loyal, Affectionate, Playful, Sociable
- ❧ Affectionate, Sensitive, Intelligent, Loyal, Vocal
- ❧ Gentle, Friendly, Greedy, Sleepy
- ❧ Mad, Lovable, Happy
- ❧ Fun, Sweet, Playful, Loving
- ❧ Real-Life Cuddly Teddy Bears

Read on to find the right puppy and, if you already have yours, learn how to take good care of the newest member of the family for the rest of his or her life, and how to build a unique bond that will become one of the most important things in your life - and certainly theirs.

2. Cavaliers, Poodles & F Numbers

The Cavapoo crossbreed results from breeding a Cavalier King Charles Spaniel with a Miniature or Toy Poodle.

In order to understand what makes your dog tick, it is important to understand his or her heritage. Each individual Cavapoo's physical appearance, health, coat, natural temperament, energy levels and reaction to the outside world varies according to his or her genetic make-up. This chapter provides a detailed insight into the parent breeds, as well as an explanation of F numbers.

....

The Cavalier

This handsome, affectionate little dog is known for its wonderful, gentle temperament, great love of humans and desire to please his owners. When listing the attributes of all the different breeds, it's hard – if not impossible - to think of one with a sweeter nature, or a dog that is more child-friendly.

The word *Companion* sums up the Cavalier in a single word. This little Love Machine has boundless affection for his or her owners and loves nothing more than snuggling up with them - preferably after a good walk. The Cavalier is at one with the world; happy with everything and everybody. As one Cavalier breeder told us: "They haven't got a bad bone in their body".

Properly socialised, they are completely non-aggressive with other dogs and infinitely patient with children – sitting accommodatingly as they are dressed up as Santa Claus or Superman – it's more often the dog that needs protecting from the kids, rather than the other way round.

Sporting Toy with a Royal Connection

Historically, the Cavalier is a strange anomaly of Toy breed and sporting dog. Its origins lie with the field Spaniel, a hardy dog bred to flush and retrieve game for the guns. The Cavalier is the only Spaniel to be classed in the Toy Group, the others are all in the Gundog (UK) or Sporting (USA) Group.

As with all dogs of sporting origins, Cavaliers love a challenge, both physical and mental, especially games and retrieving.

However, the modern Cavalier does not have the "drive" of a sporting Spaniel; he or she is far more laid back. Hundreds of years ago, Spaniels were bred down to create a smaller, gentler dog for lords and ladies. Queen Elizabeth I (1533-1603) had a "spaniel gentle" as a comforter. This type of dog was probably a forerunner to the Cavalier and was popular with aristocratic ladies as a plaything and bed warmer! It is said that Mary, Queen of Scots' little Spaniel was found hidden in her petticoats after she was beheaded.

Just over half of all of today's Cavaliers are the rich chestnut and white *Blenheims*, developed by the first Duke of Marlborough (1650-1722) who lived at Blenheim Palace. The Duke of Norfolk also kept the Blenheim type, but went on to create the black and tan. The *tricolour* (the second most popular colour today) was originally called the Prince Charles, and the *ruby* was the last colour to be developed.

In some Blenheims there is a highly-prized chestnut mark in the middle of the forehead called the Blenheim Spot or Duchess Thumb Print. Legend has it that while Sarah Churchill, Duchess of Marlborough, was awaiting news of her husband's safe return from the Battle of Blenheim (1704), she anxiously kept pressing her thumb on the head of an expecting female. The story goes that this resulted in five puppies bearing the "lucky mark" after news arrived that the battle had been won.

The Modern Cavalier

Today's dog has anything but *a Cavalier attitude* to life. Not at all domineering, stand-offish or egotistic, the Cavalier is sweet and gentle, friendly, incredibly loyal and easy to train — provided you put a bit of time in at the beginning. It's not often the word "kind" is used to describe a breed - but it sums up this one.

The Cavalier's athletic side is complemented with a kind and generous temperament with a streak of sensitivity. Many owners say that their Cavaliers are compassionate and can pick up on the emotions within their household. They are also tactile and love to be petted - for as many hours as you are prepared to give them; you'll tire of it before they do!

They will jump on your lap if you sit down or follow you from room to room like a little shadow; they love physical contact and want to be close. This desire to be close extends to other dogs too; if you have more than one, you will find that they like to sleep in piles!

They are generally excellent with other dogs and seem to have an affinity with other Cavaliers. Often happy to share their house with a cat, as long as they have been introduced at an early age, but outdoors, some take great delight in chasing small birds, squirrels and other people's cats.

Once socialised, Cavaliers are not generally noisy dogs. Some may bark when a person comes to the door, but they are not known as excessive barkers. However, if you're looking for a guard dog, then look elsewhere. If a truckload of robbers arrived to make off with the family silver, the Cavalier's main priorities would be to make friends with, and get petted by, them all.

Not only is the Cavalier a companion second to none for young and old alike, but the breed, with its soft, silky coat and trademark long ears, is also graceful and attractive. The sight of a fully-groomed Cavalier gliding around the ring at a conformation show is a beautiful sight to behold. The Cavalier does shed its coat and needs regular grooming.

Although the Cavalier King Charles Spaniel Alansmere Aquarius won Best in Show at Crufts in 1973, the breed has yet to repeat this success at America's Westminster Kennel Club Dog Show.

The breed's playful nature and sporting background mean that they can be trained in several different disciplines, including Agility, Obedience, Rally and Canine Freestyle (Dancing with Dogs). And their sensitive nature, combined with their love of humans, makes them well-suited to therapy work with disabled people, children and the elderly.

Cavaliers do not respond well to harsh voices or rough treatment, which stresses them. Neither do they like being left alone for very long; they can even become depressed if they are ignored, left alone or badly treated. Although some Cavaliers are quite brave, others can also be wimpy. Some have a low pain threshold and may squeal at the slightest discomfort.

....

Downsides to Cavaliers?

Does the Cavalier have any downsides and, with all of these amazing attributes, how come some end up in rescue centres? Although Cavaliers have all of the qualities listed, these dogs are demanding of you and your time. Here are some other things to consider:

- ❧ Cavaliers are high maintenance and expensive when it comes to their long, silky coat. They require regular grooming – anything from daily to two or three times a week - to keep them clean and matt-free. They are not hypoallergenic and so generally not suitable for people with allergies

- ❧ Cavaliers shed hair and can get wet and muddy when running free or swimming, so this is not a breed for the very house-proud

- ❧ Several health issues can affect the breed, and it is especially prone to inherited heart disease. According to animal health organisation UFAW, Cavaliers are 20 times more likely to have the heart condition Mitral Valve Disease than other breeds. Choose your Cavapoo puppy carefully and ask to see the parents' health certificates before committing. Once you have your dog, take out canine health insurance

- ❧ Like other Toy breeds, Cavaliers are prone to dental issues, so regular teeth cleaning is another necessary maintenance job

- ❧ Their floppy ears are prone to infections, so owners should make time to pluck hair out of the inside of the ears – or pay a groomer to do it

- ❧ Cavaliers are most definitely *Velcro dogs*. They like to stick to you and don't like being left alone for long. This means they are not a suitable choice for people who are regularly out of the house for many hours

- ❧ Some Cavaliers can be stubborn, requiring more time and patience to train and socialise

- ❧ Toy breeds have a reputation for being slow to housetrain. Some Cavaliers pick it up very quickly, but others take longer – vigilance on the part of the owner speeds up the process

- ❧ Although the Cavalier was bred as a companion, he still needs regular walks – up to an hour or more a day

- ❧ The Cavalier is an escape artist extraordinaire - and has NO road sense whatsoever. You need to have a secure fence and plug every little gap. This goes for Cavapoos too.

We also asked breeders and owners to sum up their Cavaliers in a few words. This is what they said:

- ❧ Gay, friendly, relaxed, tactile, willing
- ❧ Gentle, inquisitive, fearless and friendly
- ❧ Passionate, compassionate, snuggle-bunny
- ❧ Loyal, kind, best friend
- ❧ Great companions, friendly temperament and fearless
- ❧ Kind, easy, family dog, easy to train
- ❧ Active, well balanced with a gentle expression
- ❧ They leave paw prints on your heart
- ❧ Gentle, friendly, companionable, tactile
- ❧ Devoted, kind, patient
- ❧ Hairy bundle of love

Cavalier Breed Standard

What is a Breed Standard?

The **Breed Standard** is what makes a Great Dane a Great Dane and a Chihuahua a Chihuahua. It is a blueprint not only for the appearance of each breed, but also for character and temperament, how the dog moves and what colours are acceptable. In other words, it ensures that a Cavalier King Charles Spaniel looks and acts like a Cavalier King Charles Spaniel.

The breed standard is laid down by the breed societies. In the UK it's the Kennel Club, and in the USA it's the AKC (American Kennel Club) that keeps the register of pedigree (purebred) dogs. Dogs entered in conformation shows run under Kennel Club and AKC rules are judged against this ideal list of attributes. Breeders approved by the Kennel Clubs - called **Assured Breeders** in the UK - agree to produce puppies in line with the Breed Standard and maintain certain welfare conditions.

Good breeders select only the best dogs for reproduction, based on factors such as the health, looks, temperament, physical structure and character of the parents and their ancestors. They do not simply take any available male and female and allow them to randomly breed.

 The fact that a breeding Cavalier or Poodle is registered with the Kennel Club or AKC does NOT mean that his or her parents have been screened for hereditary diseases, or that you are guaranteed a healthy Cavapoo pup. A Kennel Club or AKC pedigree certificate simply means that the dog's family tree can be traced back several generations. Always ask to see health certificates.

Responsible breeders aim to reduce or eradicate genetic illnesses by screening their dogs and not breeding from the ones that carry faulty genes. In the case of Cavaliers, the major health tests cover heart and eye diseases and Syringomyelia (SM), a serious disorder which affects the brain and spine.

After World War II, there were only a handful of Cavaliers left in the world and all of today's Cavalier King Charles Spaniels are their descendants. Unfortunately, as well as passing on good genes, they also passed on some bad ones, so it is extremely important that you check the health of your future Cavapoo's Cavalier parent or ancestors. Hereditary diseases are not uncommon among unscreened dogs.

Kennel Club Breed Standard (UK)

<u>General Appearance</u>: Active, graceful and well balanced, with gentle expression.

<u>Characteristics</u>: Sporting, affectionate, absolutely fearless.

<u>Temperament</u>: Gay, friendly, non-aggressive; no tendency to nervousness.

<u>Head and Skull</u>: Skull almost flat between ears. Stop shallow. Length from base of stop to tip of nose about 3.8 cm (1½ in). Nostrils black and well developed without flesh marks, muzzle well tapered. Lips well developed but not pendulous. Face well filled below eyes. Any tendency to snipiness undesirable.

<u>Eyes</u>: Large, dark, round but not prominent; spaced well apart.

<u>Ears</u>: Long, set high, with plenty of feather.

<u>Mouth</u>: Jaws strong, with a perfect, regular and complete scissor bite, i.e. upper teeth closely overlapping lower teeth and set square to the jaws.

<u>Neck</u>: Moderate length, slightly arched.

<u>Forequarters</u>: Chest moderate, shoulders well laid back; straight legs moderately boned.

<u>Body</u>: Short-coupled with good spring of rib. Level back.

<u>Hindquarters</u>: Legs with moderate bone; well turned stifle – no tendency to cow-hocks or sickle-hocks.

<u>Feet</u>: Compact, cushioned and well feathered.

<u>Tail</u>: Length of tail in balance with body, well set on, carried happily but never much above the level of the back. Docking previously optional when no more than one-third was to be removed.

<u>Gait</u>: Free-moving and elegant in action, plenty of drive from behind. Forelegs and hind legs move parallel when viewed from in front and behind.

<u>Coat</u>: Long, silky, free from curl. Slight wave permissible. Plenty of feathering. Totally free from trimming. <u>Colours</u>: Recognised colours are:-

- <u>**Black and Tan**</u>: Raven black with tan markings above the eyes, on cheeks, inside ears, on chest and legs and underside of tail. Tan should be bright. White marks undesirable.

- <u>**Ruby**</u>: Whole coloured rich red. White markings undesirable.

- <u>**Blenheim**</u>: Rich chestnut markings well broken up, on pearly white ground Markings evenly divided on head, leaving room between ears for much valued lozenge mark or spot (a unique characteristic of the breed).

- <u>Tricolour</u>: Black and white well spaced, broken up, with tan markings over eyes, cheeks, inside ears, inside legs, and on underside of tail.

- *Any other colour or combination of colours highly undesirable.*

<u>Weight and Size</u>: Weight – 5.4–8.2 kg (12–18 lb). A small, well balanced dog well within these weights desirable.

<u>Faults</u>: Any departure from the foregoing points should be considered a fault and the seriousness with which the fault should be regarded should be in exact proportion to its degree and its effect upon the health and welfare of the dog.

<u>Note</u>: Male animals should have two apparently normal testicles fully descended into the scrotum.

Last Updated – February 2012

The **American Kennel Club Breed Standard** is very similar, but adds:

<u>General Appearance:</u> The Cavalier King Charles Spaniel is an active, graceful, well-balanced toy spaniel, very gay and free in action; fearless and sporting in character, yet at the same time gentle and affectionate.

It is this typical gay temperament, combined with true elegance and royal appearance which are of paramount importance in the breed. Natural appearance with no trimming, sculpting or artificial alteration is essential to breed type.

<u>Size:</u> Height 12 to 13 inches at the withers; weight proportionate to height, between 13 and 18 pounds. A small, well balanced dog within these weights is desirable, but these are ideal heights and weights and slight variations are permissible.

··

The Poodle

Whatever size of Poodle your Cavapoo is bred from, there is little doubt that this breed is truly unique. No other dog quite looks or acts like it, nor has the same type of coat. Not only is a Poodle the epitome of elegance when fully groomed, but this is also the second most intelligent canine on the planet after the Border Collie ...an unbeatable combination of brains AND beauty!

Some people make the mistake of thinking that the Poodle is an ornamental dog, all show and no substance, but nothing could be further from the truth. Don't let those pompoms deceive you; strip away the woolly coat from the original Standard Poodle and you have a muscular and agile hunter. And lurking inside that striking exterior is a big personality – that goes for all three sizes; nobody has told the Toy that he is tiny!

The Poodle is a more complex character than the Cavalier and super intelligent. If your Cavapoo has Poodle-like tendencies, you will need to spend time channelling that great intellect by consistent training and providing plenty of mental stimulation, such as playing games, inventing challenges or taking part in competitions or therapy work.

History of the Poodle

Although its exact origins are uncertain, it is known that the Poodle is one of the oldest dog breeds. The first ones were the large Standards, versatile and athletic working dogs bred to retrieve ducks and upland game birds from both water and land. In its hunting heyday hundreds of years ago, the Poodle was regarded as a water retriever second to none. If your Cavapoo loves water, it's the Poodle instinct coming out.

Duck hunters loved this breed with its unique woolly, water-resistant coat, webbed feet, athleticism and stamina, intelligence, trainability and supreme loyalty to its owner.

The modern day Poodle's pompoms and fancy clips actually derive from their hunting days, when bracelets of longer hair were left on the joints, neck, tail and chest to help stave off rheumatism and keep this hardy dog warm in cold water and reed beds.

We know from historical writings and paintings that the first Poodle clip was a lion-like trim. This early photograph of a hunting Poodle very clearly shows the origins of today's Continental and English Saddle clips with not only the bracelets (which later became pompoms), but also pompoms to protect the loins from cold. As the clip evolved, a topknot was introduced to keep long hair out of the Poodle's eyes when swimming. Hunters tied coloured ribbons to help identify their dogs when they were working in tall reeds.

Compare this photo with the photo on the previous page - and the similarities of the clips are evident - despite the fact that they were taken more than 100 years apart.

Although land drainage in Europe decreased Man's reliance on water retrievers as sporting dogs, there were plenty of dog fanciers who admired the Poodle's legendary intelligence, trainability and loyalty. And they set about breeding smaller Poodles which were sold as pets and companion dogs. Some became famous performing dogs. These went on to become known as Miniature and Toy Poodles.

French breeders were particularly active in experimenting with Poodles and made a major contribution to the standardisation of the different sizes - which is why the breed is often referred to as the French Poodle. They also began to trim Poodles in more outlandish styles, which became fashionable with the aristocracy. This really came to the fore during the reign of the last King of France, Louis XVI (1774-92), when he and his wife, Marie Antoinette, had Toy Poodles which they carried around like trophies. It is said that Toy Poodles were bred to be small enough to be carried around in ladies' sleeves.

The sophisticated art of Poodle trimming really took hold during Louis's reign, giving rise to the birth of professional dog groomers. This fashion spread to England and in 1896, London had a "Dogs' Toilet Club" where Poodles could be professionally clipped, brushed, combed, shampooed with the yolks of eggs and attended to by a professional chiropodist!

It is generally thought that the Miniature Poodle, as well as being bred down from the Standard as a pet, was also used in truffle hunting (*pictured, next page*). Truffles are very expensive fungi that grow underground near tree roots, and are highly prized in Europe as an exotic culinary treat.

The Modern Poodle

Sporting dogs were bred to use their initiative and also to work closely with Man. These qualities are still evident in today's Poodle, who loves a challenge - mental as well as physical. Poodles love games and, given enough exercise and stimulation, they are happy to snuggle up with you after a good romp around. They are also incredibly loyal, good-tempered and biddable (trainable), at least when you have trained them to fit in with you and your family - youngsters can be very boisterous with a mind of their own!

Another bonus with the Poodle is that, like Cavaliers, they are not generally yappy dogs - although some Toys can get carried away with the sound of their own voice if not well trained! They are not usually good guard dogs, although some will bark to alert you when the doorbell rings. Unlike the Cavalier, they do not welcome all and sundry; some Poodles can be wary or nervous of strangers until they get to know them.

The list of Poodle accomplishments – for both beauty and brains - is long and varied. The Poodle has been crowned Best in Show at Crufts and Westminster Kennel Club a total of six times at each event. And the breed's intellect, love of a challenge and eagerness to please its owner mean that Poodles can be trained to a high level.

Standards and Miniatures are particularly adaptable and have notched up notable victories in competitions such as Agility, Obedience, Canine Freestyle, Rally, Tracking and Weight Pulling.

The Poodle is one of the most sensitive of all breeds. Like Cavaliers, they are regarded as empathetic dogs; it is often reported that they are able to pick up on the mood of their owner, making the breed well-suited to therapy work. They do not respond well to harsh or loud voices, rough treatment or discord within a household, which stresses them.

What to Expect

There are three sizes of Poodle: Standard, Toy and Miniature. They are classed as one breed in North America and three breeds in the UK. The three share many characteristics already outlined. Given the right treatment and attention they deserve, Poodles make excellent companions. When owners have had a Poodle, they often won't consider a different breed.

The Cavapoo is a small to medium-sized dog and its Poodle ancestors are Miniatures or Toys. Many breeders prefer Miniatures as the Toy has a tiny, delicate structure, which can lead to health issues - or injury, especially if placed with families with young children.

But Poodles are also complex characters and can be misunderstood – by the public at large and by their owners if they don't put in the time and effort to understand and train their Poodle, particularly in the early weeks.

While they are quick and eager to learn, Poodles are slow to forget and forgive, so consistency is the key when training. They don't enjoy being scolded – a firm word is usually enough of a reprimand – and they can switch off or sulk to show their displeasure.

On the other side of the coin, they absolutely love being given a chance to shine! In the 18th and 19th centuries, Toy and Miniature Poodles became famous as popular entertainers in different countries. Stories of their tricks abound, they even played cards and dominoes! Today's owners report their Poodles opening fridge doors or getting treats out of zipped pockets - they are very quick learners.

They also have a reputation for being instinctive. Some, particularly Standards and Miniatures, have a strong prey drive and will happily chase down any small bird or mammal. However, they generally get on well with other pets when introduced properly.

It's not uncommon for male Poodles of all sizes, and some females, to have a strong desire to "mark" their territory by urinating frequently on objects. This is fine outdoors, but important that you are vigilant with housetraining early on.

Poodles are very aware of their surroundings and often wary with new people until they get to know them. They are also affectionate with their family (and this may include other animals) and can be protective.

Socialisation is extremely important for young Poodles.

Without it, some, particularly Toys, can bark too much and become fixated on, and over-protective of, their owners. While it is not unusual for Poodles to follow their owners from room to room, they should also be accepting of other people. Young Poodles benefit from lots of positive experiences with many different people, places and situations, which helps them to become relaxed in their environment. A well-socialised Poodle is a delight to be with.

Poodles are generally active by nature and enjoy being involved. Their intelligence should be channelled into exercise, training or games. Most Poodles love retrieving a ball, although some will just look at you, waiting for you to fetch it back yourself!

Miniatures (often called *Mins* in the UK and *Minis* in the USA) and Toys are more "on-the-go" compared with Standards, both in and out of the home. Minis often enjoy more exercise than many medium-sized breeds – again, much depends on individual character. Some will enjoy an hour or more a day, while others are happy with shorter walks. Toys, while being more highly strung, obviously need less exercise. They may seem happy romping around the garden or yard, but a daily walk is good for socialisation and stimulation as well as exercise.

No other breed combines a striking appearance, a hypoallergenic coat, cleverness, a great desire to please his owner, an affectionate, non-aggressive nature and a sense of humour like the Poodle.

....

Poodles as Family Pets

With the increase in allergies, one of the reasons that the Poodle has become a popular choice for families is the breed's unique low-shedding coat - there is no such thing as a "non-shedding" dog, by the way! The Poodle has a single coat of dense, curly hair and although a minimal amount of hair is actually shed, it normally falls back into the coat, along with any dander.

The coat is described as *hypoallergenic* meaning "less likely to cause allergies". This unique coat is why there are so many Doodles and Poos around today - particularly with the increase in allergies and asthma. However, anyone with allergies considering a Cavapoo should be aware that Cavaliers DO SHED and there is no 100% guarantee that you will not be allergic to a Cavapoo. If you do have allergies, it's advisable for you and your family to spend time with the individual puppy (away from the other puppies and mother) if possible before committing.

Treated well, a Poodle can develop an extremely deep bond with a child. However, children must be taught to respect the Poodle, not to tease him, or constantly wake or pick him up, and most Poodles dislike lots of loud shouting.

To help build a bond and begin to understand a dog's needs, get your child involved in walking, feeding, giving water and grooming the dog.

This is what one breeder of Toys and Miniatures had to say: "We much prefer families with young and/or noisy or boisterous children to have a Min instead of a Toy, as they're not just taller, but are generally more emotionally hardy.

"Our now 16-year-old son has autism and sensory processing disorder and our Min has naturally become his emotional assistance dog over the years.

"Our son never used to do outdoor activities as he found it too aurally overwhelming, but he now competes in Kennel Club Agility at Grade 4 with her and as he's so focused on her, he doesn't even seem to notice the noise around him.

"Our Mins have much more leeway in what they don't mind than the Toys, who are super sociable with everyone, but are definitely more sensitive. Our Toys are absolutely obsessed with children of all ages and seem particularly drawn to little toddlers, but they are so fragile in comparison that, rather than doing a temperament test on a puppy, I think it's children who need a temperament test in order to assess which size Poodle is best for them!"

The Poodle Coat and Colours

All Poodles are born with a puppy coat, which varies in texture and maintenance from an adult coat; the puppy coat is soft and wavy, whereas an adult coat is dense and curly. The texture of an adult coat can vary from soft to wiry, depending on genetics.

At around nine or 10 months old, a Poodle puppy coat starts to change to an adult coat. This process often lasts around nine months with Toys and Miniatures, although it can sometimes take over a year. A slicker or pin brush is the best tool for the job, being careful not to damage the pup's skin.

During this time it is very easy for the puppy's coat to become matted. Owners have to regularly brush their puppy to get the tangles out. If not, the coat may be ruined for life. Worst case scenario is that the whole coat has to be shaved off.

It is unlikely that a mature Poodle will be exactly the same shade as he or she when first seen as a pup. The change often happens by the time the dog is two years old. Some cream or apricot Poodle puppies may grow up to be white, reds often fade to apricot, and silvers and blues start out as black. A change or fading of coat colour is also not uncommon with Cavapoos. As far as colour goes, only *solid colours* are accepted by the Kennel Clubs. In the UK, these are: white, cream, black, brown (including chocolate), apricot, red, silver and blue. In the USA, café au lait, silver beige and grey are also accepted. You might also hear the term "champagne", which some people use to refer to a Poodle that is darker than cream and lighter than apricot.

In the Poodle world, blue is actually a "dilute" black; puppies are born black and lighten to blue. They also have black points (nose, lips, eye rims, pads, toe nails) and brown eyes, as do black and silver Poodles. Browns and café au laits have liver points. Red was the last colour to be accepted by the AKC, in 1980. The Kennel Club Breed Standard (UK) says: *"Apricots and reds to have dark eyes with black points or deep amber eyes with liver points."* In the US, black points are preferred to liver points in reds.

Downsides to Poodles?

Every breed, even the Poodle, has some drawbacks:

- Poodles are high maintenance and expensive when it comes to their wonderful coat. They require more grooming than almost any other breed. Even with a low-maintenance Puppy Clip, the dog will still have to visit the groomer's every six weeks. Unless you learn how to clip, it will cost a lot of money over your dog's lifetime

- In between trips to the groomer's, Poodles require grooming at home every few days – or even daily. This is a big, time-consuming commitment

- Their floppy ears are prone to infections, so it's recommended that owners make time to pluck hair out of the inside of the ears

- They are also prone to tooth decay and should have their teeth brushed regularly

- Some Standards and Miniatures can be full-on high energy, especially when young

- If not properly socialised, some Poodles, particularly small ones, can become highly strung, excessive barkers, over-protective or timid

- A Poodle that doesn't receive the time and attention it needs will react badly, either by becoming attention-seeking or bored and unhappy

- They need to be engaged and no Poodle likes being left alone for long periods. If you are out at work all day, consider a different breed

This is how breeders sum up their beloved Poodles:

- Funny, clever, eager to please

- Sociable, affectionate, alert

- Amazing, adorable companions

- ✤ Proud, sensitive and energetic
- ✤ Intelligent, entertaining, empathetic, malleable
- ✤ Smart, pleasing companion
- ✤ Playful, active, smart, loving
- ✤ Stylish, intelligent, perfection
- ✤ Life's best pleasure

American Kennel Club Breed Standard

General Appearance: *Carriage and Condition* - That of a very active, intelligent and elegant appearing dog, squarely built, well proportioned, moving soundly and carrying himself proudly. Properly clipped in the traditional fashion and carefully groomed, the Poodle has about him an air of distinction and dignity peculiar to himself.

Size, Proportion, Substance: *Size - The Standard Poodle* is over 15 inches at the highest point of the shoulders. Any Poodle which is 15 inches or less in height shall be disqualified from competition as a Standard Poodle.

The Miniature Poodle is 15 inches or under at the highest point of the shoulders, with a minimum height in excess of 10 inches. Any Poodle which is over 15 inches or is 10 inches or less at the highest point of the shoulders shall be disqualified from competition as a Miniature Poodle.

The Toy Poodle is 10 inches or under at the highest point of the shoulders. Any Poodle which is more than 10 inches at the highest point of the shoulders shall be disqualified from competition as a Toy Poodle. As long as the Toy Poodle is definitely a Toy Poodle, and the Miniature Poodle a Miniature Poodle, both in balance and proportion for the Variety, diminutiveness shall be the deciding factor when all other points are equal.

Proportion - To insure the desirable squarely built appearance, the length of body measured from the breastbone to the point of the rump approximates the height from the highest point of the shoulders to the ground.

Substance - Bone and muscle of both forelegs and hindlegs are in proportion to size of dog.

Head and Expression: *(a) Eyes* - very dark, oval in shape and set far enough apart and positioned to create an alert intelligent expression. Major fault: eyes round, protruding, large or very light.
(b) Ears - hanging close to the head, set at or slightly below eye level. The ear leather is long, wide and thickly feathered; however, the ear fringe should not be of excessive length.
(c) Skull - moderately rounded, with a slight but definite stop. Cheekbones and muscles flat. Length from occiput to stop about the same as length of muzzle.
(d) Muzzle - long, straight and fine, with slight chiseling under the eyes. Strong without lippiness. The chin definite enough to preclude snipiness. Major fault: lack of chin.

Teeth - white, strong and with a scissors bite. Major fault: undershot, overshot, wry mouth.

Neck, Topline, Body: *Neck* well proportioned, strong and long enough to permit the head to be carried high and with dignity. Skin snug at throat. The neck rises from strong, smoothly muscled shoulders. Major fault: ewe neck. The *topline* is level, neither sloping nor roached, from the highest point of the shoulder blade to the base of the tail, with the exception of a slight hollow just behind the shoulder.

Body -
(a) Chest deep and moderately wide with well sprung ribs.

(b) The loin is short, broad and muscular.

(c) Tail straight, set on high and carried up, docked of sufficient length to insure a balanced outline. Major fault: set low, curled, or carried over the back.

Forequarters: Strong, smoothly muscled shoulders. The shoulder blade is well laid back and approximately the same length as the upper foreleg. Major fault - steep shoulder. Forelegs - Straight and parallel when viewed from the front. When viewed from the side the elbow is directly below the highest point of the shoulder. The pasterns are strong. Dewclaws may be removed. Feet - The feet are rather small, oval in shape with toes well arched and cushioned on thick firm pads. Nails short but not excessively shortened. The feet turn neither in nor out. Major fault - paper or splay foot.

Hindquarters: The angulation of the hindquarters balances that of the forequarters. Hindlegs straight and parallel when viewed from the rear. Muscular with width in the region of the stifles which are well bent; femur and tibia are about equal in length; hock to heel short and perpendicular to the ground. When standing, the rear toes are only slightly behind the point of the rump. Major fault - cow-hocks.

Coat: *(a) Quality -* (1) Curly: of naturally harsh texture, dense throughout. (2) Corded: hanging in tight even cords of varying length; longer on mane or body coat, head, and ears; shorter on puffs, bracelets, and pompons.

(b) Clip - A Poodle under 12 months may be shown in the "Puppy" clip. In all regular classes, Poodles 12 months or over must be shown in the "English Saddle" or "Continental" clip.
In the Stud Dog and Brood Bitch classes and in a non-competitive Parade of Champions, Poodles may be shown in the "Sporting" clip. A Poodle shown in any other type of clip shall be disqualified.
(1) "Puppy" - A Poodle under a year old may be shown in the "Puppy" clip with the coat long. The face, throat, feet and base of the tail are shaved. The entire shaven foot is visible. There is a pompon on the end of the tail.

In order to give a neat appearance and a smooth unbroken line, shaping of the coat is permissible.
(2) "English Saddle" - In the "English Saddle" clip, the face, throat, feet, forelegs and base of the tail are shaved, leaving puffs on the forelegs and a pompon on the end of the tail. The hindquarters are covered with a short blanket of hair except for a curved shaved area on each flank and two shaved bands on each hindleg. The entire shaven foot and a portion of the shaven leg above the puff are visible. The rest of the body is left in full coat but may be shaped in order to insure overall balance.

(3) "Continental" In the "Continental" clip, the face, throat, feet, and base of the tail are shaved. The hindquarters are shaved with pompons (optional) on the hips. The legs are shaved, leaving bracelets on the hindlegs and puffs on the forelegs. There is a pompon on the end of the tail. The entire shaven foot and a portion of the shaven foreleg above the puff are visible. The rest of the body is left in full coat but may be shaped in order to insure overall balance.

(4) "Sporting" - In the "Sporting" clip, a Poodle shall be shown with face, feet, throat, and base of tail shaved, leaving a scissored cap on the top of the head and a pompon on the end of the tail. The rest of the body, and legs are clipped or scissored to follow the outline of the dog leaving a short blanket of coat no longer than one inch in length. The hair on the legs may be slightly longer than that on the body.

In all clips the hair of the topknot may be left free or held in place by elastic bands. The hair is only of sufficient length to present a smooth outline. "Topknot" refers only to hair on the skull, from stop to occiput. This is the only area where elastic bands may be used.

Color: The coat is an even and solid color at the skin. In blues, grays, silvers, browns, café -au-laits, apricots and creams the coat may show varying shades of the same color. This is frequently present in the somewhat darker feathering of the ears and in the tipping of the ruff.

While clear colors are definitely preferred, such natural variation in the shading of the coat is not to be considered a fault. Brown and café -au-lait Poodles have liver-colored noses, eye-rims and lips, dark toenails and dark amber eyes. Black, blue, gray, silver, cream and white Poodles have black noses, eye-rims and lips, black or self colored toenails and very dark eyes. In the apricots while the foregoing coloring is preferred, liver-colored noses, eye-rims and lips, and amber eyes are permitted but are not desirable.

Major fault: color of nose, lips and eye-rims incomplete, or of wrong color for color of dog. Parti-colored dogs shall be disqualified. The coat of a parti-colored dog is not an even solid color at the skin but is of two or more colors.

Gait: A straightforward trot with light springy action and strong hindquarters drive. Head and tail carried up. Sound effortless movement is essential.

Temperament: Carrying himself proudly, very active, intelligent, the Poodle has about him an air of distinction and dignity peculiar to himself. Major fault: shyness or sharpness.

Glossary:

Hock - tarsal joint of the hind leg corresponding to the human ankle, but bending in the opposite direction (looks like a low backwards knee on the back leg). *Cow Hocks* bend inwards (knock knees) and *Sickle Hocks* bend outwards (bow legged)

Muzzle – Upper and lower jaws

Occiput - bony bump seen at the top rear of the skull on some breeds

Parti colors – different colors, one of which is usually white

Pastern – the area below the wrist or hock but above the foot

Snipiness - a weak, pointed muzzle lacking in substance in a dog's underjaw, or fill beneath the eyes

Stifle – technically the knee, but higher than the hock and closer to the body

Stop - area between a dog's eyes, below the skull

Withers - the ridge between the shoulder blade

F Numbers Explained

The Cavapoo is a crossbreed, not a purebred (North America) or pedigree (UK). It is the product of crossing two breeds of dog: the Cavalier King Charles Spaniel and the Miniature or Toy Poodle.

Because the Cavapoo is a crossbreed (also called a hybrid), you cannot get Kennel Club or AKC registration papers with your dog - although if the parents are purebred dogs, they should have registration papers. If this is the case, ask to see the documents and take details.

You should always find out about your dog's parents and ancestry because, provided you care for him well, your dog's genes will be the major factor in deciding how healthy he will be. Cavapoos bred from healthy parents are robust dogs with a longish lifespan, estimated at 10 to 15 years. Some Cavapoos live even longer.

In the canine world, F numbers have nothing to do with photography or Formula One motor racing. They describe the generation of a crossbreed dog. The F comes from the Latin *filius* (son) and means "relating to a son or daughter."

Pictured is F1 parti Phoebe, bred by Charlotte Purkiss. Photo courtesy of owner Nivien Speith.

So, an **F1 Cavapoo** is a first generation cross; one parent is a Cavalier and the other is a Poodle, so 50% Cavalier King Charles Spaniel and 50% Poodle. That's simple enough and many of today's Cavapoos are F1 crosses with two pure breed parents. While this cross often throws a loose, wavy coat, it can also throw tighter curls, or a silky, shedding coat like the Cavalier. Some canine experts believe that this first generation cross may benefit from **hybrid vigour.** This is the belief that the first cross between two unrelated purebred lines is healthier and grows better than either parent line.

An **F2 Cavapoo** is second generation. It is generally a cross between two F1 Cavapoos, so is still 50% Cavalier King Charles Spaniel and 50% Poodle.

NOTE: With Doodles that have been on the scene longer than the Cavapoo, there are other permutations. The F numbers are worked out by always adding one to the lowest number. While an F2 could be the offspring of two first-generation doodles (F1 x F1), it could also be the product of an F1 x F2 or higher (bigger number) cross. An F3 is the offspring of one F2 parent when the other parent was F2 or higher. Further down the line there are also **multigenerations.**

Then we get on to the Bs. The B stands for *Backcross*. This occurs when a litter has been produced as a result of a backcross to one of the parent breeds – normally the Poodle (so when a Cavapoo is bred with a Poodle). This is usually done to improve coat type and increase the possibility of a low shedding coat. It is not common practice for breeders to backcross to a Cavalier King Charles Spaniel, so a typical **F1B Cavapoo** will probably be one-quarter Cavalier and three-quarters Poodle.

An **F2B** is the result of an F1 Cavapoo bred to a Cavapoo backcross (F1B). Although three generations in the making, F2Bs are technically second generation dogs.

All clear? No, well, we're moving on anyway...!

Hybrid Vigour

Hybrid Vigour (Vigor in the US), scientific name **heterosis,** is the theory, when applied to dogs, that **the first cross between two unrelated purebred lines is healthier and grows better than either parent line.** Note that this only applies to first generation or F1 crosses. Also the theory, if it's true, only applies to F1 crosses from healthy parents. Obviously, if both the Cavalier and Poodle have hereditary cataracts or luxating patellas (slipped kneecaps), there is every chance the Cavapoo will inherit - or at the very least be a carrier of - these diseases.

On the Institute of Canine Biology website, Carol Beuchat PhD says: "Mating related animals makes it more likely that offspring will inherit two copies of the same gene." She says this can cause "inbreeding depression" and a loss of: "The collection of traits that affect reproduction and lifespan, such as fertility, offspring size, pre- and post-natal mortality, maternal care, resistance to disease, and general "vigor and vitality". These effects have been documented in many thousands of studies and in all manner of organisms and although there is much yet to be learned about it, there is no debate about the fact that it is a real phenomenon in both wild and domestic animals."

Interestingly, Dr Beuchat adds that the parent dogs don't even have to be of different breeds, they can be two dogs of the same breed, but with completely unrelated bloodlines. She adds: "Many long-time dog breeders understand heterosis and use it to good effect in their breeding programs:" www.instituteofcaninebiology.org/blog/the-myth-of-hybrid-vigor-in-dogsis-a-myth

If true, a deliberately chosen healthy purebred sire and dam can give an F1 crossbreed puppy the advantage of hybrid vigour – or robustness. Due to genetics being a complicated science, there are also more variables with hybrid dogs like the Cavapoo; physical appearance and size, color and coat are just some of the inconsistencies.

Similarly, some Cavapoos are sold as non-shedding and hypoallergenic. Although many families with allergies live perfectly happily with Cavapoos, no breeder can categorically say that you will NOT be allergic to their dogs. Allergies vary from one person to the next and the odds are that even the other littermates didn't turn out exactly the same as your puppy. Spending time with the individual puppy is the way to find out.

A University of California, Davis study tracked 24 genetic disorders in more than 27,000 dogs. It revealed that the prevalence of 13 of the diseases was roughly the same in purebred dogs as it was in mixed breed dogs. However, 10 disorders were more common in purebred dogs, and just one was more common in mixed breeds. The study also found that purebred dogs that shared a similar lineage (bloodline) were more susceptible to certain inherited disorders. Read the findings at: www.ucdavis.edu/news/purebred-dogs-not-always-higher-risk-genetic-disorders-study-finds

There are also studies, such as the one published in the Journal of the American Veterinary Medical Association at http://news.vin.com/VINNews.aspx?articleId=29634, which call into question the whole notion of hybrid vigour in dogs at all!

 As scientists can't even agree on the subject, it's impossible for anyone to 100% guarantee that their Cavapoo pups have hybrid vigour. The best thing you can do is check the health screening of the parent dogs.

3. Before You Get Your Puppy

If you haven't got your puppy yet, then read this chapter before you commit to anything; it will help you find a happy, healthy puppy.

Once you have decided that the Cavapoo is your ideal dog, the best way to select a puppy is with your HEAD - and not with your heart! There are thousands of Cavapoo puppies out there, but few first-rate breeders. Unfortunately, due to the high price of puppies, the Cavapoo is one "designer crossbreed" that has attracted some people whose main aim is to make money.

With their Teddy bear looks, button noses, soft, wavy coats, affectionate and playful personalities, there are few more appealing things on this Earth than Cavapoo puppies. If you go to view a litter, the pups are sure to melt your heart and it is extremely difficult – if not downright impossible - to walk away without choosing one. So, it's essential to do your research before you visit any litters.

As you know, the Cavapoo is a crossbreed created from the Cavalier King Charles Spaniel and the Miniature or Toy Poodle. As with most breeds, the Poodle can have some genetic health issues - and there are even more affecting the Cavalier. So your number one priority should be to buy a puppy free from inherited diseases.

If you haven't yet chosen your pup yet and take only one sentence from this entire book, it is this:

Find an ethical breeder with health-tested parents - of the puppy, not the breeder! One who knows Cavapoos inside out and who does not breed lots of different types of dog. After all, apart from getting married or having a baby, getting a puppy is one of the most important, demanding, expensive and life-enriching decisions you will ever make.

Just like babies, Cavapoo puppies will love you unconditionally - but there is a price to pay. In return for their loyalty and devotion, you have to fulfil your part of the bargain. In the beginning, you have to be prepared to devote much of your day to your new puppy. You have to feed her several times a day and housetrain virtually every hour, you have to give her your attention and start to gently introduce the rules of the house as well as take care of health and welfare. You also have to be prepared to part with hard cash for regular healthcare and pet insurance.

If you are unable to devote the time and money to a new arrival, if you have a very young family, a stressful life or are out at work all day, then now might not be the right time to consider getting a puppy. Cavapoos are highly affectionate people-loving dogs that thrive on being close to their owners. If left alone too long, these "Velcro" dogs can become unhappy, bored and even destructive. This is a natural reaction and is not the dog's fault; she is simply responding to the environment, which is failing to meet her needs.

Pick a healthy pup and he or she should live for 10 to 15 years if you're lucky - so getting a Cavapoo is certainly a long-term commitment. Before taking the plunge, ask yourself some questions:

Have I Got Enough Time?

In the first days after leaving his mother and littermates, your puppy will feel very lonely and probably even a little afraid. You and your family have to spend time with your new arrival to make him feel safe and sound. Ideally, for the first few days you will be around all of the time to help him settle and to start bonding. If you work, book a couple of weeks off (this may not be possible for some of our American readers who get shorter vacations than their European counterparts), but don't just get a puppy and leave him all alone in the house a couple of days later.

Housetraining (potty training) starts the moment your pup arrives home. Then, after the first few days and once he's feeling more settled, start to introduce short sessions of a couple of minutes of behaviour training to teach your new pup the rules of the house. Cavapoo puppies want to please you and, while they are often gentle souls as adults, they are often very lively as puppies. This energy can become mischievous if not channelled - so training should start early to discourage puppy biting and jumping up.

Like Poodles, some Cavapoos can have sensitive natures and may be affected by all kinds of things: loud noises, shouting, arguments, unhappiness, other animals or new situations, to name but a few things. You'll also have to make time to slowly start the socialisation process by taking him out of the home to see buses, noisy traffic, other animals, kids, etc. - but make sure you CARRY HIM until the vaccinations have taken effect. Start socialising as soon as possible; that critical window for socialisation is all too short. The more positive experiences he is introduced to at this early stage, the better, and good breeders will already have started the process.

Once he has had the all-clear following vaccinations, get into the habit of taking him for a short walk every day – more as he gets older. While the garden or yard is fine, new surroundings stimulate interest and help to stop puppies becoming bored and developing unwanted behaviour issues. He also gets used to different experiences away from the home.

Make time right from the beginning to get your pup used to being handled, gently brushed, ears checked, and having his teeth touched and later cleaned.

We recommend – as do most good breeders - that you have your pup checked out by a vet within a couple of days of arriving home. Factor in time to visit the vet's surgery for annual check-ups as well as vaccinations, although most now last several years – check with your vet.

How Long Can I Leave My Puppy?

This is a question we get asked all of the time and one that causes much debate among new and prospective owners. All dogs are pack animals; their natural state is to be with others. So being alone is not normal for them - although many have to get used to it. The Cavapoo has not been bred to be a guard dog; he or she most definitely wants to be around you.

Another issue is the toilet; Cavapoo puppies have tiny bladders. Forget the emotional side of it, how would you like to be left for eight hours without being able to visit the bathroom? So how many hours can you leave a dog alone?

Well, a useful guide comes from the canine rescue organisations. In the UK, they will not allow anybody to adopt if they are intending to leave the dog alone for more than four or five hours a day.

Dogs left at home alone a lot get bored and, in the case of Cavapoos, i.e. a breed that thrives on companionship, they can become depressed. Of course, it depends on the character and temperament of your dog, but a lonely Cavapoo may display signs of unhappiness by barking, chewing, digging, urinating, soiling, bad behaviour, or just being plain sad and disengaged.

In terms of housetraining, a general rule of thumb is that a puppy can last without going to the toilet for **one hour or so for every month of age.** So, provided your puppy has learned the basics a three-month-old puppy should be able to last for three hours or a little longer without needing the toilet. Of course, it doesn't work like this – until housetraining kicks in, young puppies just pee at will!

A puppy or fully-grown dog must never be left shut in a crate all day. It is OK to leave a dog in a crate if he or she is happy there, but the door should not be closed for more than a couple of hours during the day. It's fine to close the crate door at night until your puppy is housetrained. A crate is a place where a dog should feel safe, not a prison.

Family and Children

Cavapoos are great dogs for first-time owners and are known for being really good with children. You may find puppyhood a challenge as baby Cavapoos can be extremely lively! But survive that and adult Cavapoos are gentle, patient, tolerant and love being with people. Of course, that comes with the usual caveat – you have to socialise your Cavapoo AND the kids! Your children will naturally be delighted about your new arrival. Cavapoo puppies are very fragile, so avoid leaving babies or toddlers and dogs alone together – no matter how well they get along.

Due to their tiny bones and delicate structure, Cavapoos bred from Toy Poodles are probably not a good choice for a family with pre-school or young children. Small kids lack co-ordination and may inadvertently poke a puppy in the eye, tread on him and break a bone or pull a joint out of place. In fact, most breeders with Toy Poodles often will not place their puppies with families with very young children. Some Cavapoo breeders prefer to breed from Miniature Poodles, as the puppies are sturdier and more robust health-wise.

Often puppies regard children as playmates - just like a child regards a puppy as a playmate; young pups and children are playful, both easily getting over-excited. A puppy may chase, jump and nip a small child – although it can be the other way round; a gentle pup may need protecting from the children! Lively behaviour is not aggression; it is normal play for puppies. See **Chapter 10. Training** on how to deal with puppy biting.

Train your pup to be gentle with your children and your children to be gentle with your puppy.

Your dog's early experiences with children should all be positive. If not, a dog may become nervous or mistrustful - and what you want around children is most definitely a relaxed dog that does not feel threatened by a child's presence.

 Discourage the kids from picking up your gorgeous new puppy at every opportunity. Constantly picking up a Cavapoo puppy can lead to the dog becoming less independent and more needy.

Teach your children respect for their dog, which is a living creature with his or her own

needs, not a toy. Cavapoos are extremely loyal; they may even become protective and watch over your children. Take things steady in the beginning and your Cavapoo will undoubtedly form a deep, lifelong bond that your children will remember throughout their lives.

Make sure puppy gets enough time to sleep – **which is most of the time in the beginning** - so don't let children (or adults!) constantly pester him. Sleep is very important to puppies, just as it is for babies. Also, allow your Cavapoo to eat at his or her own pace uninterrupted; letting youngsters play with the dog while eating is a no-no as it may promote gulping of food or food aggression.

One reason that some dogs end up in rescue centres is that owners are unable to cope with the demands of small children AND a dog. On the other hand, it is also a fantastic opportunity for you to educate your little darlings (both human and canine) on how to get along with each other and set the pattern for wonderful lasting friendships.

Single People

Many single adults own dogs, but if you live alone, be aware that getting a puppy will require a lot of dedication on your part. There will be nobody to share the responsibility, so taking on a dog requires a huge commitment and a lot of your time if the dog is to have a decent life.

If you are out of the house all day as well, it is not really fair to get a puppy, or even an adult dog – and a Cavapoo is definitely not a good choice as this hybrid absolutely thrives on interaction with humans. However, if you work from home or are at home for much of the day and can spend considerable time with the pup, then a Cavapoo will most definitely become your closest friend.

Older People

If you are older or have elderly relatives living with you, Cavapoos can be a good choice and great company, as they are usually adaptable as far as exercise goes. They are a very affectionate breed and love to snuggle up. Puppies generally require a lot of energy and patience from any owner, so if you are older and/or less mobile, an adult Cavapoo may be a better option.

Dogs can, however, be a great tonic for fit, older people. In his mid-80s my father still walked his dog for an hour to 90 minutes every day - a morning and an afternoon walk and then a short one last thing at night – even in the rain or snow. He grumbled occasionally, but it was good for him and it was good for the dog - helping to keep them both fit and socialised! They got fresh air, exercise and the chance to communicate with other dogs and their humans. My father's dog passed away, but at 89 he still walks with a friend's dog every day.

You're never alone when you've got a dog. Many older people get a canine companion after losing a loved one (a husband, wife or previous much-loved dog). A pet gives them something to care for and love, as well as a constant companion.

Bear in mind that dog ownership is not cheap, so budget for annual pet insurance, veterinary fees, a quality pet food, etc. The RSPCA in the UK has estimated that owning a dog costs an average of around £1,300 ($1,700) a year!

Other Pets

However friendly your puppy is, if you already have other pets in your household, they may not be too happy at the new arrival. Cavapoos generally get on well with other animals, but it might not be a good idea to leave your hamster or pet rabbit running loose; many young puppies have play and/or prey instincts – although if introduced slowly, they may well become best friends!

Both the Cavalier and Poodle have hunting backgrounds, so it is no surprise that some Cavapoos do have quite a strong hunting instinct outdoors, when they love to chase cats, birds and other small creatures - but once back indoors they often get along perfectly happily with other small animals sharing their home.

Karen Howe is the proud first-time owner of two F1 Cavapoos: Rodney, aged three, and two-year-old Mabel. She says: "We also own a cat, Alfie, whom they do get on with and, in the evenings, will happily settle and relax next to. However, there are times when they will chase him - this tends to occur mainly around mealtimes!

"The strong prey drive is probably the biggest surprise about my Cavapoos. Rodney is worse than Mabel; I feel she has learnt it from him! Both are avid squirrel chasers and will chase birds and most things that move - even a plastic bag blowing out to sea! For this reason, I put bells on their harnesses when walking in the woods. This scares the squirrels away so the dogs have nothing to chase, and if they do chase off, I can still hear where they are."

Karen's photo shows Rodney enjoying a relaxing moment with Alfie the cat.

Cavapoo puppies are naturally curious and playful and will sniff and investigate other pets. They may even chase them in the beginning. Depending on how lively your pup is, you may have to separate them to start off with, or put a playful Cavapoo into a pen or crate initially to allow a cat to investigate without being mauled by a hyperactive pup who thinks the cat is a great playmate.

This will also prevent your puppy from being injured. If the two animals are free and the cat lashes out, your pup's eyes could get scratched. A timid Cavapoo might need protection from a bold cat - or vice versa. A bold cat and a gentle Cavapoo will probably settle down together quickest!

If things seem to be going well with no aggression, then let them loose together after one or two supervised sessions. Take the process slowly; if your cat is stressed or frightened, he may decide to leave. Our feline friends are notorious for abandoning home because the board and lodgings are better down the road...

More than One Dog

Well-socialised Cavapoos have no problem sharing their home with other dogs. Introduce your puppy to other dogs and animals in a positive, non-frightening manner that will give him or her confidence. Supervised sessions help everyone to get along and for the other dog or dogs to accept your new pup. If you can, introduce them for the first time outdoors on neutral ground, rather than in the house or in an area that one dog regards as his own. You don't want the established dog to feel he has to protect his territory, nor the puppy to feel he is in an enclosed space and can't get away.

Everything should hopefully run smoothly. The Cavapoo's popularity is due in no small part to the lack of aggression, affectionate nature, gentle temperament and ability to get on with children and other dogs.

If you are thinking about getting more than one pup, you may wish to consider waiting until your first Cavapoo is a few months old or an adult before getting a second, especially if you are a first-time owner. This enables you to give your full attention to one dog, get housetraining out of the way and your new puppy can learn some training from the older dog. On the other hand, some owners prefer to get the messy part over and done with in one go and get two together.

One such owner is Claire Cornes, of Bedfordshire, UK, whose Cavapoos Bob and Boris **(pictured)** are now two and a half-years-old. Claire says: "Bob and Boris are F1 with a Cavalier mum and Miniature Poodle dad and they are from the same litter.

"I work full time, but was lucky enough to work from home for the first two months after they came home. I spent a lot of time training them apart when they were pups, so I got a bond with them and they didn't rely on each other. After this my friend or in-laws came and sat with them for a few hours a day. Now we have a dog walker or my in-laws are over.

"Before I got two, I spoke to other owners who also have littermates to ensure I was doing the right thing. They have never had any signs of *littermate syndrome*. Bob and Boris both have their own little character and are very different. By the way, they were sold as fox red, but have both faded, so they now look apricot with darker ears and muzzle."

Like Claire, if you are thinking of getting two puppies at the same time, you should be prepared to devote a lot of time and energy to each dog for the first few weeks and months. Owning two dogs can be twice as nice - it's also double the food and vet's bills. Here is some cautionary advice from UK rescue organisation The Doodle Trust:

"Think about why you are considering another dog. If, for example, you have a dog that suffers from separation anxiety, then rather than solving the problem, your second dog may learn from your first and you then have two dogs with the problem instead of one. The same applies if you have an unruly adolescent; cure the problem first and only introduce a second dog when your first is balanced."

"A second dog will mean double vet's fees, insurance and food. You may also need a larger car, and holidays will be more problematic. Sit down with a calculator and work out the expected expense – you may be surprised. Two dogs will need training, both separately and together. If the dogs do not receive enough individual attention, they may form a strong bond with each other at the expense of their bond with you.

"If you are tempted to buy two puppies from the same litter - DON'T! Your chances of creating a good bond with the puppies are very low and behaviour problems with siblings are very common. If you have a very active dog, would a quieter one be best to balance his high energy or would you enjoy the challenge of keeping two high energy dogs? You will also need to think of any problems that may occur from keeping dogs of different sizes and ages.

"If you decide to purchase a puppy, you will need to think very carefully about the amount of time and energy that will be involved in caring for two dogs with very different needs. A young puppy will need to have his exercise restricted until he has finished growing and will also need individual time for training. If you decide to keep a dog and female together, then you will obviously need to address the neutering issue."

At the end of the day, the decision is, of course, entirely yours. Cavapoos do especially well with other Cavapoos. Like Cavalier King Charles Spaniels, they seem to have an affinity with their own breed.

Gender

You have to decide whether you want a male or a female puppy. In terms of gender, much depends on the temperament of the individual dog - the differences WITHIN the sexes are greater than the differences BETWEEN the sexes.

One difference, however, is that females have heat cycles and, if she is intact, you will have to restrict your normal exercise routine when she comes into heat (every six months or so) to stop unwanted attention from other dogs.

Another is that some Cavapoos can be territorial and it is not unusual for some (males in particular) to 'mark' their territory by urinating. Many breeders and most, if not all, vets and rescue organisations recommend neutering pet dogs. If your dog is to remain intact – i.e. not neutered or spayed - think carefully about which gender would be most suitable.

If you already have dogs or are thinking of getting more than one, you do, however, have to consider gender. You cannot expect an unneutered male to live in a relaxed manner with an unspayed female on heat. Similarly, two uncastrated males may not always get along; there may be too much testosterone and competition. If an existing dog is neutered or spayed and you plan to have your dog neutered or spayed, then gender should not be an issue.

NOTE: Some breeders will specify that your pup has to be spayed or neutered within a certain timeframe to prevent indiscriminate breeding.

Your main points of reference in terms of size, physical appearance and temperament are the puppy's parents. Even if the father is not present, you should always see the mother and watch how she interacts with the puppies – are they really hers? Discuss with your breeder which puppy would best suit you.

Which Colour?

There are many colours of Cavapoos; some of the most common ones are:

- *Apricot* – can be light, medium or dark
- *Gold or Cream*
- *Black*
- *Black and White* - also called *Parti*
- *Ruby* – rich red
- *Blenheim* - tan/chestnut and white
- *Tricolour* - black and white with tan markings on eyebrows, cheeks, underside of tail, inside ears and legs
- *Black and Tan*

Some of these colours can be **Abstract**, with small white markings usually on the dog's chest, chin, paws, tail tip or neck, or **Parti**, with a mainly white background *(pictured)*.

If you have set your heart on a favourite colour, remember to check that all the health boxes have been ticked as well.

....

Puppy Stages

It is important to understand how a puppy develops into a fully-grown dog to help you become a good owner. **The first few months and weeks of a puppy's life will have an effect on his or behaviour and character for life.** This Puppy Schedule outlines the early stages:

Birth to seven weeks	A puppy needs sleep, food and warmth. He needs his mother for security and discipline and littermates for learning and socialization. The puppy learns to function within a pack and learns the pack order of dominance. He begins to become aware of his environment. During this period, puppies should be left with their mother.
Eight to 12 weeks	At the age of eight weeks, the brain is fully developed and **he now needs socializing with the outside world.** He needs to change from being part of a canine pack to being part of a human pack. This period is a fear period for the puppy, avoid causing him fright and pain.
13 to 16 weeks	Training and formal obedience should begin. **This is a critical period for socializing with other humans, places and situations.** This period will pass easily if you remember that this is a puppy's change to adolescence. Be firm and fair. His flight instinct may be prominent. Avoid being too strict or too soft with him during this time and praise his good behavior.
Four to eight months	Another fear period for a puppy is between seven to eight months of age. It passes quickly, but be cautious of fright or pain which may leave the puppy traumatized. The puppy reaches sexual maturity and dominant traits are established. Your Cavapoo should now understand the following commands: 'sit', 'down', 'come' and 'stay'.

Plan Ahead

Choosing the right breeder is one of the most important decisions you will make. Like humans, your puppy will be a product of his or her parents and will inherit many of their characteristics. Natural temperament and how healthy your puppy will be now and throughout his life will depend to some extent on the genes of his parents. By the way, character is formed by a combination of temperament (or *nature*) and *nurture* - and how you treat your dog influences his or her character.

Responsible breeders health test their dogs; they check the health records and temperament of the parents and only breed from suitable stock. Sound Cavapoo puppies are not cheap – health screening, socialisation and first-rate care come at a cost.

Expect to pay anything upwards of $2,000 in the US and £2,000+ in the UK for a pup from health-tested parents. See **Chapter 11. Cavapoo Health** for more info on what certificates to ask to see.

 BE PATIENT. Start looking months or even a year or more before your planned arrival. There is usually a waiting list for Cavapoo pups from health-tested parents and good breeders, so once you know you can afford a well-bred Cavapoo, then get your name down on a list.

Phone or email your selected breeders to find out about future litters and potential dates, but don't commit until you've asked lots of questions. Good breeders will also ask a lot of questions about yourself, your household and living conditions and how you will take care of their much-loved puppy.

A healthy Cavapoo will be your irreplaceable companion for the next decade or more, so why buy one from a pet shop or general advertisement? Would you buy an old car or a house with potential structural problems just because it looked pretty in a website photo or was cheap? The answer is probably no, because you know you would be storing up stress and expense in the future.

UK owner Denise Knightley has two Cavapoos, three-and-a-half-year-old *Carmen Rose, pictured (left) with Domino,* aged 18 months. She said: "Our daughter bought Carmen Rose from a home breeder through an advertisement on the Pets4Homes website. Her parents were not health-tested and only the mother was seen.

"Unfortunately, she was unable to care for her as Carmen Rose had severe medical issues; Grade 4+ patella luxation. This required surgery at just five months old and a long convalescence confined to a crate. We fell in love with Carmen Rose and agreed to keep her, then, two years later, we bought our second Cavapoo, Domino.

"This time we bought from a well-known and recommended breeder. We were on their waitlist for about eight months and visited them to see both parents. We were provided with pedigree certificates and health documents for both parents."

Visit the breeder personally at least once. However, with the vast distances sometimes involved, this is not always possible in the USA. In this case, speak at length on the phone to the breeder and ask lots of questions. Ethical breeders, like the ones involved in this book, will be happy to answer all your questions - and will have lots for you too. They will provide photos and perhaps even videos and emails of your chosen pup's progress if you can't visit.

Some will also arrange escorted "Nanny Transport" to safely deliver the pup to your home, or an agreed meeting place. If you are satisfied with the answers to your questions, and have checked the Puppy Contract and Health Guarantee on offer, then go ahead and put your name down on the waiting list. The age at which a puppy leaves a breeder varies, but Cavapoos should be at least eight weeks old. Puppies need to be given the time to physically develop and learn the rules of the pack from their mothers and litter mates. Small breeds tend to mature later than larger breeds and, for this reason, some Cavapoo breeders like to hold on to the puppies for a little longer. In some USA states it is illegal to sell a puppy less than eight weeks of age.

Keep Your Eyes Wide Open

The Cavapoo's parent breeds of Cavalier and Poodle are not without health issues. There are no cast iron guarantees that your puppy will be 100% healthy and have a good temperament. **However, choosing a Cavapoo breeder who health screens his or her breeding dogs increases these chances enormously.**

Good breeders do not sell their dogs on general purpose websites, on Gumtree, eBay, Craig's List or Freeads, in car parks or somebody else's house. Puppies in pet shops often come from puppy mills. If you live in the UK and are looking online at dogs on Pets4Homes, follow their guidelines carefully, check the health screening and see the pup with his or her mother.

There is a difference between *a hobby breeder* and a *backyard or backstreet breeder*. Both may breed just one or two litters a year and keep the puppies in their homes, but that's where the similarity ends.

Hobby or home breeders often don't have a website and you will probably find out about them via word of mouth. Good hobby breeders are usually breed enthusiasts or experts; sometimes they show their pedigree dogs. They carry out health tests and lavish care and love on their dogs. **Backyard breeders** generally have less knowledge about a breed, pay scant attention to the health and welfare of their dogs and are doing it primarily for the extra money.

Our advice is the same: check the health certificates of the parents and the health and welfare of the dogs and puppies. Ask lots of questions - are the breeders very knowledgeable and passionate about their dogs and the breed/crossbreed?

Increasingly, the way most new owners are finding their puppies is by an online search. Many breeders have their own websites, and it's worth taking time to learn how to spot the good ones from the bad ones. Here are four reasons for buying from a good breeder:

1. **Health.** Some new owners make the mistake of thinking that because they are buying a crossbreed dog, he or she will automatically be healthier than a purebred. However, genetic diseases can be passed on to crossbreed puppies too. Cavaliers have many potentially inheritable health issues - and Poodles have a few. Health testing the parents is the best way of preventing genetic disorders from being passed on.

2. **Socialisation.** Scientists and dog experts now realise that the critical socialisation period for dogs is up to the age of four months. An unstimulated puppy is likely to be less well-adjusted and more likely to have fear or behaviour issues as an adult.

3. **Temperament.** Good breeders select their breeding stock based not only on sound structure and health, but also on temperament. They will not breed from an aggressive or overly timid dog.

4. **Peace of Mind.** Most good breeders give a genetic health guarantee with their puppy of anything from a year to several years. They will also agree to take the dog back at any time in its life (although you may find it too hard to part with your beloved dog by then).

If a pup is advertised at a price that seems too good to be true; then it is. You can bet your last penny that the dam and sire are not superb examples, that they haven't been fully health screened, and that the puppies are not being fed premium quality food, nor has the breeder started the all-important socialisation and housetraining processes.

....

Caveat Emptor – Buyer Beware

Getting a puppy is such an emotional decision - and one that will hopefully have a wonderfully positive impact on you and your family's life for over a decade. Because Cavapoo puppies command such high prices, sadly there are some unscrupulous people breeding puppies.

Here is some advice to try and help you avoid the pitfalls of getting a puppy from a puppy mill, a puppy broker (somebody who makes money from buying and selling puppies) or even an importer.

If you suspect that this is the case, walk away. You can't buy a Rolls Royce or a Lamborghini for a couple of thousand pounds or dollars - you'd immediately suspect that the 'bargain' on offer wasn't the real thing. No matter how lovely it looked, you'd be right - and the same applies to Cavapoos. Here are some signs to look out for:

- ❧ Avoid websites where there are no pictures of the owners, home or environment

- ❧ If the website shows lots of photos of cute puppies with little information about the family, breeding dogs, health tests and environment, click the **X** button

- ❧ Don't buy a website puppy with a shopping cart symbol next to his picture

- ❧ See the puppy with his or her mother face-to-face. If this is not possible due to distances, speak at length on the phone with the breeder and ask questions

- ❧ Good breeders are happy to provide lots of information and at least one reference before you commit

- ❧ If the breeder is reluctant to answer your questions, look elsewhere

- ❧ Pressure selling: on the phone, the breeder doesn't ask you many questions and then says: "There are only X many puppies left and I have several other buyers interested." Walk away

- ❧ At the breeder's, ask to see where the puppy is living. If the breeding dogs are not housed in the family home, as is sometimes the case in the USA, they should be in suitable, clean buildings, not too hot or cold, with access to grass and time spent with humans

- ❧ Ask to see the other puppies from the litter

- ❧ The mother is not with the puppies, but brought in to meet you

- ❧ You hear: *"You can't see the parent dogs because......"* ALWAYS ask to see the parents and, as a minimum, see the mother and how she looks and behaves with the pups. If the pups are really hers, she will interact with them.

- ❧ If the breeder says that the dam and sire are Kennel Club or AKC registered, ask to see the registration papers

- ❧ Photographs of so-called 'champion' ancestors do not guarantee the health of the puppy

- ❧ The puppies look small for their stated age

- The person you are buying the puppy from did not breed the dog themselves. Deal with the breeder, not an intermediary

- The place you meet the puppy seller is a car park, somebody else's house or place other than the puppies' home

- The seller tells you that the puppy comes from top, caring breeders from your or another country. Good breeders don't sell their puppies through brokers

- Price – if you are offered a very cheap Cavapoo, he or she almost certainly comes from dubious stock. Anyone selling their puppies at a knock-down price has cut corners and it's often health screening

- Ask to see photos of the puppy from birth to present day

- If you get a rescue Cavapoo, make sure it is from a recognised rescue group and not a 'puppy flipper' who may be posing as a do-gooder, but is in fact getting dogs (including stolen ones) from unscrupulous sources

- NEVER buy a puppy because you feel sorry for it; you are condemning other dogs to a life of misery

- If you have any doubt, go with your gut instinct and WALK AWAY - even if this means losing your deposit. It will be worth it in the long run

Breeder Charlotte Purkiss, of Lotties Cavapoos, Hampshire, UK, adds this about websites: "Avoid websites that want money straight away to go on their waiting list. Feedback or reviews may not be genuine, so always ask if you can be put in contact with a few of them and ask lots of questions to see if the info adds up. My reviewers are always open for contact.

"If there are a lot of different breeds on the website, then you know they are breeding on a big scale, which means there is no attention to detail or one-to-one rearing. This is why puppies often develop behavioural problems that are hard to reverse – and then you may need to get a professional behaviourist involved. Your gut instinct is a good one to follow if something is just not right or adding up when looking through any website."

One first-time UK Cavapoo owner had this cautionary tale: "I initially enquired by email and was told there were three puppies available. The breeder said I needed to make a decision as other people were interested, so we paid a deposit of £1,000 (with a guarantee that "the colour won't fade," which of course it has) and I was so excited. We were told that the parents were health tested.

"When we went to collect our puppy, we arrived at a large, beautiful house with a big driveway and very smart outbuildings. The operation was so slick. We were shown into a foyer - we didn't actually see where the dogs were kept. Our puppy was in the woman's arms and the mother and father were brought in, although the mother didn't react to the puppy.

"Alarm bells were ringing at the back of my mind, but we were far too down the line to walk away. When someone handles you a gorgeous bundle of fluff, you are not going to turn it down.

"I had looked online and seen favourable reviews of the breeder. After we got our puppy, I did some more research and found out they have 38 breeding bitches producing 300 puppies a year. The puppies were just like consumable goods; the breeder didn't ask us any questions. When I criticised them online, I was issued with a solicitor's letter. I learned that other people had also had the same, which is why there are no negative reviews of this breeder.

"We were very stupid; you live and learn. After our experience, my advice is to look for a small hobby breeder, check that all the health tests have been done and see the puppy with the Mum."

 Bad breeders do not have two horns coming out of their head! Most will be perfectly pleasant when you approach them. Use this chapter to learn how to spot the signs.

Advice from the Kennel Club

Unscrupulous breeders have sprung up to cash in on the high price of "designer crossbreed" dogs and unfortunately, the Cavapoo attracts more than its fair share of breeders whose main aim is to make money. That's not to say there aren't some excellent Cavapoo breeders out there; there are. You just have to - as the ancient saying goes - separate the wheat from the chaff!

While new owners might think they have bagged "a bargain", this more often than not turns out to be false economy and an emotionally disastrous decision when the puppy develops health problems due to poor breeding, or behavioural problems due to poor temperament or lack of socialisation.

The UK's Kennel Club has issued a warning of a puppy welfare crisis, with some truly sickening statistics. As many as one in four puppies bought in the UK may come from puppy farms - and the situation is no better in North America. The KC Press release stated: "As the popularity of online pups continues to soar:

- ❖ **Almost one in five pups bought (unseen) on websites or social media die within six months**
- ❖ One in three buy online, in pet stores and via newspaper adverts - outlets often used by puppy farmers – this is an increase from one in five in the previous year
- ❖ The problem is likely to grow as the younger generation favour mail order pups, and breeders of fashionable breeds flout responsible steps."

The Kennel Club added: "We are sleepwalking into a dog welfare and consumer crisis as new research shows that more and more people are buying their pups online or through pet shops, outlets often used by cruel puppy farmers, and are paying the price with their pups requiring long-term veterinary treatment or dying before six months old. The increasing popularity of online pups is a particular concern. Of those who source their puppies online, half are going on to buy "mail order pups" directly over the internet."

The KC research found that:

- ❖ One third of people who bought their puppy online, over social media or in pet shops failed to experience "overall good health"
- ❖ Almost one in five puppies bought via social media or the internet dies before six months old
- ❖ Some 12% of puppies bought online or on social media end up with serious health problems that require expensive on-going veterinary treatment from a young age

Caroline Kisko, Kennel Club Secretary, said: "More and more people are buying puppies from sources such as the internet, which are often used by puppy farmers. Whilst there is nothing wrong with initially finding a puppy online, it is essential to then see the breeder and ensure that they are doing all of the right things. This research clearly shows that too many people are failing to do this, and the consequences can be seen in the shocking number of puppies that are becoming sick or dying. We have an extremely serious consumer protection and puppy welfare crisis on our hands."

The research revealed that the problem was likely to get worse as mail order pups bought over the internet are the second most common way for the younger generation of 18 to 24-year-olds to buy a puppy (31%). Marc Abraham, TV vet and founder of Pup Aid, said: "Sadly, if the "buy it now" culture persists, then this horrific situation will only get worse. There is nothing wrong with sourcing a puppy online, but people need to be aware of what they should then expect from the breeder.

"For example, you should not buy a car without getting its service history and seeing it at its registered address, so you certainly shouldn't buy a puppy without the correct paperwork and health certificates and without seeing where it was bred. However, too many people are opting to buy directly from third parties such as the internet, pet shops, or from puppy dealers, where you cannot possibly know how or where the puppy was raised.

"Not only are people buying sickly puppies, but many people are being scammed into paying money for puppies that don't exist, as the research showed that 7% of those who buy online were scammed in this way." The Kennel Club has a lot of info on the dos and don'ts of buying a puppy at www.thekennelclub.org.uk/paw

....

Breeders' Advice

There are good Cavapoo breeders out there, spend the time to find one - and then get your name down for the next litter.

Here's some advice from one experienced breeder in the US: "THE BAD: Shy away from the 'Puppy For Sale' internet sites that list multiple breed puppy sales, such as Puppyfind.com, Petfinder.com, nextdaypets and breeders.net. You know the sites; you click on a drop down menu to 'Select the breed you are looking for', then up pops 50 different listings of puppies from different kennels or individuals.

"These sites are used frequently by puppy millers, dog brokers and in general poor quality breeders with poor quality animals. It is a known fact that they 'bait/switch'. This means that they bait their ads with pictures of lovely puppies and/or dogs that are NOT the animal for sale and, in most cases, not even of an animal they own. Many steal pictures from reputable breeders' sites of darling pups and adults and place those pictures on their ad. Then, when someone makes a purchase, they are sent a dog that is the same breed/color and sex, but clearly NOT the one pictured!

"I have had my dogs and puppies' pictures stolen on many occasions. I have even had these people say they have a litter sired by one of our Champion stud dogs with a direct link back to my stud's page. They are dishonest, so avoid at all cost.

"THE SHODDY: Now, let's say you type in 'Cavapoo Breeders in Tennessee' or 'Georgia' or 'Florida'. What frequently pops up (for any state) is a website called (State)Cavapoobreeders.net or similar. These are **dog broker sites.**

"A dog broker is someone who finds buyers (acts as a second party) for pups produced from puppy mills and bad breeders. These online sites are jammed packed full of poorly-bred pups, highly over-priced and in most cases they are known to use the same pictures to advertise hundreds of pups of the same color/sex/breed in different states. They mislead you into thinking the puppy is located in

your state, only for you to later find out it was shipped in to you from five states away.

"Forget about warranties, forget about dealing with the breeder. By the time you get that puppy, he or she has changed hands several times and is exposed to many different pups that the broker hauls around. Not a good risk to take.

"THE WORST: pet stores, auctions and flea markets. No doubt you have heard: "Never purchase from a pet store as they are all puppy mill-bred puppies." IT IS TRUE! By the time they get to the store, they have been transformed from a feces/urine/flea-infested rag into the cutest puppy ever. Sickly, raised in cages, filth and more. Flea markets are full of Amish puppy mill pups. They are deplorable.

"Auctions are used for those pups a breeder can't find a home for. Don't fall victim to these people. I know how many of us want to reach out and save these puppies and give them a good home, but when you pay for them, you are just keeping these types of deplorable people in the breeding business and causing their dogs to suffer at the cost of being bred over and over until they die or are killed when they are no longer able to produce puppies.

"Just stay away from newspaper ads, Craigslist, eBay Pets, AKC online advertising. None of these are used by reputable breeders. Even AKC online ads are full of back yard breeders galore. Some terms you will not find on reputable breeder websites include: USDA Inspected - If you see these words run! It means they ARE NOT hobby breeders. They usually are high volume mass producers (puppy mills)."

Charlotte Purkiss has a lot of advice for potential owners: "Finding the right breeder is hard and can be a minefield, so be very vigilant. It's important you do your research, otherwise your puppy's life could be cut short due to improper care, no health testing done prior to mating, poor conditions the puppies are reared in, etc."

Pictured enjoying a day out is F1b ruby Cavapoo, Balfour, bred by Charlotte. Photo courtesy of owners Ariella Wagerman and Joshua Gertner.

"Poor breeders cut corners as they have little or no care or love for the Mum or puppies, so they rear them in what can be awful conditions. Often in outbuildings with poor sanitation, which breaks my heart. Those poor unloved Mum and babies are either alone or with lots of other breeds on the go. Some don't know who the father is if they have two or more entire males roaming, so please don't buy from these sorts of people.

"I have heard far too many bad stories in my years of breeding, due to families contacting me in absolute distress. They have either put down a deposit as they felt pressured and were hoping to save the puppy from its awful environment. Then there are the situations where they have already collected the puppy and it is very ill. It has cost thousands to get the puppy well again, but often the puppy doesn't make it; it is so upsetting.

"This is why families need to be made aware of these awful breeders who are only thinking of lining their own pockets. Don't be one of those families; do your research. The main danger signs are:

- A very unclean environment
- No up-to-date paperwork or fake documents. Always check that Kennel Club names, numbers and dates match. Also, check any DNA paperwork, make sure everything matches and never rush when looking through them
- If the breeder cannot provide the dam at any time, walk away as it may not be the puppy's mother. Usual excuses are: "Oh she's gone for walk or a ride in the car." I've heard this from many families who have experienced it when viewing puppies
- Never feel pressured to leave after a short time of visiting. I offer whole morning or afternoon sessions for each family and it's they that decide when to leave my home as there is a lot to take in
- If puppies appear to be sick or withdrawn contact the appropriate authorities

"You can expect to pay anything from £2,000 plus in the UK for a Cavapoo from health-tested parents. It may seem a lot of money, but you have to remember a top breeder puts a lot of experience, time and love into making sure a healthy puppy has been reared so you can enjoy a happy, healthy furbaby!"

One US breeder added: "It is fine to advise UK buyers not to buy a Cavapoo puppy that is raised in a building near the house, rather than in the house. However, the same does not necessarily apply to the USA, where commercial breeders may be very good and ethical and NOT puppy farms, yet keep their puppies away from the house. New owners should look for:

- Breeders who are selective whom they sell to

- Breeders who keep the pup till he or she is socially ready to leave

- Breeders who offer future support; i.e. ones that offer refunds versus just replacement

- Breeders whose health guarantee is actually more than a "no death" guarantee

- Breeders that have the same lines for over five years, so you can track health, size and temperament"

Ten Signs of a Good Breeder

1. His or her breeding dogs are health tested with certificates to prove it.

2. The area where the puppies are kept is clean and the puppies look clean.

3. Their Cavapoos appear happy and healthy. The pups have clean eyes, ears, nose and bum (butt) with no discharge. They are alert, excited to meet new people and don't shy away from visitors.

4. The breeder encourages you to spend time with the puppy's parents - or at least the mother - when you visit. He or she wants your family to meet the puppy and are happy for you to visit more than once.

5. They are very familiar with Cavapoos, although some may also have one or two other breeds - many more breeds is a warning sign.

6. They feed their adults and puppies high quality dog food and give you some to take home and guidance on feeding and caring for your puppy. They will also be available for advice afterwards.

7. They provide you with a written Puppy Contract, Health Guarantee and Puppy Pack or Going Home Bag with items to help the pup's transition. They will show you records of the puppy's visits to the vet, vaccinations, worming medication, etc. and explain what other vaccinations your puppy will need.

8. They don't always have pups available, but keep a list of interested people for the next available litter. They don't over-breed, but do limit the number of litters from their dams.

9. They will, if asked, provide references from other people who have bought their puppies; call at least one.

10. And finally ... good Cavapoo breeders want to know their beloved pups are going to good homes and will ask YOU a lot of questions about your suitability as owners.

Charlotte adds: "Make sure the breeder provides you with all the DNA health test paperwork for the parents. Puppies should have been wormed and vaccinated. Mine also have a health check certificate, issued by our vet, at eight weeks old.

Do check both documents are not fake; check the vet's signature matches on the vaccination card and health certificate. Remember it's the law now in the UK that all puppies have to be microchipped before leaving the breeder. A good breeder offers a Contact of Sale, four weeks' free pet insurance, a Cavapoo book, high quality puppy food and a puppy Welcome Home bag with essentials. I include a folder with all the health testing paperwork, toys, puppy treats and toilet training pads - but these are only to be used under complete supervision as the puppy can chew and ingest it when you're not looking. I also have the pleasure of hand knitting blankets for my fur babies in their new home!

"I'm a firm believer that puppies should be only reared in the family home, where it is a warm, loving, natural environment. The puppy learns the sounds of a family home and becomes mentally stable, which is key when transitioning to your home. The home environment should be exceptionally clean at all times, especially the mother and puppy areas. The mother and puppies themselves should be clean and have no signs of illness or distress.

"When visiting or viewing puppies, take your time to have a good look around. You will probably know if it's right or not when you see the surroundings, after being outside and inside. Walk away promptly if you feel something is not right and report it to the local council or RSPCA."

 Take your puppy to a vet to have a thorough check-up within 48 hours of purchase. If your vet is not happy with the health of the dog, no matter how painful it may be, return the pup to the breeder. Keeping an unhealthy puppy will only cause more distress and expense in the long run.

Puppy Contracts

Most good breeders provide their puppy parents with an official Puppy Contract. This protects both buyer and seller by providing information on the puppy until he or she leaves the breeder. You should also have a health guarantee for a specified time period. A Puppy Contract will answer such questions as whether the puppy:

* Is covered by breeder's insurance and can be returned if there is a health issue within a certain period of time
* Was born by Caesarean section
* Has been micro-chipped and/or vaccinated and details of worming treatments
* Has been partially or wholly toilet trained
* Has been socialised and where he or she was kept

- And what health issues the pup and parents have been screened for
- What the puppy is currently being fed and if any food is being supplied
- Details of the dam and sire

It's not easy for caring breeders to part with their puppies after they have lovingly bred and raised them, and so many supply extensive care notes for new owners, which may include details such as:

- The puppy's daily routine
- Feeding schedule
- Vet and vaccination schedule
- General puppy care
- Toilet training
- Socialisation

In the UK, The Royal Society for the Prevention of Cruelty to Animals (RSPCA) has a downloadable puppy contract (*pictured*) endorsed by vets and animal welfare organisations; you should be looking for something similar from a breeder: https://puppycontract.rspca.org.uk/home and the AKC (American Kennel Club) has this article on Puppy Contracts: www.akc.org/expert-advice/dog-breeding/preparing-a-contract-for-puppy-buyers

....

Top 10 Tips for Choosing a Healthy Cavapoo

Once you've selected your breeder and a litter is available, you then have to decide WHICH puppy to pick, unless the breeder has already earmarked a pup for you after asking lots of questions.

A breeder may try and match you with a puppy to fit in with your household, lifestyle and schedule. Here are some signs to look for when selecting a puppy:

1. Your chosen puppy should have a well-fed appearance. He or she should not, however, have a distended abdomen (pot belly) as this can be a sign of worms - or other illnesses. The ideal puppy should not be too thin either; you should not be able to see his ribs.
2. His or her nose should be cool, damp and clean with no discharge.
3. The pup's eyes should be bright and clear with no discharge or tear stain. Steer clear of a puppy that blinks a lot, this could be the sign of a problem.
4. The pup's ears should be clean with no sign of discharge, soreness or redness and no unpleasant smell.
5. Check the puppy's rear end to make sure it is clean and there are no signs of diarrhoea.
6. The pup's coat should look clean, feel soft, not matted - and puppies should smell good! The coat should have no signs of ticks or fleas. Red or irritated skin or bald spots could be a sign of infestation or a skin condition. Also, check between the toes of the paws for signs of redness or swelling.
7. Gums should be clean and pink.
8. Choose a puppy that moves freely without any sign of injury or lameness. It should be a fluid movement, not jerky or stiff, which could be a sign of joint problems.

9. When the puppy is distracted, clap or make a noise behind her - not so loud as to frighten her - to make sure she is not deaf.

10. Finally, ask to see veterinary records to confirm your puppy has been wormed and had her first injections.

If you are unlucky enough to have a health problem with your pup within the first few months, a reputable breeder will allow you to return the pup. Also, if you get the Cavapoo puppy home and things don't work out for whatever reason, some breeders will also take the puppy back – either within a limited time frame or for the whole life of the puppy, although if it is more than one year later, you cannot expect the breeder to financially reimburse you.

Picking the Right Temperament

You've picked a Cavapoo, presumably, because you love their Teddy bear looks and are attracted to the breed's many good points: its good nature, small to medium size, eagerness to please, loyalty, close bond with humans, trainability and ability to get on well with children and other animals. While Cavapoos may share many common characteristics and temperament traits, each puppy also has his own individual character, just like humans.

Visit the breeder to see how your chosen pup interacts and get an idea of his character in comparison to the littermates. Some puppies will run up to greet you, pull at your shoelaces and playfully bite your fingers.

Others will be more content to stay in the den sleeping. Watch their behaviour and energy levels. Are you an active person who enjoys lots of daily exercise or would a less energetic puppy be more suitable? Having said that, one of the attractions of Cavapoos is that they are pretty adaptable – happy to go for a long ramble in the countryside or snuggle up with you on the couch. .

A submissive dog will by nature be more passive, less energetic and also possibly easier to train. A dominant dog will usually be more energetic and lively. He or she may also be more stubborn and need a firmer hand when  training or socialising with other dogs. If you already have a dominant dog at home, you have to be careful about introducing a new dog into the household; two dominant dogs may not live comfortably together.

There is no good or bad, it's a question of which type of character will best suit you and your lifestyle. Here are a couple of quick tests to try and gauge your puppy's temperament; they should be carried out by the breeder in familiar surroundings so the puppy is relaxed. It should be pointed out that there is some controversy over temperament testing, as a dog's personality is formed by a combination of factors, which include inherited temperament, socialisation, training and environment (or how you treat your dog):

❧ The breeder puts the pup on his or her back on her lap and gently rests her hand on the pup's chest, or

❖ She puts her hands under the pup's tummy and gently lifts the pup off the floor for a few seconds, keeping the pup horizontal.

A puppy that struggles to get free is less patient than one that makes little effort to get away. A placid, patient dog is likely to fare better in a home with young children than an impatient one.

Here are some other useful signs –

❖ Watch how he interacts with other puppies in the litter. Does he try and dominate them, does he walk away from them or is he happy to play with his littermates? This may give you an idea of how easy it will be to socialise him with other dogs

❖ After contact, does the pup want to follow you or walk away from you? Not following may mean he has a more independent nature

❖ If you throw something for the puppy, is he happy to retrieve it for you or does he ignore it? This may measure willingness to work with humans

❖ If you drop a bunch of keys behind the puppy, does he act normally or does he flinch and jump away? The latter may be an indication of a timid or nervous disposition. Not reacting could also be a sign of deafness

Decide which temperament would fit in with you and your family and the rest is up to you. Whatever hereditary temperament your Cavapoo has, it is true to say that dogs that have constant positive interactions with people and other animals during the first few months of life will generally be happier and more stable.

In contrast, a puppy plucked from its family too early and/or isolated for long periods will be less happy, which may lead to behaviour issues later.

Puppies are like children. Being properly raised contributes to their confidence, sociability, stability and intellectual development. The bottom line is that a pup raised in a warm, loving environment with people is likely to be more tolerant and accepting, and less likely to develop behaviour problems.

To sum up: a good course of action would be something like this:

1. Decide to get a Cavapoo.

2. Do your research.

3. Find a good breeder whose dogs are health tested.

4. Register your interest - and WAIT until a puppy becomes available.

5. Decide on a male or female.

6. Pick one with a suitable temperament to fit in with your family.

7. Enjoy 10 to 15 years with a beautiful, healthy Cavapoo.

Some people pick a puppy based on how the dog looks. If coat colour, for example, is very important to you, make sure the other boxes are ticked as well.

4. Bringing Puppy Home

Getting a new puppy is so exciting. You can't wait to bring your little bundle of joy home. Before that happens, you probably dream of all the things you and your fluffy little soul mate are going to do together; going for walks in the countryside, snuggling down by the fire, playing games together, setting off on holiday, maybe even taking part in organised activities or local dog shows.

Your pup has, of course, no idea of your big plans, and the reality when he or she arrives can be a bit of a shock for some owners!

Puppies are wilful little critters with minds of their own and sharp teeth. They leak at both ends, chew anything in sight, constantly demand your attention, nip the kids or anything else to hand, may cry a lot for the first few days and don't pay a blind bit of notice to your commands. There is a lot of work ahead before the two of you develop a unique bond.

Your pup has to learn what is required before he or she can start to meet some of your expectations - and you have to learn what your pup needs from you.

....

Once your new arrival lands in your home, your time won't be your own, but you can get off to a good start by preparing things before the big day. Here's a list of things to think about getting beforehand (your breeder may supply some of these):

Puppy Checklist

- ✓ A dog bed or basket
- ✓ Bedding – a Vetbed or Vetfleece would be a good choice, you can buy one online
- ✓ A towel or piece of cloth which has been rubbed on the puppy's mother to put in the bed
- ✓ A puppy gate and/or pen to initially contain the pup in one area of the house
- ✓ A crate if you decide to use one
- ✓ A collar or harness with identification tag and lead (leash)
- ✓ Food and water bowls, preferably stainless steel
- ✓ Puppy food – find out what the breeder is feeding and stick with that to start with
- ✓ Puppy treats, healthy ones like carrots or apple are best, no rawhide
- ✓ Newspapers, and a bell if you decide to use one, for potty training
- ✓ Poo(p) bags
- ✓ Toys and chews suitable for puppies
- ✓ A puppy coat if you live in a cool climate
- ✓ Old towels for cleaning/drying your puppy and partially covering the crate

AND PLENTY OF TIME!

Later on you'll also need grooming tools, (see **Chapter 13. Grooming**), dog shampoo, flea and worming products and maybe a travel crate. Many good breeders provide Puppy Packs to take home; they contain some or all of the following items:

- ✓ Registration certificate
- ✓ Pedigree certificate
- ✓ Buyer's Contract
- ✓ Information pack with details of vet's visits, vaccinations and wormings, parents' health certificates, diet, breed clubs, etc.
- ✓ Puppy food
- ✓ ID tag/microchip info
- ✓ Blanket that smells of the mother and litter
- ✓ Soft toy that your puppy has grown up with, possibly a chew toy as well
- ✓ Collar or harness and lead (sometimes)
- ✓ Four or five weeks' free insurance

Puppy Proofing Your Home

Before your puppy arrives, you may have to make a few adjustments to make your home safe and suitable. Puppies are small bundles of instinct and energy when they are awake, with little common sense and even less self-control. Young Cavapoos love to play and have a great sense of fun. They may have bursts of energy before they run out of steam and spend much of the rest of the day sleeping. As one breeder says: They have two speeds – ON and OFF!

Make sure there are no poisonous plants which your pup might chew and check there are no low plants with sharp leaves or thorns which could cause eye or other injuries. There are literally dozens of plants which can harm a puppy if ingested, including azalea, daffodil bulbs, lily, foxglove,

hyacinth, hydrangea, lupin, rhododendron, sweet pea, tulip and yew. The Kennel Club has a list of some of the most common ones at http://bit.ly/1nCv1qJ and the ASPCA has an extensive list for the USA at: http://bit.ly/19xkhoG Also, fence off any sharp plants, such as roses, which can injure a dog's eyes.

If you have a garden or yard that you intend letting your puppy roam in, make sure that every little gap has been plugged. You'd be amazed at the tiny holes puppies can escape through - and Cavapoo puppies don't have any road sense. *Pictured with her head stuck in a tiny gap in the fence is Laura Lambert's Dolly, who had to be rescued. Fortunately, she was unharmed.*

Avoid leaving your puppy unattended in the garden or yard if you live near a road, as dognapping is on the increase, partly due to the high cost and resale value of dogs. In the UK, some 2,000 dogs are now being stolen each year. The figures are much higher for the US where the AKC reports that dog thefts are on the rise and warns owners against leaving their dog unattended – including tying them up outside a store.

Puppies are little chew machines and puppy-proofing your home involves moving any breakable or chewable - including your shoes. Lift electrical cords, mobile phones and remote controls, etc. out of reach and block off any off-limits areas of the house, such as or your bedroom, with a child gate or barrier, especially as he or she may be shadowing you first few days. Just as with babies, it's up to you to keep them safe and set the boundaries – bo physically, in terms of where they can wander, and also in terms of behaviour – but gently and o step at a time.

Create an area where puppy is allowed to go, perhaps one or two rooms, preferably with a hard floor which is easy to clean, and keep the rest of the house off-limits, at least until housetraining (potty training) is complete. The designated area should be near a door to the garden or yard for housetraining. Restricting the area also helps the puppy settle in. She probably had a den and an area to run around in at the breeder's. Suddenly having the freedom of the whole house can be quite daunting - not to mention messy!

You can buy a barrier specifically made for dogs or use a baby gate, which may be cheaper. Although designed for infants, they work perfectly well with dogs; you might find a second-hand one on eBay. Choose one with narrow vertical gaps or mesh, and check that your puppy can't get his head stuck between the bars, or put a covering or mesh over the bottom of the gate initially. You can also make your own barrier, but bear in mind that cardboard and other soft materials will get chewed.

Gates can be used to keep the puppy enclosed in a single room or specific area or put at the bottom of the stairs. The gaps between the bars of some safety gates and pens are sometimes too big to keep very small puppies contained. One alternative is Dreambaby Retractable Gate, which has mesh instead of bars. It can be bought at Argos in the UK or at Amazon.com in the USA.

A puppy's bones are soft, and studies have shown that if pups are allowed to climb or descend stairs regularly, or jump on and off furniture, they can develop joint problems later in life.

 Don't underestimate your puppy! Young Cavapoos can be lively and determined; they can jump and climb, so choose a barrier higher than you think necessary.

The puppy's designated area or room should not be too hot, cold or damp and it must be free from draughts. Little puppies can be sensitive to temperature fluctuations and don't do well in very hot or very cold conditions. If you live in a hot climate, your new pup may need air conditioning in the summertime.

Just as you need a home, so your puppy needs a den. This den is a haven where your pup feels safe, particularly in the beginning after the traumatic experience of leaving his or her mother and littermates. Young puppies sleep for 18 hours or longer a day at the beginning; this is normal. You have a couple of options with the den; you can get a dog bed or basket, or you can use a crate, which can also speed up potty training. **See Chapter 7. Crate Training and Housetraining** for getting your Cavapoo used to - and even to enjoy - being in a crate.

It may surprise some American readers to learn that normal practice in the UK has often been to initially contain the puppy in the kitchen or utility room, and later to let the dog roam around the house at will. Some owners do not allow their dogs upstairs, but many do.

Most puppies' natural instinct is not to soil the area where they sleep. Put plenty of newspapers down in the area next to the den and your pup should choose to go to the toilet here if you are not

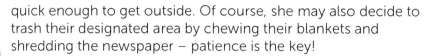

quick enough to get outside. Of course, she may also decide to trash their designated area by chewing their blankets and shredding the newspaper – patience is the key!

Some owners prefer to create a safe penned area for their pup, rather than use a crate, while others use both a pen and a crate. You can make your own barriers or buy a manufactured playpen. Playpens come in two types - mesh or fabric, *pictured.* A fabric pen is easy to put up and take down, but can be chewed so may not last long. A metal mesh pen can be expanded and will last longer, but is not quite as easy to put up or take down.

One breeder said: "A play pen can be used in much the same way as a crate and has an advantage of being very versatile in separating eating, sleeping and - in the early days - toileting. They are ideal for the busy Mum or Dad who has other things on their mind and can't possibly watch the puppy, children and try and tidy the house or prepare dinner. Again, it is peace of mind for the owner, knowing the pup is safe and not chewing anything it shouldn't."

If you have young children, the time they spend with the puppy should be limited to a few short sessions a day. Plenty of sleep is **essential** for the normal development of a young dog. You wouldn't wake a baby every hour or so to play, and the same goes for puppies. Wait a day or two - preferably longer – before inviting friends round to see your gorgeous little puppy. However excited you are, your new arrival needs a few days to get over the stress of leaving mother and siblings and to start bonding with you.

For puppies to grow into well-adjusted dogs, they have to feel comfortable and relaxed in their new surroundings and need a great deal of sleep. They are leaving the warmth and protection of their mother and littermates and while confident, well-socialised puppies may settle in right away, other puppies may feel sad. It is important to make the transition from the birth home to your home as easy as possible. Your pup's life is in your hands. How you react and interact with her in the first few days and weeks will shape your relationship and her character for the years ahead.

Chewing and Chew Toys

There are some things you can't move out of puppy's way, like kitchen cupboards, doors, sofas, fixtures and fittings, so don't leave your pup unattended for any length of time where she can chew something which is hard to replace. Chew toys are a must – avoid giving old socks, shoes or slippers or your pup will naturally regard your footwear as fair game, and rawhide chews can get stuck in a dog's throat or stomach.

A safe alternative to real bones or plastic chew bones are natural reindeer antler chew toys *(pictured, right),* which have the added advantage of calcium. Other natural chews preferred by some breeders include ears, dried rabbit pelt and tripe sticks – all excellent for teething puppies - once you have got over the gross factor!

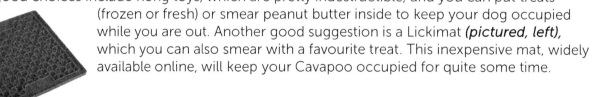

Other good choices include Kong toys, which are pretty indestructible, and you can put treats (frozen or fresh) or smear peanut butter inside to keep your dog occupied while you are out. Another good suggestion is a Lickimat *(pictured, left),* which you can also smear with a favourite treat. This inexpensive mat, widely available online, will keep your Cavapoo occupied for quite some time.

Bully sticks (*pictured*) are dog treats made from ...a bull's penis or pizzle! If you can get the picture of their source out of your mind, you might want to consider buying some as a healthy treat for your dog. Unlike rawhide, bully sticks are highly digestible, break down easily in the stomach and are generally considered safe for all dogs. They are made from 100% beef, normally contain no additives or preservatives, come in different sizes and dogs love 'em. Puppies should be supervised while eating bully sticks or any other treats.

Dental bones are great for cleaning your dog's teeth, but many don't last for very long with a determined chewer; one that can is the Nylabone Dura Chew Wishbone, which is made of a type of plastic infused with flavours appealing to dogs. Get the right size and throw it away if it starts to splinter after a few weeks.

The Zogoflex Hurley and the Goughnut are both strong and float, so good for swimmers – and you'll get your money back on both if your Cavapoo destroys them! For safety, the Goughnut has a green exterior and red interior, so you can tell if your dog has penetrated the surface - as long as the green is showing, you can let your dog "goughnuts."

A natural hemp or cotton tug rope is another option, as the cotton rope acts like dental floss and helps with teeth cleaning. It is versatile and can be used for fetch games as well as chewing.

Puppies' stomachs are sensitive - so be careful what goes in. Even non-poisonous garden plants can cause intestinal blockages and/or vomiting. Like babies, pups can quickly dehydrate if they are vomiting or have diarrhoea. If either continues for a couple of days, seek medical advice.

The First Few Days

Before you collect your puppy, let the breeder know what time you will arrive and ask her not to feed the pup for a couple of hours beforehand - unless you have a very long journey, in which case the puppy will need to eat something. She will be less likely to be car sick and should be hungry when she lands in her new home. The same applies to an adult dog moving to a new home.

When you arrive, ask for an old towel or toy which has been with the pup's mother – you can leave one on an earlier visit to collect with the pup. Or take one with you and rub the mother with it to collect her scent and put this with the puppy for the first few days. It will help her to settle in. In the US, some puppies are flown to their new homes; good breeders still provide a Puppy Pack which includes something with the mother's scent and a toy.

Make sure you get copies of any health certificates relating to the parents. Again, good breeders have a Contract of Sale or Puppy Contract which outlines everyone's rights and responsibilities – see **Chapter 3. Before You Get Your Puppy** for details. It should also state that you can return the puppy if there are health issues within a certain time frame – although if you have picked your puppy carefully, it should not come to this. The breeder will also give you details of worming and any vaccinations, as well as an information sheet.

Find out exactly what the breeder is feeding and how much. You cannot suddenly switch a pup's diet; their digestive systems cannot cope with a sudden change. In the beginning, stick to whatever the pup is used to. Again, good breeders will send some food home with the puppy.

The Journey Home

Bringing a new puppy home in a car can be a traumatic experience. Your puppy will be sad at leaving his or her mother, brothers and sisters and a familiar environment. Everything will be strange and frightening and he or she may well whimper and whine - or even bark - on the way home. If you can, take somebody with you on that first journey – some breeders insist on having somebody there to hold and cuddle the pup to make the journey less traumatic. Under no circumstances have the puppy on your lap while driving. It is simply too dangerous - a Cavapoo puppy is extremely cute, often wriggly and far too distracting.

Have an old towel between your travel companion and the pup as (s)he may quite possibly pee - the puppy, not the passenger!

If you have to travel any distance, take a crate – either a purpose-made travel crate or a wire crate which she will use at home.

Photo of one-year-old Pip, bred by Charlotte Purkiss, safe in her crate in the back of the car, courtesy of James Tuthill.

Travel crates can be soft canvas or hard plastic. A plastic one should have holes in the sides to allow air flow. Cover the bottom of the crate with a waterproof material and then put a comfortable blanket on top. You can put newspapers in half of the crate if the pup is partly housetrained.

If you have a journey of more than a couple of hours, make sure that you take water to give the puppy en route. She may need the toilet, but don't let her outside on to the ground as she is not yet fully vaccinated.

Arriving Home

As soon as you arrive home, let your puppy into the garden or yard and when she 'performs,' praise her for her efforts. These first few days are critical in getting your puppy to feel safe and confident in her new surroundings. Spend time with the latest addition to your family, talk to her often in a reassuring manner. Introduce her to her den and toys, slowly allow her to explore and show her around the house – once you have puppy-proofed it.

Cavapoo puppies are extremely curious - and amusing, you might be surprised at their reactions to everyday objects. Puppies explore by sniffing and mouthing, so don't scold for chewing. Instead, put objects you don't want chewed out of reach and replace them with chew toys. Some puppies can be more "mouthy" than others; if yours is like this, make sure she has safe toys to chew.

Almost all Cavapoo owners say that theirs get on well with other animals. However, it is important that you introduce them to each other in the right conditions. Do it slowly and in supervised sessions on neutral territory or outdoors where there is space so neither feels threatened - preferably once the pup has got used to her new surroundings, not as soon as you walk through the door. Gentleness and patience are the keys to these first few days, so don't over-face pup.

Have a special, gentle puppy voice and use her new name frequently - and in a pleasant, encouraging manner. **Never use her name to scold** or she will associate it with bad things. The sound of her name should always make her want to pay attention to you as something good is going to happen - praise, food, playtime, and so on.

Resist the urge to pick the puppy up – no matter how irresistible she is! Let her explore on her own legs, encouraging a little independence - this is important for Cavapoos. Cavapoo pups are tiny and it is so tempting to pick them up and cuddle them all the time, but this will only encourage them to become "clingy".

One of the most important things at this stage is to ensure that your puppy has enough sleep – **which is nearly all of the time** - no matter how much you want to play with her, cuddle her or watch her antics when awake. If you haven't decided what to call your new puppy yet, 'Shadow' might be a good suggestion, as he or she will follow you everywhere! Many puppies from different breeds do this, but Cavapoos like to stick close to their owners – both as puppies and adults. Our website receives many emails from worried new owners. Here are some of the most common concerns:

- My puppy won't stop crying or whining
- My puppy is shivering
- My puppy won't eat
- My puppy is very timid
- My puppy follows me everywhere, she won't let me out of her sight
- My puppy sleeps all the time, is this normal?

These behaviours are quite common at the beginning. They are just a young pup's reaction to leaving her mother and littermates and entering into a strange new world. It is normal for puppies to sleep most of the time, just like babies. It is also normal for some puppies to whine a lot during the first couple of days. A few puppies might not whine at all. If they are confident and have been well socialised and partly housetrained by the breeder, settling in will be much easier.

Make your new pup as comfortable as possible, ensuring she has a warm (but not too hot), quiet den away from draughts, where she is not pestered by children or other pets. Handle her gently, while giving her plenty of time to sleep. Some breeders recommend keeping the pup in a crate near your bed for the first couple of nights, so she knows she is not alone. If she makes sad little whimpering noises or barks, talk softly and gently stroke her. Resist the urge to pick her up and cuddle her every time or she will learn that crying always gives her the reward of your attention.

A puppy will think of you as her new mother and it is quite normal for them to want to follow you everywhere, but after a few days start to leave your pup for short periods of a few minutes, gradually building up the time. A puppy unused to being left alone at all can grow up to have separation anxiety - see **Chapter 8. Cavapoo Behaviour** for more information.

If your routine means you are normally out of the house for a few hours during the day, get your puppy on a Friday or Saturday so she has at least a couple of days to adjust to her new surroundings. A far better idea is to book time off work to help your puppy to settle in, if you can, or if you don't work, leave your diary free for the first couple of weeks.

Helping a new pup to settle in is virtually a full-time job. This can be a frightening time for some puppies. Is your puppy shivering with cold or is it nerves? Avoid placing your pup under stress by making too many demands. Don't allow the kids to pester the pup and, until they have learned how to handle a dog, don't allow them to pick her up unsupervised, as they could inadvertently damage her delicate little body.

If your pup won't eat, spend time gently coaxing. If she leaves her food, take it away and try it later. Don't leave it down all of the time or she may get used to turning her nose up at it. Some Cavapoos are notoriously fussy eaters. Breeder Laura Koch says: "Cavapoos would rather play than eat, so the first few days it's important to hand-feed kibble or play in the bowl with your finger while sitting with them so they think they are eating with a sibling."

If your puppy is crying, it is probably for one of the following reasons:

- ❧ She is lonely

- ❧ She is hungry

- ❧ She wants attention from you

- ❧ She needs to go to the toilet

If it is none of these, then physically check her over to make sure she hasn't picked up an injury. Try not to fuss too much! If she whimpers, reassure her with a quiet word. If she cries loudly and tries to get out of her allotted area, she probably needs to go to the toilet. Even if it is the middle of the night, get up and take her outside. Praise her if she goes to the toilet.

The strongest bonding period for a puppy is between eight and 12 weeks of age. The most important factors in bonding with your puppy are TIME and PATIENCE, even when he or she makes a mess in the house or chews something. Remember, your Cavapoo pup is just a baby (dog) and it takes time to learn not to do these things.

Spend time with your pup and you will have a loyal friend for life. Cavapoos are very focused on their humans and that emotional attachment may grow to become one of the most important aspects of your life – and certainly his or hers.

Where Should the Puppy Sleep?

Where do you want your new puppy to sleep? You cannot simply allow a pup to wander freely around the house – at least not in the beginning. Ideally, she will be in a contained area, such as a pen or crate, at night. While it is not acceptable to shut a dog in a cage all day, you can keep your puppy in a crate at night until housetrained. Even then, some adult dogs still prefer to sleep in a crate.

You also have to consider whether you want the pup to permanently sleep in your bedroom or elsewhere. If it's the bedroom, do not allow her to jump on and off beds and/or couches or race up and down stairs until she has stopped growing, as this can cause joint damage.

Some breeders recommend putting the puppy in a crate (or similar) next to your bed for the first two or three nights before moving her to the permanent sleeping place. Knowing you are close and being able to smell you will help overcome initial fears. She may still cry when you move her further away or out of your bedroom, but that should soon stop - you just have to block your ears for a couple of nights! She will have had those few days to get used to her new surroundings and feeling safe with you.

Eight or nine-week-old puppies can't go through the night without needing to pee (and sometimes poo); their bladders simply aren't up to it. To speed up housetraining, consider getting up half way through the night from Day One for the first week or so to let your pup outside for a pee. Just pick her up, take her outside with the minimum of fuss, praise the pee and put her back into the crate. After that, set your alarm for an early morning wake-up call.

NOTE: While I and many breeders recommend getting up in the night in the beginning, some breeders are against it, as they don't believe it speeds up housetraining. Ask your own breeder's advice on this one.

We definitely don't recommend letting your new pup sleep on the bed. She will not be housetrained and also a puppy needs to learn her place in the household and have her own safe place. It's up to you whether you decide to let her on the bed when she's older.

Photo of Winston enjoying forty winks on the floor courtesy of Lindsey McDonald.

If you do allow your dog to sleep in the bedroom but not on the bed, be aware that it is not unusual for some Cavapoos - like many other types of dog — to snuffle, snore, fart and - if not in a crate - pad around the bedroom in the middle of the night and come up to the bed to check you are still there! None of this is conducive to a good night's sleep.

While it is not good to leave a dog alone all day, it is also not healthy to spend 24 hours a day together. Cavapoos can become very clingy and while this is very flattering for you, it actually means that the dog is more nervous and less sure of herself when you are not there. She becomes too reliant on you and this increases the chances of separation anxiety when you do have to leave her.

Breeder Laura Koch endorses this: "It is very important with the Cavapoos NOT to overly bond with them the first day or two; one must give them plenty of space and independent time to learn to entertain themselves. If not, this can set them up for separation anxiety."

A Cavapoo puppy that is used to being on her own every night is less likely to develop attachment issues, so consider this when deciding where she should sleep. If you decide you definitely DO want your pup to sleep in the bedroom from Day One, put her in a crate or similar with a soft blanket covering part of the crate initially. Put newspapers inside and set your alarm clock.

Puppy Tips

We asked a number of Cavapoo breeders and owners what advice they have for bringing a puppy home, starting with Tracey Nott: "It's a big step for both the puppy and its owners. Plan ahead for collecting your puppy and bringing it home; if you can, visit the breeder a number of times to familiarise yourself with the dog.

"Make sure your puppy has a quiet place it can call its own to sleep undisturbed. If there is a blanket with the mother's scent, let the puppy have that in its bed. You may experience some signs of distress to start with, so comfort your puppy, but do not pamper too much. We provided Ethel with a bed in a suitably-sized crate to start with, which included puppy pads and water. Be careful if you give any toys as they can chew and swallow bits. Arrange to see your vet early on so they can assess your puppy and record their details in case of an emergency."

Claire Cornes, whose Cavapoos Bob and Boris are from the same litter: "The first few months were very hard, especially with two; you need eyes in the back of your head! Please ensure you do your research before getting a puppy; it's hard work, you need a lot of time, patience and lots of love.

"They slept in the kitchen in their playpen for the first nine months. We then went on holiday where they slept close to our room. When we got home they kept waking at 4am, and they eventually ended up in our room. They have a bed on the floor, but spend most nights at the bottom of my bed! One thing which surprises me about Cavapoos is how fussy they can be with food - this only applies to their dinner. They are hungry, but getting them to eat can be tricky. Don't spend a fortune on different foods; make dinnertime fun, use Kongs, games, etc. to get them to eat."

Val Boshart: "Millie *(pictured)* at first was very timid (which is still a big part of her personality when she is faced with new situations), but about one-and-a half-days in, it seemed like her batteries had been put in. Suddenly she was zooming around her pen, jumping, nipping and acting quite wild. She sure shocked us!

"It was fun to see how comfortable she felt, and we immediately began working on stopping the nipping and giving her opportunities to get that energy out, like running in the backyard. We tried to keep the first couple days quite calm, but did invite a couple friends to stop by here and there to ensure she would keep meeting new people and wouldn't have any social issues. That was her favorite part, and she still loves visitors!"

Here are some more comments: "Make sure you have all wires away and install stair gates if needed. I recommend a playpen and medium-sized crate, with toys only being allowed in there under supervision. Anything on the puppy's level that can be chewed or knocked over needs to be moved out of reach.

"Your garden should be all properly fenced in and any poisonous plants removed. Small shingle or stones can be a hazard to puppies, as they have been known to swallow them, so be aware and avoid or cover them over until the pup is a lot older.

"Max settled in within a couple of days, although he did cry for two nights. We did cuddle him and talk to him a lot. I left a blanket with his mother before we collected him and put it in his bed. I also put one of my tops in his bed when he was left on his own."

"Cavapoos are fearless at first and need help with getting down from furniture."

"Archie slept in the kitchen until he could be trusted to sleep an entire night. Now he is allowed to sleep in the lounge with access to the kitchen where his water bowl is. We have never used a crate."

"I fell in love with Harper instantly, so the bond was there straight away, I think this helped her settle in and also helped me to adjust to a new puppy. My tips would be to ignore the bad behaviour and give lots of praise for the good. Another tip I found - I used to wrap an old top of mine around a hot water bottle and pop into her crate on a night, I found that this helped settled her in as she could smell my scent and felt the warmth, so it was like I was close by."

"She was smelly when she arrived, but that was down to her breeder. My advice is to remain calm, play, cuddle and crate-train immediately if that is your intention. I cover the crate with a blanket and leave a night light on, I also left classical music on and took her out for potty before bedtime. You have to accept that it will be the dog's main carer that does all the training work and make sure the household knows the rules to prevent puppy confusion. It was a tad stressful juggling family responsibilities with training puppy that doesn't understand time!"

"Take everything at puppy's pace, but start as you mean to go on. Ignore any behaviour you don't want, or remove your attention for a minute, then give lots of praise when they do the right things. Play some games with the food if they won't eat. They will be nippy to start but it does pass! Just be consistent."

Pictured is F1 Dolly doing what all puppies love to do...chew! Photo courtesy of Laura Lambert.

....

Top Tips For Working Cavapoo Owners

We don't recommend getting a Cavapoo if you are out at work all day, as Cavapoos are companion dogs that thrive on interaction with humans. But if you're determined to get one when you're out for extended periods, here are some tips:

1. If you can afford it, leave him at doggie day care where he can socialise with other dogs. If you can't, come home during your lunch break or employ a dog walker (or neighbour) to take him out for a walk in the middle of the day.

2. Do you know anybody you could leave your dog with during the day? Consider leaving your dog with a reliable friend, relative or neighbour who would welcome the companionship of a dog without the full responsibility of ownership.

3. Take him for a walk before you go to work – even if this means getting up at the crack of dawn – and spend time with him as soon as you get home. Exercise generates serotonin in the brain and has a calming effect. A dog that has been exercised will be less anxious and more ready for a good nap.

4. Leave him in a place of his own where he feels comfortable. If you use a crate, leave the door open. You may need to restrict access to other areas of the house to prevent him coming to harm or chewing things you don't want chewed. If possible, leave him in a room with a view of the outside world; this will be more interesting than staring at four blank walls.

5. Make sure that it does not get too hot during the day and there are no cold draughts.

6. Leave toys available to play with to prevent destructive chewing. Stuff a Kong toy with treats or peanut butter to keep him occupied or buy a Lickimat.

7. **Make sure he has access to water at all times.** Dogs cannot cool down by sweating; they do not have many sweat glands (which is why they pant, but this is much less efficient than perspiring) and can die without sufficient water.

8. Consider getting a companion for your Cavapoo, bearing in mind that this will involve even more of your time and twice the expense.

9. Consider leaving a radio or TV on very softly in the background. The 'white noise' can have a soothing effect on some pets. If you do this, select your channel carefully – try and avoid one with lots of bangs and crashes or heavy metal music!

10. Stick to the same routine before you leave your dog home alone. This will help him to feel secure. Before you go to work, get into a daily habit of getting yourself ready, then feeding and exercising your Cavapoo. Dogs love routine. But don't make a huge fuss of him when you leave as this can also stress the dog; just leave the house calmly.

Similarly, when you come home, your Cavapoo may feel starved of attention and be pleased to see you. Greet him normally, but try not to go overboard by making too much of a fuss as soon as you walk through the door. Give a pat and a stroke then take off your coat and do a few other things before turning your attention back to your dog. Lavishing too much attention on your Cavapoo the second you walk through the door may encourage needy behaviour or separation anxiety.

Vaccinations and Worming

It is a good idea to have your Cavapoo checked out by a vet within a couple of days of picking him up. In fact, some Puppy Contracts stipulate that the dog should be examined by a vet within a certain time frame – often 48 hours. This is to everyone's benefit and, all being well, you are safe in the knowledge that your puppy is healthy, at least at the time of purchase. Keep your pup on your lap away from other dogs in the waiting room as he or she will not yet be fully protected against canine diseases.

Vaccinations

All puppies need immunisation and currently the most common way of doing this is by vaccination. An unimmunised puppy is at risk every time he meets other dogs as he has no protection against potentially fatal diseases – another point is that it is unlikely a pet insurer will cover an unvaccinated dog.

It should be stressed that vaccinations are generally quite safe and side effects are uncommon. If your Cavapoo is unlucky enough to be one of the **very few** that suffer an adverse reaction, here are some signs to look out for; a pup may exhibit one or more of these:

MILD REACTION - Sleepiness, irritability and not wanting to be touched. Sore or a small lump at the place where he was injected. Nasal discharge or sneezing. Puffy face and ears.

SEVERE REACTION - Anaphylactic shock. A sudden and quick reaction, usually before leaving the vet's, which causes breathing difficulties. Vomiting, diarrhoea, staggering and seizures.

A severe reaction is rare. There is a far greater risk of your Cavapoo either being ill and/or spreading disease if he or she does not have the injections.

The usual schedule is for the pup to have the first vaccination at eight or nine weeks of age, usually before leaving the breeder. This gives protection from a number of diseases in one shot.

In the UK these are Distemper, Canine Parvovirus (Parvo), Infectious Canine Hepatitis (Adenovirus) and Leptospirosis. Most vets also recommend vaccinating against Kennel Cough (Bordetella). In the US this is known as DHPP. Puppies in the US also need vaccinating separately against Rabies. There are optional vaccinations for Coronavirus and - depending on where you live and if your dog is regularly around woods or forests - Lyme Disease.

A puppy requires a second vaccination two to four weeks later. He or she is clear to mix with other animals two weeks after the second vaccinations.

- ❖ Boosters for Distemper, Parvo and Canine Hepatitis are every three years
- ❖ Boosters for Leptospirosis are every year.

Leptospirosis is a bacterial infection that attacks the body's nervous system and organs. It is spread through infected rat pee and contaminated water, so dogs are at risk if they swim in or drink from stagnant water or canals. Outbreaks can often happen after flooding.

Diseases such as Parvo and Kennel Cough are highly contagious and you should not let your new arrival mix with other dogs - unless they are your own and have already been vaccinated - until two weeks after his last vaccination, otherwise he will not be fully immunised. Parvovirus can also be transmitted by fox faeces.

The vaccination schedule for the USA is different, depending on which area you live in and what diseases are present. Full details can be found by typing *"AKC puppy shots"* into Google, which will take you to this page: www.akc.org/content/health/articles/puppy-shots-complete-guide

You shouldn't take your new puppy to places where unvaccinated dogs might have been, like the local park. This does not mean that your puppy should be isolated - far from it. This is an important time for socialisation. It is OK for the puppy to mix with other dogs that you 100% know are up-to-date with their vaccinations and annual boosters. Perhaps invite a friend's dog round to play in your yard/garden to begin the socialisation process.

Once your puppy is fully immunised, you have a window of a few weeks when it's the best time to introduce him to as many new experiences as possible - dogs, people, traffic, noises, other animals, etc. This critical period before the age of four and a half to five months is when he is at his most receptive to socialisation. It is important that all of the experiences are **positive** at this stage of life; don't frighten or over-face your little puppy. Socialisation should not stop after a few months, but should continue for the rest of your dog's life.

The vet should give you a record card or send you a reminder when a booster is due, but it's also a good idea to keep a note of the date in your diary. Tests have shown that the Parvovirus vaccination gives most animals at least seven years of immunity, while the Distemper jab provides immunity for at least five to seven years. In the US, many vets now recommend that you take your dog for a 'titer' test once he has had his initial puppy vaccinations and one-year booster.

Titres (Titers in the USA)

Some breeders and owners feel strongly that constantly vaccinating our dogs is having a detrimental effect on our pets' health. Many vaccinations are now effective for several years, yet some vets still recommend annual "boosters".

One alternative is titres. The thinking behind them is to avoid a dog having to have unnecessary repeat vaccinations for certain diseases as he or she already has enough antibodies present. Known as a VacciCheck in the UK, they are still relatively new here; they are more widespread in the USA.

Not everybody agrees with titres. One English vet we spoke to commented that a titre is only good for the day on which it is carried out, and that antibody levels may naturally drop off shortly afterwards, possibly leaving the animal at risk. He added that the dog would still need vaccinating against Leptospirosis. His claim is strongly refuted by advocates of titre testing.

To 'titre' is to take a blood sample from a dog (or cat) to determine whether he or she has enough antibodies to guarantee immunity against a particular disease, usually Parvovirus, Distemper and Adenovirus (Canine Hepatitis). If so, then an annual injection is not needed. Titering is not recommended for Leptospirosis, Bordetella or Lyme Disease, as these vaccines provide only short-term protection. Many US states also require proof of a Rabies vaccination.

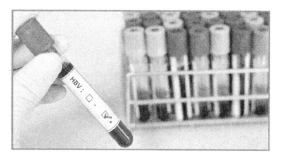

The vet can test the blood at the clinic without sending off the sample, thereby keeping costs down for the owner. A titre for Parvovirus and Distemper currently costs around $100 or less in the US, and a titre test in the UK costs as little as £40.

Titre levels are given as ratios and show how many times blood can be diluted before no antibodies are detected. So, if blood can be diluted 1,000 times and still show antibodies, the ratio would be 1:1000, which is a 'strong titre,' while a titre of 1:2 would be 'weak.' A *strong (high) titre* means that your dog has enough antibodies to fight off that specific disease and is immune from infection. A **weak titre** means that you and your vet should discuss revaccination - even then your dog might have some reserve forces known as 'memory cells' which will provide antibodies when needed. (If you are going on holiday and taking your dog to kennels, check whether the kennel accepts titre records; many don't as yet).

One UK dog breeder said: "Most people don't realise that there are tests you can do to ensure that you don't over-vaccinate or over-worm your dog. It is well known that, although very rare, all vaccinations can have potential adverse reactions. These can range from mild problems such as cystitis to a severe autoimmune disease. There are also a lot of discussions going on as to whether the over-vaccination of dogs may be linked to the increased rates of cancers.

"When my puppies go to their new homes, I tell all my owners to follow their vet's advice about worming and vaccinating, as the last thing new owners require is to be at odds with their vets. However, a few owners do express concern about all the chemicals we are introducing into our puppies' lives and if they do, I explain how I try to give my dogs a chemical-free life, if possible, as adult dogs. All dogs must have their puppy vaccinations.

"Instead of giving my adult dogs their core vaccinations for Canine Distemper, Parvovirus and Adenovirus (Hepatitis) every three years, I just take my dogs down to the local vet and ask them to do something called a titre test, also known as a VacciCheck. They take a small amount of blood and send it to a lab and the lab checks for antibodies to the diseases. If they have antibodies to the diseases, there is no reason to give dogs a vaccination. If a puppy has its puppy vaccinations, it is now thought that the minimum duration of immunity is between seven and 15 years.

"However, you should note that there is a separate vaccination for Leptospirosis and Canine Parainfluenza, which is given annually. Leptospirosis is recommended by the BSAVA (British Small Animal Veterinary Association). Leptospirosis is more common in tropical areas of the world and not that common in England. In order to make a decision about whether to give this to your dog annually, you need to talk to your vet and do some research yourself so you can make an informe decision. It may be that Leptospirosis is a problem in your area.

If you want to do some of your own research, then Ronald Schulz and Catherine O'Driscoll are some of the leading authorities on vaccinations and The Pet Welfare Alliance is also a good source of information."

She added: "We vaccinate our children up to about the age of 16. However, we don't vaccinate adults every one to three years, as it is deemed that the vaccinations they receive in childhood will cover them for a lifetime. This is what is being steadily proved for dogs and we are so lucky that we can titre test our dogs so we don't have to leave it to chance."

Another breeder added: "A healthy Cavapoo is dependent on the owner feeding, maintaining, training and exercising the dog. Some factors in ill health are considered to be environmental and this is beyond the control of the breeder. However, I do not vaccinate my dogs beyond the age of four to five years, I now have them titre tested. Every dog I have titre tested aged five to 10 years has been immune to the diseases vaccinated against when younger. I believe many vets over-vaccinate. Also, many dogs are given too many flu and worming chemicals."

The (UK) Kennel Club now includes titre testing information into its Assured Breeder Pack, but has yet to include it under its general information on vaccines on its website. The AKC (American Kennel Club) discusses titering here: www.barkingbulletin.com/great-akc-wellness-plus-benefit and there is more info at: www.embracepetinsurance.com/waterbowl/article/titer-testing

....

Worming

All puppies need worming (technically, deworming). A good breeder will give the puppies their first dose of worming medication at around two weeks old, then probably again at five and eight weeks before they leave the litter – or even more often. Get the details and inform your vet exactly what treatment, if any, your pup has already had.

The main worms affecting puppies are roundworm and tapeworm. In certain areas of the US, the dreaded heartworm can also pose a risk. If you live in an affected area, discuss the right time to start heartworm medication when you visit your vet for puppy vaccinations – it's usually from a few months old. The pill should be given every month when there is no heavy frost (frost kills mosquitos that carry the disease); giving it all year round gives the best protection. The heartworm pill is by prescription only and deworms the dog monthly for heartworm, round, hook, and whip worm.

Roundworm can be transmitted from a puppy to humans – often children - and can in severe cases cause blindness, or miscarriage in women, so it's important to keep up to date with worming. Worms in puppies are quite common; they are often picked up through their mother's milk. If you have children, get them into the habit of washing their hands after they have been in contact with the puppy – lack of hygiene is the reason why children are most susceptible.

Most vets recommend worming a puppy once a month until he is six months old, and then around every two to three months. If your Cavapoo is regularly out and about running through woods and fields, it is important to stick to a regular worming schedule, as he is more likely to pick up worms than one which spends less time in the Great Outdoors.

Fleas can pass on tapeworms to dogs, but a puppy would not normally be treated unless it is known for certain he has fleas - and then only with caution. You need to know the weight of your puppy and then speak to your vet about the safest treatment to get rid of the parasites. It is not usually worth buying a cheap worming or flea treatment from a supermarket, as they are usually far

.han more expensive vet-recommended
, such as **Drontal.** NOTE: Drontal cannot be given to
ies.

ple living in the US have contacted our website claiming
ite treatment **Trifexis** has caused severe side effects, and
ath, to their dogs. Although this evidence is only anecdotal,
you might want consider avoiding Trifexis to be on the safe side -
even if your vet recommends it.

Breeders must worm their puppies as they are all born with worms picked up from the mother's milk. However, there are ways to reduce worming treatments for adult dogs. Following anecdotal reports of some dogs experiencing side effects with chemical wormers, more owners are looking to use natural wormers on their dogs. If you go down this route, check exactly which worms your chosen herbal preparation deals with – it may not be all of them.

Also, a method of reducing worming medication by testing your dog's stools is becoming more popular. You send a small sample of your dog's poo(p) off in an envelope every two to three months. If the result is positive, your dog needs a worming treatment, but if negative, no treatment is necessary. In the UK this is done by veterinary labs like Wormcount www.wormcount.com and similar options are available in the USA – there is even a "fecal worm test" available at just over $20 from Amazon.com.

5. Cavapoos for People with Allergies

Allergies are on the increase. Amazingly, 50 million Americans are allergy sufferers, according to the Asthma and Allergy Foundation of America. They affect as many as 30% of adults and 40% of children according to the American College of Allergy, Asthma, and Immunology. Of these, some 10 million people are pet allergy sufferers. In fact, allergic disease, including asthma, is the fifth leading chronic disease in the U.S. in people of all ages and the third most common chronic disease in children aged under 18.

In the UK, pets are the second most common cause of allergy in the home, with 40% of asthmatic children reacting to dogs. According to Allergy UK, each year the number of people affected increases by 5% and half of all sufferers are children. The UK is one of the top three countries in the world for the most allergies, with 50% of youngsters having one or more allergy within the first 18 years of life (Journal of Clinical & Experimental Allergy.)

It's a common misconception that people are allergic to animal hair, but that's not true. What they are actually allergic to are proteins - or allergens. These are secreted by the animal's oil glands and then shed with the **dander**, which is dead skin cells (like dandruff).

They are also found in dog saliva and urine, and if you are allergic to either, it is unlikely you will ever to be able to successfully share your home with a dog, even a hypoallergenic breed.

This is what Allergy UK has to say: "Dog and cat allergen is found in the animals' saliva, sweat and urine. Animals frequently groom themselves, so the allergens coat the hair and skin cells (dander) which, when shed, spread throughout the home or other buildings. Once the saliva dries, it becomes airborne very easily.

"These allergens can be very persistent in the environment, with detectable levels found in homes where no pets have lived for many years, and dog allergen can be found in schools, having been brought there on the clothing and shoes of pupils and teachers. Cat allergen in particular is very 'sticky' in this way.

"In dogs, routine and proper grooming, preferably outdoors, has been shown to greatly decrease shedding of hair and may decrease skin irritation and secondary bacterial infection. Grooming, preferably by someone other than the sensitive individual, should therefore be an important part of a management strategy for dog-allergic patients."

It is possible for many pet allergy sufferers to enjoy living with a dog without spending all of their time sneezing, wheezing, itching or breaking out in rashes. Millions of people are proving the case. Any dog can cause an allergic reaction, although you stand a far higher chance of having no reaction to a dog which is a regarded as low-shedding and hypoallergenic. By the way, there is no such thing as a **non-shedding dog**; all dogs shed some hair.

NOTE: The definition of 'hypoallergenic' is "**having a decreased tendency** to provoke an allergic reaction." This does not mean that hypoallergenic dogs won't provoke a reaction in some people. That's because, without the human and the dog spending time together, it is impossible to say that a specific allergy sufferer will NOT have a reaction to a specific puppy. Every dog is different; every person's allergy is different. This is why some breeders won't let their dogs go to allergy sufferers; they simply don't want to see their beloved pup out of a home if the sneezing starts.

Cavapoo Coats and Allergies

You are either already the proud owner of a Cavapoo or you are thinking about becoming one, and if you're reading this, you or someone you know probably has allergies. Cavapoos make excellent family pets; they look cute, have cheerful temperaments, get along well with people and other dogs and you've heard that they are non-shedding and "hypoallergenic".

The Poodle, with its tightly curled wool coat, is regarded as a minimal shedder and a "hypoallergenic" breed. This is one of the main reasons why Poodle hybrids like the Cavapoo have become so popular – there are now oodles of Doodles and piles of Poos! The Cavapoo cannot truly be regarded as a hypoallergenic crossbreed, as some dogs have coats similar to the Cavalier, which is not hypoallergenic and does shed hair. However, there is plenty of anecdotal evidence that individual Cavapoos with wool or wavy coats shed little to no hair and do not trigger a reaction in many allergy sufferers.

Having said that, there is no breed that will never cause an allergic reaction in someone. This is particularly true with crossbreeds including the Cavapoo, as there are even more variables than with a purebred dog – even puppies in the same litter can look different, be different sizes and have different coat types. The Cavapoo can have several different types of coat:

- ❉ **Long and silky** like the Cavalier
- ❉ **Wiry** similar to some Terriers
- ❉ **Wool** with tight curls like the Poodle; this is low-shedding
- ❉ **Fleece or Wavy** which is the most common and is also low shedding

You may be surprised to learn that all of these dogs *pictured below* are Cavapoos. Notice the difference in size, appearance and coat type. From left to right: tightly-curled coat similar to the Poodle, Cavalier-type coat, popular wavy coat, wiry Terrier-like coat.

Most prospective owners are looking for puppies with **wavy** coats, as these combine hypoallergenic coat qualities with the classic Teddy bear look *(photo second from right).*

Recently there has been a breakthrough in genetics. A test has been developed to determine coat type and some breeders at the cutting edge, particularly in the US, are testing their breeding dogs with the aim of consistently producing hypoallergenic Cavapoo puppies. Scientists have identified a particular allele, or gene variant, called MC5R that affects the degree of shedding in various breeds. (It's never quite that simple, as the degree of shedding is actually regulated by a combination of genes!)

However, further research has found a link between the shedding allele, named the SD locus, and the **Furnishings** or **Improper Coat** allele, F locus. ("Furnishings" are longer eyebrows and moustache).

Dogs that inherit two copies of the **Improper Coat** allele - described as **F/F** - have the lowest level of shedding. Those that inherit two copies of the SD locus, **SD/SD,** shed most.

Although there are no guarantees, when good Cavapoo breeders select their breeding stock, coat is an important factor — whether through scientific tests or by knowing the characteristics of their breeding stock. In the future, more breeders will use the **Improper Coat** genetic test as it is relatively easy and inexpensive and takes much of the guesswork out. This will undoubtedly have an influence on how our Cavapoos look in the future.

Laura Koch, of Petit Jean Puppies, Arkansas, USA, is one breeder who tests: "We do DNA genetic coat testing on our Poodles to make sure they will produce a low to non-shedding F1 Cavapoo.

"Since some Poodles can carry an Improper Coat gene(IC), it's very important to test the genetics behind the Poodle being used for breeding F1 Cavapoos.

"Poodles should be F/F for full furnishings, but some actually carry the IC (Improper Coat) gene and are carrying one gene for furnishings and one gene for no furnishings. These are still purebred poodles. But it's very important that a breeder uses Poodles that are fully furnished and carry two genes and are FF. If they do not, they could produce shedding pups in both F1 and F1b. The slick-face Cavalier already carries the IC gene, so the Poodle should be fully furnished."

Pictured is F1 Petit Jean Puppy, Prada, courtesy of Heather Darnell. Prada is hypoallergenic; her mother was scientifically tested for the low-shedding coat gene.

....

Choosing a puppy

Selecting an experienced breeder is essential. He or she knows her dogs and is, in all likelihood, breeding for a no or low-shedding coat. The more experience breeders have, the more likelihood they have of knowing which dogs will produce low shedding puppies — especially if they carry out the **Improper Coat** genetic test.

If you decide you can't live without a dog, you have to put in extra time to make sure you pick the right puppy and make adjustments to your home as well to increase your chances of successfully living together. Allergies are all about tolerance loads - and a dog could tip you over the edge if your body is already battling triggers from other fronts.

Allergy sufferers should be aware that they may be fine with a Cavapoo puppy because tiny puppies often don't shed. But the coat changes in adolescence and this could trigger a reaction later on. It would be distressing if you were suddenly allergic to your one-year-old Cavapoo who has become a dearly-loved member of your family. If you have any doubts at all about a puppy - even a tiny reaction — please don't get him.

For those people with severe allergies, the only way to discover what triggers them is to undergo a series of medical tests and immunisation therapy. Remember:

No dog is totally non-shedding. No dog is totally hypoallergenic

Two further points to consider are that people's pet allergies vary greatly. Sufferers may react differently to different dogs within a breed or crossbreed, or even litter. A person may be fine with one puppy, yet have a reaction to his brother or sister. In broad terms, all dogs - even so-called 'hairless' dogs - have hair, dander, saliva and urine. Therefore all dogs *can* cause allergic reactions, but not all dogs do.

If a dog is shedding minimal amounts of hair, then the dander remains trapped within the coat. Hypoallergenic dogs shed very little - you might find the *occasional* dog hair or small fur ball around the house - which is why they have to be clipped.

If you have friends or neighbours with a Cavapoo, spend some time inside their house with their dog, stroke the dog, touch your face with the same hand, allow the dog to lick you - do you have a reaction? Did you have a reaction the following day? Rub the dog with a cloth, take it home and rub your face with it the following day. Any reaction? Look on Facebook for Poo or Doodle get-togethers in your area, ask if you can go along and meet some Cavapoos.

Once you have chosen your breeder, ask if you can visit the litter – this shouldn't be a problem in the UK. Once there, handle the dog, rub your hands on your face and lick your hands after you have touched the dog in order to absorb as much potential allergen as you can on your short visit. Take an old towel or piece of cloth and rub the puppy with it. Take this home with you and handle it to see if you get a delayed reaction - which can occur up to 48 hours later. You should also do this if you are buying a puppy or dog online. Once you've visited the dog and taken a cloth or towel home, wait at least 48 hours to see if you have a reaction before committing to buy. An honest seller will not have a problem with this; they will want to see their puppy settled in a suitable home.

If, as may be the case in the US, you cannot visit the breeder personally, ask if she will send a towel or cloth with the dog's saliva and hair on - just as Labradoodle creator Wally Conron did decades ago before sending the first hypoallergenic Doodle puppy all the way from Australia to Miami, Florida.

Check with the breeder to see if you can return the pup within a certain time period were you to have a reaction back at home. However, you cannot expect the breeder to take the dog back if the allergies only occur once the dog has reached adulthood.

Photo of this handsome fellow courtesy of Calla Lily Cavapoo.

Oklahoma hobby breeder Windie, who is also a Registered Nurse, added: "Cross-sensitivity was one method we used when people came to our home to do our "allergy play with the puppy test." One specific example was a family who came with their three children, one of whom had "dog allergies." We were going to test the child's tolerance to the Cavapoo, and we had no more than sat down on the floor when I saw a hive starting to appear on her forehead.

"We removed the puppies, her mommy administered Benadryl and she recovered just fine. They had a friend who had a Cavapoo and she had had no reactions to that dog. The Cavapoo cross is Cavalier to Poodle, and therefore we have the Cavalier dander burden in our home environment.

"So, we tried again. This time with an over-the-counter puppy coat allergy wash, and we met at a park instead of our home. The girl had no reaction and they were able to add a Cavapoo to their family."

....

Top 12 Tips for Reducing Pet Allergens

Here's an interesting fact: everyone with pet allergies can tolerate a certain amount of allergens (things they are allergic to). If that person is just below his or her tolerance, any additional allergen will push him or her over the edge, thus triggering a reaction. So if you reduce the general allergen load in the home, you'll be much more successful when you bring your dog home. Here are some tips for doing just that:

1. Get a HEPA air cleaner in the bedroom and/or main living room. HEPA stands for High Efficiency Particle Air - a type of air filter that removes 99.97% of all particles.

2. Use a HEPA vacuum cleaner. Neither the HEPA air nor vacuum cleaner is cheap, but if you suffer allergies and really want to share your life and home with a dog, they are worth considering. Both will dramatically improve the quality of the air you breathe in your home. Regardless of what vacuum you use, clean and dust your home regularly.

3. Carpets and curtains trap allergens and dust, so consider having hard floor coverings and blinds in the rooms where you spend most time.

4. **Keep the dog out of your bedroom**. We spend around a third of our lives here and keeping animals out can greatly reduce allergic reactions.

5. Wash your hands with an antibacterial soap after handling the dog and before eating – and make sure your children do the same. Avoid contact with other dogs and always wash your hands after you have handled any dog, including your own.

6. Get a non-allergic member of your family to brush your dog regularly - always outdoors - and regularly clean the bedding. Avoid using normal washing powder, as it may trigger a reaction in dogs with sensitive skin.

7. Do not allow your dog on the couch, bed or any other furniture. Have clean seat covers or blankets which are washed regularly if your dog travels in the car.

8. Keep your dog's skin healthy by regularly feeding a good multivitamin and a fatty acid supplement, such as Omega 3 fish oil.

9. You can try 'Allergy Control Solutions' that alter animal allergens to make them less reactive. They can be sprayed on carpets and soft furnishings, and can be added to water when washing fabrics or clothing.

10. Wipe your dog's underbelly and paws with a damp cloth - or hose him down - after walks, particularly in spring and summer when there are more allergens around.

11. Consider using a dander-reducing treatment such as Allerpet *(pictured)*, which helps to cleanse the dog's hair of dander, saliva and sebaceous gland secretions. There are also products to reduce allergens from carpets, curtains and furniture.

12. If your allergies are chronic, seek medical help to determine the nature of them and discuss immunotherapy or medication. There are medical advances being made in the treatment of allergies and a range of tablets, sprays and injections are currently available.

Experts aren't sure whether bathing your dog has any effect on allergy symptoms. Some studies have shown that baths reduce the amount of airborne dander, while others haven't found a difference. We wouldn't recommend bathing your dog more than once a month unless he has a skin problem, as this could cause dry skin, which would then be shed. What is clear is that a dirty dog is more likely to cause allergies.

Of course, the only sure-fire way to GUARANTEE no allergic reaction is not to have a dog, but that's not what you want to hear! It wasn't what we wanted to hear either when we decided to get another dog more than 13 years ago, knowing that one of our family members had allergies. We followed the advice given in this chapter before we got our dog and can honestly say that we have never had a problem. It pays to do your homework.

6. Crate Training and Housetraining

Crates are becoming increasingly popular with owners everywhere. They can help with housetraining (potty training), give you and puppy short breaks from each other and keep the dog safe at night or when you are not there. Many breeders, trainers, behaviourists and people who show and compete use them.

Getting Your Dog Used to a Crate

The first thing to remember is that a crate is not a prison and should only be used in a humane manner. It's important to spend time getting your puppy or adult dog used to crate so he comes to regard it as his own safe little haven.

Crates may not be suitable for every dog. Cavapoos are not like hamsters or pet mice that can adapt to life in a cage; they are "Velcro" dogs that like sticking close to you.

Being caged for long periods is a miserable existence for any dog, but particularly the Cavapoo, who is reliant on human contact for happiness. A crate should never be used as a means of confinement because you are out of the house all day.

Looking very much at home in her crate is two-year-old apricot F1, Cookie. Photo by Kit Lam.

A couple of other points with crates:

1. Always remove your dog's collar before leaving him inside when you are not there. Sadly, dogs have been known to die after their collars got caught and they panicked.

2. If the door is closed, your puppy must have access to water while inside. Non-spill water bowls are available from pet stores and online, as are bowls that attach to the bars.

It you do decide to use a crate - perhaps to put your dog in for short periods while you leave the house, or at night, especially in the beginning - the best place for it is in the corner of a room away from cold draughts or too much heat. And because Cavapoos like to be near their family, which is you and/or any other dogs, avoid putting the crate in a utility room or garage away from everybody else or your Poo will feel lonely and isolated.

Dogs can't sweat like humans and many Cavapoos shed only very lightly, so they can overheat. When you buy a crate, get a wire one that is robust and allows air to pass through, like Cookie's, not a plastic one that may get very hot.

 Covering the crate with an old blanket is a good way of creating a den for your new puppy, especially at night. Only cover on three sides - leave the front uncovered - and leave a gap at the bottom all the way round to allow air to flow.

The crate should be large enough to allow your dog to stretch out flat on his side without being cramped, and he should be able to turn round easily and to sit up without hitting his head on the top. Cavapoos vary in size, but you are probably looking at around a 30" crate for a fully-grown dog, or 36" if your Cavapoo is a big 'un like Cookie! If you only intend buying one, get the right size for an adult and divide it until your puppy grows into the full-sized crate.

Here is Midwest Pet Products sizing guide for crates, based on the anticipated adult weight of your dog (with Cavapoos, that's anything from 12lb to 25lb, or 5.4kilos to 11.3kilos): www.midwestpetproducts.com/midwestdogcrates/dog-crate-sizes

You have a number of options when it comes to deciding where to put the crate. Perhaps consider leaving it in the kitchen or another room (preferably one with an easy-to-clean surface) where there are people during the day. If you have noisy children, you have to strike the balance between putting the crate somewhere where the pup won't feel isolated, yet is able to get some peace and quiet from the kids.

You could bring it into your bedroom for the first couple of nights until the puppy settles. Some breeders advise putting the crate right next to the bed for the first night or two – even raised up next to the bed, so the puppy doesn't feel alone, and some owners even sleep next to the crate on the floor for a night!

A couple of nights with broken sleep is worth it if it helps the young pup to settle in, as he or she will often then sleep through the night quicker. After that, you could put the crate in a nearby place where the dog can hear or smell you at night-time, such as the landing, or you could leave it in the same place, e.g. the kitchen, 100% of the time. Ask your breeder for guidance.

It is only natural for any dog to whine in the beginning. He is not crying because he is in a cage. He would cry if he had the freedom of the room and was alone - he is crying because he is separated. However, with patience and the right training, he will get used to it and dogs often come to regard the crate as a favourite place. Some owners make the crate their dog's only bed, so he feels comfortable and safe in there. Not every owner wishes to use a crate, but used correctly they can:

- ❧ Create a canine den
- ❧ Be a useful housetraining tool
- ❧ Give you a bit of a break
- ❧ Limit access to the rest of the house until potty trained
- ❧ Be a place for the dog to nap or sleep
- ❧ Be a safe way to transport your dog in a car

If you use a crate right from Day One, initially cover half of it with a blanket to help your puppy regard it as a den. He also needs bedding and it's a good idea to put a chew in as well. A large crate may allow your dog to eliminate at one end and sleep at the other, but this may slow down his housetraining. So, if you are buying a crate that will last for a fully-grown Cavapoo, get adjustable crate dividers – or make them yourself (or put a box inside, preferably wood as cardboard will get chewed) - to block part of it off while he is small so that he feels safe and secure, which he won't do in a very big crate.

You can order a purpose-made crate mat or a *'Vet Bed'* (widely available) to cover the bottom and then put bedding on top. Vet Beds are widely used by veterinarians to make dogs feel warm, secure and cosy when receiving treatment, but they're just as good for using in the home. They are made from double-strength polyester with high fibre density to retain extra heat and allow air to permeate. They have drainage properties, so if your pup has an accident, he or she will stay dry. They are also a good choice for older dogs as the added heat is soothing for aging muscles and joints, and for any dogs recovering from surgery or treatment. Another added advantage of a Vet Bed is that you can wash it often and it shouldn't deteriorate. Bear in mind that a bored or lively Cavapoo puppy is a little chew machine so, at this stage, don't spend a lot of money on a fluffy floor covering for the crate, as it is likely to get destroyed.

Many breeders recommend **not** putting newspapers in one part of the crate, as this encourages the pup to soil the crate. If you bought your puppy from a good breeder, she will probably already have started the housetraining process, and eight to 12-week-old pups should be able to last a couple of hours without needing the toilet. Some people say that a pup can last one hour or so without needing to urinate for every month of age. During the night, set your alarm clock to get up after four or five hours to let the pup out to do his or her business for the first week. You might hate it, but it can speed up housetraining.

For the very house-proud, crates aren't the most attractive objects to have in your home. There are, however, some chic alternatives now available for the style-conscious owner. We particularly like the 36" Fido Studio Dog Crate available in the UK from Omlet www.omlet.co.uk

Admittedly, it's not cheap, but not only does it look good, it also boasts "the world's first doggie wardrobe" (the closed section on the left) where you can store your dog's coats, toys, blankets, etc. *Photo of Pip, bred by Charlotte Purkiss, of Lotties Cavapoos, Hampshire, UK, in her Omlet crate, courtesy of James Tuthill.*

Once you've got your crate, you'll need to learn how to use it properly so that it becomes a safe, comfortable den for your dog. Many breeders will have already started the process but, if not, here's a tried-and-tested method of getting your dog firstly to accept a crate, and then to actually want to spend time in there. These are the first steps:

1. Drop a few tasty puppy treats around and then inside the crate.
2. Put your puppy's favourite bedding or toy in there.
3. Keep the door open.
4. Feed your puppy's meals inside the crate. Again, keep the door open.

Place a chew or treat INSIDE the crate and close the door while your puppy is OUTSIDE the crate. He will be desperate to get in there! Open the door, let him in and praise him for going in. Fasten a long-lasting chew inside the crate and leave the door open. Let your puppy go inside to spend some time eating the chew.

After a while, close the crate door and feed him some treats through the mesh. At first just do it for a few seconds at a time, then gradually increase the time. If you do it too fast, he may become distressed. Slowly build up the amount of time he is in the crate. For the first few days, stay in the room, then gradually leave for a short time, first one minute, then three, then 10, 30 and so on.

Next Steps

5. Put your dog in his crate at regular intervals during the day - maximum two hours.

6. Don't crate only when you are leaving the house. Place the dog in the crate while you are home as well. Use it as a 'safe' zone.

7. By using the crate both when you are home and while you are gone, your dog becomes comfortable there and not worried that you won't come back, or that you are leaving him alone. This helps to prevent separation anxiety later in life.

8. If you are leaving your dog unattended, give him a chew and remove his collar, tags and anything else that could become caught in an opening or between the bars.

9. Make it very clear to any children that the crate is NOT a playhouse for them, but a 'special room' for the dog.

10. Although the crate is your dog's haven and safe place, it must not be off-limits to humans. You should be able to reach inside at any time.

The next point is important:

11. Do not let your dog immediately out of the crate if he barks or whines, or he will think that this is the key to opening the door. Wait until the barking or whining has stopped for at least 10 or 20 seconds before letting him out.

 One breeder puts a Smart Pet Love Snuggle Puppy in the crate with the new puppy. The Snuggle Puppy (available from Amazon) is a safe soft toy with a heartbeat. She added: "In their new home, the puppies have the heartbeat sound like they had from laying on mum. We've had really good feedback from families about the Snuggle Puppies".

A puppy should not be left in a crate for long periods except at night-time, and even then he has to get used to it first. Whether or not you decide to use a crate, the important thing to remember is that those first few days and weeks are a critical time for your puppy. Try and make him feel as safe and comfortable as you can. Bond with him, while at the same time gently and gradually giving him positive experiences with new places, humans and other animals.

Cookie sleeps in her crate at night, which is covered with a blanket. She has plenty of room to move around and the front is left open. Photo by Kit Lam.

Special travel crates are useful for the car, or for taking your dog to the vet's or a show. Choose one

with holes or mesh in the side to allow free movement of air rather than a solid plastic one, in which a dog can soon overheat. Alternatively, you can buy a metal grille to keep your dog or dogs confined to the back on the car.

A crate is one way of transporting your Cavapoo in the car. Put the crate on the shady side of the interior and make sure it can't move around; put the seatbelt around it. If it's very sunny and the top of the crate is wire mesh, cover part of it so your dog has some shade and put the windows up and the air conditioning on. Don't leave your Cavapoo unattended in a vehicle for more than a few minutes, especially if it's hot as they can overheat very quickly - or be targeted by thieves.

Allowing your dog to roam freely inside the car is not a safe option, particularly if you - like me – are a bit of a 'lead foot' on the brake and accelerator! Even though it looks cute, try to avoid letting your dog put his head out of the window, as wind pressure can cause an ear infection or bits of dust, insects, etc. can fly into his unprotected eyes; he can also slip and hurt himself or fly forward if you brake suddenly.

Cavapoo Breeders and Owners on Crates

Traditionally crates have been more popular in North America than in the UK and the rest of Europe. In the UK, dogs have more commonly been allowed to roam free inside the home and run off-lead (leash) for much of the time outdoors. But habits are changing and more owners are using crates on both sides of the Atlantic. This is perhaps because people's perception is shifting, particularly in the UK, from regarding the crate as a cage to thinking of it as a safe haven and a useful tool to help with housetraining and transport.

Without exception, the breeders we contacted believe that a crate should not be used for punishment or to imprison a dog all day while away from the house. This is cruel for any dog, but particularly a social dog that craves company like the Cavapoo.

Another option that can be used instead of - or in conjunction with - a crate is a pen. Not everybody has the space, but if you do, a pen is a good way of giving your puppy a bit more freedom, while keeping him or her safe and contained.

Dayna Rosindale, owner of two-and-a-half-year-old female Harper, used a pen and says: "I do think crates are a good idea, but only if introduced from Day One. Personally, I wouldn't close the door as I never needed to with Harper. I left the door open so she had the freedom to wander around the playpen *(pictured).* I felt this worked a lot better for us both. The pen was kept in the kitchen and we kept up with this routine till she was fully housetrained, which was about five months old. Now she sleeps on my bed!"

The key to successful crate training is to spend time enticing the dog into the crate so that he or she starts to enjoy spending time in there - most puppies will not initially like being in a crate and patience, alongside the right techniques, are essential. If the breeder has already got your puppy used to a crate, then you're part way there already.

One such breeder is Charlotte Purkiss, who says: "Crate training is a must. I do it from five weeks old and use a small crate in the puppies' big pen. The puppies are in our open plan dining room so they can hear all the noises. The door of the crate is never closed, so it offers freedom for puppies to come and go at their leisure without being frightened. I do this so families can decide if to continue to crate or not after leaving me. The feedback has been very positive from families who have carried on crating.

"When I myself have a new puppy to add to my family, I crate until eight months or until they no longer need it, but everyone is different on how they do things. I personally crate at night and if I have to go out for a short time - around an hour – I close the door to the crate. If I am going out for any longer, I place a pen around crate, leaving the door of the crate open. You should not allow any toys or food inside the crate, just a small water bowl. Never leave a collar on or any clothing, as there is a risk of items getting caught up. I believe a plastic bed is safer, as a puppy could eat the filling of other beds; hence why I recommend no toys at all.

"With crate sizes, I recommend a medium size for a Cavapoo. Covering the crate from a young age gives puppies a sense of their own space and security. Crate covers are often used, but I recommend just using a big blanket over as puppies can chew the material or ties of crate covers. The blanket only goes only on three sides and just three-quarters down so air is able to flow even if door is closed. I use stair gates around the house as this gives a more open feel when you have to go out and leave them, as closing doors can cause anxiety."

Clare Cornes, owner of F1 brothers Bob and Boris: "We started with a playpen, and moved to a very large crate as they could climb out of the playpen! They were always shut in crate at night until they came in with us. When we were out they had the run of the kitchen from seven months. If you want to crate-train, make it a happy place; start by feeding them dinner, treats and playing in the crate, and leave them with an item of your worn clothing. Also, leave them in the crate during the day whilst you are there so they know it's a safe place and don't use it as a punishment."

Trevor and Tracey Nott, owners of four-year-old Ethel: "We did use a crate - although no longer do so – and would recommend the use of one as a starting point for any new pup. The length of time and use depend on whether you want your pet to permanently sleep in a bed in the crate."

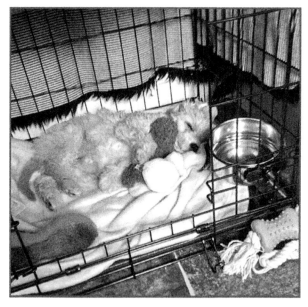

Max's owner Beverley Burlison: "Max slept in his crate for the first three months. He has a bed which he sleeps in during the day, but he sleeps in our bedroom at night."

Hilary Morphy: "Teddy was wonderful - the breeder had crate-trained him so he was quite happy in there *(as shown by this photo of Teddy somewhat relaxed in his crate!)*

"She sent him with a puppy pack including a blanket that had been rubbed on his Mum. He slept through at night - perfect! I had his crate on the landing so he could see me and I could hear him. The fact he was used to a crate made such a difference. It was his personal space and he kept going in there to sleep or nap - I left the door open unless I was going out or it was night-time."

Karen Howe, owner of Rodney and Mabel: "When Rodney first came home it was all very exciting and overwhelming at the same time. I worried if I was doing things right, although I think I was much more relaxed with Mabel a year later. I was very lucky that they both were used to sleeping in a crate; so we had minimal crying and they both slept well from the start.

"They both slept in crates in our spare room from the start. When they were pups I did used to close the door at night or when going out. They were never left for more than three hours at a time. I had a cover over mine and try to make it as cosy as possible. When I first got Mabel they were in separate crates next to each other for the first six weeks, then they shared a crate with a pen attached to it. Now they have the whole spare room with the crate door open and full access to the spare room."

Denise Knightley, owner of Carmen Rose and Domino: "In both cases our puppies had road trips of about five hours before we got them home. We were given bedding and toys which were familiar to them and carried the scent of their mother and siblings. We made sure that the house was quiet and calm and placed them into their beds in their crates so that they became accustomed to this as a safe area."

"We used a 'Snuggle Puppy' with a heated pad inside and we covered their crates at night to protect them from any draughts and to give them a safe and secure space with no distractions. We put a puppy pad in their crate overnight in case of any accidents and we hooked a water bowl on the inside of their crate so that they could drink if necessary. We gave them a few doggie white chocolate buttons when it was time to go to sleep and we have continued with this routine. Both girls scuttle off to their beds every night when they see the Tupperware with the bedtime chocolate buttons! We have never left a light on or played music or the TV.

"We only used a crate for about six months and only used it overnight or for the odd hour if we had to pop out during the day when we couldn't be sure that they wouldn't chew something or injure themselves. I don't think that crates should be used as a punishment and we were careful not to shut them into their crates if they had had an accident around the house or if they'd been naughty."

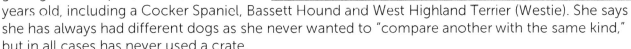

Now she no longer sleeps in a crate, Domino (left) enjoys nothing more than napping on Denise's luxurious leather sofa with next door's Cockapoo, Sheldon, pictured.

June Hicks had several dogs before getting her Cavapoo, Archie, now two years old, including a Cocker Spaniel, Bassett Hound and West Highland Terrier (Westie). She says she has always had different dogs as she never wanted to "compare another with the same kind," but in all cases has never used a crate.

Rebecca Seabrook rescued Max when he was 10 months old through the UK's Doodle Trust about a year ago. She discovered he was frightened to go outdoors, having originally been confined to the house by his previous owners. Rebecca says: "We do have a crate, but it does not have a door on and we call it "Max's Cave" and it is where he goes when he wants some time alone. Now he is getting older, we are finding he is not using it so much."

Gina Desmond, of New York, is the owner of three-year-old Duncan, her first dog and says: "When Duncan arrived home, we let him explore for a while and take in all the smells. Bedtime was difficult. We put his crate in our bedroom and when it was time to turn the lights off he started crying. For that first night, my husband and I actually slept on the floor next to his crate. It was a big transition for Duncan so we wanted him to feel as safe as possible.

"For the second night, we moved the crate next to our bed so we could put our hands down to him if he needed comfort. Over the course of the first week, Duncan and the crate moved back to their intended corner of our bedroom. I think it's an adjustment for everyone, the humans and the pup. Consistency is key.

"We used a crate during potty training and over time used it less and less – now we no longer use any type of crate. One thing we learned was to make sure the crate isn't too big (or too small). Puppies think of their crate as their bed and personal space. So if the crate size is just right, they will not go potty inside. But, if they have room to do their business in one corner and sleep in the other, they will. Just make sure you are taking them out to relieve themselves often enough. Puppies can only hold their bladder for as many hours as they are months old.

"A crate should be a safe space for your puppy. Make it into a positive experience and NEVER use the crate as punishment. We would give Duncan treats for going inside the crate on his own. We would never reward crying. Cavapoos are smart. If you are letting your pup out of the crate every time they cry, they will learn to cry all of the time so get their way - we learned this the hard way!

"The same goes for night-time. As Duncan got better with potty training we noticed he was still waking up in the middle of the night to go potty, but he didn't always need to go. He just knew that if he cried in the middle of the night we would wake up with him. So we eventually caved and let him sleep in bed. They are VERY smart dogs! I love having Duncan sleep in bed, but it was definitely important to make sure he was properly potty trained first."

Lindsey McDonald and Alex Kostiw: "Winston (now aged 15 months, *pictured*) slept in his crate the first few nights and still does now. He sleeps so much better in it, though occasionally he is allowed to sleep upstairs, especially if he has a poorly tummy.

"In the beginning, we found it easier to sit with our back to the crate or lie down and pretend to sleep next to it until he fell asleep. After the first few nights we found it easier to settle him if we set an alarm to take him out for toilet rather than him waking us. We went by a rule of about one hour per month of age, plus an extra hour - and it worked really well. At nine weeks: bed at 11pm, toilet at 1.30am and back in crate, toilet at 4.30 to 5am and then up to bed for snuggles until about 8am.

"We still put Winston in his crate for short bursts every day during the day. It started with me in the same room and worked up to me out of the room. We didn't leave him in his crate for more than one-and-a-half to two hours at a time when little."

US owner Val Boshart: "We crate-trained Millie and she slept in our bedroom. The first day we worked on getting her comfortable with the crate, rewarding her with treats and praising her as we closed the door and opened it back up. We added pieces of clothing that smelled like us, a soft towel and her favorite toy, and put her to bed around 9pm with the lights off in our room.

"She cried at first, so I slept on the floor next to her, soothing her with my voice when needed and poking my fingers in her crate so she could smell and lick me. I never opened the door, made sure she knew we were there and she was not alone. The second night, I did the same thing from bed. By the third or fourth night, she was sleeping through the night! We eventually moved her crate to another room. What has been key has been consistency - same bedtime routine and morning routine every day.

"Millie *(pictured)* went through a sleep regression, starting when she went through her first heat at seven to eight months old until a few weeks after she was spayed. That was a tough time! She would wake up at night and cry, but we knew she wasn't hungry or didn't need the bathroom. Once her hormones had settled down after her surgery, she went back to normal, like it had never happened.

"We try to use her crate for only when we are out of the house and overnight for bed. During the day, we don't keep her in there for longer than four to five hours at a time - and she has adjusted her schedule to know to sleep during this period and we rarely hear a peep. At night, she is usually in her crate for closer to seven hours without issue, as she's fast asleep. In the past couple of months, she is starting to like her crate more and more. At night, she will sometimes jump off our bed and put herself to sleep in her crate, which is so sweet. She always needs her special stuffed octopus in there with her!"

Housetraining

How easy are Cavapoos to housetrain (potty train)? Well, you will not be surprised to hear that... it varies!

Fairly or unfairly, Toy breeds have a reputation of being slower than some other larger breeds to potty train. This isn't because they are less intelligent; far from it. It's simply that their little bodies can take longer to mature. The Cavalier King Charles Spaniel is classed as a Toy breed, as is the Toy Poodle; a Miniature Poodle is not. Either way, your Cavapoo will have some Toy breed parentage. Some Cavapoos pick up potty training extremely quickly – within a week or two. We only mention the Toy breed aspect to help you understand what may be going on if your puppy seems to be a bit slow on the uptake.

Potty training varies according to the individual dog, how much effort the breeder has put in and, most importantly, how vigilant you are prepared to be in the beginning. The speed and success of housetraining often depends largely on the time and effort YOU are prepared to put in at the beginning. Provided the breeder has already started the process, the more vigilant you are during the early days, the quicker your dog will be housetrained. It's as simple as that. Taking the advice in this chapter and being consistent with your routines and repetitions is the quickest way to get results.

Of course, if yours is a rescue Cavapoo, he or she may have picked up some bad habits before arriving at your home. In such cases, time and patience are needed to help the dog forget the old ways before he or she can begin to learn the new ones.

You have five big factors in your favour when it comes to toilet training a Cavapoo:

1. They want to please their owners.
2. They are biddable (willing to learn).
3. Most would do anything for praise or a treat.
4. Dogs do not naturally soil their beds.
5. The Cavapoo is a clean breed.

From about the age of three weeks, a pup will leave his sleeping area to go to the toilet. Most good breeders will have already started the housebreaking process, so when you pick up your little bundle of joy, all you have to do is ensure that you carry on the good work.

If you're starting from scratch when you bring your puppy home, your new arrival thinks that the whole house is his den and doesn't realise that this is not the place to eliminate. Therefore, you need to gently and persistently teach him that it is unacceptable to make a mess inside the home. Cavapoos, like all dogs, are creatures of routine - not only do they like the same things happening at the same times every day, but establishing a regular routine with your dog also helps to speed up obedience and toilet training.

 Dogs are tactile creatures, so they will pick a toilet area that feels good under their paws. Many dogs like to go on grass - but this will do nothing to improve your lawn, so you should think carefully about what area to encourage your puppy to use. You may want to consider a small patch of crushed gravel in your garden, or a particular corner of the garden or yard away from any attractive plants.

Some breeders advise against using puppy pads at all, and certainly for weeks on end, as puppies like the softness of the pads. Long-term use may also encourage them to eliminate on other soft areas - such as carpets or bed. However, there are plenty of breeders and owners that do use puppy pads for a limited period, alongside regularly taking the puppy outside. They gradually reduce the area covered by the pads over a period of a couple of weeks, and a few dogs living in apartments permanently use puppy pads.

Follow these tips to speed up housetraining:

1. **Constant supervision** is essential for the first week or two if you are to housetrain your puppy quickly. This is why it is important to book time off work when you bring him home, if you can. Make sure you are there to take him outside regularly. If nobody is there, he will learn to urinate or poo(p) inside the house.

2. **Take your pup outside at the following times:**

   * As soon as he wakes – every time

   * Shortly after each feed

   * After a drink

   * When he gets excited

   * After exercise or play

   * Last thing at night

   * Initially every hour - whether or not he looks like he wants to go

You may think that the above list is an exaggeration, but it isn't! Housetraining a pup is almost a full-time job in the beginning. If you are serious about toilet training your puppy quickly, then clear your diary for a week or two and keep your eyes firmly glued on your pup...learn to spot that expression or circling motion just before he makes a puddle - or worse – on your floor.

3. Take your pup to **the same place** every time, you may need to use a lead (leash) in the beginning - or tempt him there with a treat. Some say it is better to only pick him up and dump him there in an emergency, as it is better if he learns to take himself to the chosen toilet spot. Dogs naturally develop a preference for going in the same place or on the same surface. Take or lead him to the same patch every time so he learns this is his toilet area.

No pressure – be patient. You must allow your distracted little darling time to wander around and have a good sniff before performing his duties – but do not leave him, stay around a short distance away. Unfortunately, puppies are not known for their powers of concentration; it may take a while for him to select the perfect bathroom spot!

4. **Housetraining is reward-based.** Give praise and/or a treat immediately after he has performed his duties in the chosen spot. Cavapoos like to please you and love praise, and reward-based training is the most successful method for quick results.

5. **Share the responsibility.** It doesn't have to be the same person who takes the dog outside all the time. In fact, it's easier if there are a couple of you, as this is a very time-demanding business. Just make sure you stick to the same principles, command and patch of ground.

6. **Stick to the same routine.** Dogs understand and like routine. Sticking to the same times for meals, short exercise sessions, playtime, sleeping and toilet breaks will help to not only housetrain him quicker, but also help him settle into his new home.

7. **Use the same word** or command when telling your puppy to go to the toilet – or while he is in the act. He will gradually associate this phrase or word with toileting and you will even be able to get him to eliminate on command after some weeks.

8. **Use your voice if you catch him in the act indoors.** A short sharp negative sound is best - NO! ACK! EH! It doesn't matter, as long as it is loud enough to make him stop. Then start running enthusiastically towards your door, calling him into the garden and the chosen place and patiently wait until he has finished what he started indoors. It is no good scolding your dog if you find a puddle or unwanted gift in the house but don't see him do it; he won't know why you are cross with him. Only use the negative sound if you actually catch him in the act.

9. **No punishment.** Accidents will happen at the beginning, do not punish your pup for them. He is a baby with a tiny bladder and bowels, and housetraining takes time - it is perfectly natural to have accidents early on. Remain calm and clean up the mess with a good strong-smelling cleaner to remove the odour, so he won't be tempted to use that spot again. Dogs have a very strong sense of smell; use a special spray from your vet or a hot solution of washing powder to completely eliminate the odour. Smacking or rubbing his nose in it can have the opposite effect - he will become afraid to do his business in your presence and may start going secretly behind the couch or under the bed, rather than outside.

10. **Look for the signs.** These may be:

    a. Whining

    b. Sniffing the floor in a determined manner

    c. Circling and looking for a place to go

    d. Walking uncomfortably - particularly at the rear end!

Take him outside straight away, and try not to pick him up all the time. He has to learn to walk to the door himself when he needs to go outside.

11. **If you use puppy pads, only do so for a short time** or your puppy will get to like them.

12. **Use a crate at night-time** and, for the first few nights, set your alarm clock. An eight-week-old pup should be able to last a few hours if the breeder has already started the process. For the first few nights, consider getting up four or five hours after you go to bed to take the pup outside, gradually increasing the time by 15 minutes. By the age of four or five months a Cavapoo pup should be able to last through (a short night) without needing the toilet –

provided you let him out last thing at night and first thing in the morning. Before then, you will have a lot of early mornings!

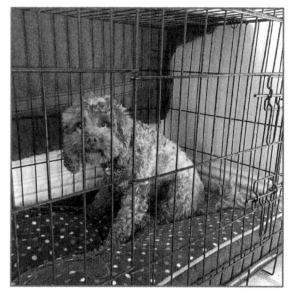

If using a crate, remember that during the day the door should not be closed until your pup is happy with being inside. At night-time it is acceptable to close the door. Consider keeping the pup close to you for the first two or three nights. He needs to believe that the crate is a safe place and not a trap. If you don't want to use a crate, then use pet gates, section off an area inside one room or use a puppy pen to confine your pup at night.

Photo of Flossie, bred by Charlotte Purkiss.

And finally, one British breeder added this piece of advice: "If you are getting a puppy, invest in a good dressing gown and an umbrella!"

....

Advice From the Experts

Good breeders provide new owners with information to take home that helps them to understand their puppy's needs. In her Notes For Buyers one breeder says: "Your puppy has already started to ask to go out when she needs the toilet; in any case you will need to take her outside regularly. Typically, this would be every time she wakes up as well as after meals.

"Watch for the signs: searching the ground and sniffing is a good indication she needs to pass water. Puppies have relatively small bladders. Always choose the same place in the garden; remain with the puppy until she has performed and then give her plenty of praise. Remember, accidents will happen. If you catch her in the act, simply take her outside and then praise her for her efforts. Never shout at or hit your puppy as this will cause confusion and is likely to make matters worse.

"During the times when puppy has no access to the garden, it is a good idea to place some newspaper on the floor. The newspaper could be moved nearer and nearer to the outside door until puppy realises to go to the door to ask to go out. Puppy training pads are also available from pet shops, although we find that puppies prefer to rip them up rather than to use them for their correct purpose!"

Here is the routine from another breeder: "We have a pretty strict routine for toilet training which is a little intensive, but not unreasonable. It definitely works. They learn that 10pm till 6am is sleep time, which any new home could do. This matters as obviously they learn through conditioning. So, with a sleep routine, they know how long it is until they next can pee and near 10pm they know it's nearly bedtime, so learn quickly to pee then.

"Then, during the day, it's a case of taking them out every two hours on the hours so 6am, 8am, 10am and so on... I find that every time they go out, they pee so therefore they would probably struggle waiting longer. It's also important that they don't have free reign to go outside whenever they feel like it (unsupervised) which is tempting in summer months, but it's absolutely vital to notice every time they pee and when they do one to let them know what they're doing. "Go toilet" is what we use. Then reward immediately. Eventually, you'll be able to ask them to "Go toilet" as they've formed the association.

"This doesn't mean they categorically can't go longer than two hours, but it's better to set them up to win rather than fail. We then don't have a specified age where the length of time is extended as that's definitely an individual basis, so when they stop going every time you take them out, the time can be very gradually increased."

Another breeder added: "Some breeders do not advocate putting newspaper in the crate for the puppy to toilet. I agree, as by doing this it makes it much harder to get the puppy fully toilet trained. The idea of getting up in the night to toilet the puppy may not suit everyone. What we do is to use a fairly spacious puppy pen at night for a young puppy and not a crate. We have a bed at one end and newspaper at the far end where the puppy can eliminate. We still have a crate for the puppy to go in during the day if he so wishes and we leave the door open. This then becomes his own little den. But at night he is put in the playpen. By the time the puppy is about four-and-a-half to five months old we find that they can usually go all night without toileting and so we then put them in a crate at night."

If breeders have already started housetraining - either inside or outside the house – they may have a phrase that they already use, such as "Go toilet!" or "Go potty!" Ask your breeder if she has started the process and what phrase she uses to encourage the pups to eliminate.

Here are some Cavapoo owners' personal experiences, starting with Denise Knightley: "Cavapoos are relatively easy to housetrain as long as you are consistent in taking them outside at very regular intervals in the first four to six weeks that you have them at home as puppies. We used a crate overnight for both dogs until they were about six months old and we usually let them out for their last toilet break about 11pm and then took them out again by 6am."

Trevor and Tracey Nott: "It took Ethel just three to four weeks. We feel that you must be disciplined in your approach to this task, i.e. consistent with verbal commands and choice of words for instruction, as well as encouraging the dog to go out if he or she has eaten, wakes up or has not been out for a couple of hours."

June Hicks: "It didn't take long at all, as at the time I had another mature dog in the house who set an example."

ond: "It took about one month for Duncan (at three months old) to understand the would say it took us a further three solid months before we were really comfortable that 't have an accident in the house. When we first got him, my husband and I each took a om work so he had one of us home for two full weeks to get a kick start on house-nink this was important for his transition and our bonding. If you are able to do something like this I highly recommend it. It's exhausting, but worth it!

"We were told puppies can hold their bladder for as many hours as they are months old, so when we got Duncan he could technically hold his bladder for three hours at a time. We used this reference as part of our schedule to take him outside. At night, we would crate-train him and take him out once in the middle of the night or early morning. We always made sure he went potty right before bed. If he was wandering freely around our apartment, we had to watch him closely for a few months. Otherwise we had him in a gated-off area that had a pee pad.

"Tip: Positive reinforcement. We never punished Duncan for accidents but we always made sure to reward when he went potty outside or on his pee pad. We rewarded him with a treat he loved that was ONLY used for potty training. If we happened to catch him going potty inside, we would pick him up quickly and bring him outside. If he finished his business outside he was heavily rewarded, but if not we had no reaction."

Hilary Morphy: "Teddy only took about a week to housetrain!! I got him in the August, so just left the doors open and he learned very quickly to go outside. The fact I was at home all the time obviously helped."

Bell Training

Bell Training is a potty training method which can work particularly well with Cavapoos. There are different types of bells, the simplest are widely available online and cost just a few dollars or pounds. They consist of a series of adjustable bells that hang on a nylon strap from the door handle *(pictured, right)*. Another option is a small metal bell attached to a metal hanger which fixes low down on the wall next to the door with two screws *(pictured, left).*

The technique is quite simple and is based on first getting your dog to touch the bell, then to ring it, then to learn to ring it when he wants to go outside. As with all training involving young puppies, do it in short bursts of five to 10 minutes or your easily-distracted little student will switch off! Here is one tried and tested method:

❧ Show your dog the bell, either on the floor, before it is fixed anywhere or by holding it up. Point to it and give the command "Touch" or "Ring" and let her explore by touch.

❧ Reward her with praise and a treat when she pushes it with her nose – you can rub on something tasty, like peanut butter, to make it more interesting

❧ Take the bell(s) away after four or five repetitions and repeat this session, so two or three times a day for several days; Cavapoos are naturally curious

❧ When you point to the bell, give the command and she touches it every time with her nose or paw, you are ready to move on to the next stage

* Fix the bell to the door handle or wall, pull it towards your dog while holding it in your hand and give the "Touch" or "Ring" command. When she makes the bell(s) ring, say "Yes!" or "Good Girl/Boy" enthusiastically and give a treat − or praise, whatever motivates her most, and take her outside immediately

* Give her further praise and a treat when she then pees or poops outside

* To speed things up, you can place a treat just outside the door while she is watching. Then close the door and give the "Touch" or "Ring" command

* The next time you think she needs the toilet, walk to the door, point to the bell and give the command; give her a treat if she rings it, let her out again immediately and reward again after potty

* You must start by ringing the bell yourself EVERY time you open the door to let her outside to potty.

Tip Some Cavapoos can get carried away by their own success and will ring the bell any time they want your attention or fancy a wander outdoors! Make sure that you ring the bell EVERY time she goes out through this door to potty, but DON'T ring the bell if she is going out to play - and ignore it if you know she doesn't need to toilet and is only ringing to demand your attention.

Here are some Bell Training testimonials from Cavapoo owners, starting with Karen Howe: "Housetraining now seems like a distant memory but I think Rodney was around four months old when he was fully housetrained. Mabel was younger and seemed to pick it up a lot quicker due to having Rodney's lead to follow. She just very easily slotted into his routine. I also learned the second time around not to bother using puppy pads and to just teach her to go straight outside.

"I used toilet bells with both of them; I found Rodney wouldn't bark to let me know he needed to go outside, so if I wasn't watching him, I wouldn't know. Therefore every time we went out I rang the bells with his paw and he very quickly picked up the idea to ring them to ask to go out. We still use them now."

Beverley Burlison: "Max *(pictured enjoying the view from the driving seat)* was totally housetrained within a month. We have attached a cat bell to the patio door which he rings by knocking it with his paw; this lets us know he wants to be outside."

Claire Cornes: "Bob was trained within a few weeks, Boris took much longer. I used toilet training bells; they tap the bell when they want to go outside. They are still using it now and I would recommend this method as they pick it up so quickly."

Kit Lam: "It took two weeks to housetrain Cookie. Hang a door bell by the exit door, set your phone alarm for every 20 to 30 minutes and take them out to potty...gradually extending the duration in between potty trips. Ignore them until they have done their toilet business and then reward them. Also take them out 20 minutes after they have eaten or had a drink."

Dayna Rosindale: "From Day One Harper was weeing in the garden. We did have accidents in the house, but I trained her to go to the door and she would paw the door chain every time she needed to go out. I believe it's the same technique as bell training."

Val Boshart: The day we brought Millie home, we set her on the grass and she went to the bathroom immediately. From there, the biggest thing was anticipating her needs and setting her up for success with a routine and frequent outdoor access. We had a very short period of accidents, most often occurring when we gave her too much freedom and let her intelligence give us a false sense of confidence - after all, she was still a baby!

"Once she was big enough to reach it, we bell-trained her so she could let us know when she needed to go out. This has been fantastic, as it removes any barking or scratching at the door and she's positively rewarded for asking to go out. Occasionally, she also uses it when she just wants to go exploring in the back yard!"

Lindsey McDonald and Alex Kostiw: "Winston was fully housetrained by about 18 weeks. We rang the bells on the back door before opening it EVERY TIME and took him out on the lead. We didn't say anything until he started to go. Then we would introduce the command words as he was going, with lots of praise. We still use the lead when it is dark and still have to sometimes go out with him to remind him why he is there.

"Our best housetraining tip is: go out and stay out until they do something, whatever the weather! We toilet-trained in December, January and February, through two lots of snow, thunderstorms, torrential rain and very windy weather. He will now go out whatever the weather, and will be quick if it's horrible. By the way, Winston does have a strong prey drive. He loves to wait for the pigeons to land in the garden, then will go nuts at the back door, ringing the bells incessantly for the door to be opened! And he loves to chase birds and squirrels in the park."

....

As you have read, housetraining varies from one Cavapoo to the next. The important thing as a new owner is to BE VIGILANT. Your Cavapoo is very trainable and really wants to learn. Time spent housetraining during the first month will reap rewards.

A trigger can be very effective to encourage your dog to perform his or her duties. Some people use a clicker or a bell - we used a word; well, two, actually. Within a week or so I trained our last puppy to urinate on the command of "Wee wee!" Think very carefully before choosing the words, as I often feel an idiot wandering around our garden last thing at night shouting "WEE WEE!!" in an encouraging manner...Although I'm not sure that the American "GO POTTY!!" sounds any better!

7. Feeding a Cavapoo

To keep your dog's biological machine in good working order, it's important to supply the right fuel, as the correct diet is an essential part of keeping your dog fit and healthy. Feeding is a very important topic for Cavapoo owners, perhaps more so than for owners of many other dogs.

This is because when it comes to food - unlike the lovable Labrador - most Cavapoos are not canine dustbins. In fact, many Cavapoos are fussy eaters, some have intolerances and, as a consequence, Cavapoo forums are full of owners seeking advice on the best food for their fussy/sensitive dog.

Having said that, some Cavapoos are greedy, and nearly all of them love treats. Puppies are no different; some will gobble down anything put in front of them, while owners of other Cavapoo puppies are at their wits' end trying to tempt them to eat.

The topic of feeding can be something of a minefield; owners are bombarded with endless choices as well as countless adverts from dog food companies, all claiming that theirs is best. There is not one food that will give every single dog the healthiest coat and skin, the brightest eyes, the most energy, the best digestion, the least gas, the longest life and stop her from scratching or having skin problems.

Dogs are individuals, just like people, which means that you could feed a quality food to a group of dogs and find that most of them thrive on it, some do not do so well, while a few might get an upset stomach or even an allergic reaction. The question is: "Which food is best for **my** Cavapoo?"

If you have been given a recommended food from a breeder, rescue centre or previous owner, stick to this as long as your dog is doing well on it. A good breeder knows which food her dogs thrive on. If you do decide - for whatever reason - to change diet, then this must be done gradually. There are several things to be aware of when it comes to feeding:

1. Food is a big motivator for many dogs, making a powerful training tool. You can use feeding time to reinforce a simple command on a daily basis.

2. Greedy dogs have no self-control when it comes to food, so it is up to you to control your dog's intake. Dogs of all breeds, including Cavapoos, can have food sensitivities or allergies - more on this topic later.

3. Some dogs do not do well on diets with a high grain content. There is enough anecdotal evidence from owners to know that this is true of some Cavapoos.

4. One of the main reasons for flatulence (farting!) is the wrong diet.

5. There is evidence that some dogs thrive on home-cooked or raw diets, particularly if they have been having issues with manufactured foods, but you need the time and money to stick to them.

6. With processed dried foods (kibble), you often get what you pay for, so a more expensive food is usually – but not always - more likely to provide better nutrition in terms of minerals, nutrients and high quality meats. Cheap foods often contain a lot of grain; read the list of ingredients to find out. Dried foods tend to be less expensive than some other foods. They have improved a lot over the last few years and some of the best ones are now a good choice for a healthy, complete diet. Dried foods also contain the least fat and most preservatives. Foods such as Life's Abundance dry formulas do not contain any preservatives.

7. Sometimes elderly dogs just get bored with their diet and go off their food. This does not necessarily mean that they are ill, simply that they have lost interest and a new food should be gradually introduced.

One of our dogs had inhalant allergies. He was fed a quality dried food which the manufacturers claimed was 'hypoallergenic,' i.e. good for dogs with allergies. Max did well on it, but not all dogs thrive on dried food. We tried several other foods first; it is a question of owners finding the best food for their dog. If you got your dog from a good breeder, they should be able to advise you. As you will read later in this chapter, many Cavapoo owners have found that their dogs do best on a home-cooked diet.

Beware foods described as 'premium' or 'natural' or both, these terms are meaningless. Many manufacturers blithely use these words, but there are no official guidelines as to what they mean. However, **"Complete and balanced"** IS a legal term and has to meet standards laid down by AAFCO (Association of American Feed Control Officials) in the USA.

Always check the ingredients on any food sack, packet or tin to see what is listed first; this is the main ingredient and it should be meat or poultry, not grain. If you are in the USA, look for a dog food endorsed by AAFCO. In general, tinned foods are 60-70% water and often semi-moist foods contain a lot of artificial substances and sugar. Choosing the right food for your dog is important; it will influence health, coat, longevity and sometimes even temperament.

There are three stages of your dog's life to consider when feeding: *Puppy, Adult* and *Senior* (also called Veteran). Some manufacturers also produce a *Junior* feed for adolescent dogs. Each represents a different physical stage of life and you should choose the right food during each particular phase. This does not necessarily mean that you have to feed Puppy, then Junior, then Adult, then Senior food; some owners switch their young dogs to Adult formulas fairly soon. Ask your breeder for his or her advice on the right time to switch.

A pregnant female will require a special diet to cope with the extra demands on her body; this is especially important as she nears the latter stages of pregnancy.

Most breeders and owners feed their Cavapoos twice a day; this helps to stop a hungry dog gulping food down in a mad feeding frenzy and also reduces the risk of Bloat although this is not a major concern for Cavapoos (see **Chapter 11. Cavapoo Health**). Some owners of fussy eaters or older dogs who have gone off their food give two different meals each day to provide variety. One meal could be dried kibble, while the other might be home-made, with fresh meat, poultry and vegetables, or a tinned food - or a mix of the two for both meals. If you do this, make sure the combined meals provide a balanced diet and that they are not too rich in protein – especially with young or old dogs.

Food allergies are a growing problem in the canine world generally. Sufferers may itch, lick or chew their paws and/or legs, rub their face or get 'hot spots'. They may also get frequent ear infections as well as redness and swelling on their face. Switching to a grain-free diet can help to alleviate the symptoms, as your dog's digestive system does not have to work as hard. In the wild, a dog or wolf's staple diet would be meat with some vegetable matter from the stomach and intestines of the herbivores (plant-eating animals) that she ate – but no grains. Dogs do not efficiently digest corn or wheat - both of which are often staples of cheap commercial dog food. Grain-free diets provide carbohydrates through fruits and vegetables, so a dog still gets all the necessary nutrients.

NOTE: Although there is no conclusive scientific proof, there is emerging anecdotal evidence that the recent trend for grain-free diets has, in some cases, resulted in a Taurine (amino acid) deficiency, causing the enlarged heart disease DCM (Dilated Cardiomyopathy). One breeder added: "We only recommend no corn or wheat. Good grains are OK, but some gluten-free foods add bad starches like potatoes or peas." So, if you are looking at grain-free food for your dog, try and avoid those made with large quantities of various legumes (peas, chickpeas, lentils, etc.).

20 Tips For Feeding Your Cavapoo

1. If you do choose a manufactured food, don't pick one where meat or poultry content is NOT the first item listed on the bag or tin. Foods with lots of cheap cereals or sugar are not the best choice.

2. Some Cavapoos suffer from sensitive skin, 'hot spots' or allergies. A cheap food, often bulked up with grain, will only make this worse. If this is the case, bite the bullet and choose a high quality – usually more expensive – food, or consider a raw or home-cooked diet. You'll probably save money in vets' bills in the long run and your dog will be happier. A food described as 'hypoallergenic' on the sack means 'less likely to cause allergies.'

3. Consider feeding your dog twice a day, rather than once. Smaller feeds are easier to digest and reduce flatulence (gas). Puppies need to be fed more often; discuss exactly how often with your breeder.

4. Establish a feeding regime and stick to it. Dogs like routine. If you are feeding twice a day, feed once in the morning and then again at tea-time. Stick to the same times of day. Do not give the last feed too late, or your dog's body will not have chance to process or burn off the food before sleeping. She will also need a walk or letting out in the garden or yard after her second feed to allow her to empty her bowels. Feeding at the same times each day helps your dog establish a toilet regime.

5. Some owners practise 'free feeding,' which allows the dog to eat when he or she wants. However, if your Cavapoo is fussy, consider taking away any uneaten food between meals. (Even then some Cavapoos can still refuse to eat). Most Cavapoos enjoy their food, but any dog can become fussy if food is available all day. Imagine if your dinner was left on the table for hours. Returning to the table two or three hours later would not be such a tempting prospect, but coming back for a fresh meal would be far more appetising.

    Also, when food is left all day, some dogs take the food for granted and lose their appetite. They start leaving food and you are at your wits' end trying to find something they will actually eat. Put the food bowl down twice a day and take it up after 20 minutes – even if there is some left. If she is healthy and hungry, she'll look forward to her next meal and soon stop leaving food. If a Cavapoo does not eat anything for a couple of days, it either means that she is unwell or you will have to try a different diet.

NOTE: The exception to this is with very young puppies – under three months – where the breeder might recommend free feeding so the dog can eat at will. Also, some fussy eaters do better with free feeding. IMPORTANT: Dishes must be washed daily and old uneaten food thrown away.

6. If your puppy is a fussy eater, don't be too quick to switch foods. Try removing the bowl between meals, so (s)he is hungry when it's time for the next meal. Switching foods too quickly or tempting a young dog with treats can be a sure-fire way of encouraging fussy eating.

7. Some Cavapoo owners find that their dog eats better if the food is presented on a small plate.

8. If your dog is a fussy eater, try giving the teatime feed after a long walk when your dog is more likely to be hungry. (Wait until an hour after vigorous exercise).

9. Do not feed too many titbits (tidbits) and treats between meals. Extra weight will place extra strain on your Cavapoo's heart, other organs and joints, causing a detrimental effect on health and even lifespan. It also throws a balanced diet out of the window if they are cheap and unhealthy. Try to avoid feeding your dog from the table or your plate, as this encourages attention-seeking behaviour, begging and drooling.

10. If you feed leftovers, feed them INSTEAD of a balanced meal, not as well as - unless you are feeding a raw diet. High quality commercial foods already provide all the nutrients, vitamins, minerals and calories that your dog needs. Feeding titbits or leftovers may be too rich for your Cavapoo in addition to her regular diet and cause gas, scratching or other problems, such as obesity. You can feed your dog vegetables as a healthy low-calorie treat.

 Get your puppy used to eating raw carrots, pieces of apple, etc. as a treat and she will continue to enjoy them as an adult. If you wait until she's fully grown before introducing them, she may well turn her nose up.

11. Never give your dog cooked bones, as these can splinter and cause choking or intestinal problems.

12. Avoid rawhide, as dogs, particularly those that rush their food, have a tendency to swallow without first nibbling it down into smaller pieces. Rawhide also contains glue and chemicals which are toxic in large quantities. Personally, I would never give rawhide to a dog.

13. NEVER feed the following items to your dog: grapes, raisins, chocolate, onions, Macadamia

nuts, any fruits with seeds or stones, tomatoes, avocadoes, rhubarb, tea, coffee or alcohol. All of these are poisonous to dogs.

14. If you switch to a new food, do the transition gradually. Unlike humans, dogs' digestive systems cannot handle sudden changes. Begin by gradually mixing some of the new food in with the old and increase the proportion so that after seven to eight days, all the food is the new one. The following ratios are recommended by Doctors Foster & Smith Inc: Days 1-3 add 25% of the new food, Days 4-6 add 50%, Days 7-9 add 75%, Day 10 feed 100% of the new food. By the way, if you stick to the identical brand, you can change flavours in one go.

NOTE: The exception is when switching to a raw diet as raw and processed or cooked food are digested at different rates, and the stomach produces different acids for the digestion of each. Raw takes around four hours to digest, whereas kibble takes 12 hours. To switch to raw, give the last bowl of kibble then start feeding raw the following day.

Our photo, courtesy of owner Karen Howe, shows Rodney and Mabel happily tucking in together.

15. If you have more than one dog, consider feeding them separately. Cavapoos normally get on well with other dogs, but feeding dogs together can sometimes lead to food aggression from one dog either protecting her own food or trying to eat the food designated for another.

16. Check your dog's faeces (aka stools, poo or poop!). If her diet is suitable, the food should be easily digested and produce dark brown, firm stools. If your dog produces soft or light stools, or has a lot of gas or diarrhoea, then the diet may not suit her, so consult your vet or breeder for advice.

17. Feed your dog in stainless steel or ceramic dishes. Plastic bowls don't last as long and can also trigger an allergic reaction around the muzzle in some sensitive dogs. Ceramic bowls are best for keeping water cold. Elevated bowls with narrow tops (*pictured,* available on Amazon, eBay, etc.) are good if your Cavapoo has long Spaniel-like ears, as they keep ears out of food and drink.

18. Keep your dog's weight in check. Obesity can lead to the development of serious health issues, such as heart disease, diabetes and high blood pressure. Although weight varies from dog to dog, a good rule of thumb is that your Cavapoo's tummy should be higher than her rib cage. If her belly is level or hangs down below it, she is overweight.

19. Some owners feed vitamins and/or supplements to help keep their Cavapoos healthy, particularly if they have skin issues. Check with your breeder or vet as to which, if any, to feed. These may include fish oil for the coat, a probiotic to aid digestion, or glucosamine for joints.

20. And finally, always make sure that your dog has access to clean, fresh water. Change the water and clean the bowl regularly – it gets slimy!

Many breeders feed their adult dogs twice a day, others feed just once, and yet others feed some dogs once a day and some dogs twice a day. As one US breeder put it: "They are not all made from the same cookie cutter." Start your dog on twice-daily feeds from four to six months old and, if he or she seems to be thriving on this regime, stick to it.

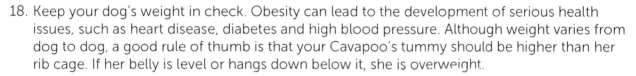

Types of Dog Food

We are what we eat. The right food is a very important part of a healthy lifestyle for dogs as well as humans. Here are the main options explained:

Dry dog food - also called kibble, is a popular and relatively inexpensive way of providing a balanced diet – look for *"Complete and Balanced"* on the packet in the UK. However, kibble was created for the convenience of owners, not dogs, and it doesn't suit all dogs. Kibble comes in a variety of flavours and with differing ingredients to suit the different stages of a dog's life. Cheap foods are often false economy, particularly if your Cavapoo does not tolerate grain/cereal very well. You may also have to feed larger quantities to ensure she gets sufficient nutrients.

Canned food - another popular choice – and it's often very popular with dogs too. They love the taste and it generally comes in a variety of flavours. Canned food is often mixed with dry kibble, and a small amount may be added to a dog that is on a dry food diet if she has lost interest in food. It tends to be more expensive than dried food and many owners don't like the mess. These days there are hundreds of options, some are very high quality and made from natural, organic ingredients and contain herbs and other beneficial ingredients. A part-opened tin can sometimes smell when you open the fridge door. As with dry food, read the label closely. Generally, you get what you pay for and the origins of cheap canned dog food are often somewhat dubious. Some dogs can suffer from diarrhoea or soft stools and/or gas with too much tinned or soft food.

Freeze-Dried *(pictured)* - This is made by a special process which freezes the food, then removes the moisture before vacuum packing. The product is sealed with an oxygen-absorbing substance to increase shelf life. It doesn't need a fridge and can be kept at room temperature for up to six months. Usually with a very high meat content and no grain, many freeze-dried meals contain high quality, natural, human-grade ingredients. So what's the catch?

........Price! If you can afford it, freeze-dried will not only give you a quality, natural food, but your dog will love it. Many raw feeders use freeze-dried and it's also handy for those travelling with their dogs.

Home-Cooked - Some owners want the ability to be in complete control of their dog's diet, know exactly what their dog is eating and to be sure that his or her nutritional needs are being met. Feeding your dog a home-cooked diet of meat and vegetables can be time-consuming and more expensive than kibble, and the difficult thing is sticking to it once you have started out with the best of intentions. But many owners think the extra effort is worth it. If you decide to go ahead, spend the time to become proficient and learn about canine nutrition to ensure your dog gets all the vital nutrients and right amount of calories. You can also buy ready-made frozen home-cooked food from companies such as Butternut Box.

We have several friends with itchy dogs who are all now doing better having switched from a commercial, dried dog food to a home-cooked diet - usually involving chicken and vegetables.

Semi-Moist - These are commercial dog foods shaped like pork chops, salamis, bacon *(pictured)*, burgers or other meaty foods and they are the least nutritional of all dog foods. They are full of sugars, artificial flavourings and colourings to help make them visually appealing. Cavapoos don't care two hoots what their food looks like, they only care how it smells and tastes; the shapes are designed to appeal to humans. While you may give your dog one as an occasional treat, they are not a diet in themselves and do NOT provide the nutrition your dog needs. Steer clear of them for regular feeding.

The Raw Diet

If there is one thing which is guaranteed to divide opinion, it is the raw diet! There is anecdotal evidence that some dogs thrive on a raw diet, particularly those with allergies or food intolerances - although scientific proof is lagging behind. However, I also know several breeders (of different breeds) who have tried feeding raw and say their dogs did badly on it, and some say their dogs actually dislike the taste.

Given that our dog, Max, had allergies for many years, I would say that had he been younger, I would have tried him on a home-cooked or raw diet – but that's just personal opinion.

When we talk about a raw diet, we are referring to uncooked meat, poultry and vegetables. This may be fed in the natural state, which requires more work on the part of the owner, or bought pre-prepared, so all you have to do is open the packet.

Many Cavapoos thrive on a high quality dried commercial dog food or a mix of cooked/raw and kibble. We are not suggesting that everybody rushes out and feeds their dog a raw diet. Due to various factors, the time and expense involved, the raw diet is certainly not for every dog. We are simply providing the information here for anyone considering feeding raw. This may include owners who are fans of a natural diet or who have a Cavapoo that has skin issues or is not doing well on a commercially-prepared kibble. In these circumstances, a raw diet is one of the options for owners to consider.

Claims made by fans of the raw diet include:

- ❖ Reduced symptoms of - or less likelihood of - allergies, and less scratching
- ❖ Better skin and coats
- ❖ Easier weight management
- ❖ Improved digestion
- ❖ Less doggie odour and flatulence
- ❖ Higher energy levels
- ❖ Reduced risk of Bloat
- ❖ Helps fussy eaters
- ❖ Fresher breath and improved dental health
- ❖ Drier and less smelly stools, more like pellets
- ❖ Overall improvement in general health and less disease
- ❖ Most dogs love a raw diet

Raw food emulates the way dogs ate before the existence of commercial kibble, which may contain artificial preservatives and excessive protein and fillers – causing a reaction in some dogs. Dry, canned and other styles of processed food were mainly created as a means of convenience - for the owner, not the dog!

However, nowadays, you also have the option of buying packets or boxes of balanced, ready-made raw meals for your dog. Made by companies such as such as Paleo Ridge or Naturaw, these meals can even be individually tailored to suit your dog. There is also the freeze-dried option if you don't fancy handling raw meats and poultry.

Some nutritionists believe that dogs fed raw whole foods tend to be healthier than those on other diets. They say there are inherent beneficial enzymes, vitamins, minerals and other qualities in meats, fruits, vegetables and grains in their natural forms that are denatured or destroyed when cooked. Many also believe dogs are less likely to have allergic reactions to the ingredients on this diet. Frozen food can be a valuable aid to the raw diet. The food is highly palatable and made from high quality ingredients. The downsides are that not all pet food stores stock it, it can be expensive and you have to remember to defrost it.

Critics of a raw diet say that the risks of nutritional imbalance, intestinal problems and food-borne illnesses caused by handling and feeding raw meat outweigh any benefits. Owners must pay strict attention to hygiene when preparing a raw diet.

 A raw diet made at home from scratch may not be a good option if you have young children in the house, due to the risk of bacterial infection from the raw meat. The dog may also be more likely to ingest bacteria or parasites such as Salmonella, E. Coli and Ecchinococcus.

There are two main types of raw diet, one involves feeding raw, meaty bones and the other is known as the BARF diet (*Biologically Appropriate Raw Food* or *Bones And Raw Food),* created by Dr Ian Billinghurst.

Raw Meaty Bones

This diet is:

* Raw meaty bones or carcasses, if available, should form the bulk of the diet

* Table scraps both cooked and raw, such as vegetables, can be fed

* As with any diet, fresh water should be constantly available. **NOTE: Do NOT feed cooked bones, they can splinter**

Australian veterinarian Dr Tom Lonsdale is a leading proponent of the raw meaty bones diet. He believes the following foods are suitable:

* Chicken and turkey carcasses, after the meat has been removed for human consumption

* Poultry by-products, including heads, feet, necks and wings

* Whole fish and fish heads

* Sheep, calf, goat, and deer carcasses sawn into large pieces of meat and bone

* Other by-products, e.g. pigs' trotters, pigs' heads, sheep heads, brisket, tail and rib bones

* A certain amount of offal can be included in the diet, e.g. liver, lungs, trachea, hearts, tripe

He says that low-fat game animals, fish and poultry provide the best source of food for pet carnivores. If you feed meat from farm animals (cattle, sheep and pigs), avoid excessive fat and bones that are too large to be eaten.

Some of it will depend on what's available locally and how expensive it is. If you shop around you should be able to source a regular supply of suitable raw meaty bones at a reasonable price. Start with your local butcher or farm shop. When deciding what type of bones to feed your Cavapoo, one point to bear in mind is that dogs are more likely to break their teeth when eating large knuckle bones and bones sawn lengthwise than when eating meat and bone together. You'll also need to think about WHERE you are going to feed your dog. A dog takes some time to eat a raw bone and will push it around the floor, so the kitchen may not be the most suitable or hygienic place. Outside is one option, but what do you do when it's raining?

Establishing the right quantity to feed your Cavapoo is a matter of trial and error. You will reach a decision based on your dog's activity levels, appetite and body condition. High activity and a big appetite show a need for increased food, and vice versa.

A very approximate guide, based on raw meaty bones, for the average dog is 15%-20% of body weight per week, or 2%-3% a day. So, if your Cavapoo weighs 16lb (7.27kg), he or she will require 2.4lb-3.2lb (1kg-1.45kg) of carcasses or raw meaty bones weekly. **These figures are only a rough guide** and relate to adult pets in a domestic environment. Pregnant or lactating females and growing puppies may need much more food than adult animals of similar body weight. Table scraps should be fed as an extra component of the diet.

Photo, courtesy of Kit Lam, shows two-year-old F1 Cookie enjoying a raw bone.

Dr Lonsdale says: "Wherever possible, feed the meat and bone ration in one large piece requiring much ripping, tearing and gnawing. This makes for contented pets with clean teeth. Wild carnivores feed at irregular intervals, in a domestic setting regularity works best and accordingly I suggest that you feed adult dogs and cats once daily. If you live in a hot climate I recommend that you feed pets in the evening to avoid attracting flies.

"I suggest that on one or two days each week your dog may be fasted - just like animals in the wild. On occasions you may run out of natural food. Don't be tempted to buy artificial food, fast your dog and stock up with natural food the next day. Puppies...sick or underweight dogs should not be fasted (unless on veterinary advice)."

Table scraps and some fruit and vegetable peelings can also be fed, but should not make up more than one-third of the diet. Liquidising cooked and uncooked scraps in a food mixer can make them easier to digest.

Things to Avoid:

- Excessive meat off the bone - not balanced
- Excessive vegetables - not balanced
- Small pieces of bone - can be swallowed whole and get stuck
- Cooked bones, fruit stones (pips) and corn cobs - get stuck
- Mineral and vitamin additives - create imbalance
- Processed food - leads to dental and other diseases
- Excessive starchy food - associated with Bloat
- Onions, garlic, chocolate, grapes, raisins, sultanas, currants - toxic to pets
- Milk - associated with diarrhoea. Animals drink it whether thirsty or not and can get fat

Points of Concern

- Old dogs used to processed food may experience initial difficulty when changed on to a natural diet. Discuss the change with your vet first

- Raw meaty bones are not suitable for dogs with dental or jaw problems

- This diet may not be suitable if your dog gulps her food, as the bones can become lodged internally, larger bones may prevent gulping

- The diet should be varied, any nutrients fed to excess can be harmful

- Liver is an excellent foodstuff, but should not be fed more than once weekly

- Weight bearing bones shouldn't be given as they damage teeth. One breeder added: "My general rule is that if I can cut it with poultry shears, they can eat it; anything harder should be avoided

- Other offal, e.g. ox stomachs, should not make up more than half of the diet

- Whole fish are an excellent source of food, but avoid feeding one species of fish constantly. Some species, e.g. carp, contain an enzyme which destroys thiamine (vitamin B1)

- If you have more than one dog, do not allow them to fight over the food, feed them separately if necessary

- Be prepared to monitor your dog while she eats the bones, especially in the beginning, and do not feed bones with sharp points

- Make sure that children do not disturb the dog when feeding or try to take the bone away

- Hygiene: Make sure the raw meaty bones are kept separate from human food and clean thoroughly any surface the uncooked meat or bones have touched. This is especially important if you have children. Feeding bowls are unnecessary, your dog will drag the bones across the floor, so feed them outside if you can, or on a floor that is easy to clean

- Puppies can and do eat diets of raw meaty bones, but you should consult the breeder or a vet before embarking on this diet with a young dog

You will need a regular supply of meaty bones - either locally or online - and you should buy in bulk to ensure a consistency of supply. For this you will need a large freezer. You can then parcel up the bones into daily portions. You can also feed frozen bones; some dogs will gnaw them straight away, others will wait for them to thaw.

More information is available from the website www.rawmeatybones.com and I would strongly recommend discussing the matter with your breeder or vet first before switching to raw meaty bones.

The BARF diet

A variation of the raw meaty bones diet is the BARF created by Dr Ian Billinghurst, who owns the registered trademark 'Barf Diet'. A typical BARF diet is made up of 60%-75% of raw meaty bones (bones with about 50% meat, such as chicken neck, back and wings) and 25%-40% of fruit and vegetables, offal, meat, eggs or dairy foods. Bones must not be cooked or they can splinter inside the dog. There is a great deal of information on the BARF diet on the internet.

 Only start a raw diet if you have done your research and are sure you have the commitment and money to keep it going. There are numerous websites and canine forums with information on switching to a raw diet and everything it involves.

Food Allergies

Dog food allergies affect about one in 10 dogs. They are the third most common canine allergy for dogs after atopy (inhaled or contact allergies) and flea bite allergies. While there's no scientific evidence of links between specific breeds and food allergies, there is anecdotal evidence from owners that some Cavapoos can be sensitive to, and suffer a reaction from, certain foods.

Food allergies affect males and females in equal measure as well as neutered and intact pets. They can start when your dog is five months or 12 years old - although the vast majority start when the dog is between two and six years old. It is not uncommon for dogs with food allergies to also have other types of allergies.

If your dog is not well, how do you know if the problem lies with her food or not? Here are some common symptoms to look out for:

- Itchy skin (this is the most common). Your dog may lick or chew her paws or legs and rub her face with her paws or on the furniture, carpet, etc.
- Excessive scratching
- Ear infections (***pictured***)
- Hot patches of skin – 'hot spots'
- Hair loss
- Redness and inflammation on the chin and face
- Recurring skin infections
- Increased bowel movements (maybe twice as often as usual)
- Skin infections that clear up with antibiotics but recur when the antibiotics run out

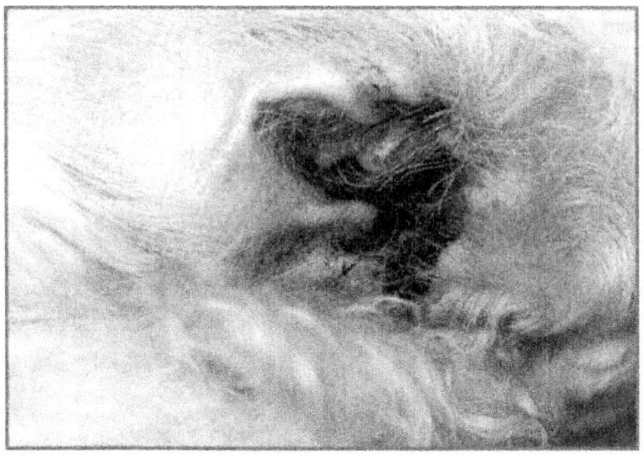

Allergies or Intolerance?

There's a difference between dog food allergies and dog food intolerance (sensitivity):

Typical reactions to allergies are skin problems and/or itching

Typical reactions to intolerance are diarrhoea and/or vomiting

Dog food intolerance can be compared to people who get diarrhoea or an upset stomach from eating spicy food. Both can be cured by a change to a diet specifically suited to the individual, although a food allergy may be harder to get to the root cause of. As they say in the canine world: "One dog's meat is another dog's poison".

With dogs, certain ingredients are more likely to cause allergies than others. In order of the most common triggers across the canine world in general they are: **Beef, dairy products, chicken, wheat, eggs, corn, and soy (soya).**

There is also increasing evidence that some dogs cannot tolerate the preservatives and other chemicals in dried dog food.

Unfortunately, these most common offenders are also the most common ingredients in dog foods! In the past, dogs were often put on a rice and lamb kibble diet, which were thought to be less likely to cause allergies. However, the reason was simply because they were not traditionally included in many dog food recipes - therefore fewer dogs had reactions to them.

It is also worth noting that a dog is allergic or sensitive to an **ingredient**, not to a particular brand of dog food, so it is very important to read the ingredients label on the sack or tin. If your Cavapoo has a reaction to beef, for example, she will react to any food containing beef, regardless of how expensive it is or how well it has been prepared.

 Food intolerances frequently start when a dog is less than one year old. If your Cavapoo starts scratching, has diarrhoea, ear infections or other symptoms, don't think that because she has always had this food that the problem lies elsewhere. It may be that she has developed an intolerance to the food as her body matures.

Symptoms of food allergies are well documented. Unfortunately, the problem is that these conditions may also be symptoms of other issues such as environmental or flea bite allergies, intestinal problems, mange, and yeast or bacterial infections. You can have a blood test on your dog for food allergies, but many veterinarians now believe that this is not accurate enough.

The only way to completely cure a food allergy or intolerance is total avoidance. This is not as easy as it sounds. First you have to be sure that your dog does have a food allergy, and then you have to discover which food is causing the reaction.

Blood tests are not thought to be reliable and, as far as I am aware, the only true way to determine exactly what your dog is allergic to, is to start a food trial. If you don't or can't do this for the whole 12 weeks, then you could try a more amateurish approach, which is eliminating ingredients from your dog's diet one at a time by switching diets – remember to do this over a period of a week.

A food trial is usually the option of last resort, due to the amount of time and attention that it requires. It is also called *'an exclusion diet'* and is the only truly accurate way of finding out if your dog has a food allergy and what is causing it. Before embarking on one, try switching dog food.

If you wish to stick with commercial dog food, try switching to a grain-free, hypoallergenic one – preferably with natural (not chemical) preservatives. Although usually more expensive, hypoallergenic dog food ingredients do not include common allergens such as wheat protein or soya, thereby minimising the risk of an allergic reaction. Many may have less common ingredients, such as venison, duck or types of fish.

Here are some things to look for in a high-quality food:

- ❧ Meat or poultry as the first ingredient
- ❧ Vegetables
- ❧ Natural herbs such as rosemary or parsley
- ❧ Oils such as rapeseed (canola) or salmon.

Here's what to avoid if your dog is showing signs of a food intolerance:

- ❧ Corn, corn meal, corn gluten meal
- ❧ Meat or poultry by-products (as you don't know exactly what these are or how they have been handled)

- Artificial preservatives including BHA, BHT, Propyl Gallate, Ethoxyquin, Sodium Nitrite/Nitrate and TBHQBHA

- Artificial colours, sugars and sweeteners like corn syrup, sucrose and ammoniated glycyrrhizin

- Powdered cellulose

- Propylene glycol

If you can rule out all of these and you've tried switching diet without much success, then a food trial may be your only option.

....

Food Trials

Before you embark on one of these, you need to know that they are a real pain-in-the-you-know-what to monitor. You have to be incredibly vigilant and determined, so only start one if you 100% know you can see it through to the end, or you are wasting your time. It is important to keep a diary during a food trial to record any changes in your dog's symptoms, behaviour or habits.

A food trial involves feeding one specific food for 12 weeks, something the dog has never eaten before, such as rabbit and rice or venison and potato. Surprisingly, dogs are typically NOT allergic to foods they have never eaten before. The food should contain no added colouring, preservatives or flavourings.

There are a number of these commercial diets on the market, as well as specialised diets that have proteins and carbohydrates broken down into such small molecular sizes that they no longer trigger an allergic reaction. These are called *'limited antigen'* or *'hydrolysed protein'* diets.

Home-made diets are another option as you can strictly control the ingredients. The difficult thing is that this must be the **only thing** the dog eats during the trial. Any treats or snacks make the whole thing a waste of time. During the trial, you shouldn't allow your dog to roam freely, as you cannot control what she is eating or drinking when out of sight outdoors. Only the recommended diet must be fed. Do NOT give:

- Treats

- Rawhide

- Pigs' ears

- Cows' hooves

- Flavoured toothpastes

- Flavoured medications (including heartworm treatments) or supplements

- Flavoured plastic toys

If you want to give a treat, <u>use a foodstuff included</u> in the recommended diet." (Tinned diets can be frozen in chunks or baked and then used as treats). If you have other dogs, either feed them all on the trial diet or feed the others in an entirely different location. If you have a cat, don't let the dog near the cat litter tray. And keep your dog out of the room when you are eating — not easy with a hungry Cavapoo! But even small amounts of food dropped on the floor or licked off of a plate can ruin a food trial, meaning you'll have to start all over again.

Although beef is the food most likely to cause allergies in the general dog population, there are plenty of stories to suggest that the ingredient most likely to cause a problem in many dogs is grain – just visit any canine internet forum to see that this is true.

'Grain' is wheat or any other cultivated cereal crop. Some dogs also react to starch, which is found in grains and potatoes (also bread, pasta, rice, etc.).

Some breeds (especially the Bully breeds, e.g. Bulldogs, Boxers, Pugs, Bull Terriers and French Bulldogs) can be prone to a build-up of yeast in the digestive system. Foods that are high in grains and sugar can cause an increase in unhealthy bacteria and yeast in the stomach. This crowds out the good bacteria in the stomach and can cause toxins to occur that affect the immune system.

And when the immune system is not functioning properly, the itchiness related to food allergies can cause secondary bacterial and yeast infections, which, in Cavapoos, may show as ear infections, hot spots, reddish or dark brown tear stains or other skin disorders. Symptoms of a yeast infection also include:

❖ Itchiness

❖ A musty smell

❖ Skin lesions or redness on the underside of the neck, the belly or paws

Although drugs such as antihistamines and steroids will temporarily help, they do not address the root cause. Wheat products are also known to produce flatulence, while corn products and feed fillers may cause skin rashes or irritations. Switching to a grain-free diet may help to get rid of yeast and bad bacteria in the digestive system. Introduce the new food over a week or so and be patient, it may take two to three months for symptoms to subside – but you will definitely know if it has worked after 12 weeks.

 Some owners give their dogs a daily spoonful of natural or live yoghurt, as this contains healthy bacteria and helps to balance the bacteria in a dog's digestive system - by the way, it can work for humans too! And plenty of owners whose Cavapoos have struggled with conventional kibble have switched to a home-cooked or raw diet with some success.

It is also worth noting that some of the symptoms of food allergies - particularly the scratching, licking, chewing and redness - can also be a sign of inhalant or contact (environmental) allergies, which are caused by a reaction to such triggers as pollen, grass or dust. Some dogs are also allergic to flea bites - see **Chapter 12. Skin and Allergies** for more details.

If you suspect your dog has a food allergy, the first port of call should be to the vet to discuss the best course of action. However, many vets' clinics promote specific brands of dog food, which may or may not be the best for your dog. Don't buy anything without first checking every ingredient on the label.

The website www.dogfoodadvisor.com provides useful information with star ratings for grain-free and hypoallergenic dogs' foods, or www.allaboutdogfood.co.uk if you are in the UK, or www.veterinarypartner.com/Content.plx?P=A&S=0&C=0&A=2499 for more details about canine food trials. We have no vested interest in these sites or their recommended products, but have found them to be good sources of unbiased information.

How Much Food?

This is another question I am often asked. The answer is ... there is no easy answer! The correct amount of food for a dog depends on a number of factors:

- ❖ Breed
- ❖ Gender
- ❖ Age
- ❖ Health
- ❖ Environment
- ❖ Number of dogs in the house
- ❖ Quality of the food
- ❖ Natural energy levels
- ❖ Amount of daily exercise
- ❖ Whether your dog is working, competing, performing a service or simply a pet

Some breeds have a higher metabolic rate than others, and energy levels vary tremendously from one dog to the next. Some individual Cavapoos are energetic, while others are more laid back. Generally:

- ❖ Smaller dogs have faster metabolisms so require a higher amount of food per pound of body weight
- ❖ Dogs that have been spayed may be more prone to putting on weight
- ❖ Growing puppies and young dogs need more food than senior dogs with a slower lifestyle

Every dog is different; you can have two Cavapoos with different body shapes, energy levels and capacity for exercise. The energetic dog will burn off more calories.

Maintaining a healthy body weight for dogs – and humans – is all about balancing what you take in with how much you burn off. If your dog is exercised two or three times a day and/or has regular play sessions with other dogs, she will need more calories than a couch potato Cavapoo. Certain health conditions such as heart disease, an underactive thyroid, diabetes and arthritis can all lead to dogs gaining weight, so their food has to be adjusted accordingly.

Just like us, a dog kept in a very cold environment will need more calories to keep warm than a dog in a warm climate, as they burn extra calories to keep themselves warm. Here's an interesting fact: a dog kept on her own is more likely to be overweight than a dog kept with other dogs, as she receives all of the food-based attention.

Manufacturers of cheaper foods usually recommend feeding more to your dog, as much of the food is made up of cereals, which are not doing much except bulking up the weight of the food – and possibly triggering allergies in your Cavapoo. The daily recommended amount listed on the dog food sacks or tins is generally too high – after all, the more your dog eats, the more they sell!

Because there are so many factors involved, there is no simple answer. However, below we have listed the recommended feeding amount for dogs for James Wellbeloved's hypoallergenic kibble, which we feed.

Adult Cavapoos, both male and female, can be expected to weigh between 12lb to 25lb (5.4kg to 11.3kg) when fully grown - although one or two can be even bigger.

In the chart, the number on the left is the dog's adult weight. The numbers on the right are the amount of daily food that an average dog with average energy levels requires.

NOTE: This Canine Feeding Chart gives only very general guidelines; your dog may need more or less than this. Use the chart as a guideline only and if your dog loses or gains weight, adjust meals accordingly.

PUPPY

Size type	Expected adult body weight in kg (lb)	Daily serving in grams (ounces)					
		2 mths	3 mths	4 mths	5 mths	6 mths	> 6 mths
Small	5kg (11lb)	95g (3.5oz)	110g (3.9oz)	115g (4oz)	115g (4oz)	110g (3.9oz)	Change to Adult or Small Breed Junior
Small	10kg (22lb)	155g (5.5oz)	185g (6.5oz)	195g (6.9 oz)	190g (6.7oz)	185g (6.5oz)	Change to Adult or Small Breed Junior

JUNIOR

Size type	Expected adult body weight in kg (lb)	Daily serving in grams (ounces)							
		6 mths	7 mths	8 mths	10 mths	12 mths	14 mths	16 mths
Small	10kg (22lb)	195g (6.9 oz)	185g (6.5oz)	175g (6.2oz)	160g (5.6oz)	Change to Adult		

ADULT

Size type	Bodyweight in kg (lb)	Daily serving in grams (ounces)		
		High activity	Normal activity	Low activity
Small	5-10kg (11-22lb)	115-190g (4-6.7oz)	100-170g (3.5-6oz)	85-145g (3-5.1oz)
Medium	10-15 (22-33lb)	190-255g (6.7-9oz)	170-225g (6-7.9oz)	145-195g (5.1-6.9oz)

SENIOR

Size type	Bodyweight in kg (lb)	Daily serving in grams (ounces)	
		Active	Normal
Small	5-10kg (11-22lb)	105-175g (3.7-6.2oz)	90-150g (3.2-5.3oz)
Medium	10-15kg (22-33lb)	175-235g (6.2-8.3oz)	150-205g (3.2-7.2oz)

Canine Bloat

Bloat is known by several different names: twisted stomach, gastric torsion or Gastric Dilatation-Volvulus (GDV). It occurs mainly in larger breeds, however, there have been cases of smaller dogs getting Bloat. It is one reason why owners often feed their dogs twice a day - particularly if they are greedy gulpers.

Tips to avoid Bloat:

❧ Buy an elevated feeding bowl, which will not only keep your Cav's ears out of the food, but many people believe helps to prevent bloat. If you have a gulper, consider buying a bowl with nobbles in *(pictured)* and moisten your dog's food – both of these will slow her down

❧ Feed twice a day rather than once

❧ Diet - avoid dog food with high fats or which use citric acid as a preservative, also avoid tiny pieces of kibble

❧ Don't let your dog drink too much water just before, during or after eating. Remove the water bowl just before mealtimes, but be sure to return it soon after

❧ Stress can possibly be a possible trigger, with nervous (and aggressive) dogs being more susceptible; maintain a peaceful environment for your dog, particularly around mealtimes

❧ IMPORTANT: Avoid vigorous exercise just before or after eating, allow one hour either side of mealtimes before strenuous exercise

Bloat can kill a dog in less than one hour. If you suspect your Cavapoo has bloat, get him or her into the car and off to the vet IMMEDIATELY. Even with treatment, mortality rates range from 10% to 60%. With surgery, this drops to 15% to 33%.

Overweight Dogs

Any dog can become overweight given too much food, too many treats and not enough exercise. It is very hard to resist those beautiful, big brown pleading eyes when it comes to food - *as is beautifully demonstrated here by Cookie.* Fortunately, owner Kit Lam has trained Cookie to enjoy

healthy raspberries as a treat. In fact, she loves them so much that Kit has had to fence off the raspberry bushes in her garden to stop Cookie scoffing the lot!

It is far easier to regulate your dog's weight and keep it at a healthy level than to try and slim down a voraciously hungry Cavapoo when he or she becomes overweight. Sadly, overweight and obese dogs are susceptible to a range of illnesses and even a shortened lifespan. According to James Howie, Veterinary Advisor to Lintbells, some of the main ones are:

Heart and lung problems – fatty deposits within the chest cavity and excessive circulating fat play important roles in the development of cardio-respiratory and cardiovascular disease.

Joint disease – excessive body weight may increase joint stress, which is a risk factor in joint degeneration (arthrosis), as is cruciate disease (knee ligament rupture). Joint disease tends to lead to a reduction in exercise that then increases the likelihood of weight gain which reduces exercise further. A vicious cycle is created. Overfeeding growing dogs can lead to various problems, including the worsening of hip dysplasia. Weight management may be the only measure required to control clinical signs in some cases.

Diabetes – resistance to insulin has been shown to occur in overweight dogs, leading to a greater risk of diabetes mellitus.

Tumours – obesity increases the risk of mammary tumours in female dogs.

Liver disease – fat degeneration may result in liver insufficiency.

Reduced lifespan - one of the most serious proven findings in obesity studies is that obesity in both humans and dogs reduces lifespan.

Exercise intolerance – this is also a common finding with overweight dogs, which can compound an obesity problem as fewer calories are burned off and are therefore stored, leading to further weight gain. Obesity also puts greater strain on the delicate respiratory system of Cavapoos, making breathing even more difficult for them.

Cavapoos are extremely loyal companions and very attached to their humans, who regard them as members of the family. However, beware of ascribing too many human characteristics to your lovable Cavapoo. Scientists have shown that dogs regarded as 'family members' (i.e. anthropomorphised) by the owner are at greater risk of becoming overweight. This is because attention given to the dog often results in food being given as well. The important thing to remember is that many of the problems associated with being overweight are reversible. Increasing exercise increases the calories burned, which in turn reduces weight. If you do put your dog on a diet, the reduced amount of food will also mean reduced nutrients, so he or she may need a supplement during this time.

Feeding Puppies

It's important to start out on the right foot with your baby Cavapoo by getting him or her interested in food right from the beginning - as they can soon become fussy eaters. Feeding your pup the right diet is important to help his or her young body and bones grow strong and healthy.

Puppyhood is a time of rapid growth and development, and puppies require different levels of nutrients to adult dogs.

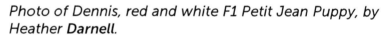

Photo of Dennis, red and white F1 Petit Jean Puppy, by Heather Darnell.

Initially, pups get all their nutrients from their mother's milk and then they are gradually weaned from three or four weeks of age. Many owners prefer to stick with the food provided and recommended by the breeder. If your pup is doing well on this, there is no reason to change. However, if you do change food, it should be done very gradually by mixing in a little more of the new food each day over a period of seven to 10 days.

If at any time your puppy starts being sick, has loose stools or is constipated, slow the rate at which you are switching him over. If she continues vomiting, seek veterinary advice quickly - within a day or two - as she may have a problem with the food you have chosen. Puppies quickly dehydrate if they are vomiting or have diarrhoea.

Because of their special nutritional needs, only give your puppy a food that is approved either just for puppies or for all life stages. If a feed is recommended for adult dogs only, it won't have enough protein, and the balance of calcium and other nutrients will not be right for a pup. Puppy food is very high in calories and nutritional supplements, so you want to switch to a junior or adult food once she leaves puppyhood, which is at about six months old. Feeding puppy food too long can result in obesity and orthopaedic problems.

Getting the amount and type of food right for your pup is important. Feeding too much will cause him to put on excess pounds, and overweight puppies are more likely to grow into overweight adults. As a very broad guideline, Cavapoos normally mature (physically) into fully developed adults at around 18 months to two years old - females tend to mature slightly earlier than males - although both sexes can behave like puppies for much longer!

DON'T:

❧ Feed table scraps from the table. Your Cavapoo will get used to begging for food, it will also affect a puppy's carefully balanced diet

❧ Feed food or uncooked meat that has gone off. Puppies have sensitive stomachs

DO:

❧ Check the weight of your growing puppy to make sure she is within normal limits for her age. There are charts available on numerous websites, just type *"puppy weight chart"* into Google – you'll need to know the exact age and current weight of your puppy

❧ Take your puppy to the vet if she has diarrhoea or is vomiting for two days or more

❧ Remove her food after it has been down for 15 to 20 minutes. Food available 24/7 encourages fussy eaters

How Often?

Most puppies have small stomachs but big appetites, so feed them small amounts on a frequent basis. Establishing a regular feeding routine with your puppy is good, as this will also help to toilet train her. Get her used to regular mealtimes and then let her outside to do her business straight away when she has finished. Puppies have fast metabolisms, so the results may be pretty quick!

Don't leave food out so puppy can eat it whenever she wants; you need to be there for the feeds because you want her and her body on a set schedule. Smaller meals are easier for her to digest and energy levels don't peak and fall so much with frequent feeds. There is some variation between recommendations, but as a general rule of thumb:

❧ Up to the age of three or four months, feed your puppy three or four times a day

❧ Then three times a day until she is four to six months old

❧ Twice a day until she is one year old

❧ Then once or twice a day for the rest of her life

 Cavapoos are very loving companions. If your dog is not responding well to a particular family member, a useful tactic is to get that person to feed the dog every day. The way to a dog's heart is often through his or her stomach!

Feeding Seniors

Once your adolescent dog has switched to an adult diet she will remain on it for several years. However, as a dog moves towards old age, her body has different requirements to those of a young dog. This is the time to consider switching to a senior diet. Generally, a dog is considered to be older or senior when in the last third of normal life expectancy. Some owners of large breeds, such as Great Danes (with an average lifespan of nine years) switch their dogs from an adult to a senior diet as young as six or seven years old.

A Cavapoo's average lifespan is 10 to 15 years, which is quite a wide variation. Genetics and general care play a role in longevity; look for signs of your dog slowing down or having joint problems. You can describe any changes to the vet at your dog's annual check-up, rather than having the expense of a separate consultation.

Dogs, generally, are living longer than they did 30 years ago. There are many factors that contribute to a longer life, including better immunisation and veterinary care, but one of the most important factors is better nutrition.

As a dog ages her metabolism slows, her joints stiffen, her energy levels decrease and she needs less exercise, just as with humans. An adult diet may be too rich and have too many calories, so it may be the time to move to a senior diet. Having said that, some dogs stay on a normal adult diet all of their lives – although the amount is usually decreased and supplements added, e.g. for joints.

Just like me, your Cavapoo will thicken around the waist as she gets older! Keep her weight in check even though it may be harder, as she will not be burning off as many calories and some older dogs become more food-focussed with age. Obesity in old age only puts more strain on the body - especially joints and organs - and makes any health problems even worse. Getting an older dog to slim down can be very difficult. It is much better not to let your Cavapoo get too chunky than to put her on a diet. But if she is overweight, put in the effort to shed the extra pounds. This is one of the single most important things you can do to increase your Cavapoo's quality AND length of life.

Other changes in canines are again similar to those in older humans and as well as stiff joints or arthritis, they may move more slowly and sleep more. Hearing and vision may not be so sharp and organs don't all work as efficiently as they used to; teeth may have become worn down or decayed. When this starts to happen, it is time to consider feeding your old friend a senior diet, which will take these changes into account. Specially formulated senior diets are lower in protein and calories but help to create a feeling of fullness.

Older dogs are more prone to constipation, so senior diets are often higher in fibre - at around 3% to 5%. Wheat bran can also be added to regular dog food to increase the amount of fibre - but do not try this if your Cavapoo has a low tolerance to grain. If your dog has poor kidney function, then a low phosphorus diet will help to lower the workload for the kidneys.

Ageing dogs may have additional needs, some of which can be catered for with supplements, e.g. glucosamine and chondroitin, which help joints. Two popular joint supplements in the UK are GWF Joint Aid for dogs, used by several breeders, and Lintbell's Yumove. If your dog is not eating a complete balanced diet, then a vitamin/mineral supplement is recommended to prevent any deficiencies. Some owners also feed extra antioxidants to an older dog – ask your vet's advice on your next visit. Antioxidants are also found naturally in fruit and vegetables.

While some older dogs suffer from obesity, others have the opposite problem – they lose weight and are disinterested in food. If your old dog is getting thinner and not eating well, firstly get her checked out by the vet to rule out any possible diseases. If she gets the all-clear, your next challenge is to tempt her to eat. She may be having trouble with her teeth, so if she's on a dry food, try smaller kibble or moistening it with water or gravy.

An old dog of ours loved his twice daily feeds until he got to the age of 10 when he suddenly lost interest in his hypoallergenic kibble. We tried switching flavours within the same brand, but that didn't work. After a short while we mixed his daily feeds with a little gravy and a spoonful of tinned dog food – Bingo! He started wolfing it down again and was as lively as ever.

At 12 he started getting some diarrhoea, so we switched again and for the last year of his life he was mainly on home-cooked chicken and rice with some Senior kibble, which worked well.

Some dogs can tolerate a small amount of milk or eggs added to their food, and home-made diets of boiled rice, potatoes, vegetables and chicken or meat with the right vitamin and mineral supplements can also be good. See **Chapter 16. Caring for Senior Cavapoos** for more information on looking after an ageing Cavapoo.

Reading Dog Food Labels

A NASA scientist would have a hard job understanding some manufacturers' labels, so it's no easy task for us lowly dog owners. Here are some things to look out for on the manufacturers' labels:

❖ The ingredients are listed by weight and the top one should always be the main content, such as chicken or lamb. Don't pick one where grain is the first ingredient; it is a poor-quality feed. Some dogs can develop grain intolerances or allergies, and often it is specifically wheat they have a reaction to

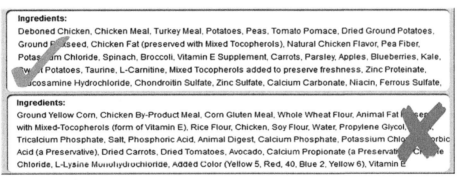

❖ High on the list should be meat/poultry or meat/poultry by-products, these are clean parts of slaughtered animals, not including meat. They include organs, blood and bone, but not hair, horns, teeth or hooves

❖ Chicken meal (dehydrated chicken) has more protein than fresh chicken, which is 80% water. The same goes for beef, fish and lamb. So, if any of these meals are number one on the ingredient list, the food should contain enough protein

❖ A certain amount of flavourings can make a food more appetising for your dog. Choose a food with a specific flavouring, like *'beef flavouring'* rather than a general *'meat flavouring'*, where the origins are not so clear

❖ **Guaranteed Analysis** – This guarantees that your dog's food contains the labelled percentages of crude protein, fat, fibre and moisture. Keep in mind that wet and dry dog foods use different standards. (It does not list the digestibility of protein and fat and this can vary widely depending on their sources). While the Guaranteed Analysis is a start in understanding the food quality, be wary about relying on it too much. One pet food manufacturer made a mock product with a guaranteed analysis of 10% protein, 6.5% fat, 2.4% fibre, and 68% moisture (similar to what's on many canned pet food labels) – the ingredients were old leather boots, used motor oil, crushed coal and water!

GUARANTEED ANALYSIS

Crude protein (min.)	28.00 %
Crude fat (min.)	12.00 %
Crude fiber (max.)	4.50 %
Moisture (max.)	11.00 %
Docosahexaenoic acid (DHA) (min.)	0.05 %
Calcium (min.)	1.20 %
Phosphorus (min.)	1.00 %
Omega-6 fatty acids* (min.)	2.20 %
Omega-3 fatty acids* (min.)	0.30 %
Glucosamine* (min.)	500 mg/kg
Chondroitin sulfate* (min.)	500 mg/kg

* Not recognized as an essential nutrient by the AAFCO Dog Food Nutrient Profiles.

❖ Find a food that fits your dog's age, breed and size. Talk to your breeder, vet or visit an online Cavapoo forum and ask other owners what they are feeding their dogs

❖ If your Cavapoo has a food allergy or intolerance to wheat, check whether the food is gluten free; all wheat contains gluten

❖ Natural is best. Food labelled *'natural'* means that the ingredients have not been chemically altered, according to the FDA in the USA. However, there are no such guidelines governing foods labelled *'holistic'* – so check the ingredients and how it has been prepared

❖ In the USA, dog food that meets minimum nutrition requirements has a label that confirms this. It states: *"[food name] is formulated to meet the nutritional levels established by the AAFCO Dog Food Nutrient Profiles for [life stage(s)]"*

Even better, look for a food that meets the minimum nutritional requirements *'as fed'* to real pets in an AAFCO-defined feeding trial, then you know the food really delivers the nutrients that it is *'formulated'* to. AAFCO feeding trials on real dogs are the gold standard. Brands that do costly feeding trials (including Nestlé and Hill's) indicate so on the package.

NOTE: Look for the words *'Complete and Balanced'* on a commercial food. Dog food labelled *'supplemental'* isn't complete and balanced. Check with your vet if in doubt.

If it all still looks a bit baffling, you might find the following websites, mentioned earlier, very useful. The first is www.dogfoodadvisor.com run by Mike Sagman. He has a medical background and analyses and rates hundreds of brands of dog food based on the listed ingredients and meat content. You might be surprised at some of his findings. The second is www.allaboutdogfood.co.uk run by UK canine nutritionist David Jackson.

Food for Thought

Dogs are individuals; one Cavapoo will do really well on commercial kibble, while another is a fussy eater and a third has a reaction to a certain food. We asked a number of breeders and owners to share their experiences of feeding their Cavapoos. Laura Koch, of Petit Jean Puppies, Arkansas, US: "We feed NutriSource Small/Medium Breed Puppy and have had great results. After 12 months we transition slowly to the Adult formula.

"Cavapoos would rather play than eat, so the first few days it's important to hand-feed kibble or play in the bowl with your finger while sitting with them, so they think they are eating with a sibling. We are seeing more chicken allergies with today's dogs than in past years."

US hobby breeder Windie, of Calla Lily Cavapoo, Oklahoma, also feeds NutriSource: "We feed age-relevant Small Breed NutriSource Chicken and Rice, and Royal Canin. We have never tried raw or home-cooked, it's too tricky to be fully assured that they are getting their full nutrition, especially during their first puppy year. If people want to change to the BARF or raw diet after the puppy is one year old, they should make sure that the diet is nutritionally balanced. We encourage our families to simply be nutritionally fully informed.

"We have no experience of intolerances, but Cavapoos appreciate sweeter flavors, and if their treats are more palatable to them than their dog food, they will entirely boycott eating their dog food. They are incredibly smart, and will self-manage if they find something that they find more pleasing."

UK F1 Cavapoo Teddy, who is nearly six years old now, has shown a reaction to chicken. Owner Hilary Morphy says: "Teddy is fed on Burns Fish and Rice (dry food) twice a day. He started on Chicken and Rice, but after one or two problems, the vet referred him for tests and he was found to be intolerant of chicken. It's not classed as an allergy, but his symptoms were that he seemed to have a lot of reflux and it went once we changed his food."

UK breeder Charlotte Purkiss, Lotties Cavapoos: "I feed a high quality dry food and vary the diet by buying different flavours, plus I add fresh chicken often as I feel variety is nice. As for raw feeding, I'm against it and wouldn't personally feed mine on it, but that's just my preference as everyone is going to have their own ideas of feeding. I, personally, have not experienced Cavapoos being sensitive to foods."

June Hicks, owner of 22-month-old Archie, **pictured**: "I always feed dried food that is age appropriate, with access to water and added raw vegetables such as carrots."

Beverley Burlison, owner of two-year-old Max: "Max is fed a mixture of dried food and chicken or liver. We researched into the dried food which has a high meat content with no cereal."

Dayna Rosindale, owner of two-and-a-half-year-old Harper: "I tried a raw diet, which Harper enjoyed to start with. But then after a few months she went off it, so decided to try some other things. Now she has a Weetabix with goat's milk in the morning and her second meal is Guru food with Harrington's wet meat. This works well for Harper as she has different flavours and seems to eat every meal."

Denise Knightley, owner of Domino and therapy Cavapoo Carmen Rose: "Mine are fussy eaters. We use a frozen complete wet food called Butternut Box, which we thaw and warm in the microwave, and we also offer Royal Canin complete dry food if they have not eaten their wet food. Sometimes they will go days without eating! Sometimes they will eat roast chicken or tuna but we have the most success with the complete wet food.

"As Carmen Rose is a therapy dog, I am not allowed to feed her raw food nor unpasteurised milk in case of any cross-contamination and transferral to vulnerable children and/or the sick or elderly."

Karen Howe, from Essex, UK, owner of Rodney and Mabel: "Rodney was quite a fussy eater and so mealtimes were difficult as he would quite happily just miss a meal. I found that being strong and just taking his food up after 15 minutes meant that he realised quite quickly if he didn't eat it he would have to wait until the next meal. Mabel, however, was quite the opposite and would gobble her meals in seconds. This was brilliant for Rodney as he realised that if he didn't eat it, Mabel would and so he hasn't missed a meal since she arrived home! My tip would be start as you mean to go on and stick with it, but most of all enjoy them while they are little as they grow so quickly."

Karen recently switched her Cavapoos to a raw diet after Rodney was diagnosed with seasonal allergies. He also takes a Piriton antihistamine tablet. She says: "Although it hasn't completely cured him, the raw diet has definitely helped and made his paw licking more manageable. I feed raw completes from Naturaw, which contain no vegetables. I also ensure that his treats are all grain-free, as I do notice a flare-up in his licking if he has had treats with grain in them. I have noticed many benefits of switching them both to a raw diet; their coats are glossy and soft, their teeth are cleaner, they poo less and when they do poo, it is solid and doesn't really smell. They also absolutely love it and clear every bowl. I definitely wouldn't switch back now."

Tracey and Trevor Nott, from Devon, UK, owners of five-year-old-Ethel: "Ethel eats a mix of cooked chicken (sometimes non-oily fish) and dried dog food which has been crushed. She tends to be fussy about her diet - not sure if some of that is our fault! Cavapoos can be prone to plaque due to the jaw alignment so, like all our dogs, we encourage her to gnaw on bones, eat an occasional biscuit treat and a Dentastix at night.

"We are also currently experimenting using a pet toothbrush and paste. We have found that she has a sensitive stomach and so her stools can be very soft - so if you're not into washing a dog's bottom, be cautious about what you give your Cavapoo!" *Ethel is pictured here as a puppy.*

Raspberry-eating Cookie's owner Kit Lam added: "I originally fed Butternut Box, which is home-cooked and delivered frozen. I'm currently doing an elimination diet as she's showing signs of an allergy. I'm using one single protein and it is raw."

Claire Cornes, owner of brothers Bob and Boris: "I have recently moved to raw in the past two weeks; Bob was really poorly, and was tested for pancreatitis. The vet advised that dogs can get allergies to things from two years old. Bob and Boris have been on the same brand food since 10 weeks old, and no change in recipe. I put it down to an allergy, not that it has been tested. So far, two weeks on raw and Bob has had no further issues! I feed a raw complete food."

Lindsey McDonald and Alex Kostiw, UK owners of 18-month-old Winston: "We would not object to feeding raw, but just don't have the freezer space, and also travel quite a bit, which would prove problematic. We do, however, try to feed as close to raw as possible. We are currently feeding Eden semi-moist kibble (the only kibble he has stuck with more than three weeks) with Forthglade wet as a topper. We reduce his food as he has quite a few natural treats. He won't eat food first thing, so has a piece of dehydrated duck and a piece of dehydrated sweet potato for breakfast. We also give him a daily fishy cube to help his teeth, as well as natural dried meat products.

"Cavapoos are notoriously fussy, so when Winston was growing up, he was fed wet meat only. We started on Lily's Kitchen and moved to Nature's Menu when he was nearing one year old. Both have a range of flavours (Winston prefers dark meat) and you can feed the Adult flavours from four months old. This meant we could change the flavour every day for variety and keep him interested."

US owner, Val Boshart, owner of nine-month-old Millie, added: "We had Millie on NutriSource, but have always had issues with her interest in food. She loves treats and things like carrots, frozen pumpkin, watermelon and more - but it's been a tough task to get her to eat her dry food regularly. We finally got in a good routine by leaving it in her crate overnight. She didn't have distractions and had access when she decided she was hungry. We would also add water and some Fortlfora, Probiotic supplement for the dietary management of puppies and adult dogs with diarrhea, to her food to give it a mushier consistency, which she loves.

"We have had some issues with loose stool, so in those cases, we give her rice and canned chicken, which is her absolute favorite. In the past it seems to have been Giardia-related, but this latest bout isn't caused by that so we had to switch her to some canned food, plus put her on medication. We're in the thick of it, so we don't have any solves yet!"

Gina Desmond, from New York City is the owner of three-year-old Duncan, her first dog, **(pictured),** and says: "Feeding is something that I am constantly researching to make sure I am providing Duncan with the best diet. We feed him a mix of the dry food brands Ziwi and Nutrish. Ziwi is a New Zealand-based company that focuses on a high protein diet. Nutrish offers a variety of natural ingredients all US-based (nothing from China).

"Neither brand has ever had any recalls and, through my research, I feel they give Duncan the most variety of nutrients into his diet. Specifically, we like the Lamb and Mackerel Ziwi dry food (or beef), and the chicken, veggie and brown rice Nutrish flavor."

....

As you have just read, no single food is right for every Cavapoo; you must decide on the best for yours. If you have a puppy, initially stick to the same food as the breeder. The best test of a food is how well your dog is doing on it.

If your Cavapoo is happy and healthy, interested in life, has enough energy, is not too fat and not too thin, doesn't scratch a lot and has healthy-looking stools, then...

Congratulations, you've got it right!

8. Cavapoo Behaviour

Just as with humans, a dog's personality is made up of a combination of temperament and character. While every Cavapoo is an individual, there are also certain shared character traits. Understanding your dog, what makes him tick and why he behaves like that will give you a greater understanding of - and ultimately a deeper bond with - your dog.

....

Temperament is the nature – or inherited characteristics - a dog is born with; a predisposition to act or react in a certain way. Getting your puppy from a good breeder is so important, as they not only produce puppies from physically healthy dams and sires (mothers and fathers), but also look at the temperament of the dogs and only breed from those with good traits.

Character varies from one dog to the next. It develops through the dog's life and is formed by a combination of temperament and environment, or **nurture and nature.** How you treat your dog will have a huge effect on his or her personality and behaviour. Starting off on the right foot with good routines is very important; so treat your dog well, spend lots of time with him or her, while also leaving your puppy alone for short periods, and make time for plenty of socialisation and exercise. All dogs need different environments, scents and experiences to keep them stimulated and well-balanced.

Despite being bred as companion dogs, Cavapoos have ancestry from working dogs on both sides - the Cavalier King Charles Spaniel and the Poodle, and this is often exhibited in their behaviour. Some have a fairly strong prey drive (instinct to chase small birds and mammals), many love swimming and all enjoy running free off the lead (leash).

When training your Cavapoo, set your dog set up for success; praise good behaviour, use positive methods and keep sessions short and fun. At the same time, all dogs should understand the "No" (or similar) command. Just as with children, a canine has to learn boundaries to adapt successfully and to be content with his or her environment. Be consistent so your dog learns the guidelines quickly. All of these measures will help your dog grow into a happy, well-adjusted and well-behaved adult that is a delight to be with.

If you adopt a Cavapoo from a rescue centre, you may need a little extra patience. These eager-to-please people-loving dogs may arrive with some baggage. They have been abandoned by their previous owners for a variety of reasons and may very well still carry the scars of that trauma. They may feel nervous and insecure, needy or aloof, and may not know how to behave in a house or interact with a loving owner. Your time and patience is needed to teach these poor animals to trust again and to become happy in their new forever homes.

....

Understanding Canine Emotions

As pet lovers, we are all too keen to ascribe human characteristics to our dogs; this is called *anthropomorphism* – "the attribution of human characteristics to anything other than a human being." Most of us dog lovers are guilty of that, as we come to regard our pets as members of the family - and Cavapoos certainly regard themselves as members of the family! An example of anthropomorphism might be that the owner of a male dog might not want to have him neutered because he will "miss sex", as a human might if he or she were no longer able to have sex.

This is simply not true. A male dog's impulse to mate is entirely governed by his hormones, not emotions. If he gets the scent of a female on heat, his hormones (which are just body chemicals) tell him he has to mate with her. He does not stop to consider how attractive she is or whether she is **'the one'** to produce his puppies. No, his reaction is entirely physical, he just wants to dive in there and get on with it!

It's the same with females. When they are on heat, a chemical impulse is triggered in their brain making them want to mate – with any male, they aren't at all fussy. So don't expect your little princess to be all coy when she is on heat, she is not waiting for Prince Charming to come along - the tramp down the road or any other scruffy pooch will do! It is entirely physical, not emotional.

Food is another example. A dog will not stop to count the calories of that lovely treat (you have to do that). No, he or she is driven by food and just thinks about getting the food or the treat. Most non-fussy eaters will eat far too much, given the opportunity.

Cavapoos are not only very attractive dogs, they are also extremely loving and eager to please you, not to mention quirky. If yours doesn't make you laugh from time to time, you must have had a humour by-pass. All of this adds up to one thing: a hugely engaging and affectionate family member that it's all too easy to reward - or spoil.

It's fine to treat your dog like a member of the family - as long as you keep in mind that she is a dog and not a human. Understand her mind, patiently train her to learn her place in the household and that there are household rules she needs to learn – like not jumping on the couch when soaking wet or covered in mud - and you will be rewarded with a companion who is second to none and fits in beautifully with your family and lifestyle.

Dr Stanley Coren is a psychologist well known for his work on canine psychology and behaviour. He and other researchers believe that in many ways a dog's emotional development is equivalent to that of a young child. Dr Coren says: "Researchers have now come to believe that the mind of a dog is roughly equivalent to that of a human who is two to two-and-a-half years old. This conclusion holds for most mental abilities as well as emotions.

"Thus, we can look to human research to see what we might expect of our dogs. Just like a two-year-old child, our dogs clearly have emotions, but many fewer kinds of emotions than found in adult humans. At birth, a human infant only has an emotion that we might call excitement. This indicates how excited he is, ranging from very calm up to a state of frenzy. Within the first weeks of life the excitement state comes to take on a varying positive or a negative flavour, so we can now detect the general emotions of contentment and distress.

"In the next couple of months, disgust, fear, and anger become detectable in the infant. Joy often does not appear until the infant is nearly six months of age and it is followed by the emergence of shyness or suspicion. True affection, the sort that it makes sense to use the label "love" for, does not fully emerge until nine or ten months of age."

So, our Cavapoos truly love us – but we knew that already!

A Study of Canine Emotion

According to Dr Coren, dogs can't feel shame, so if you are housetraining your puppy, don't expect him to be ashamed if he makes a mess in the house, he can't; he simply isn't capable of feeling shame. But he will not like it when you ignore him when he's behaving badly, and he will love it when you praise him for eliminating outdoors. He is simply responding to your reaction with his simplified range of emotions.

Dr Coren also believes that dogs cannot experience guilt, contempt or pride. I'm not a psychology expert, but I'm not sure I agree. Take a Cavapoo to a local dog show, obedience class or agility competition, watch him perform and maybe win a rosette and applause - is the dog's delight something akin to pride? Cavapoos can certainly experience joy. They love your attention and praise; is there a more joyful sight for you both than when your Cavapoo runs towards you, tail wagging like crazy, with those big, loving eyes that say you're the best person in the world?

If you want to see a happy dog, just watch Cavapoos running free, swimming or snuggling up on the sofa with you. And when they dash off and return with the ball, isn't there a hint of pride there? The Cavapoo is one of the most gentle and friendly of dogs and they can certainly show empathy - "the ability to understand and share the feelings of another." They can pick up people's moods and emotions, which is one reason why they make excellent therapy dogs.

One emotion that all dogs can experience is jealousy. It may display itself by possessive or aggressive behaviour over food, a toy or a person, for example. An interesting article was published in the PLOS (Public Library of Science) Journal in 2014 following an experiment into whether dogs get jealous. Building on research that shows that six-month old infants display jealousy, the scientists studied 36 dogs in their homes and video recorded their actions when their owners displayed affection to a realistic-looking stuffed canine *(pictured).*

Over three-quarters of the dogs were likely to push or touch the owner when they interacted with the decoy! The envious mutts were more than three times as likely to do this for interactions with the stuffed dog compared to when their owners gave their attention to other objects, including a book. Around a third tried to get between the owner and the plush toy, while a quarter of the put-upon pooches snapped at the dummy dog! The researchers think that the dogs believed that the stuffed dog was real. They cite the fact that 86% of the dogs sniffed the toy's rear end during and after the experiment!

"Our study suggests not only that dogs do engage in what appear to be jealous behaviours, but also that they were seeking to break up the connection between the owner and a seeming rival," said Professor Christine Harris from University of California in San Diego. "We can't really speak of the dogs' subjective experiences, of course, but it looks as though they were motivated to protect an important social relationship. Many people have assumed that jealousy is a social construction of human beings - or that it's an emotion specifically tied to sexual and romantic relationships," said Professor Harris. "Our results challenge these ideas, showing that animals besides ourselves display strong distress whenever a rival usurps a loved one's affection."

Typical Cavapoo Traits

Every dog is different, of course, but there are also shared traits. Here are some typical characteristics - some of them also apply to other breeds, but put them all together and you have a blueprint for the Cavapoo.

1. Cavapoos are one of the most gentle of all breeds.

2. They are intelligent.

3. They are friendly with everyone and love to be petted or made a fuss of.

4. Because they are friendly with everyone, they do not make good guard dogs.

5. Cavapoos are extremely playful and love toys and games. Some can become almost obsessive about their toys.

6. They were bred for companionship and are "Velcro" dogs; they like to stick close to you.

7. It is not uncommon for Cavapoos to suffer from separation anxiety if they have not got used to being on their own from puppyhood or if left alone too often.

8. Cavapoos are extremely keen to please and "biddable", meaning they can be easily trained - provided the owner puts in the time.

9. Praise, praise and praise is the way to train a Cavapoo; they do not respond well to rough treatment or loud, harsh voices, which can lead to timidity.

10. Cavapoos are extremely patient and gentle with children – it may be the dog that needs protecting from the kids!

11. Provided they are fully socialised, Cavapoos are non-aggressive with other dogs.

12. Because they are gentle, relatively easy to train and get along well with people of all ages and other animals, they are considered good first-time dogs.

13. They are sensitive dogs and can pick up on emotions.

14. Some can be a bit "wimpy", so socialisation is important to give the dog confidence.

15. The Cavapoo's forebears are Spaniels and Poodles - both of which were originally bred as working dogs. Some still retain sporting instincts and enjoy chasing small mammals and birds when outdoors. However, most would not harm a rabbit, bird or other small creature if they caught one.

16. Even if they chase things outdoors, most Cavapoos live happily with cats and other animals inside the house when introduced at a young age.

17. Again, due to their sporting heritage and the intelligence of the Poodle, Cavapoos are happiest with mental as well as physical challenges.

Photo of F1 Bertie Lee courtesy of Janice Shapiro.

18. Many, although not all, Cavapoos have an instinctive love of water, which comes from the Poodle side.

19. Cavapoos often love playing in the snow – although their feet may need gently "de-icing" afterwards.

20. All Cavapoos love running off the lead (leash) with their noses to the ground. Most are adaptable when it comes to exercise. They can go hiking for hours or snuggle up on the sofa all day.

21. They enjoy being the centre of attention.

22. A few Cavapoos can be a little nervous around new people, dogs and situations. (Poodles can also be wary of strangers until they get to know them). Socialisation from an early age is the key. The more varied **positive** experiences a dog has when young, the more comfortable and relaxed he or she will be as an adult. Don't constantly pick your Cavapoo up unless there is a danger of injury; panicky owners trigger a fear response in their dogs.

23. They are highly affectionate, forming deep bonds. Unlike some breeds, they often bond with the entire family, rather than just one person.

24. A Cavapoo will 100% steal your heart - OK, that's not very scientific, but ask anyone who owns one!

....

Cause and Effect

As you've read, properly socialised and trained, well-bred Cavapoos make superb canine companions. Once you've had one, no other dog seems quite the same, which is why owners often choose another Cavapoo as their second dog.

But any dog can develop behaviour problems given a certain set of circumstances. There are numerous reasons for this; every dog is an individual with his or her own temperament and environment, both of which influence the way the dog interacts with the world. Poor behaviour can **result** from a number of factors, including:

❧ Poor breeding
❧ Lack of socialisation
❧ Lack of training
❧ Lack of exercise or mental challenges
❧ Being left alone too long
❧ Not being left alone at all
❧ Being badly treated
❧ A change in living conditions
❧ Anxiety or fear
❧ Being spoiled

Unwanted behaviour may **show** itself in a number of different ways, including:

❧ Nervousness/neurotic behaviour
❧ Chewing or destructive behaviour
❧ Jumping up

- Constantly demanding attention
- Being over-protective or jealous
- Incessant barking
- Biting or nipping
- Growling
- Soiling or urinating inside the house
- Aggression towards humans or other dogs
- Mounting humans or other dogs
- Separation anxiety

NOTE: Further information on dealing with chewing and puppy biting can be found in **Chapter 10. Training.**

10 Ways to Avoid Bad Behaviour

Different dogs have different reasons for exhibiting bad behaviour; there is no single cure for everything. Your best chance of ensuring your dog does not become badly behaved is to start out on the right foot and follow these simple guidelines:

1. **Buy from a good breeder**. They use their expertise to match suitable breeding pairs, taking into account factors such as good temperament, health, appearance and being "fit for function."

2. **Start socialisation right away**. We now realise the vital role that early socialisation plays in developing a well-rounded adult dog. Lack of socialisation is one of the major causes of unwanted behaviour, timidity or aggression. It is essential to expose your puppy to other people, places, animals and experiences as soon as possible; it will go a long way towards helping her become a stable, happy and trustworthy companion.

Photo of Buddy and Holly courtesy of Sarah King

IMPORTANT: Socialisation does not end at puppyhood. Dogs are social creatures that thrive on sniffing, seeing, hearing and even licking. While the foundation for good behaviour is laid down during the first few months, good owners reinforce social skills and training throughout a dog's life.

Cavapoos like to be involved and be the centre of attention and it is important they learn when young that they are not also the centre of the universe! Socialisation helps them to learn their place in that universe and to become comfortable with it.

3. **Start training early** - you can't start too soon. Like babies, puppies have incredibly enquiring minds that absorb a lot of new information quickly. Start teaching your puppy to learn her own name as well as some simple commands a couple of days after bringing her home.

4. **Basic training should cover several areas:** housetraining, chew prevention, puppy biting, simple commands like 'sit', 'come' or 'here', 'stay' and familiarising her with a collar or harness and lead. Adopt a gentle approach and keep training sessions short. Cavapoos are sensitive to you and your mood and do not respond well to harsh words or treatment. Start with five or 10 minutes a day and build up. Puppy classes or adult dog obedience classes are a great way to start, but make sure you do your homework afterwards. Spend a few minutes each day reinforcing what you have both learned in class - owners need training as well as dogs!

5. **Reward your dog for good behaviour.** All behaviour training should be based on positive reinforcement; so praise and reward your dog when she does something good. Cavapoos love to please their owners; this trait and their intelligence speeds up the training process. The main aim of training is to build a good understanding between you and your dog.

6. **Ignore bad behaviour**, no matter how hard this may be. If, for example, your dog is chewing his way through your shoes, the couch or toilet rolls or eating things she shouldn't, remove her from the situation and then ignore her. For some dogs even negative attention is some attention. Remove yourself from the room so he learns that you give attention when you want to give it, **not** when he demands it. The more time you spend praising and rewarding good behaviour, while ignoring bad behaviour, the more likely she is to respond. If your pup is a chewer – and nearly all are - make sure there are durable toys and chews to occupy her.

7. **Take the time to learn what sort of temperament your dog has.** Is (s)he by nature a nervous or confident boy/girl? What was she like as a puppy, did she rush forward or hang back? Does she fight to get upright when on her back or is she happy to lie there? Is she a couch potato or a ball of fire? Your puppy's temperament will affect her behaviour and how she responds to the world. A timid Cavapoo will certainly not respond well to a loud approach on your part, whereas an energetic, strong-willed one will require more patience, exercise and mental stimulation.

8. **Exercise and stimulation.** A lack of either is another major reason for dogs behaving badly. Regular daily exercise as well as indoor or outdoor games and toys are all ways of stopping your dog from becoming bored or frustrated.

9. **Learn to leave your dog.** Just as leaving your dog alone for too long can lead to problems, so can being with her 100% of the time. Cavapoos are very reliant on humans for their happiness, but they also need to learn that being alone for short periods is fine too, and not a cause for anxiety. When a dog becomes over-reliant on you, she gets stressed when you leave; this is called *separation anxiety*. Start a few days after she arrives home by leaving her alone for a few minutes and gradually extend the time so that you can eventually leave her for up to four hours.

10. **Love your Cavapoo – but don't spoil her,** however difficult that might be. Resist the urge to pick her up all the time or to give too much attention or treats. Don't constantly respond to her demands for attention or allow her to behave as she wants inside the house.

Separation Anxiety

It's not just dogs that experience separation anxiety - people do too. About 7% of adults and 4% of children suffer from this disorder. Typical symptoms for humans are:

- ❧ Distress at being separated from a loved one
- ❧ Fear of being alone

Our canine companions aren't much different to us. When a dog leaves the litter, her owners become her new family or pack. It's estimated that as many as 10% to 15% of dogs suffer from separation anxiety. It is an exaggerated fear response caused by being parted from their owner. Cavapoos bred from Toy Poodles can be more clingy than those bred from Miniature Poodles. **Separation anxiety is on the increase and recognised by behaviourists as the most common form of stress for dogs. Millions of dogs suffer from it.**

Tell-Tale Signs

Does your Cavapoo do any of the following?

- ❧ Get anxious or stressed when you're getting ready to leave the house?
- ❧ Howl, whine or bark when you leave?
- ❧ Tear up paper or chew furniture or other objects?
- ❧ Dig, chew, or scratch at the carpet, doors or windows trying to join you?
- ❧ Soil or urinate inside the house, even though she is housetrained? (This **only** occurs when left alone)
- ❧ Exhibit restlessness - such as licking her coat excessively, pacing or circling?
- ❧ Greet you ecstatically every time you come home – even if you've only been out to the garage?

- ❧ Wait by the window or door until you return?
- ❧ Dislike spending time alone in the garden or yard?
- ❧ Refuses to eat or drink if you leave her?
- ❧ Howl or whine when one family member leaves - even though others are still in the room or car?

If so, she or he may suffer from separation anxiety. Fortunately, in many cases this can be cured.

Photo of Cookie courtesy of Kit Lam, who says: "Cookie gets a little anxious when I leave her, but she does settle down quite quickly."

NOTE: Cavapoos are known as "shadow" or "Velcro" dogs, they like to stick close and often follow their owners around the house. This is not necessarily a sign of separation anxiety in the Cavapoo - unless they get visibly distressed when you leave the house. However, if they even want to follow you into the toilet, this can be a sign that separation anxiety is developing.

Causes

Dogs are pack animals and being alone is not a natural state for them. A puppy will emotionally latch on to her new owner, who has taken the place of mother and siblings. Puppies should be patiently taught in a structured way to get used to short periods of isolation if they are to be comfortable with it. It is also important for them to have a den where they feel safe - this may be a crate or dog bed where they can sleep in peace and quiet.

One thing that surprises some owners, particularly first-time owners, is just how much love they feel for their Cavapoo, and this is reciprocated by the dog. Dogs are truly life enhancing. In the beginning you are setting patterns for the future and it is all too easy to give a lovable Cavapoo pup a huge amount of attention and cuddles, pick them up a lot, and not leave them alone for any length of time.

As the dog reaches adolescence, this can lead to behaviour issues, as the dog thinks he or she has the upper hand or becomes anxious about you not being there – or both. It may lead to attention-seeking behaviour, excessive barking, fussiness with food or separation anxiety.

There are several causes of separation anxiety, including:

- ❖ Being left for too long by owners who are out of the house for most of the day
- ❖ Not being left alone for short periods when young
- ❖ Poor socialisation with other dogs and people, resulting in too much focus and dependence on the owner

- ❖ Boredom - Cavapoos are intelligent and most need mental as well as physical exercise
- ❖ Leaving a dog too long in a crate or confined space
- ❖ Being over-indulgent with your dog; giving her too much attention
- ❖ Making too much of a fuss when you leave and return to the house
- ❖ Mistreatment in the past; a dog from a rescue centre may have insecurities and feel anxious when left alone
- ❖ Wilful behaviour due to a lack of training

Symptoms do not usually develop in middle-aged dogs, although dogs that develop symptoms when young may be at risk later on. Separation anxiety is common in elderly dogs. Pets age and, like humans, their hearing, sense of smell and sight often deteriorates. When they do, a dog can become more dependent on its owners and anxious when separated from them - or even out of view.

Tip It may be very flattering and cute that your dog wants to be with you all the time, but insecurity and separation anxiety are forms of panic, which is distressing for the dog. If your dog starts showing the first signs, help her become more self-reliant and confident; she will be happier and more relaxed.

Every dog is different, but here are some techniques that have proved effective in helping some dogs with separation anxiety:

Tips to Combat Separation Anxiety

1. After the first few days, leave your new puppy or adult dog for short periods, starting with literally a minute or two and gradually lengthening the time you are out of sight.

2. Tire your dog out before leaving her. Take her for a walk or play a game and, if you can, leave her with a view of the outside world, e.g. in a room with a patio door or low window.

3. Keep arrivals and departures low key and don't make a big fuss. Don't say hello or goodbye – either in words or body language, and don't sneak in and out of the house either.

4. Leave your dog a 'security blanket,' such as an old piece of clothing you have recently worn that still has your scent on it, or leave a radio on - not too loud - in the room with the dog. Avoid a heavy rock station! If it will be dark when you return, leave a lamp on a timer. One breeder leaves a TV on low, on the same channel, so her dogs become familiar with the same programmes. This also cuts out any background noise such as traffic, people and barking dogs.

5. Associate your departure with something good. As you leave, give a rubber toy, like a Kong filled with a tasty treat, or a frozen treat, or spread her favourite treat over a Lickimat (available on Amazon). This may take her mind off your departure - some dogs may refuse to touch the treat until you return home! Give her the treat when you are at home as well, so she doesn't just associate it with being left.

6. If your dog is used to a crate, try crating her when you go out. Many dogs feel safe there, and being in a crate can also help to reduce destructiveness. Always take the collar off first. Pretend to leave the house, but listen for a few minutes. NEVER leave a dog in a crate with the door closed all day; two or three hours are long enough during the day.

Warning: if your dog starts to show major signs of distress, remove her from the crate immediately as she may injure herself.

7. Structure and routine can help to reduce anxiety in your dog. Carry out regular activities, such as feeding and exercising, at the same time every day.

   Dogs read body language very well; many Cavapoos are intuitive. They may start to fret when they think you are going to leave them. One technique is to mimic your departure routine when you have no intention of leaving. So put your coat on, grab your car keys, go out of the door and return a few seconds later. Do this randomly and regularly and it may help to reduce your dog's stress levels when you do it for real.

Photo of Dolly relaxing at home courtesy of Laura Lambert.

8. Some dogs show anxiety in new places; get her better socialised and used to different environments, dogs and people.

9. However lovable your Cavapoo is, if she is showing early signs of anxiety when separating from you, do not shower her with attention all the time when you are there. She will become overly dependent on you.

10. If you have to leave the house for a few hours at a time, ask a neighbour or friend to call in - or drop the dog off with them.

11. Getting another dog to keep the first one company can help, but first ask yourself whether you have the time and money for two or more dogs. Can you afford double the vet and food bills?

Sit-Stay-Down

Another technique for helping to reduce separation anxiety is to practise the common "sit-stay" or "down-stay" exercises using positive reinforcement. The goal is to be able to move briefly out of your dog's sight while she is in the "stay" position.

Through this your dog learns that she can remain calmly and happily in one place while you go about your normal daily life. You have to progress slowly with this. Get your dog to sit and stay and then walk away from her for five seconds, then 10, 20, a minute and so on. Reward your dog with a treat or toy every time she stays calm.

Then move out of sight or out of the room for a few seconds, return and give her the treat if she is calm, gradually lengthen the time you are out of sight. If you're watching TV with your Cavapoo snuggled up at your side and you get up for a snack, say "stay" and leave the room. When you come back, give her a treat or praise her quietly. It is a good idea to practise these techniques after exercise or when your dog is a little sleepy (but not exhausted), as she is likely to be more relaxed.

Canine separation anxiety is NOT the result of disobedience or lack of training. It's a psychological condition; your dog feels anxious and insecure.

NEVER punish your dog for showing signs of separation anxiety – even if she has chewed your best shoes. This will only make her worse.

NEVER leave your dog unattended in a crate for long periods or if she is frantic to get out, it can cause physical or mental harm. If you're thinking of leaving an animal all day in a crate while you are out of the house, get a rabbit or a hamster - not a dog.

....

Excessive Barking

Dogs, especially youngsters and adolescents, sometimes behave in ways you might not want them to, until they learn that this type of unwanted behaviour doesn't earn any rewards. Cavapoos are not known for barking a lot, but like any dog, they can get into the habit of barking too much if you don't put a stop to it. Dogs from the Toy Group, such as the Toy Poodle, can become yappy if it isn't nipped in the bud.

Some puppies start off by being noisy from the outset, while others hardly bark at all until they reach adolescence or adulthood. Some may be triggered by other, noisier dogs in the household. On our website we hear from owners worried that their young dogs are not barking enough. However, we get far more posts from owners whose dogs are barking too much.

We had one dog that hardly barked at all until he was two years old. We needn't have worried, by the time he got to five or six years old, he loved the sound of his own voice! We have been in contact with several Cavapoo owners in a similar position; their dog hardly barked when young and now barks too much. If that's the case, then try **the Speak and Shush** technique outlined later in this chapter.

Some Cavapoos will bark if someone comes to the door – and then welcome them like best friends - while others remain quiet.

There can be a number of reasons a dog barks too much. She may be lonely, bored or demanding your attention. She may be possessive and over-protective and so barks (or howls) her head off when you leave or others are near you. She may have picked up the habit from other dogs.

Excessive, habitual barking is a problem best corrected early on before it gets out of hand and drives you and your neighbours nuts. The problem often develops during adolescence or early adulthood (before the age of two or three) as your dog becomes more confident.

If your barking dog is an adolescent, she is probably still teething, so get a good selection of hardy chews, and healthy chew treats to keep her occupied and gnawing. But give her these when she is quiet, not when she is barking.

Your behaviour can also encourage excessive barking. If your dog barks non-stop for several seconds or minutes and then you give her a treat to quieten her, she associates barking with getting a nice treat.

A better way to deal with it is to say in a firm voice: **"Quiet"** after she has made a few barks. When she stops, praise her and she will get the idea that what you want her to do is stop. The trick is to stop the bad behaviour straight away before it becomes ingrained.

If she's barking to get your attention, ignore her. If that doesn't work, leave the room and don't allow her to follow you, so you deprive her of your attention. Do this as well if her barking and attention-seeking turns to nipping. Tell her to **"Stop"** in a firm voice - not shouting - remove your hand or leg and, if necessary, leave the room.

As humans, we can use our voice in many different ways: to express happiness or anger, to scold, to shout a warning, and so on. Dogs are the same; different barks and noises give out different messages. **Listen** to your dog and try and get an understanding of Cavapoo language. Learn to recognise the difference between an alert bark, an excited bark, a demanding bark, a high pitched bark, an aggressive bark or a plain "I'm barking 'coz I can bark" bark!

If your dog is barking at other dogs, arm yourselves with lots of treats and spend time calming your dog down. With Cavapoos, this is rarely pure aggression, it is more often a fear response – especially if they are on a lead (leash), as they know they cannot escape so are trying to make themselves look and sound fierce to the other dog or dogs.

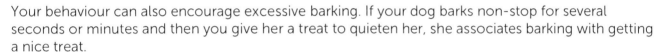

Listen to the tone of the bark, a high-pitched bark is usually a sign of fear or nervousness. Ears flattened back on the head are another sign of nerves or fear.

When she starts to bark wildly at another dog while on the lead, distract her by letting her sniff a treat in your hand. Make your dog sit and give a treat. Talk in a gentle manner and keep showing and giving her a treat for remaining calm and not barking. Get her to focus her attention and gaze on you and the treat, not the other dog. There are several videos on YouTube that show how to deal with this problem in the manner described here.

Speak and Shush!

Cavapoos are not good guard dogs, most of them couldn't care less if somebody breaks in and walks off with the family silver – they are more likely to greet with the burglar with a wagging tail and approach for a treat or a pat as the villains make off with your prize possessions!

But if you do have a problem with excessive barking when visitors arrive, the Speak and Shush technique is one way of getting a dog to quieten down. If your Cavapoo doesn't bark and you want her to, a slight variation of this method can also be used to get her to bark as a way of alerting you that someone is at the door. We have used this method very successfully.

When your dog barks at an arrival at your house, gently praise her after the first few barks. If she persists, gently tell her that that is enough. Like humans, some dogs can get carried away with the sound of their own voice, so try and discourage too much barking from the outset. The Speak and Shush technique teaches your dog or puppy to bark and be quiet on command.

"Yes, I live on the third floor ... but I have never heard any howling sounds."

Get a friend to stand outside your front door and say "Speak" - or "Woof" or "Alert". This is the cue for your accomplice to knock or ring the bell – don't worry if you both feel like idiots, it will be worth the embarrassment!

When your dog barks, praise her profusely. You can even bark yourself in encouragement! After a few good barks, say "Shush" and then dangle a tasty treat in front of her nose. She will stop barking as soon as she sniffs the treat, because it is physically impossible for a dog to sniff and woof at the same time.

Praise your dog again as she sniffs quietly and then give her the treat. Repeat this routine a few times a day and your Cavapoo will quickly learn to bark whenever the doorbell rings and you ask her to speak.

Eventually your dog will bark AFTER your request but BEFORE the doorbell rings, meaning she has learned to bark on command. Even better, she will learn to anticipate the likelihood of getting a treat following your "Shush" request and will also be quiet on command.

With Speak and Shush training, progressively increase the length of required shush time before offering a treat - at first just a couple of seconds, then three, five, 10, 20, and so on. By alternating instructions to speak and shush, the dog is praised and rewarded for barking on request and also for stopping barking on request.

If you want your dog to be more vocal, you need to have some treats at the ready, waiting for that rare bark. Wait until she barks - for whatever reason - then say "Speak" or whatever word you want to use, praise her and give her a treat. At this stage, she won't know why she is receiving the treat. Keep praising her every time she barks and give her a treat. After you've done this for several days, hold a treat in your hand in front of her face and say "Speak".

Your dog will probably still not know what to do, but will eventually get so frustrated at not getting the treat that she will bark. At which point, praise her and give her the treat. We trained a Labrador to do this in a week or so and he barked his head off when anybody came to the door or whenever we give him the command: "Speak".

 Always use your 'encouraging teacher voice' when training; speak softly when instructing your dog to Shush, and reinforce the Shush with whisper-praise. The softer you speak, the more your dog will be likely to pay attention. Cavapoos respond very well to training when it is fun, short and reward-based.

Dealing with Aggression

Some breeds are more prone to aggression than others; fortunately, this issue is not often seen in Cavapoos, so feel free to skip this section. However, given certain situations, any dog can growl, bark or even bite. Sometimes a dog learns unwanted behaviour from another dog or dogs, but often it is because the dog feels insecure or has become too territorial or protective of her owner, toys or food.

NOTE: Puppy biting is not aggression; all puppies bite; they explore the world with their noses and mouths. It is, however, important to train your cute little pup not to bite, as he may cause injury to someone if he or she continues to bite when fully grown.

Any dog can bite when under stress and, however unlikely it may seem, so can Cavapoos. Here are some different types of aggressive behaviour:

- Growling at you or other people
- Snarling or lunging at other dogs
- Growling or biting if you or another animal goes near her food
- Being possessive with toys
- Growling if you pet or show attention to another animal
- Marking territory by urinating inside the house
- Growling and chasing other small animals
- Growling and chasing cars, joggers or strangers
- Standing in your way, blocking your path
- Pulling and growling on the lead

As well as snarling, lunging, barking or biting, look out for other physical signs, such as raised hackles, top lip curled back to bare the teeth, ears up and tail raised.

One reason for aggression can be that the dog has not been fully socialised, and so feels threatened or challenged. Rather than being comfortable with new situations, other dogs or intrusions, she responds using "the best form of defence is attack" philosophy and displays aggressive behaviour to anything or anyone she is unsure of.

If the aggression is rooted in fear, it may stem from a bad experience the dog has suffered. I know a number of naturally non-aggressive dogs that have started to growl and snarl at other dogs in later life, after they have been the victim of an attack by another dog or dogs.

An owner's treatment of a dog can be a further reason. An owner that shouts, uses physical violence or reprimands the dog too often, can result in snapping or other unwanted behaviour from the dog. Aggression breeds aggression. Dogs can also become aggressive or depressed if they are consistently left alone, cooped up, under-fed or under-exercised.

Many dogs are more combative on the lead (leash). This is because they cannot run away; fight or flight. They know they can't escape, and so make themselves as frightening as possible and bark or growl to warn off the other dog or person. Train your dog from an early age to be comfortable walking on the lead. And socialisation is, of course, vital — the first four to five months of a puppy's life is the critical time.

If your dog **suddenly** shows a change of behaviour and becomes aggressive, have her checked out by a vet to rule out any underlying medical reason for the crankiness, such as earache or toothache. Raging hormones can be another reason for aggression or a change in behaviour.

A further reason is they have been spoiled by their owners and have come to believe that the world revolves around them. Not spoiling your Cavapoo and teaching her what is acceptable behaviour in the first place is the best preventative measure. Early training, especially during puppyhood and adolescence - before he or she develops unwanted habits - can save a lot of trouble in the future.

Professional dog trainers employ a variety of techniques with a dog that has become aggressive. Firstly, they will look at the causes and good trainers use reward-based methods to try and cure aggressive or fearful dogs. *Counter conditioning* is a positive training technique used by many professionals to help change a dog's aggressive behaviour towards other dogs.

A typical example would be a dog that snarls, barks and lunges at other dogs while on the lead. It is the presence of other dogs that is triggering the dog to act in a fearful or anxious manner. Every time the dog sees another dog, he or she is given a tasty treat to counter the aggression. With enough steady repetition, the dog starts to associate the presence of other dogs with a tasty treat.

Properly and patiently done, the final result is a dog that calmly looks to the owner for the treat whenever he or she sees another dog while on the lead. Whenever you encounter a potentially aggressive situation, divert your Cavapoo's attention by turning her head away from the other dog and towards you, so that she cannot make eye contact with the other dog.

Aggression Towards People

Desensitisation is the most common method of treating aggression. It starts by breaking down the triggers for the behaviour one small step at a time. The aim is to get the dog to associate pleasant things with the trigger, i.e. people or a specific person whom she previously feared or regarded as a threat.

This is done through using positive reinforcement, such as praise or treats. Successful

desensitisation takes time, patience and knowledge. If your dog is starting to growl at people, there are a couple of techniques you can try to break her of this bad habit before it develops into full-blown biting.

One method is to arrange for some friends to come round, one at a time. When they arrive at your house, get them to scatter kibble on the floor in front of them so that your dog associates the arrival of people with tasty treats. As they move into the house, and your dog eats the kibble, praise your dog for being a good boy or girl. Manage your dog's environment. Don't over-face him.

Most Cavapoos love children, but if yours is at all anxious around them, separate them or carefully supervise their time together in the beginning. Children typically react enthusiastically to dogs and some dogs may regard this as frightening or an invasion of their space. One contributor said: "Our Cavapoo bit our son on his face when he was cuddling her. She can be asleep and he wraps his arms around her. It's an instinctive reaction because he doesn't respect her space. (He doesn't walk or feed her)."

Some dogs, particularly spoiled ones, may show aggression towards people other than the owner. Several people have written to our website on this topic and it usually involves a partner or husband. Often the dog is jealous of the attention the owner is giving to the other person, or it could be that the dog feels threatened by him; this is more common with Toy breeds.

If it happens with your Cavapoo, the key is for the partner to gradually gain the trust of the dog. He or she should show that they are not a threat by speaking gently to the dog and giving treats for good behaviour. Avoid eye contact, as the dog may see this as a challenge. If the subject of the aggression lives in the house, then let this person give the dog his daily feeds.

A crate is also a useful tool for removing an aggressive dog from the situation for short periods of time, allowing him out gradually and praising good behaviour. As with any form of aggression, the trick is to take steps to deal with it **immediately.**

In extreme cases, when a dog exhibits persistent bad behaviour that the owner is unable to correct, a canine professional may be the answer. However, this is not an inexpensive option. Far better to spend time training and socialising your dog as soon as you get him or her.

....

Coprophagia (Eating Faeces)

It is hard for us to understand why a dog would want to eat his or any other animal's faeces (stools, poop or poo, call it what you will), but it does happen. There is plenty of anecdotal evidence that some dogs love the stuff.

Nobody fully understands why dogs do this, it may simply be an unpleasant behaviour trait or there could be an underlying reason. It is also thought that the inhumane and useless potty training technique of "sticking the dog's nose in it" when he has eliminated inside the house can also encourage coprophagia.

If your dog eats poop from the cat litter tray - a problem several owners have contacted us about - the first thing to do is to place the litter tray somewhere where your dog can't get to it – but the cat can. Perhaps on a shelf or put a guard around it, small enough for the cat to get through, but not your dog.

Our dog sometimes eats cow or horse manure when out in the countryside. He usually stops when we tell him to and he hasn't suffered any after effects – so far. But again, this is a very unpleasant habit as the offending material sticks to the fur around his mouth and has to be cleaned off. Sometimes he rolls in the stuff and then has to be washed down.

Think of it as a product recall!

You may find that your Cavapoo will roll in fox poo to cover the fox's scent. Try and avoid areas you know are frequented by foxes if you can, as their faeces can transmit several diseases, including Canine Parvovirus or worms – neither of these should pose a serious health risk if your dog is up to date with vaccinations and worming treatments.

Vets have found that canine diets with low levels of fibre and high levels of starch increase the likelihood of coprophagia. If your dog is exhibiting this behaviour, first check that the diet you are feeding is nutritionally complete. Look at the first ingredient on the dog food packet or tin – is it corn or meat? Does he look underweight? Check that you are feeding the right amount.

If there is no underlying medical reason, you will have to try and modify your dog's behaviour. Remove cat litter trays, clean up after your dog and do not allow him to eat his own faeces. If it's not there, he can't eat it.

One breeder told us of a dog that developed the habit after being allowed to soil his crate as a pup, caused by the owners not being vigilant in their housetraining. The puppy got used to eating his own faeces and then continued to do it as an adult, when it became quite a problem.

Don't reprimand the dog for eating faeces. A better technique is to cause a distraction while he is in the act and then remove the offending material.

NOTE: Coprophagia is sometimes seen in pups aged between six months to a year and often disappears after this age.

Cavapoo Quirks

All breeds are different, all Cavapoos are different. Here are some comments:

"Archie loves walking on his hind legs thinking he is human. He also likes to hide on the chair under the kitchen table."

"Duncan loves to please; he also loves to eat treats. The moment we grab a treat from the jar, he performs a medley of tricks all at once to earn his treat as soon as possible. Sometimes he gets so excited he does the medley twice!"

"My pair love their toy box, every evening about 7pm they rummage in the box for a toy. Many will be taken out and left on the floor. Once the right toy is found, it will be shaken around the room with a little dance before they play with it! It makes me laugh every day."

"Max does not bark a lot for attention. When he wants to be fed he will sit in front of my husband and stare at him - even at 7am when we are sometimes sleeping. When he wants to play after his early evening nap, Max will drop a toy at Steve's feet and give a single bark, this normally lasts up to an hour. He loves his toys (he has a fair few). They are kept in his toy box, which he will pick them out of one by one. Max often comes to work with me, which he treats like a home from home. He loves looking out of the window at home and at our caravan!"

"When we or her best friends enter the house, we all have to sit on the stairs and make a fuss of Ethel while she "talks to" us. She will paw at her dish to tell you there's no water and barks to let you know if she wants something, i.e. go outside, feeding time."

"Millie's favorite place to drink is the tub! She requests a drink by sitting nicely outside of the shower curtain. When we pull it back, she'll put her front paws on the edge to ask to go in! Sometimes she will drink for a minute or more, even though she always has fresh water available in her bowl. I guess it tastes better fresh from the tub!

"We bought her a collapsible soft playpen to give her a break from her crate, and she hated it. We thought it had been a waste of money until a couple months in, she started using it as a bouncy house! Once or twice a day, she will walk into it and start jumping and flipping it and scratching and having the best time. It will travel all around our living room as she romps around. It's quite the scene!

"Millie's favorite way to greet a new person is by flopping onto her back and requesting a belly rub. It doesn't matter who the person is - she loves everyone. We think Millie thinks she's a person. At dog parks she sometimes finds a canine companion to play with, but first she needs to say hi to every owner. If we can't find her in the big play area, we always check the benches - she's usually getting pets from someone's mom or dad.

"Every morning, before we go outside for Millie to use the bathroom, she has to grab one of her toys from her crate and bring it with us... We can't go unless her friends come too!"

"Harper is so affectionate that she is obsessed with my sister's baby bump. Every time Harper sees my sister, she cuddles up to her baby bump; it's like she knows there is a baby in there and wants to be as close to her as possible. It's so loving to see. She's going to make a good auntie."

"He's a mummy's boy and I love that. He goes mad when friends come to the house or we go out with them. He knows all his toys by name and I can ask him to bring 'Walter' and he goes to his toy box and runs back with Walter."

"Max is so mad he can be running around the house with a toy in his mouth as happy as Larry and jumping all over the furniture then he jumps all over us... he just wants love when jumping over us!"

"Rodney and Mabel are both very loving lapdogs. Every evening without fail, they will both snuggle on my lap and so are also known as "The Cavapoo Blanket"! It's the warmest, most gorgeous blanket you will ever have."

"Cookie likes to sit in the hen run. She likes to think it's her own personal zoo where she can watch the hens go about their daily business. She is also very good at herding them back into their area if they escape the hen section of the paddock - although I think she's playing chase rather than herding! Given the chance, she would chase them, but she is wary of the cockerel. Each and every time she plays in the hen area she knows she has to stand by the outdoor taps to have her feet washed before she's allowed back in!"

"We love the Doodle dash! This is a short period of time where your pup will tear around the house and/or garden, generally doing laps, expelling any last bits of energy remaining before crashing out hard! Cherish these Doodle dashes in the early days as they become far less frequent as they get older, but on the rare occasion they still happen they bring such a smile to your face."

"Our families have all reported that they search and search for a great hiding place for their favorite toy, then to place it in clear view and sit and guard it because they can't find the perfect spot. So funny!"

....

This chapter provides just a general overview of canine behaviour. If your Cavapoo exhibits persistent behavioural problems, particularly if he or she is aggressive towards people or other dogs, consider seeking help from a reputable canine behaviourist, such as those listed the Association of Professional Dog Trainers, at: http://www.apdt.co.uk (UK) or https://apdt.com (USA).

Check they use positive reinforcement techniques - the old Alpha-dominance theories of forcefully imposing your will on a dog have largely been discredited and, even if they hadn't, a Cavapoo will not respond well to this type of treatment.

....

9. Exercise

One thing all dogs have in common – including every Cavapoo ever born - is that they need daily exercise. Even if you have a large garden or back yard where your dog can run free, there are still lots of benefits to daily walks.

One of the great things about Cavapoos is that, like the Cavalier King Charles Spaniel, they are very adaptable. They love going for long walks, but are equally happy to lounge around at home if you have to skip a walk. But don't think that because yours is happy to snuggle up on the sofa with you that they don't need regular exercise – THEY DO.

Start exercise patterns early so your dog gets used to a routine. **Dogs love routine.** Daily exercise helps to keep your Cavapoo happy, healthy and free from disease. It:

* Strengthens respiratory and circulatory systems
* Helps get oxygen to tissue cells
* Helps keep a healthy heart
* Wards off obesity
* Keeps muscles toned and joints flexible
* Aids digestion
* Releases endorphins that trigger positive feelings
* Helps to keep dogs mentally stimulated and socialised

Another way of keeping your dog exercised, mentally stimulated and happy is to take part in an activity, such as Obedience, Agility, therapy work, Canine Freestyle/Heelwork to Music (dancing) or other canine activities which challenge dogs. And even if you don't do any official competitions, Cavapoos love to show off by learning new tricks and commands.

Lapdogs or Hunters?

The answer is ... a mixture of both! How much hunter and how much lapdog depends largely on your dog's bloodlines. The Cavapoo is part Spaniel, which is a hardy dog bred to flush birds like pheasant, partridge and woodcock from dense undergrowth and then retrieve the game for the guns. A working Spaniel can run all day long with its nose to the ground. Although the Cavalier King Charles Spaniel has been developed as a companion dog, some still retain a degree of sporting instinct.

The Poodle was originally bred to work as a water retriever, and although its heyday as Europe's working retriever par excellence was a couple of hundred years ago, it is surprising how much instinct is passed down through the generations.

Cavapoos do, however, differ from their hard-working ancestors in that they are far more reliant on humans for their happiness than sporting and working dogs, which tend to be a bit more independent.

How Much Exercise?

The amount of exercise each adult Cavapoo needs varies tremendously from one dog to the next. It depends on various factors, including:

- Temperament
- Natural energy levels
- Bloodline
- Your living conditions
- Whether your dog is kept with other dogs
- What he or she gets used to

One of the big advantages of Cavapoos is that they are happy to fit in with your lifestyle; they enjoy short and long walks but are not bouncing off the walls if they miss one. They are known for being very playful; in fact one breeder says that puppies often prefer playing to eating - and enjoy toys and games, which help to stop them getting bored and mischievous.

Some of your dog's natural temperament and energy level will depend on the bloodline - ask the breeder how much exercise he or she recommends. But the good news is that even high-energy Cavapoos love nothing more than snuggling up on the couch with you.

As a rule of thumb with adult dogs, a minimum of an hour a day spread over at least two walks will keep your dog exercised and stimulated - although Cavapoos can take much more exercise and if you have the time, will love more. If a dog is taking part in obedience or agility events, then owners may exercise and train their Cavapoos in short, high energy sessions.

Owning more than one dog - or having friends with dogs - is a great way for them to get more exercise. A couple of dogs running round together will get far more exercise than one on her own. If you already have a Cavapoo and are looking for a second dog, consider another Cavapoo, as they seem to have a natural affinity with their own kind.

Photo of Cavapoos Domino and Carmen Rose enjoying a walk in the country, courtesy of Denise Knightley.

A fenced garden or yard is a definite advantage for a Cavapoo - but should not be seen as a replacement for daily exercise away from the home, where a dog can experience new places, scents, other people and dogs. Of course, if you live in an apartment, you may have no outside space, so it is doubly important to make the time to give your Poo outdoor exercise.

Your Cavapoo will enjoy going for walks on the lead (leash), but will enjoy it far more when (s)he is allowed to run free, following a scent, chasing a ball or going for a swim. If your dog is happy just to amble along beside you, think about playing some games to raise her heartbeat, build muscle and get her fit. If you want to hike or take part in agility with your dog, build up time and distance gradually. Exercise within your dog's limits - on both land and water - this loyal breed WILL want to keep up with you, regardless of how fit he or she is, and you don't want your beloved pooch to struggle.

If they are not in the mood for a walk, or if it is raining outside, some Cavapoos will lay on the ground and refuse to go anywhere! While it's OK to skip the odd walk, try not to let your dog dictate to you; regular exercise is important, and skipping too many walks will only make the dog more lazy, not less.

The Cavapoo loves to run free. You must, however, make sure it's safe to let her off the lead, away from traffic and other hazards - and only after she has learned the recall. There are reports in both the UK and North America about increasing numbers of dog attacks, even dog parks and public parks. If you are at all worried, avoid popular dog walking areas and find other places where your dog can exercise safely.

Mental Stimulation

Without mental challenges, dogs can become bored, unresponsive, destructive, attention-seeking and/or depressed. Cavapoos are known for being playful. Combine this with the intelligence of the Poodle and you have a dog that enjoys a mental as well as physical challenge. Have plenty toys and chews and factor in some regular play time with your dog – even gentle play time for old dogs.

Our photo shows Archie relaxing with his bottle of beer, chicken leg and ball-on-a-rope toys, courtesy of June Hicks.

If your dog's behaviour deteriorates, ask yourself are: "Is she getting enough exercise?" and "Am I leaving her alone for too long?"

Cavapoos are natural retrievers, i.e. they love fetching things back to you. As well as throwing a toy or ball, you can make it more interesting by hiding the object and training your dog to find it. Try and avoid sticks, which can splinter in the mouth. Playing in the garden or yard with toys or balls is also a good way to let off steam. If you play Frisbee, don't overdo it - especially with young, growing dogs, as this can lead to joint damage.

A Cavapoo at the heart of the family getting regular exercise and mental stimulation is a happy dog and loving companion second to none.

Cavapoos and Water

All Cavapoos are part Poodle, which was originally bred as a water dog. Many Cavapoos have inherited a love of water. If your dog does enjoy swimming, it is an excellent way to exercise; many veterinary clinics now use water tanks not only for remedial therapy, but also for canine recreation. It is also a great way for high energy Cavapoos to blow off some steam.

Remember that swimming is a lot more strenuous for a dog than walking or even running. Don't constantly throw that ball into the water for long periods - your Cavapoo will fetch it back until she drops. Your dog should exercise within her limits; overstretching could place a strain on the heart. Don't forget to gently dry under your Cavapoo's ear flaps after swimming to reduce the risk of ear infections. Not all Cavapoos like water and not all are natural swimmers – yours might not have inherited "the water gene"!

Some dogs have a natural fear of water. Never force a dog into water that doesn't want to go; you will only make her even more fearful. If you live near water and/or want your dog to enjoy it, introduce her while still a puppy.

Start off by getting the feet wet and paddling in the shallows, NOT by throwing a ball into water. Allow a young dog to build up confidence. Once used to getting wet feet, throw an object (preferably not one that will float into deep water) into the shallows and encourage your Cavapoo to fetch. You can even get into the shallow water yourself to give encouragement. Then gradually throw the object into slightly deeper water. All of this should be done over a period of time on separate visits, not in a single day. Avoid very cold weather and choppy water.

Like a child, if a young dog gets frightened of water or loses confidence, he or she is unlikely to want to go swim as an adult. If you are regularly near water, you might want to get a life vest, which will keep your dog afloat even when exhausted.

....

Establish a Routine

Establish an exercise regime early in your dog's life. If possible, get your dog used to a walk or walks at the same time every day, at a time that fits in with your daily routine and gradually build that up as the puppy reaches adulthood. For example, take your dog out after her morning feed, then again in the afternoon and a toilet trip last thing at night. Whatever routine you decide on, stick to it.

A dog that has been used to an hour of two of exercise a day will soon become bored and unhappy if your routine changes and she's only getting a couple of 10-minute walks a day. If you don't feel you have enough time to give your Cavapoo the exercise she needs, consider employing a daily dog walker, if you can afford it, or take her to doggie day care once or twice a week. As well as the exercise, she will love the interaction with other dogs.

To those owners who say their dog is happy and getting enough exercise playing in the yard or garden, just show her the lead (leash) and see how she reacts. Do you think she is excited at the prospect of leaving the home and going for a walk? Of course she is. Cavapoos are very curious and love investigating interesting new scents and places, which is why you need to plug every little gap in your fence – they will be off given half a chance!

Older dogs still need exercise to keep their body, joints and systems functioning properly. They need a less strenuous regime – they are usually happier with shorter walks, but still enough to keep them physically and mentally active. Again, every dog is different; some are willing and able to keep on running to the end of their lives, others slow right down. If your old or sick dog is struggling, she will show you that she's not up to it by stopping and looking at you or sitting/lying down and refusing to move. If she's healthy and does this, she is just being lazy!

Regular exercise can add months or even years to a dog's life.

Many Cavapoos love snow, but it can sometimes present problems with clumps of snow and ice building up on paws, ears, legs and tummy. Salt or de-icing products on roads and pathways can also cause irritation – particularly if he or she tries to lick it off - as they can contain chemicals that are poisonous to dogs. If your dog gets iced up, you can bathe paws and anywhere else affected in lukewarm - NOT HOT - water.

If your dog spends a lot of time in snow, you might invest in a quality paw wax or a pair of canine snow boots *(pictured)*, which are highly effective in preventing snow and ice balls forming on paws – provided you can get the boots to stay on!

Exercising Puppies

There are strict guidelines to stick to with puppies. It's important not to over-exercise young pups as their bones and joints are still soft and cannot tolerate a lot of stress. Too much impact can cause permanent damage. So, playing Fetch or Frisbee for hours on end with your young Cavapoo is definitely not a good plan, nor is allowing a pup to freely run up and down stairs in your home. You'll end up with an injured dog and a pile of vet's bills.

Just like babies, puppies have different temperaments and energy levels; some will need more exercise than others. Start slowly and build it up. The worst danger is a combination of over-exercise and overweight when puppy is growing.

Don't take your pup out of the yard or garden until the all-clear after the vaccinations - unless you carry him or her around to start the socialisation process. Begin with daily short walks on the lead. Puppies have enquiring minds. Get yours used to being outside the home environment and experiencing new situations as soon as possible. The general guideline for exercise is:

Five minutes of on-lead exercise per month of age

- 🐾 So, a total of 15 minutes when three months (13 weeks)
- 🐾 30 minutes when six months (26 weeks) old, etc.

This applies until around one year to 18 months old, when most of their growing has finished. Slowly increase the time as she gets used to being exercised and this will gradually build up muscles and stamina.

It is OK for your young pup to have free run of your garden or yard, provided it has a soft surface such as grass. This does not count in the five minutes per month rule. If the yard is stone or concrete, limit the time your dog runs around on it, as the hard surface will impact joints. It is also fine for your pup to run freely around the house to burn off energy - although not up and down stairs or jumping on and off furniture.

A pup will take things at her own pace and stop to sniff or rest. If you have other dogs, restrict the time pup is allowed to play with them, as she won't know when she's had enough. When older, your dog can go out for much longer walks.

UK breeder Charlotte Purkiss, of Lotties Cavapoos, added: "For the first 18 months whilst the puppy's bones are soft and developing, it's best not to over-exert and put strain on the joints which, in turn, could lead to luxating patella. Daily gentle walking is great, just not constant fast and hard running/chasing in the puppy stage as too much is a big strain."

And when your little pup has grown into a beautiful adult Cavapoo with a skeleton capable of carrying him or her through a long and healthy life, it will have been worth all the effort:

A long, healthy life is best started slowly

....

Cavapoo Exercise Tips

- 🐾 Don't over-exercise puppies or allow them to race up and down stairs
- 🐾 Aim for at least one walk away from the house every day
- 🐾 Vary your exercise route – it will be more interesting for both of you
- 🐾 Triple check the fencing around your garden or yard to prevent The Great Escape

- If you want your dog to retrieve, don't fetch the ball or toy back yourself or he will never learn. Train him by giving praise or a treat when he brings the ball or toy back to your feet

- Do not throw a ball or toy repeatedly for a dog if he shows signs of over-exertion. Your Cavapoo will fetch to please you and because it's great fun. Stop the activity after a while - no matter how much he begs you to throw it again

- The same goes for swimming, which is an exhausting exercise for a dog. Ensure any exercise is within your dog's capabilities – look out for heavy panting. Gentle swimming, if your dog enjoys it, is an excellent activity for Cavapoos. It's also beneficial for older dogs as it is low impact on joints

- Don't strenuously exercise your dog straight after or within an hour of a meal as this can cause Bloat. More normally seen in deep-chested dogs, Canine Bloat can affect any breed and is extremely serious, if not fatal. See **Chapter 11. Cavapoo Health** for details

- Cavapoos need play time as well as walk time. It keeps their minds exercised – and they love the interaction with their beloved owner

- Exercise old dogs more gently - especially in cold weather when it is harder to get their bodies moving. Have a cool-down period after exercise to reduce stiffness and soreness; it helps to remove lactic acids from the dog's body. Our 13-year-old loves a body rub

- If you throw a stick, don't let your dog chew it to bits, as splinters can get lodged in the mouth – or worse

- Make sure your dog has constant access to fresh water. Dogs can only sweat a tiny amount through the pads of their paws, they need to drink water to cool down

Admittedly, when it is pouring down with rain, freezing cold (or scorching hot), the last thing you want to do is to venture outdoors with your dog. And in all likelihood, your Cavapoo may not be too keen either!

But make the effort; the lows are more than compensated for by the highs. Exercise helps you bond with your dog, keep fit, see different places and meet new companions - both canine and human. In short, it enhances both your lives.

Socialisation

Your adult dog's character will depend largely on two things: inherited temperament and environment, or **nature and nurture**. And one absolutely essential aspect of nurture is socialisation.

Scientists now realise the importance that socialisation plays in a dog's life. There is a fairly small window that is regarded as the optimum time for socialisation - and this is up to the age of four to five months.

Socialisation actually begins from the moment the puppy is born and the importance of picking a good breeder cannot be over-emphasised. Not only will he or she breed for good temperament and health, but the canine mother will be well-balanced, friendly and unstressed and the pup will learn a lot in this positive environment.

Most young animals, including dogs, are naturally able to get used to their everyday environment until they reach a certain age. When they reach this age, they become much more suspicious of things they haven't yet experienced. This is why it often takes longer to train an older dog.

When you think about it, humans are not so different. Babies and children have a tremendous capacity to learn, we call this early period our "formative years". As we age, we can still learn, but not at the speed we absorbed things when very young. Also, as we get older we are often less receptive to new ideas or new ways of doing things.

This age-specific natural development allows a puppy to get comfortable with the normal sights, sounds, people and animals that will be a part of his life. It ensures that he doesn't spend his life jumping in fright, snapping, or growling at every blowing leaf. The suspicion that dogs develop later also ensures that they react with a healthy dose of caution to new things that could really be dangerous - Mother Nature is clever!

Socialisation means "learning to be part of society", or "integration". When we talk about socialising puppies, it means helping them learn to be comfortable within a human society that includes many different types of people, environments, buildings, traffic, sights, noises, smells, animals, other dogs, etc. It is essential that your dog's introductions to new things are all **positive**. Negative experiences lead to a dog becoming fearful and untrusting.

Your dog may already have a wonderful temperament, but he still needs socialising to avoid him thinking that the world is tiny and it revolves around him - which in turn leads to unwanted adult behaviour traits. Cavapoos can be demanding enough of your attention without developing a "Little Emperor" complex as well!

Good socialisation helps puppies – whether bold or timid - to learn their place in society and become more relaxed and integrated adults. It gives your dog confidence and teaches him not to be afraid of new experiences. The ultimate goal of socialisation is to have a happy, well-adjusted dog that you can take anywhere.

Photo of Dolly, courtesy of Laura Lambert.

Ever seen a therapy dog in action and noticed how incredibly well-adjusted to life they are? This is no coincidence. These dogs have been extensively socialised and are ready and able to deal in a calm manner with whatever situation they encounter. They are relaxed and comfortable in their own skin - just like you want your dog to be.

Start socialising your puppy as soon as you bring her home; start around the house and garden and, if it is safe, carry her out of the home environment. Regular socialisation should continue until your dog is around 18 months of age. After that, don't just forget about it; socialisation isn't only for puppies, it should continue throughout your dog's life. As with any skill, if it is not practised, your dog will become less proficient at interacting with other people, animals and environments.

Developing the Well-Rounded Adult Dog

Dogs that have not been properly integrated are more likely to react with fear or aggression to unfamiliar people, animals and experiences. Cavapoos that are relaxed around strangers, other dogs, honking horns, cats, farm animals, cyclists, veterinary examinations, traffic, crowds and noise are easier to live with than dogs who find these situations challenging or frightening. And if you are planning on taking part in canine competitions, get her used to the buzz of these events early on.

Well-socialised dogs live more relaxed, peaceful and happy lives than dogs that are constantly stressed by their environment.

Socialisation isn't an "all or nothing" project. You can socialise a puppy a bit, a lot, or a whole lot. The wider the range of positive experiences you expose him to when young, the better his chances are of becoming a more relaxed adult. Don't over-face your little puppy.

Socialisation should never be forced, but approached systematically and in a manner that builds confidence and curious interaction. If your pup finds a new experience frightening, take a step back, introduce him to the scary situation much more gradually, and make a big effort to do something he loves during the situation or right afterwards.

For example, if your puppy seems to be frightened by noise and vehicles at a busy road, a good method would be to go to a quiet road, sit with the dog away from - but within sight of - the traffic. Every time he looks towards the traffic say "YES" and reward him with a treat. If he is still stressed, you need to move further away. When your dog takes the food in a calm manner, he is becoming more relaxed and getting used to traffic sounds, so you can edge a bit nearer - but still just for short periods until he becomes totally relaxed. Keep each session short and **positive.**

Meeting Other Dogs

When you take your gorgeous and vulnerable little pup out with other dogs for the first few times, you are bound to be a bit apprehensive. To begin with, introduce your puppy to just one other dog – one that you know to be friendly, rather than taking him straight to the park where there are lots of dogs of all sizes racing around, which might frighten the life out of your timid little darling.

On the other hand, your puppy might be full of confidence right from the off, but you still need to approach things slowly. If your puppy is too cocksure, he may get a warning bite from an older dog, which could make him more anxious when approaching new dogs in the future.

Always make initial introductions on neutral ground, so as not to trigger territorial behaviour. You want your Cavapoo to approach other dogs with friendliness, not fear. From the first meeting, help both dogs experience good things when they're in each other's presence. Let them sniff each other briefly, which is normal canine greeting behaviour. As they do, talk to them in a happy, friendly tone of voice; never use a threatening tone.

Don't allow them to sniff each other for too long as this may escalate to an aggressive response. After a short time, get the attention of both dogs and give each a treat in return for obeying a simple command, such as "Sit" or "Stay." Continue with the "happy talk", food rewards and simple commands.

Learn to spot the difference between normal rough and tumble play - *as shown in this photo* – and interaction that may develop into fear or aggression.

Here are some signs of fear to look out for when your dog interacts with other canines:

- Running away or freezing on the spot
- Licking the lips
- Lips pulled back
- Trembling
- Panting – this can be a sign of stress or pain
- Frantic/nervous behaviour, e.g. excessive sniffing, drinking or playing frenetically with a toy
- A lowered body stance or crouching
- Lying on his back with paws in the air – this is a submissive gesture, as is submissive urination
- Lowering of the head or turning the head away, when you may see the whites of the eyes as the dog tries to keep eyes on the perceived threat
- growling
- Hair raised on his back (raised hackles)
- Tail lifted in the air
- Ears high on the head

Some of these responses are normal. A pup may well crouch on the ground or roll on to his back to show other dogs he is not a threat. Try not to be over-protective, your puppy has to learn how to interact with other dogs. Don't be too quick to rush in and pick up your puppy, he or she will sense your anxiety. If the situation looks like escalating into something more aggressive, calmly distract the dogs or remove your puppy – don't shout or shriek. Dogs will pick up on your fear and this in itself could trigger an unpleasant situation.

Another sign to look out for is eyeballing. In the canine world, staring a dog in the eyes is a challenge and may cause an aggressive response. This is more relevant to adult dogs, as a young pup will soon be put in her place by bigger or older dogs; it is how they learn. The rule of thumb with puppy socialisation is to keep a close eye on your pup's reaction to whatever you expose him to so that you can tone things down if he seems at all frightened.

Always follow up a socialisation experience with praise, petting, a fun game or a special treat. One positive sign from a dog is the play bow *(pictured),* when he goes down on to his front elbows but keeps his backside up in the air. This is a sign that he's feeling friendly towards the other dog and wants to play. Relaxed ear and body position and wagging tail are other positive signs.

Although Cavapoos are not naturally aggressive dogs, aggression is often grounded in fear, and a dog that mixes easily is less likely to be combative. Similarly, without frequent and new experiences, some Cavapoos can become timid and nervous. Take your new dog everywhere you can. You want him to feel relaxed and calm in any situation, even noisy and crowded ones. Take treats with you and praise him when he reacts calmly to new situations.

Once settled into your home, introduce him to your friends and teach him not to jump up. If you have young children, it is not only the dog that needs socialising! Youngsters also need training on how to act around dogs, so both parties learn to respect the other.

An excellent way of getting your new puppy to meet other dogs in a safe environment is at a puppy class. We highly recommend this for all puppies. Ask around locally if any classes are being run. Some vets and dog trainers run classes for very junior pups who have had all their vaccinations. These help pups get used to other dogs of a similar age.

....

Walkies!

Charlotte Purkiss adds: "The adult stage is the prime time of life for enjoying exercise before dogs reach their senior stage, so let them run free and enjoy the freedom of energy with the wind in their ears!"

Different owners describe their daily exercise routines with their Cavapoos: "I take mine 40 minutes to an hour twice a day. They love interacting with other dogs and are looking to play and make friends."

"As puppies we kept to about five minutes exercise for every month of age. Since they were fully grown at about one year old, they have at least two hours of mainly off-lead exercise every day. Our Cavapoos are particularly keen to chase birds, pigeons, seagulls, crows and will chase and swim after ducks! They do not seem to be interested in cats, rabbits, deer, sheep, horses, etc. They are totally non-confrontational with other dogs and socialise well."

"On weekdays we jog for 30 mins in the morning, they then have a 45-minute off-lead walk at lunchtime! At weekends they can get anything from one to two off-lead walks a day. They love other dogs."

"Lifestyle is a big thing for potential dog owners to consider. During the early months, follow the recommendations for the breed, say five minutes of exercise per month of age while the pup is growing. Ethel enjoys frequent walks, but up to an hour is satisfactory. She tends to be people-friendly rather than friends with other animals - she will give chase to cats and birds."

"On weekdays, we take Duncan for walks every morning before work. He has a dog walker that comes every afternoon for a 45-minute walk and then we go for a brief walk after work. If it is a nice day we go to the dog park. I wouldn't say he needs a lot of exercise throughout the day, especially compared to other breeds. On the weekends, Duncan explores New York city with us all day.

"Duncan wants to play with everyone and everything, even the pigeons walking on the sidewalk. He loves to chase them, but if they don't fly away, he backs off. He doesn't want to hurt them, he only likes the chase!"

Photo of Duncan, bred by Petit Jean Puppies, enjoying a day at the beach courtesy of Gina Desmond.

"Millie prefers to take a couple of 20-minute walks as well as play a good long game of Fetch inside or outside, depending on the weather. We have tried to find activities where she can entertain herself, but she prefers to play Fetch with one of us! She does not have an intense prey drive, though she occasionally surprises us - once, she brought a dead mouse into the house from the garden. Yikes! In general, she adores other dogs and we're not quite sure she knows other types of animals exist, as she largely ignores cats, squirrels, etc."

"Max is walked for approximately 20 minutes on a morning (if he will go out!). Otherwise about 40 minutes at lunchtime; his evening walk is anywhere from 20 minutes, often though he will turn around and make it clear he has had enough. On a weekend he will easily walk at least three miles at a time. We have a coastal holiday home which we go to at least twice a month and we go for beach walks, which he loves.

"Max socializes with other breeds of dogs at a weekly day care, but can get jealous if I fuss over other dogs. Once he sees a bird or a rabbit he will give chase and it is difficult to recall him."

"Harper has 20 minutes every morning, a 10-minute lunchtime walk and then on an evening it can be anything from 20 to 60 minutes depending on the weather. On a weekend I tend to do one long walk for around an hour on a Saturday and/or Sunday. Harper doesn't seem too interested in prey, she loves other dogs and loves to play. She has a little brother, George the Cavachon, and these two are inseparable and get along wonderfully."

"We go out at 7.30am and meet friends with dogs and are out for about an hour. Some of the other dogs are on leads, but Teddy is good on recall so is off the lead on the park. In the afternoon he gets another walk which can vary from 20 minutes to two hours.

"He's friendly with other dogs and loves people. When he meets a puppy or a dog who jumps up at

him, he's a bit wimpy! Teddy gets on with other dogs but hates cats. It's my fault; I don't like the local cats who use my garden as a toilet. I shoo them away and so he barks at them."

"We do two lots of 45 to 60-minute walks a day and ball play. Cookie chases most birds and squirrels, she likes dogs her own size and enjoys watching the hens in the garden."

"I walk Dolly for 40 minutes, two miles, every day. She's not keen on walking in wind and rain and neither am I, so we tend to miss some of those day out and she's fine, it doesn't bother her. Our longest walk has been about six miles and she managed absolutely fine."

"Rodney and Mabel have a good hour-long walk every day, generally with some off-lead time, sometimes longer at the weekend. They also enjoy playtime at home or in the garden."

"Winston gets between one to two hours of walks a day, plus play times and ball play indoors. At least one of his walks will be more of a "Sniffari", where he can sniff to his heart's content and wear his mind out more than physical exercise."

Our photo shows Winston ready to head out on a Sniffari, courtesy of Lindsey McDonald and Alex Kostiw.

10. Training

Training a young dog is not unlike bringing up a child. Put lots of time in early on to work together for a better mutual understanding and you will be rewarded with a well-adjusted, sociable individual who is a joy to live with and you can take anywhere.

Dogs are not clones and you can get some that are more independent-minded, but generally Cavapoos really want to please their owners, they enjoy showing off and are very receptive to training. This won't magically happen overnight, you have to make time for training. Cavapoos are super family dogs and make wonderful companions, but let yours behave exactly how he or she wants and you may finish up with an attention-seeking adult who rules your life.

Cavapoos are highly motivated by reward – especially praise as well as treats - and this is a big bonus when it comes to training. Your dog WANTS to please you and enjoys learning. All you have to do is spend the time teaching her what you want her to do, then repeat the actions so it becomes second nature. The secret of good training can be summed up in four words:

- ❧ Consistency
- ❧ Praise
- ❧ Patience
- ❧ Reward

 Don't always use treats with your Cavapoo; praise or play time is often enough reward; police and other service dogs are trained to a very high level with only a ball for reward. If you do use treats, try getting your pup used to a small piece of carrot or apple as a healthy low-calorie alternative to traditional dog treats.

Many owners would say that Cavapoos have empathy (the ability to pick up on the feelings of others). All of them respond well to your encouragement and a positive atmosphere, they do not respond well to shouting or heavy-handed training methods. Cavapoos are certainly 'biddable', i.e. willing to learn, provided you make it clear exactly what you want them to do; don't give conflicting signals.

They enjoy socialising and love a challenge. Cavapoos can excel as therapy dogs - see Denise Knightley's story at the end of this chapter on how Cavapoo Carmen Rose is helping young children. They also do well in Obedience and Agility, which not only keeps their bodies exercised, but their minds too.

The Intelligence of Dogs

Psychologist and canine expert Dr Stanley Coren has written a book called *The Intelligence of Dogs* in which he ranks the breeds. He surveyed dog trainers to compile the list and used *Understanding of New Commands* and *Obeying First Command* as his standards of intelligence. He says there are three types of dog intelligence:

- Adaptive Intelligence (learning and problem-solving ability). This is specific to the individual and is measured by canine IQ tests

- Instinctive Intelligence. This is specific to the individual and is measured by canine IQ tests

- Working/Obedience Intelligence. This is breed-dependent

He divides dogs into six groups and the brainboxes of the canine world are the 10 breeds ranked in the 'Brightest Dogs' section of his list. It will come as no surprise to anyone who has ever been into the countryside and seen sheep being worked by a farmer and his right-hand man (his dog) to learn that the Border Collie is the most intelligent of all dogs. Number Two is the Poodle, followed by the German Shepherd Dog, Golden Retriever, Doberman Pinscher, Shetland Sheepdog, Papillon, Rottweiler and Australian Cattle Dog. All dogs in this class:

- Understand New Commands with Fewer than Five Repetitions

- Obey a First Command 95% of the Time or Better

Fans of Cavalier King Charles Spaniels may be disappointed to learn that their beloved breed is languishing alongside the Akita at Number 73 out of 138 in the fourth group, described as 'Average Working/Obedience Intelligence, Understanding of New Commands: 25 to 40 repetitions. Obey First Command: 50% of the time or better.' The full list can be seen here: https://en.wikipedia.org/wiki/The_Intelligence_of_Dogs

By the author's own admission, the drawback of this rating scale is that it is heavily weighted towards obedience-related behavioural traits, which are often found in working dogs, rather than understanding or creativity (found in hunting dogs). As a result, some dogs, such as the Bully breeds – Bulldogs, Mastiffs, Bull Terriers, Pugs, French Bulldogs, etc. - are ranked quite low on the list, due to their independent or stubborn nature.

Both the Poodle and the Cavalier are willing to learn: the Poodle to show off his fearsome intelligence and the gentle Cavalier to please you. Your Cavapoo will be a mixture of the two. However, if yours has more of a Poodle brainbox, not only has he or she the capacity to learn very quickly, but you will also have to find ways of challenging that active mind. Boredom can lead to mischief.

Whichever breed your Cavapoo takes after, it's true to say that you are starting out with a dog that has the intelligence to pick up new commands quickly and the desire to please you. All you have to do is convince her that good things will happen when she obeys your commands!

Five Golden Rules

1. Training must be reward-based, not punishment based.
2. Keep sessions short or your dog will get bored.
3. Never train when you are in a rush or a bad mood.
4. Training after exercise is fine, but never train when your dog is exhausted.
5. Keep sessions fun; **give your Cavapoo a chance to shine!**

Energetic or independent Cavapoos may try to push the boundaries when they reach adolescence, i.e. as they come out of puppyhood and before they mature into adults, and some may act like spoiled children if allowed to. If you have a high spirited, high energy dog, you have to use your brain to think of ways that will make training challenging and to persuade your dog that what you want her to do is actually what SHE wants to do!

She will come to realise that when she does what you ask of her, something good happens – verbal praise, pats, play time, treats, etc. You need to be firm with a strong-willed or stubborn dog, but all training should still be carried out using positive techniques.

Establishing the natural order of things is not something forced on a dog through shouting or violence; it is brought about by mutual consent and good training.

Cavapoos are happiest and behave best when they are familiar and comfortable with their place in the household. If you have adopted an older dog, you can still train her, but it will take a little longer to get rid of bad habits and instil good manners. Patience and persistence are the keys here.

Socialisation is a very important aspect of training. Your puppy's breeder should have already begun this process with the litter and then it's up to you to keep it going when puppy arrives home. Young pups can absorb a great deal of information, but they are also vulnerable to bad experiences.

They need exposing – in a positive manner - to different people, other animals and situations; if not, they can find them very frightening when they do finally encounter them later. They may react by cowering, urinating, barking, growling or even snapping.

If they have a lot of good experiences with other people, places, noises, situations and animals before four or five months old, they are less likely to either be timid or nervous or try to establish dominance later. Don't just leave your dog at home in the early days, take her out and about with you, get her used to new people, places and noises. Dogs that miss out on being socialised can pay the price later.

All pups are chewers. If you are not careful, some young pups and adolescents will chew through anything – wires, phone chargers, remote controls, bedding, rugs, etc. Young dogs are not infrequent visitors to veterinary clinics to have "foreign objects" removed from their stomachs. Train your young pup only to chew the things you give her – so don't give her your old slippers, an old piece of carpet or anything that resembles something you don't want her to chew, she won't know the difference between the old and the new. Buy purpose-made long-lasting chew toys.

Jumping up is another common issue. Cavapoos are generally enthusiastic about life, so it's often a natural reaction when they see somebody. You don't, however, want your dog to jump up on Granny when she has just come back from a romp through the muddy woods and a swim in a dirty pond (your dog, not Granny!). While still small, teach your dog not to jump up!

A puppy class is one of the best ways of getting a pup used to being socialised and trained. This should be backed up by short sessions of a few minutes of training a day back home.

Cavapoos are a good choice for first-time dog owners, and anybody prepared to put in a fair bit of time can train one. But if you do need some professional one-on-one tuition (for you and the dog), choose a trainer registered with the Association of Professional Dog Trainers (APDT) or other positive reward-based training school, as the old Alpha-dominance theories have gone out the window.

When you train your dog, it should never be a battle of wills; it should be a positive learning experience for you both. Bawling at the top of your voice or smacking should play NO part in training any dog, but especially one as sensitive and loving as the Cavapoo.

15 Training Tips

1. **Start training and socialising straight away**. Like babies, puppies learn quickly and it's this learned behaviour that stays with them through adult life. Puppy training should start with just a few minutes a day a couple of days after arriving home.

2. **Your voice is a very important training tool.** Your dog has to learn to understand your language and you have to understand him. Commands should be issued in a calm, authoritative voice - not shouted. Praise should be given in a happy, encouraging voice, accompanied by stroking or patting. If your dog has done something wrong, use a stern voice, not a harsh shriek. This applies even if your Cavapoo is unresponsive at the beginning.

3. **Avoid giving your dog commands you know you can't enforce.** Every time you give a command you don't enforce, he learns that commands are optional. One command equals one response. Give your dog only one command - twice maximum - then gently enforce it. Repeating commands will make him tune out, and teach him that the first few commands are a bluff. Telling your dog to **"SIT, SIT, SIT, SIT!!!"** is neither efficient nor effective. Say a single "SIT", gently place him in the Sit position and praise him.

4. **Train your dog gently and humanely.** Cavapoos are sensitive by nature and do not respond well to being shouted at or hit. Keep training sessions short and upbeat so the whole experience is enjoyable for you and for him. If obedience training is a bit of a bore, pep things up a bit by "play training" by using constructive, non-adversarial games.

5. **Do not try to dominate your dog.** Training should be mutual, i.e. your dog should do something because he WANTS to do it and he knows that you want him to do it. As one breeder said, in all her years of raising Cavapoos, she had never once come across an Alpha Cavapoo. Cavapoos are not interested in dominating you – although they might try and push the boundaries.

6. **Begin training at home around the house and garden/yard**. How well your dog responds at home affects his behaviour away from the home as well. If he doesn't respond well at home, he certainly won't respond any better out and about where there are 101 distractions, e.g. interesting scents, people, food scraps, other dogs and small animals or birds.

7. **Mealtimes are a great time to start training.** Teach Sit and Stay at breakfast and dinner, rather than just putting the dish down and letting him dash over immediately. At first, he won't know what you mean, so gently place him into the sit position while you say "Sit." Place a hand on his chest during the "Stay" command - gradually letting go – and then give him the command to eat, followed by encouraging praise - he'll soon get the idea.

8. **Use his name often and in a positive manner** so he gets used to the sound of it. He won't know what it means at first, but it won't take long before he realises you're talking to him.

9. **DON'T use his name when reprimanding, warning or punishing.** He should trust that when he hears his name, good things happen. He should always respond to his name with enthusiasm, never hesitancy or fear. Use words such as "No", "Ack!" or "Bad Boy/Girl" in a stern (not shouted) voice instead. Some parents prefer not to use "No" with their dog, as they use it so often around the kids that it can confuse the pup! When a puppy is corrected by his mother, e.g. – if he bites her – she growls to warn him not to do it again. Using a short sharp sound like **"Ack!"** can work surprisingly well; it does for us.

10. **Don't give your dog lots of attention (even negative attention) when he misbehaves.** Cavapoos love attention and if yours gets lots when he jumps up on you, you are inadvertently reinforcing bad behaviour. If he jumps up demanding your attention, push him away, use the command "No" or "Down" and then ignore him. If necessary, leave the room so he learns that when he has displeased you, he is deprived of your presence.

11. **Timing is critical.** When your puppy does something right, praise him immediately. If you wait a while, he will have no idea what he has done right. Similarly, when he does something wrong, correct him straight away.

12. **If he has an "accident" in the house, don't shout and definitely don't rub his nose in it.** This will only make things worse and encourage your dog to fear you. He may even start hiding and peeing or pooping behind the sofa or other inappropriate places.

    If you catch him in the act, use your "No!" or "Ack!" sound and immediately carry him out of the house. Then use your toilet command and praise or give a treat when he performs. If your pup is constantly eliminating indoors, you are probably not keeping a close enough eye on him or not picking up on the signs.

13. **In the beginning, give your dog attention when YOU want to – not when he wants it.** When you are training, give your puppy lots of positive attention when he is good. But if he starts jumping up, nudging you constantly or barking to demand your attention, ignore him. Don't give in to the demands. Wait a while and pat him when you are ready and AFTER he has stopped demanding your attention.

14. **You can give a Cavapoo TOO MUCH attention in the beginning.** This may create a rod for your own back when they grow into needy adults that are over-reliant on you. They may even develop Separation Anxiety, which is stressful for both dog AND owner.

15. **Start as you mean to go on.** In terms of training, treat your cute little pup as though he were fully-grown. Introduce the rules you want him to live by as an adult. If you don't want your dog to take over your couch or bed or jump up at people when he is an adult, train him not to do it while still young. You can't have one set of rules for a pup and one set for a fully-grown dog; he won't understand.

    Also make sure that everybody in the household sticks to the same set of rules. If the kids let him jump on the couch and you don't, your dog will not know what is allowed and what isn't.

Teaching Basic Commands

The three Ds

The three Ds – **Distance**, **Duration** and **Distraction** – are the cornerstone of a good training technique.

Duration is the length of time your dog remains in the command.

Distance is how far you can walk away without your dog breaking the command.

Distraction is the number of external stimuli - such as noise, scents, people, other animals, etc. - your dog can tolerate before breaking the command.

Only increase one of the Three Ds at a time. For example, if your new pup has just learned to sit on command, gradually increase the time by a second or two as you go along. Moving away from the dog or letting the kids or the cat into the room would increase the Distance or Distraction level and make the command too difficult for your pup to hold.

If you are teaching the Stay, gradually increase EITHER the distance OR the time (s)he is in the Stay position; don't increase both at once. Start off by training your dog in your home before moving into the garden or yard where there are more distractions - even if it is quiet and you are alone, outdoor scents and sights will be a big distraction for a young dog. Once you have mastered the commands in a home environment, progress to the park.

 The key to successful training is to implement the Three Ds progressively and slowly. Don't expect too much too soon. Work within your dog's capabilities, move forward one tiny step at a time and thereby set your dog up to consistently succeed, not fail.

....

The Sit

Teaching the Sit command to your Cavapoo is relatively easy. Teaching a young pup to sit still for a few seconds is a bit more difficult! If your little protégé is very distracted and/or high energy, it may be easier to put him on a lead (leash) to hold his attention in the beginning.

Stand facing each other and hold a treat between your thumb and fingers just an inch or so above his head and let him sniff it. Don't let your fingers and the treat get much further away or you might have trouble getting him to move his body into a sitting position. In fact, if your dog jumps up when you try to guide him into the Sit, you're probably holding your hand too far away from his nose. If your dog backs up, you can practise with a wall behind him.

As he reaches up to sniff it, move the treat upwards and back over the dog towards his tail at the same time as saying **"Sit."**. Most dogs will track the treat with their eyes and follow it with their noses, causing their snouts to point straight up.

As his head moves up toward the treat, his rear end should automatically go down towards the floor. TaDa! (drum roll!).

The second he sits, say "Yes!" Give him the treat and tell your dog (s)he's a good boy/girl. Stroke and praise him for as long as he stays in the sitting position. If he jumps up on his back legs and paws you while you are moving the treat, be patient and start all over again. At this stage, don't expect your bouncy little pupil to sit for more than a nanosecond!

Another method is to put one hand on his chest and with your other hand, gently push down on his rear end until he is sitting, while saying "Sit". Give him a treat and praise; even though you have made him do it, he will eventually associate the position with the word 'sit'.

Once your dog catches on, leave the treat in your pocket (or have it in your other hand). Repeat the sequence, but this time your dog will just follow your empty hand. Say "Sit" and bring your empty hand in front of your dog's nose, holding your fingers as if you had a treat. Move your hand exactly as you did when you held the treat.

When your dog sits, say "Yes!" and then give him a treat from your other hand or your pocket.

Gradually lessen the amount of movement with your hand. First, say "Sit" then hold your hand eight to 10 inches above your dog's face and wait a moment. Most likely, he will sit. If he doesn't, help him by moving your hand back over his head, like you did before, but make a smaller movement this time. Then try again. Your goal is to eventually just say "Sit" without having to move or extend your hand at all.

Once your dog reliably sits on cue, you can ask him to sit whenever you meet and talk to people (it may not work straight away, but it might help to calm him down a bit). The key is anticipation. Give your dog the cue before he gets too excited to hear you and before he starts jumping up on the person just arrived. Generously reward him the instant he sits. Say "Yes" and give treats/praise every few seconds while he holds the Sit.

Whenever possible, ask the person you're greeting to help you out by walking away if your dog gets up from the sit and lunges or jumps towards them. With many consistent repetitions of this exercise, your dog will learn that lunging or jumping makes people go away, and polite sitting makes them stay and give attention.

You can practise training your bouncy Cavapoo not to jump up by arranging for a friend to come round, then for him or her to come in and out of the house several times. Each time, show the treat, give the Sit command (initially, don't ask your dog to hold the sit for any length of time), and then allow him to greet your friend. Ask your friend to reach down to pat your dog, rather than standing straight and encouraging the dog to jump up for a greeting.

If your dog is still jumping up, you can use a harness and lead inside the house to physically prevent him from jumping up at people, while still training him to sit when someone arrives. Treats and praise are the key. You can also use the "Off" command - and reward with praise or a treat for success - when you want your dog NOT to jump up at a person, or not to jump up on furniture.

"Sit" is a useful command and can be used in a number of different situations. For example, when you are putting his lead on, while you are preparing the food, when he returned the ball you have just thrown, when he is jumping up, demanding attention or getting over-excited.

The Stay

This is a very useful command, but it's not so easy to teach a lively and distracted young Cavapoo pup to stay still for any length of time. Here is a simple method to get your dog to stay; if you are training a young dog, don't ask him to stay for more than a few seconds at the beginning.

This requires concentration from your dog, so pick a time when he's relaxed and well exercised, or just after a game or mealtimes - but not too exhausted to concentrate.

1. Tell your dog to sit or lie down, but instead of giving a treat as soon as he hits the floor, hold off for one second. Then say "Yes!" in an enthusiastic voice and give him a treat. If your dog bounces up again instantly, have two treats ready. Feed one right away, before he has time to move; then say "Yes!" and feed the second treat.

2. You need a release word or phrase. It might be "Free!" or "Here!" or a word that you only use to release your dog from this command. Once you've given the treat, immediately give your release cue and encourage your dog to get up. Then repeat the exercise, perhaps up to a dozen times in one training session, gradually wait a tiny bit longer before releasing the treat. (You can delay the first treat for a moment if your dog bounces up).

3. A common mistake is to hold the treat high and then give the reward slowly. As your dog doesn't know the command yet, he sees the treat coming and gets up to meet the food. Instead, bring the treat toward your dog quickly - the best place to deliver it is right between his front paws. If you're working on a Sit-Stay, give the treat at chest height.

4. When your dog can stay for several seconds, start to add a little distance. At first, you'll walk backwards, because your dog is more likely to get up to follow you if you turn away from him. Take one single step away, then step back towards your dog and say "Yes!" and give the treat. Give him the signal to get up immediately, even if five seconds haven't passed. The stay gets harder for your dog depending on how long it is, how far away you are, and what else is going on around him.

5. Remember **Distance, Duration, Distraction.** For best success in teaching a Stay, work on one factor at a time. Whenever you make one factor more difficult, such as distance, ease up on the others at first, then build them back up. So, when you take that first step back from your dog, adding distance, you should cut the duration of the stay.

6. Once he's mastered the Stay with you alone, move the training on so that he learns to do the same with distractions. Have someone walk into the room, or squeak a toy or bounce a ball once. A rock-solid stay is mostly a matter of working slowly and patiently to start with. Don't go too fast - the ideal scenario is that your Cavapoo never breaks out of the Stay position until you release him.

If he does get up, take a breather and then give him a short refresher, starting at a point easier than whatever you were working on when he cracked. If you think he's tired or had enough, leave it for the day and come back later – just **finish off on a positive note** by giving one very easy command you know he will obey, followed by a treat reward. Don't use the Stay command in situations where it is unpleasant for your dog. For instance, avoid telling him to stay as you close the door behind you on your way to work. Finally, don't use Stay to keep a dog in a scary situation.

Cavapoos can do so much more than sit and stay, so don't underestimate your dog! They are biddable and their great desire to please their owners means that they can be trained in different fields. Their gentle nature makes then suitable for therapy work; they can also be trained for agility, canine freestyle (dancing with dogs), rallying, obedience and other canine competitions.

Down

There are a number of different ways to teach this command, which here means for the dog to lie down. (If you are teaching this command, then use the **"Off"** command to teach your dog not to jump up). This does not come naturally to a young pup, so it may take a little while to master the Down command. Don't make it a battle of wills and, although you may gently push him down, don't physically force him down against his will. This will be seen as you asserting dominance in an aggressive manner and your Cavapoo will not like it.

1. Give the "Sit" command.

2. When your dog sits, don't give him the treat immediately, but keep it in your closed hand. Slowly move your hand straight down toward the floor, between his front legs. As your dog's nose follows the treat, just like a magnet, his head will bend all the way down to the floor.

3. When the treat is on the floor between your dog's paws, start to move it away from him, like you're drawing a line along the floor. (The entire luring motion forms an L-shape).

4. At the same time say "Down" in a firm manner.

5. To continue to follow the treat, your dog will probably ease himself into the Down position. The instant his elbows touch the floor, say "Yes!" and immediately let him eat the treat. If your dog doesn't automatically stand up after eating the treat, just move a step or two away to encourage him to move out of the Down position. Then repeat the sequence above several times. Aim for two short sessions of five minutes per day.

If your dog's back end pops up when you try to lure him into a Down, quickly snatch the treat away. Then immediately ask your dog to sit and try again. It may help to let your dog nibble on the treat as you move it toward the floor. If you've tried to lure your dog into a Down, but he still seems confused or reluctant, try this trick:

1. Sit down on the floor with your legs straight out in front of you. Your dog should be at your side. Keeping your legs together and your feet on the floor, bend your knees to make a 'tent' shape.

2. Hold a treat right in front of your dog's nose. As he licks and sniffs the treat, slowly move it down to the floor and then underneath your legs. Continue to lure him until he has to crouch down to keep following the treat.

3. The instant his belly touches the floor, say "Yes!" and let him eat the treat. If your dog seems nervous about following the treat under your legs, make a trail of treats for him to eat along the way.

Some dogs find it easier to follow a treat into the Down from a standing position.

❧ Hold the treat right in front of your dog's nose, and then slowly move it straight down to the floor, right between his front paws. His nose will follow the treat

❧ If you let him lick the treat as you continue to hold it still on the floor, your dog will probably plop into the Down position

✤ The moment he does, say "Yes!" and let him eat the treat (some dogs are reluctant to lie on a cold, hard surface. It may be easier to teach yours to lie down on a carpet). The next step is to introduce a hand signal. You'll still reward him with treats, though, so keep them nearby or hidden behind your back.

1. Start with your dog in a Sit.

2. Say "Down".

3. Without a treat in your fingers, use the same hand motion you did before.

4. As soon as your dog's elbows touch the floor, say "Yes!" and immediately get a treat to give him. Important: Even though you're not using a treat to lure your dog into position, you must still give him a reward when he lies down. You want your dog to learn that he doesn't have to see a treat to get one.

5. Clap your hands or take a few steps away to encourage him to stand up. Then repeat the sequence from the beginning several times for a week or two. When your dog readily lies down as soon as you say the cue and then use your new hand signal, you're ready for the next step. You probably don't want to keep bending all the way down to the floor to make your Cavapoo lie down. To make things more convenient, you can gradually shrink the signal so that it becomes a smaller movement. To make sure your dog continues to understand what you want him to do, you'll need to progress slowly.

6. Repeat the hand signal, but instead of guiding your dog into the Down by moving your hand all the way to the floor, move it almost all the way down. Stop moving your hand when it's an inch or two above the floor. Practise the Down exercise for a day or two, using this slightly smaller hand signal. Then you can make your movement an inch or two smaller, stopping your hand three or four inches above the floor.

7. After practising for another couple of days, you can shrink the signal again. As you continue to gradually stop your hand signal farther and farther from the floor, you'll bend over less and less. Eventually, you won't have to bend over at all. You'll be able to stand up straight, say "Down," and then just point to the floor.

Your next job is a bit harder - it's to practise your dog's new skill in many different situations and locations so that he can lie down whenever and wherever you ask him to. Practise in calm places at first, like different rooms in your house or in your garden/yard when there's no one else around. Then increase the distractions; so do some sessions at home when family members are moving around, on walks and then at friends' houses, too. *Our photo shows three-year-old F1 Rodney giving a beautiful demonstration of "Down", courtesy of Karen Howe.*

The Recall

This basic command is perhaps the most important command of all and one that you can teach right from the beginning. If your dog won't come back, you are limiting both your lives. A dog who responds quickly and consistently can enjoy freedoms that other dogs cannot. Although you might spend more time teaching this command than any other, the benefits make it well worth the investment. Cavapoos love to run free, but you can't allow that in open spaces until he or she has learned the recall.

Whether you're teaching a young puppy or an older Cavapoo, the first step is always to establish that coming to you is the best thing he can do. **Any time your dog comes to you whether you've called him or not, acknowledge that you appreciate it**. You can do this with praise, affection, play or treats. This consistent reinforcement ensures that your dog will continue to "check in" with you frequently.

1. Start off a short distance away from your dog.

2. Say your dog's name followed by the command "Come!" in an enthusiastic voice. You'll usually be more successful if you walk or run away from him while you call. Dogs find it hard to resist chasing after a running person, especially their owner.

3. He should run towards you. NOTE: Dogs tend to tune us out if we talk to them all the time. Whether you're training or out for an off-lead walk, refrain from constantly chattering to your dog - no matter how much of a brilliant conversationalist you are! If you're quiet much of the time, he is more likely to pay attention when you call him. When he does, praise him.

4. Often, especially outdoors, a young dog will start running towards you but then get distracted and head off in another direction. Pre-empt this situation by praising your puppy and cheering him on when he starts to come to you and **before** he has a chance to get distracted. Your praise will keep him focused so that he'll be more likely to come all the way to you. If he stops or turns away, you can give him feedback by saying "Uh-uh!" or "Hey!" in a different tone of voice (displeased or unpleasantly surprised). When he looks at you again, smile, call him and praise him as he approaches you.

5. When your puppy comes to you, give him the treat BEFORE he sits down or he may think that the treat was earned for sitting, not coming to you.

6. Another method is to use two people. You hold the treats and let your dog sniff them while the accomplice holds on to the dog by his harness. When you are about 10 or 15 yards away, get your helper to let the dog go, and once he is running towards you, say "COME!" loudly and enthusiastically. When he reaches you, stop, bend down and make a fuss of him before giving a treat. Do this several times. The next step is to give the "COME" command just BEFORE get your helper to release the dog, and by doing this repetitively, the dog begins to associate the command with the action.

> **Tip** "Come" or a similar word is better than "Here" if you intend using the "Heel" command, as "Here" and "Heel" sound too similar.

Progress your dog's training in baby steps. If he's learned to come when called in your kitchen, you can't expect him to be able to do it straight away at the park or on the beach when surrounded by distractions. When you first use the recall this outdoors, make sure there's no one around to distract your dog. It's a good idea to consider using a long training lead - or to do the training within a safe, fenced area. Only when your dog has mastered the recall in a number of locations and in the face of various distractions can you expect him to come to you regularly.

Puppy Biting and Chewing

All puppies spend a great deal of time chewing, playing, and investigating objects. And it's natural for them to explore the world with their mouths and needle-sharp teeth. When puppies play with people, they often bite, chew, nip and mouthe on people's hands, limbs and clothing. Play biting is normal for puppies; they do it all the time with their littermates. They also bite moving targets with their sharp teeth; it's a great game.

But when they arrive in your home, they have to be taught that human skin is sensitive and body parts are not suitable biting material. Biting is not acceptable, not even from a puppy, and can be a real problem initially, especially if you have children. When your puppy bites you or the kids, he is playing and investigating; he is NOT being aggressive. Even though the breed has a reputation for being non-aggressive, a lively young Cavapoo can easily get carried away with energy and excitement. This is when puppy biting can develop into a problem if it isn't checked.

Make sure every time you have a play session, you have a soft toy nearby and when he starts to chew your hand or feet, clench your fingers (or toes!) to make it more difficult and distract him with a soft toy in your other hand. Keep the game interesting by moving the toy around or rolling it around in front of him. (He may be too young to fetch it back if you throw it). He may continue to chew you, but will eventually realise that the toy is far more interesting and lively than your boring hand.

If he becomes over-excited and too aggressive with the toy, if he growls a lot, stop playing with him and walk away. When you walk away, don't say anything or make eye or physical contact with your puppy. Simply ignore him, this is extremely effective and often works within a few days.

If your pup is more persistent and tries to bite your legs as you walk away, thinking this is another fantastic game, stand still and ignore him. If he still persists, say "No!" in a very stern voice, then praise him when he lets go. If you have to physically remove him from your trouser leg or shoe, leave him alone in the room for a while and ignore demands for your attention if he starts barking.

Although you might find it quite cute and funny if your puppy bites your fingers or toes, it should be discouraged at all costs. You don't want your Cavapoo doing this as an adolescent or adult, when he can inadvertently cause real injury.

Here are some tips to deal with puppy biting:

* Puppies growl and bite more when they are excited. Don't allow things to escalate, so remove your pup from the situation before he gets too excited by putting him in a crate or pen

* Don't put your hand or finger into your pup's mouth to nibble on; this promotes puppy biting

* Limit your children's play time with pup - and always supervise the sessions in the beginning. Teach them to gently play with and stroke your puppy, not to wind him up

- Don't let the kids (or adults) run round the house with the puppy chasing – this is an open invitation to nip at the ankles
- If your puppy does bite, remove him from the situation and people – never smack her

 Many Cavapoos are sensitive and another method that can be very successful is to make a sharp cry of "OUCH!" when your pup bites your hand – even when it doesn't hurt.

This has worked very well for us. Most pups will jump back in amazement, surprised to have hurt you. Divert your attention from your puppy to your hand. He will probably try to get your attention or lick you as a way of saying sorry. Praise him for stopping biting and continue with the game. If he bites you again, repeat the process. A sensitive dog should soon stop biting you.

You may also think about keeping the toys you use to play with your puppy separate from other toys. That way he will associate certain toys with having fun with you and will work harder to please you. Cavapoos are playful and you can use this to your advantage by teaching your dog how to play nicely with you and the toy and then by using play time as a reward for good behaviour.

As mentioned, puppies explore the world by putting things into their mouths. Other reasons for chewing is that it is a normal part of the teething process, and some adolescent and adult dogs chew because they are bored - usually due to lack of exercise and/or mental stimulation. If puppy chewing is a problem it is because your pup is chewing on something you don't want him to. So, the trick is to keep him, his mouth and sharp little teeth occupied with something he CAN chew on, such as a durable toy – see **Chapter 4. Bringing Puppy Home** for more information.

You might also consider freezing peanut butter and/or a liquid inside a Kong toy. Put the Kong into a mug, plug the small end with peanut butter and fill it with gravy before putting it into the freezer. (Check the peanut butter doesn't contain the sweetener xylitol as this can is harmful to dogs). Don't leave the Kong and your Cavapoo on your precious Oriental rug! This will keep your pup occupied for quite a long time. It is also worth considering giving the dog a frozen Kong or Lickimat when you leave the house if your dog suffers from separation anxiety. There are lots of doggie recipes for Kongs and other treats online.

Clicker Training

Clicker training is a method of training that uses a sound - a click - to tell an animal when she does something right. The clicker is a tiny plastic box held in the palm of your hand, with a metal tongue that you push quickly to make the sound. The clicker creates an efficient language between a human trainer and a trainee.

First, a trainer teaches a dog that every time she hears the clicking sound, she gets a treat. Once the dog understands that clicks are always followed by treats, the click becomes a powerful reward. When this happens, the trainer can use the click to mark the instant the animal performs the right behaviour. For example, if a trainer wants to teach a dog to sit, he'll click the instant her rump hits the floor and then deliver a tasty treat. With repetition, the dog learns that sitting earns rewards.

So, the 'click' takes on huge meaning. To the animal it means: "What I was doing the moment my trainer clicked, that's what he wants me to do." The clicker in animal training is like the winning buzzer on a game show that tells a contestant he's just won the money! Through the clicker, the trainer communicates precisely with the dog, and that speeds up training.

Although the clicker is ideal because it makes a unique, consistent sound, you do need a spare hand to hold it. For that reason, some trainers prefer to keep both hands free and instead use a one-syllable word like **"Yes!"** or **"Good!"** to mark the desired behaviour. In the steps below, you can substitute the word in place of the click to teach your pup what the sound means.

It's easy to introduce the clicker to your Cavapoo. Spend half an hour or so teaching her that the sound of the click means "Treat!" Here's how:

1. Sit and watch TV or read a book with your dog in the room. Have a container of (healthy) treats within reach.

2. Place one treat in your hand and the clicker in the other. (If your dog smells the treat and tries to get it by pawing, sniffing, mouthing or barking at you, just close your hand around the treat and wait until he gives up and leaves you alone).

3. Click once and immediately open your hand to give your dog the treat. Put another treat in your closed hand and resume watching TV or reading. Ignore your dog.

4. Several minutes later, click again and offer another treat.

5. Continue to repeat the click-and-treat combination at varying intervals, sometimes after one minute, sometimes after five minutes. Make sure you vary the time so that your dog doesn't know exactly when the next click is coming. Eventually, she'll start to turn toward you and look expectantly when she hears the click - which means she understands that the sound of the clicker means a treat is coming her way.

If your dog runs away when she hears the click, you can make the sound softer by putting it in your pocket or wrapping a towel around your hand that's holding the clicker. You can also try using a different sound, like the click of a retractable pen or the word "Yes!"

Clicker Training Basics

Once your dog understands the connection between the click and the treat, you're ready to start:

1. Click just once, right when your pup does what you want her to do. Think of it like pressing the shutter of a camera to take a picture of the behaviour.

2. Remember to follow every click with a treat. After you click, deliver the treat to your puppy's mouth as quickly as possible.

3. It's fine to switch between practising two or three behaviours within a session, but work on one command at a time. For example, say you're teaching your dog to sit, lie down and raise her paw. You can do 10 repetitions of sit and take a quick play break. Then do 10 repetitions of down and take another quick break. Then do 10 repetitions of stay, and so on. Keep training sessions short and stop before you or your dog gets tired of the game.

 When training, always set your dog up to succeed, not fail. If she has been struggling with a new command, end training sessions on a good note with something she CAN do.

Collar, Harness and Lead (Leash) Training

You have to train your dog to get used to a collar and/or harness and lead (leash), and then she has to learn to walk nicely beside you. Teaching these manners can be challenging because young Cavapoos are lively and don't necessarily want to walk at the same pace as you! All dogs will pull on a lead initially. This isn't because they want to show you who's boss, it's simply that they are excited to be outdoors and are forging ahead.

Many Cavapoo owners prefer to use a body harness instead. Harnesses work very well with Cavapoos; they take the pressure away from the dog's sensitive neck area and distribute it more evenly around the body. Many owners use harnesses, although the dogs may also have a collar with an ID tag. Harnesses with a chest ring for the lead can be effective for training. When your dog pulls, the harness turns her around.

Another option is to start your dog on a small lightweight collar and then change to a harness once she has learned some lead etiquette. Some dogs don't mind collars, some will try to fight them, while others will slump to the floor! You need to be patient and calm and proceed at a pace comfortable to her; don't fight your dog and don't force the collar on.

1. If you start your puppy off with a collar, you need a small, lightweight one - not one she is going to grow into. You can buy one with clips to start with, just put it on and clip it together, rather than fiddling with buckles, which can be scary when she's wearing a collar for the first time. Stick to the principle of positive reward-based training and give a treat or praise once the collar is on, not after you have taken it off. Then gradually increase the length of time you leave the collar on.

IMPORTANT: If you leave your dog in a crate, or leave her alone in the house, take off the collar. She is not used to it and it may get caught on something, causing panic or injury to your dog.

2. Put the collar on when there are other things that will occupy her, like when she is going outside to be with you, or in the home when you are interacting with her. Or put it on at mealtimes or when you are doing some basic training. Don't put the collar on too tight, you want her to forget it's there; you should be able to get two fingers underneath. Some pups may react as if you've hung a two-ton weight around their necks, while others will be more compliant. If yours scratches the collar, get her attention by encouraging her to follow you or play with a toy to forget the irritation.

3. Once your puppy is happy wearing the collar, introduce the lead. Many owners prefer an extending or retractable lead for their Cavapoo, but you might want to consider a fixed-length lead to start training her to walk close to you. Start off in the house or garden; don't try to go out and about straight away. Think of the lead as a safety device to stop her running off, not something to drag her around with. You want a dog that doesn't pull, so don't start by pulling her around; you don't want to get into a tug-of-war contest.

4. Attach the lead to the collar and give her a treat while you put it on. The minute it is attached, use the treats (instead of pulling on the lead) to lure her beside you, so that she gets used to walking with the collar and lead. As well as using treats you can also make good use of toys to do exactly the same thing - especially if your dog has a favourite. Walk around the house with the lead on and lure her forwards with the toy.

   It might feel a bit odd but it's a good way for your pup to develop a positive relationship with the collar and lead with the minimum of fuss. Act as though it's the most natural thing in the world for you to walk around the house with your dog on a lead – and just hope that the neighbours aren't watching! Some dogs react the moment you attach the lead and they feel some tension on it – a bit like when a horse is being broken in for the first time. Drop the lead and allow her to run round the house or yard, dragging it after her, but be careful she doesn't get tangled and hurt herself. Try to make her forget about it by playing or starting a short fun training routine with treats. Treats are a huge distraction for most young dogs. While she is concentrating on the new task, occasionally pick up the lead and call her to you. Do it gently and in an encouraging tone.

5. The most important thing is not to yank on the lead. If it gets tight, just lure her back beside you with a treat or a toy while walking. All you're doing is getting her to move around beside you. Remember to keep your hand down (the one holding the treat or toy) so your dog doesn't get the habit of jumping up at you. If you feel she is getting stressed when walking outside on a lead, try putting treats along the route you'll be taking to turn this into a rewarding game: good times are ahead... That way she learns to focus on what's ahead of her with curiosity and not fear.

Take collar and lead training slowly, give your pup time to process all this new information about the lead. Let her gain confidence in you, and then in the lead and herself. Some dogs can sit and decide not to move! If this happens, walk a few steps away, go down on one knee and encourage her to come to you using a treat, then walk off again.

For some pups, the collar and lead can be restricting and they will react with resistance. Some dogs are perfectly happy to walk alongside you off-lead, but behave differently when they have one on. Proceed in tiny steps if that is what your puppy is happy with, don't over face her, but stick at it if you are met with resistance. With training and patience, your puppy will learn to walk nicely on a lead; it is a question of when, not if.

Harnesses

These are very popular with owners of Cavapoos as they do not put any strain on the neck. There are several different options:

* **Front-clip or training harness** - this has a lead attachment in front of the harness at the centre of your dog's chest. Dog trainers often choose this type as it helps to discourage your dog from pulling on the lead by turning her around

* **Back-clip** – this is generally the easiest for most dogs to get used to and useful for small dogs with delicate throats that are easily irritated by collars. This type is for calm dogs or ones that have already been trained not to pull on the lead

* **Comfort wrap or step-in harness** - lay the harness on the ground, have your dog step in, pull the harness up and around her shoulders and then clip her in; simple!

* **Soft or vest harness** - typically made of mesh and comes in a range of colours and patterns. Some slip over the head and some can be stepped into

* **No-pull harness** - similar to a training harness, designed to help discourage your dog from pulling. The lead attachment ring is at the centre of the dog's chest and the harness tightens pressure if the dog pulls, encouraging him to stay closer to you. Some styles also tighten around the dog's legs

* **Auto or car harness** - these are designed for car travel and have an attachment that hooks into a seat belt

Pictured wearing a harness is Lotties Cavapoo Phoebe, courtesy of Nivien Speith.

When choosing a harness, decide what its primary purpose will be – is it instead of or in addition to a collar? Do you need one that will help to train your dog, or will a back-clip harness do the job? You want to make sure that it is a snug fit for your dog, and if it's a front clip, that it hangs high on your dog's chest. If it dangles too low, it can't help control forward momentum. Make sure the harness isn't too tight or too difficult to get on. It shouldn't rub under your dog's armpits or anywhere else. If possible, take your dog to try on a few options before buying one for the first time.

 If you've never used a harness before, it's easy to get tangled up while your pup is bouncing around, excited at the prospect of a walk. It's a good idea to have a few "dry runs" without the dog!

Lay the harness on the floor and familiarise yourself with it. Learn which bits the legs go through, which parts fit where and how it clicks together once the dog is in. If you can train your Cavapoo to step into the harness, then even better...!

Walking on a Lead

There are different methods, but we have found the following one to be successful for quick results. Initially, the lead should be kept fairly loose. Have a treat in your hand as you walk, it will encourage your dog to sniff the treat as she walks alongside. She should not pull ahead as she will want to remain near the treat.

Give her the command **"Walk"** or **"Heel"** and then proceed with the treat in your hand, keep giving her a treat every few steps initially, then gradually extend the time between treats. Eventually, you should be able to walk with your hand comfortably at your side, periodically (every minute or so) reaching into your pocket to grab a treat to reward your dog.

If your dog starts pulling ahead, first give her a warning, by saying "No" or "Steady" or a similar command. If she slows down, give her a treat. But if she continues to pull ahead so that your arm becomes fully extended, stop walking and ignore your dog. Wait for her to stop pulling and to look up at you. At this point reward her for good behaviour before carrying on your walk.

If your pup refuses to budge, DON'T drag her. This will ultimately achieve nothing as she will learn to resent the lead. Coax her along with praise and, if necessary, treats so that when she moves forward with you, it is because SHE wants to and not because she has been dragged by somebody 10 or 20 times bigger.

Be sure to quickly reward your dog any time she doesn't pull and walks with you with the lead slack. If you have a lively young pup who is dashing all over the place on the lead, try starting training when she is already a little tired, after a play or exercise session – but not exhausted.

Another method is what dog trainer Victoria Stillwell describes as the Reverse Direction Technique. When your dog pulls, say **"Let's Go!"** in an encouraging manner, then turn away from her and walk off in the other direction, without jerking on the lead. When she is following you and the lead is slack, turn back and continue on your original way.

It may take a few repetitions, but your words and body language will make it clear that pulling will not get your dog anywhere, whereas walking calmly by your side - or even slightly in front of you - on a loose lead will get her where she wants to go.

There is an excellent video (in front of her beautiful house!) which shows Victoria demonstrating this technique and highlights just how easy it is with a dog that's keen to please. It only lasts three minutes: https://positively.com/dog-behavior/basic-cues/loose-leash-walking

Breeders and Owners on Training

We asked breeders and owners how easy Cavapoos are to train and if they have any tips. This is what they said: "They love to be trained and enjoy all the attention and interaction that they receive. A pocket full of tiny treats always helps."

"Food is a huge driver for my two, they will do anything for liver, cheese or sausage! They are very quick learners - sometimes too clever for their own good! My advice is to do a little training every day and continue, even when they are older."

"Ours is incredibly treat-motivated. She will do anything for a little treat and learns extremely quickly when rewards are involved. We teach her the trick and reward her each time she successfully completes it. We weave in a few other tricks and come back to the new one to test her retention. We spend about 10 minutes a day reinforcing these commands with low-calorie treats. We continue to work on these in more and more distracting situations, but she learns best first in an environment where she can focus. She loves praise - but loves treats more!"

Our photo, courtesy of Laura Lambert, shows Dolly looking rather pleased with herself as she walks beautifully on the lead.

"As a puppy he was quick to learn. He is motivated by praise and treats."

"Harper went to puppy class all the way up to intermediate classes. She was the highest scoring puppy in the class for puppy training! She's highly motivated by treats, especially sausages and ham cut up into little chunks. I found her very easy to train and I loved it just as much as she did. My tips would be make sure that you squeeze plenty of training in when they are still young and have treats on hand."

"Carmen Rose is food-oriented and has been very easy to train. Recall was easy using high-value treats like liver, cheese or chicken. Domino is not very interested in treats, but she is totally ball-obsessed and this makes her easy to train as she will do anything for the chance to chase and retrieve her ball. She would retrieve her ball for hours on end if she could."

"We found ours difficult to train. She is very good on the lead. We walk her constantly on the lead and say STOP and she will, she will not come back for the recall if there are any distractions."

"Rodney and Mabel are motivated by food. They will do anything for a treat, which means they have been fairly easy to obedience train. Sometimes they will also do things for a favourite toy. We attend fun agility every week, which they love. The only tips I can give are: be consistent and make it fun."

"Cavapoos are extremely clever. Winston is very much food-orientated, but only when he wants to be. A ball is the highest in the pecking order, though. He has been very easy to train, and we find that if we don't keep his mind active throughout the day then he can become very mischievous. Consistency is key, and all members of the household need to be on the same page."

"We have only trained Ethel *(pictured)* to basic home obedience, but we found she was easy to train, treats work well as a reward. The level of fuss and attention you give the dog depends on the individual dog's temperament. Consistency of your voice, use of body language and command words are all very important.

"We recommend that anyone who doesn't have experience of puppy training attends a recognised training class - for the owner's benefit as well as their dog."

"The motivation was treats. He was very easy to train we took him to one-to-one training. Please socialise your puppy both with dogs and people and take them to training classes."

"I advise all my families to sign up to obedience classes as a must. Cavapoos are so easy to train at home too, as they love to please - but always for a treat each time."

"They just want to please. I took him to all kinds of classes and he mixed very well with the other puppies and then dogs. I think it's essential - even though you've owned other dogs before and think you can train a puppy yourself - going to classes really is the best way."

....

We strongly recommend that all new owners book their puppy or rescue dog on to a basic training course.

Your Cavapoo will really enjoy the experience and, as well as learning basic obedience, he or she will learn how to socialise with other dogs. It is also the best, least expensive way for owners to learn how to train their dog properly. Many local veterinary clinics now run puppy training classes.

Once you have mastered the basics, you can go on to learn more and win certificates on the Canine Good Citizen Dog Scheme

More details are at: www.thekennelclub.org.uk/training/good-citizen-dog-training-scheme in the UK

For the USA, AKC training clubs are listed here: http://webapps.akc.org/obedience-training-club/#/

GENERAL NOTE: If your puppy is in a hyperactive mood or extremely tired, he is not likely to be very receptive to training.

CREDIT: With thanks to the American Society for the Prevention of Cruelty to Animals for assistance with parts of this chapter. The ASPCA has a lot of good advice and training tips on its website at: **www.aspca.org**

Once you have a Cavapoo, the world's your oyster!

....

Therapy Cavapoo Changes Lives

By Denise Knightley

Denise Knightley's love affair with our canine companions goes back as far as she can remember. Here she tells of her journey from a dog-obsessed child walking the neighbour's pets to taking part in Agility and Obedience competitions with Rottweilers and a German Shepherd Dog before getting involved with therapy work, and how **her Cavapoo Carmen Rose is helping to enhance children's lives.**

....

I was a dog-crazy child living in a house with two budgies and a cat called Cindy. My earliest memories are of standing by our front gate every morning waiting for an elderly neighbour to walk past with his tricolour Shetland sheepdog (Sheltie) called Rob Roy. He looked like a miniature Lassie and I was totally besotted with him.

My parents were both from large working class families born and brought up in London during World War II and any animals kept at home were destined for the pot! From the age of seven or eight I would walk the neighbour's Golden Retriever imagining that he was mine. I went on to walk different breeds, including a gorgeous Old English Sheepdog, another Golden and a Dalmatian.

When my father became a highly successful businessman, he bought a large country house in 60 acres of woodland and decided that they should have a couple of dogs to provide extra security. After taking advice from the RSPCA, my parents narrowed their choice of breed down to Irish Wolfhound, Rottweiler or Standard Poodle, all of which look imposing and have a deep bark, but are intelligent and easy to train. They chose the Rottweiler. I couldn't believe they were actually getting a dog just as I was leaving for university... I did forgive them eventually! They subsequently got a second Rottie and we were all totally smitten with them. I took on their training when I was home and competed in Obedience Trials and Agility competitions.

Obedience and Agility

I finally got my own dog, Beau, a long-haired German Shepherd, at the age of 30. She was beautiful, extremely friendly and very clever and we enjoyed obedience and agility whenever we could. Both obedience and agility trials are great training for the handler and the dog. They help to build a close bond and trust and create responsible owners, and dogs who can safely be taken anywhere and really enjoy their active lives.

Agility is tremendous fun for both of you... but you must be able to laugh at yourself because you will spend a lot of time crawling on your hands and knees trying to encourage your willing, but confused, dog how to negotiate tunnels, seesaws and how to jump hurdles! Beau had a long and happy life until the age of 14 years.

We got a chocolate Labrador puppy, Truffle, *(pictured with Carmen Rose)* when Beau was about 10 years old The puppy seemed to rejuvenate her and they were the best of friends.

Truffle was totally motivated by food and this made her very easy to train. A typical

Labrador, she was friendly, keen to please and absolutely loved swimming. Luckily, we live very close to a canal so she was able to indulge her passion for swimming most days. Although I don't shoot game I took her to gundog classes and she proved to be a talented retriever of decoys, especially through water.

....

Pets as Therapy

In 2013 I reduced to a four-day week and decided to spend the free day doing some voluntary work to "give something back to the community." My vet suggested Truffle would be a perfect therapy dog and I loved the idea of spending a whole day with my dog helping people. I contacted the UK charity Pets as Therapy (PAT) and completed an application form.

The dogs and cats don't need any formal training, but they have to pass a comprehensive assessment. This includes a temperament test as well as reactions to unexpected noises and a willingness to be stroked and groomed and have their paws and faces touched as well. The dog mustn't be noisy, excitable, greedy or snatch at food and should remain by your side without demanding attention whilst you're carrying out a conversation. You need to keep your dog clean and well-groomed with short claws to avoid any unintentional scratches of delicate skin.

The whole process took several months before we were accepted as one of the charity's 5,000 volunteers. At this time PAT had just started Read2Dogs, a new initiative with the Kennel Club, and I was asked if I'd like to volunteer in schools instead of the more common visits to hospitals, hospices and care homes. This appealed to me, as I'm a university lecturer and feel very comfortable in an educational setting. Also, my parents had recently been diagnosed with dementia (Dad) and Parkinson's (Mum) and I felt that volunteering with young children would be uplifting.

Truffle and I worked once a week in a mainstream primary school and also volunteered to cover fundraising events, local shows and some one-off visits to care homes, universities and teacher development days if we had any free time.

Truffle was a great favourite at school; she opened the school fete and even made a guest appearance in the nativity play – as a donkey! Truffle loved her school visits as she got lots of fuss and quite a few extra treats too. I retired her from PAT when she reached 12 years old.

As Truffle was entering old age, our journey with Cavapoos began. Our daughter, Olivia, bought a puppy, Carmen Rose, in 2015. Unfortunately, at the tender age of five months, the pup was diagnosed with a severe luxating patella (grade 4+) and underwent major surgery to correct this and associated orthopaedic issues.

Our daughter was studying at university and unable to look after Carmen Rose properly during her eight-week convalescence, when she had to be mostly confined to a crate, so we had looked after her at our home. This is when we fell in love with her happy little personality.

We ended up keeping her permanently, and two years later bought another Cavapoo, Domino. This time we researched thoroughly and chose a breeder who health-tested the parent dogs for Poodle and Cavalier King Charles Spaniel issues such as PRA and MRD (eye diseases) to try to minimise the risk of buying another Cavapoo with health problems. Carmen Rose and Domino are thick as thieves and although Carmen Rose is not as agile as her best friend, they play together all day and often share a bed at night. *Pictured on the previous page having a bath together.*

I decided to learn how to groom as I was concerned that a groomer may accidentally cause further injury to Carmen's leg and, alongside my day job at the uni, I enrolled on a course at the local agricultural college. I studied Dog Grooming one day a week for two years and qualified at Levels 2 and 3. I now clip and style my girls and thoroughly enjoy it, knowing that they're not suffering any stress at a commercial groomer - and I'm saving a fortune too.

Carmen Rose is a very pretty little Cavapoo with a sunny personality and my local PAT co-ordinator asked me to have her assessed. The charity is particularly keen to have small dogs as they are easier to place on a chair or hospital bed to comfort someone.

Socialisation is very important. I take both of my Cavapoos into shops, pubs, cafés, on trains and anywhere I can really to get them used to different places. My beautician allows them to join me for manicures and pedicures too, and they just slumber quietly on my lap while I'm being pampered. My hairdresser is always upset if I show up without them now as all her other clients look forward to seeing them too. Acclimatising your dogs to a variety of different experiences, strange people and other dogs helps them to become more settled and confident and better therapy dogs.

Carmen Rose passed the PAT assessment with flying colours and showed an aptitude for working with young children, being totally unfazed by crowds of youngsters around her. We now attend a local primary school once a week to help children aged four to 11 years with their reading.

....

Enhancing Lives

Carmen Rose took her new role in her stride; I think I was more nervous than she was. We had to have an interview with the Headteacher before we started. He admitted on the phone that he preferred cats to dogs - but Carmen Rose soon won him over and he remains one of her biggest

fans. She gets very excited when she realises we're going into school and makes squeaky guinea pig noises until we get settled on our rug in the library!

Photo shows a young child reading to Carmen Rose and Denise (head blurred for legal reasons).

The reading is normally on a one-to-one basis, but some children read in small groups with us, and the reading aloud helps them to form friendships and gain confidence too.

Carmen Rose helps young children with a range of issues, such as ADHD, autism, Asperger's, dyslexia and phobias, such as children who have a fear of dogs. We have our regular readers every week and sometimes Carmen Rose is called on to comfort another child who may be having a bad day. She seems to know instinctively what to do and normally just curls up quietly in their lap enjoying being stroked and cuddled.

I've chosen to sit in the open-plan school library with Carmen Rose so all of the children and staff get to see her at some point as they walk around the school. Most call her by name or wave at her - she does wave back (with a little help from me!)

In school a lot of the children like to choose books that they think that Carmen Rose will enjoy, hence we hear lots of stories featuring dogs and cats and they like to show her the pictures too. Despite her best efforts, Carmen Rose sometimes falls asleep while she's listening to stories and if the children notice, I just say that she's closed her eyes to concentrate on the story. This works well ...until she starts snoring!

We worked with one young girl who was an elective mute. She chose not to speak in public, although we were told that she did speak at home. I was unsure how we could help, but agreed to work with her on a weekly basis. At first, she sat away from us on her own and silently held up her book to show the pictures.

After a few weeks I managed to get her to brush Carmen Rose and to undo her collar and lead and stroke her under her PAT uniform. After many months of this interaction, I was one day amazed to see her pick up Carmen Rose's ear and start to whisper to her. Incredibly she has now chosen to "speak" to Carmen Rose and they have a special bond. Hopefully, she'll one day choose to speak to me too.

Denise is pictured at home with Domino (left) and Carmen Rose.

We are currently working with a young boy who is absolutely terrified of dogs, to the extent that his parents are concerned he may run blindly into the road to get away from a passing dog. He had a traumatic experience in a local park when a man lost control of his dog and screamed at it when he thought that it was going to attack the boy and his family. Although nothing happened and nobody was harmed, the boy was frightened and he's convinced that he will be attacked by any dog.

Initially, he sat at the far end of the library and watched other children reading to Carmen Rose. His class teacher asked if he'd like to read to her too and he has got closer and closer until he will now sit right next to Carmen and allow her to sniff him and rest her paws on his leg.

He has told his Mum that he loves Carmen Rose because she's just like a living teddy bear - and also because she has no teeth. She does, of course, have a full set of teeth, but he has convinced himself that she hasn't, so at the moment we're not challenging that perception.

We have also volunteered at a local care home and we met some lovely older people who miss having a pet with them.

Carmen Rose is a great favourite amongst the residents and happily jumps up on their beds to say hi if they're unable to move around themselves. Some residents started to hide their biscuits and cake to feed Carmen Rose every week. I had to ask them to stop, as not only was CR getting fatter, but also the care home manager said they were having problems with ants in cupboards and drawers!

The Read2Dogs scheme is a regular commitment as most schools include the reading sessions in their curriculum and expect you to attend every week at the same time. Visits to care homes, events and hospitals, etc. can be less frequent and on different days.

I'm still working now but I envisage dropping down to two days a week in the near future and then I'd like to share both my Cavapoos through the PAT Read2Dogs scheme. I will soon put Domino forward to be assessed as a PAT dog too, as she has a very calm and gentle nature and I think she will also bring a lot of joy into people's lives.

I am constantly in awe of the connection between my dogs and the children and I'm so pleased that I fell into this role in life as it's hugely rewarding to see the difference that we make to children's lives.

....

The UK's Pets as Therapy website gives full details on volunteering and you can request an application pack online at: https://petsastherapy.org/join-us/join-pat-dog The criteria are: "All breeds of dog can become part of a PAT Team, they must have been with their owner for at least six months, be over nine months of age and be able to pass the temperament assessment. All pets must be fully vaccinated."

A PAT Spokesperson added: "The charity was started by Lesley Scott Ordish in 1983. We now have about 6,500 volunteers and we visit about 160,000 people every single week – nationwide including England, Wales, Scotland and Northern Ireland. We visit care and nursing homes, hospices, hospitals and day care centre as well as main stream schools and special needs schools on both Read2Dogs and therapy works.

"If you have a look at the website under About Us there is a lot of useful information there, and under FAQ there are a number of Fact Sheets which are helpful. On the Contacts page, go to PAT Team Support Area and click on Speakers note for more info"

In the USA there are many thousands of therapy dogs performing a wide variety of roles in the community. The AKC has a full list of over 100 recognised pet therapy groups online at: www.akc.org/sports/title-recognition-program/therapy-dog-program/therapy-dog-organizations or type "AKC Recognized Therapy Organizations" into Google.

....

11. Cavapoo Health

Health has a major impact on an animal's quality of life and should always be a consideration when choosing and raising a dog. The first step is to select a puppy from a breeder who produces Cavapoos that are sound in both body and temperament – and this involves health screening - and secondly, to play your part in keeping your dog healthy throughout his or her life.

NOTE: This chapter is intended to be used as a medical encyclopaedia to help you to identify potential health issues and act promptly in the best interests of your dog. Please don't read it thinking your Cavapoo will get lots of these ailments – he or she WILL NOT!

....

It is becoming increasingly evident that genetics can have a huge influence on a person's health and life expectancy – which is why so much time and money is currently being devoted to genetic research. A human is more likely to suffer from a hereditary illness if the gene - or genes - for that disorder is passed on from parents or grandparents. That person is said to have a 'predisposition' to the ailment if the gene(s) is in the family's bloodline. Well, the same is true of dogs – crossbreeds as well as pure breeds.

There is not a single breed without the potential for some genetic weakness. For example, German Shepherd Dogs are more prone to hip problems than many other breeds, and 30% of Dalmatians have problems with their hearing. If you get a German Shepherd or a Dalmatian, your dog will not automatically suffer from these issues, but if he or she comes from unscreened parents, the dog will statistically be more likely to have them than a dog from a breed with no history of the complaint.

In other words, 'bad' genes can be inherited along with good ones.

Many people make the mistake of thinking that if they get a Cavapoo, he or she will automatically be healthier than a pedigree (pure bred) dog because the gene pool is larger. **This is simply not true.**

It is true that an F1 Cavapoo comes from two totally different gene pools – one from Cavaliers and one from Poodles. This means that, compared with many purebreds, there is a bigger gene pool with no inbreeding and this is a good thing. However, a Poodle with defective genes bred to a Cavalier with defective genes will produce a Cavapoo puppy with health issues.

For example, if you breed a Poodle with Progressive Retinal Atrophy (PRA) to a Cavalier with PRA, the likelihood of the Cavapoo puppy being born with PRA is 100%. If the parents are both carriers, but don't actually have the eye disease themselves, the resulting Cavapoo puppies will have a 25% or being born with PRA, a 50% chance of carrying the disease and only a 25% chance of being completely free of it.

This is why getting a puppy from health-tested parents is so important – and it's not just PRA, there are other diseases a Cavapoo's parents should be tested for.

Just because a puppy's parents are registered with the Kennel Club in the UK or AKC in the USA and have pedigree certificates, it does not mean that they have passed any health tests.

A pedigree certificate's only guarantee is that the puppy's parents can be traced back several generations and the ancestors were all purebred Cavaliers or Poodles. Many pedigree (purebred) dogs have indeed passed health tests, but prospective buyers should always find out **exactly** what health screening the sire and dam (mother and father) have undergone. Ask to see original certificates - and what, if any, health guarantees the breeder is offering with the puppy.

NOTE: "Vet Checked" does NOT mean health tested.

What Responsible Breeders Test For

You may think that more than £2,000 or $2,000 is a lot to pay for a puppy from health-tested parents. But when you read just how much genetic testing good Cavapoo breeders carry out, you begin to realise some of the costs and research involved in producing a litter of puppies free from hereditary diseases. And in the long run, when your Cavapoo grows up to be healthy and pain-free and lives to a ripe old age, it will have been well worth the initial expense.

US breeder Laura Koch, of Petit Jean Puppies, says: "Our main focus is to produce the healthiest puppies possible, so we test for everything we can find to rule out genetic disease. We test our Cavaliers and Poodles with Embark Vet for 160 diseases and also offer color, coat furnishings and breed identity. We also get certification from the Orthopedic Foundation for Animals (OFA) by testing for patellas (knees), cardiac (heart) and eyes.

To me, the two main concerns with the Cavalier are heart problems and Degenerative Myelopathy (DM). DM is a recessive neurological condition where the older dog loses total control of its hind. It's very common, unfortunately, but it can be bred out with DNA-testing by the breeders. Since it is so prevalent in Cavies, we make sure that if they carry one allele of the disease, we make sure to breed to a Poodle that is Clear for DM, and this way it can't be passed on.

"Episodic Falling Syndrome is another Cavalier disease, but because the Poodle does not carry this, it will not be passed on."

This healthy, handsome chap is Luis, a larger F1 Cavapoo from a Miniature Poodle and a Cavalier, bred by Laura. Photo courtesy of Heather Darnell.

"Mitral Valve Disease (MVD) is the most fatal condition for Cavaliers. To rule out this disease, the Cavalier Health Organization recommends following your bloodlines for over five years and only breeding clear dogs. OFA exams and oscillation by specialist vets can give you Cardiac Certifications.

"Syringomyelia (SM) is a painful disease Cavies are prone to and the only way to rule this disease out is an MRI scan by a specialist. Some studies currently show measuring the dome of the skull is helpful to determine the possibility. A wide flat skull is less likely to have SM as compared to a domed skull.

"Eyes should be examined by a veterinary ophthalmologist once a year to rule out eye issues such as PRA, Entropion, Ectropion, Cataracts and others. Since the Poodle can carry these same problems, this is very important.

"We also have our Cavaliers' hearts checked annually in case of any change. The OFA does not require this for certification; we just feel they need to be monitored since the breed is so prone to heart disease.

"The Poodle's main concern is Luxating Patellas (loose knees) and Progressive Retinal Atrophy (PRA) which is an eye condition that can bring on early onset of problems such as juvenile cataracts. Another concern similar to the Cavalier is Degenerative Myelopathy, so it is very important to test both parents for this.

"Luxating Patellas is a small breed fault that should not be bred and should be found in only pet quality dogs, not breeding prospects. Von Willebrand's disease (VWD) is a bleeding disorder which should also be ruled out with DNA testing."

UK breeder Charlotte Purkiss, of Lotties Cavapoos, says: "On the Poodle side, Lenny is our stud dog. We don't own him, but have known the trusted owner for many years. He is a Kennel Club red Toy Poodle with a kind, gentle and sweet nature. He is extensively DNA-health tested as follows: DNA CLEAR – Neonatal Encephalopathy, DNA CLEAR – Von Willebrand's type 1, DNA CLEAR – Degenerative Myelopathy, DNA CLEAR – PRA, DNA CLEAR – RCD4 PRA (LOPRA – late onset PRA).

"Lenny's parents' mating COI (Co-efficiency Of Inbreeding) score is wonderfully low and that's what I look for when finding a good stud dog, as this shows his parents were a perfect match for mating.

"Make sure the breeder provides you with all the health testing paperwork. On the Cavalier side, this should include certificates for Dry Eye/Curly Coat and Episodic Falling Syndrome. The Cavalier should also have up-to-date annual heart score done by a professional cardiologist and an eye test by an eye specialist. These both need to be carried out yearly right before dam comes into season and if either tests fail, the dog be taken off the breeding programme.

"Copies of all the health certificates are included in puppies' Going Home folders, and shown at the four- week litter viewings. Also, my puppies are vaccinated and a Health Check certificate is issued by my vet at eight weeks old. Do check both documents are not fake, check the vet's signature matches on the vaccination card and health certificate."

If you have already got your dog, don't worry! There is plenty of advice in this book on how to take good care of your dog. Feeding a quality food, monitoring your dog's weight, regular grooming and check-overs, plenty of exercise, socialisation and stimulation will all help to keep him or her in tiptop condition. Good, responsible owners can certainly help to extend the life of their Cavapoo.

....

Cavapoo Insurance

Insurance is another point to consider for a new puppy or adult dog. The best time to get pet insurance is BEFORE you bring your Cavapoo home and before any health issues develop. Don't wait until you need to seek veterinary help - bite the bullet and take out annual insurance.

If you can afford it, take out life cover. This may be more expensive, but will cover your dog throughout his or her lifetime - including for chronic (recurring and/or long term) ailments, such as eye, heart or joint problems, ear infections and cancer.

Insuring a healthy puppy or adult dog is the only sure-fire way to ensure vets' bills are covered before anything unforeseen happens - and you'd be a rare owner if you didn't use your policy at least once during your dog's lifetime. According to the UK's Bought By Many, monthly cover for a healthy nine-week-old Cavapoo puppy varies from around £20 to £30, depending on where you live, how much excess you are willing to pay and the amount of total vets' bills covered per year. In the UK, Bought By Many offers policies from insurers More Than at: https://boughtbymany.com/offers/cavapoo-pet-insurance They get groups of single breed owners together, so you have to join the Cavapoo Group, but it claims you'll get a 10% saving on normal insurance. We are not on commission - just trying to save you some money! There are numerous companies out there offering pet insurance. Read the small print and the amount of excess; a cheap policy may not always be the best long-term decision.

I ran a few examples for US pet insurance on a nine-week-old Cavapoo pup and came back with quotes from $30 to $41, depending on location, amount of coverage in dollars and deductible. With advances in veterinary science, there is so much more vets can do to help an ailing dog - but at a cost. Surgical procedures can rack up bills of thousands of pounds or dollars.

According to www.PetInsuranceQuotes.com these are some treatment costs: Mitral Valve Disease $15,000-$20,000, Heart Murmur $100-$20,000, Progressive Retinal Atrophy (PRA) $2,000-$3,000 per eye, Luxating Patella $1,500-$3,000, and Epilepsy $200-$15,000. ($1.30 = approximately £1 at the time of writing).

PetInsuranceQuotes rates insurance companies based on coverage, cost, customer satisfaction and the company itself and came up with the top eight: 1.Healthy Paws, 2.Embrace, 3.Trupanion, 4.ASPCA, 5.Petplan, 6.Nationwide, 7.PetsBest, 8.Figo.

Of course if you make a claim, your monthly premium will increase, but if you have a decent insurance policy BEFORE a recurring health problem starts, your dog should continue to be covered if the ailment returns. You'll have to decide whether the insurance is worth the money. On the plus side, you'll have peace of mind if your beloved Cavapoo falls ill and you'll know just how much to fork out every month.

Another point to consider is that dogs are at increasing risk of theft by criminals, including organised gangs. With the purchase price of puppies rising, dognapping has shot up. More than 1,900 dogs were stolen in the UK in 2017. Some 49% of dogs are snatched from owners' gardens and 13% from people's homes. Check that theft is included on the policy. Although nothing can ever replace your favourite companion, good insurance will ensure you are not out of pocket.

....

Three Health Tips

1. **Buy a well-bred puppy** - A responsible breeder selects their stock based on:

   * General health and DNA testing of the parents

   * Conformation (physical structure)

   * Temperament

   Although well-bred puppies are not cheap, believe it or not, committed Cavapoo breeders are not doing it for the money, often incurring high bills for health screening, stud fees, veterinary costs, specialised food, etc. The main concern of a good breeder is to produce healthy, handsome puppies with good temperaments that are "fit for function".

Better to spend time beforehand choosing a good puppy than to spend a great deal of time and money later when your wonderful pet bought from an online advert or pet shop develops health problems due to poor breeding, not to mention the heartache that causes. **Chapter 4. Bringing Puppy Home** has detailed information on how to find him or her and the questions to ask.

- ❉ Don't buy from a pet shop - no reputable breeder allows her pups to end up in pet shops

- ❉ Don't buy a puppy from a small ad on a general website

- ❉ Don't buy a pup or adult dog unseen with a credit card - you are storing up trouble and expense for yourself. (If you have selected a reputable breeder located many states away in the USA and can't travel to see the puppy, make sure you ask lots of questions)

2. **Get pet insurance as soon as you get your dog -** Don't wait until your dog has a health issue and needs to see a vet. Most insurers will exclude all pre-existing conditions on their policies. When choosing insurance, check the small print to make sure that all conditions are covered and that if the problem is recurring, it will continue to be covered year after year. When working out costs, factor in the annual or monthly pet insurance fees and trips to a vet for check-ups, annual vaccinations, etc.

   Some breeders provide free insurance for the first few weeks in their Puppy Pack - ask yours if this is the case.

3. **Find a good vet -** Ask around your pet-owning friends, rather than just going to the first one you find. A vet that knows your dog from his or her puppy vaccinations and then right through their life is more likely to understand your dog and diagnose quickly and correctly when something is wrong. If you visit a big veterinary practice, ask for the vet by name when you make an appointment.

We all want our dogs to be healthy - so how can you tell if yours is? Well, here are some positive things to look for in a healthy Cavapoo:

....

Signs of a Healthy Cavapoo

1. **Eyes -** A Cavapoo's eyes should not be too prominent or too close together. They should be round in shape and dark brown with very dark rims. Paleness around the eyeball (conjunctiva) could be a sign of underlying problems. A red swelling in the corner of one or both eyes could be cherry eye. Sometimes the dog's third eyelid (the nictating membrane) is visible at the eye's inside corner - this is normal. There should be no thick, green or yellow discharge from the eyes. A cloudy eye could be a sign of cataracts.

2. **Nose –** A dog's nose is an indicator of health symptoms. Normal nose colour is black, although some Cavapoo pups are born with pink patches that usually turn black during the first year, sometimes called a 'butterfly nose'. Regardless of colour, the nose should be moist and cold to the touch as well as free from clear, watery secretions.

   Any yellow, green or foul smelling discharge is not normal - in younger dogs this can be a sign of canine distemper. A pink nose or 'snow nose' may appear in winter due to a lack of Vitamin D, but the nose usually returns to a darker colour during summer – it happens more often with lighter coloured Cavapoos. A 'Dudley nose' or 'putty nose' is one where the nose, the area around the eyes and the feet lack any pigment from birth to old age and appear pink. Some dogs' noses turn pinkish with age; this is because their bodies are producing less pigment and is not a cause for concern. Avoid getting a Cavapoo puppy with small, pinched nostrils, as these may cause breathing difficulties.

Photo of Domino's black, shiny nose courtesy of Denise Knightley.

3. **Ears** – If you are choosing a puppy, gently clap your hands behind the pup (not so loud as to frighten him) to see if he reacts. If not, this may be a sign of deafness. Also, ear infections – sometimes known as "otitis" - can be a problem with Cavapoos and other breeds with floppy, hairy ears. A pricked-up ear allows air to circulate, while a folded ear flap creates a warm, moist haven for mini horrors such as bacteria and mites.

   The ear flap can also trap dirt and dust and should be inspected during your regular grooming routine. An unpleasant smell, redness or inflammation are all signs of infection. Some wax inside the ear – usually brown or yellowy - is normal; excessive wax or crusty wax is not. Tell-tale signs of an infection are scratching the ears, rubbing them on the floor or furniture, or shaking the head a lot, often accompanied by an unpleasant smell.

4. **Mouth** – Gums should be a healthy pink or black colour, or a mixture. A change in colour can be an indicator of a health issue. Paleness or whiteness can be a sign of anaemia or lack of oxygen due to heart or breathing problems (this is hard to tell with black gums). Blue gums or tongue are a sign that a dog is not breathing properly. Red, inflamed gums can be a sign of gingivitis or other tooth disease. Again, your dog's breath should smell OK. Young dogs will have sparkling white teeth, whereas older dogs will have darker teeth, but they should not have any hard white, yellow, green or brown bits.

5. **Coat and Skin** – These are easy-to-monitor indicators of a healthy dog. Any dandruff, bald spots, a dull lifeless coat, a discoloured or oily coat, or one that loses excessive hair, can all be signs that something is amiss. Skin should be smooth without redness. If a puppy or adult dog is scratching, licking or biting himself a lot, he may have a condition that needs addressing before he makes it worse. Open sores, scales, scabs, red patches or growths can be a sign of a problem. Signs of fleas, ticks and other external parasites should be treated immediately. Check there are no small black specks, which may be fleas, on the coat or bedding.

6. **Weight** – A general rule of thumb is that your dog's stomach should be above the bottom of his rib cage when standing, and you should be able to feel his ribs beneath his coat without too much effort. If the stomach is level or hangs below, your dog is overweight - or may have a pot belly, which can also be a symptom of other conditions.

7. **Temperature** – The normal temperature of a dog is 101°F to 102.5°F. (A human's is 98.6°F). Excited or exercising dogs may run a slightly higher temperature. Anything above 103°F or below 100°F should be checked out. The exceptions are female dogs about to give birth that will often have a temperature of 99°F. If you take your dog's temperature, make sure he or she is relaxed and **always** use a purpose-made canine thermometer.

8. **Stools** - Poo, poop, business, faeces - call it what you will - it's the stuff that comes out of the less appealing end of your Cavapoo on a daily basis! It should be firm and brown, not runny, with no signs of worms or parasites. Watery stools or a dog not eliminating regularly are both signs of an upset stomach or other ailments. If it continues for a couple of days, consult your vet. If puppies have diarrhoea they need checking out much quicker as they can quickly dehydrate.

9. **Energy** – Cavapoos are lively, engaged dogs. Yours should have good amounts of energy with fluid and pain-free movements. Lack of energy or lethargy – if it is not the dog's normal character – could be a sign of an underlying problem.

10. **Smell** – If there is a musty, 'off' or generally unpleasant smell coming from your Cavapoo's body, it could be a sign of a yeast infection. There can be a number of reasons for this; often the ears require attention or it can sometimes be an allergy to a certain food. Another not uncommon cause is that one of the anal glands has become blocked and needs expressing, or squeezing - a job best left to the vet or groomer unless you know what you are doing! Whatever the cause, you need to get to the root of the problem as soon as possible before it develops into something more serious.

11. **Attitude** – A generally positive attitude is a sign of good health. Cavapoos are playful, so symptoms of illness may include one or all of the following: a general lack of interest in his or her surroundings, tail not wagging, lethargy, not eating food and sleeping a lot (more than normal). The important thing is to look out for any behaviour that is out of the ordinary for your individual dog.

So now you know some of the signs of a healthy dog – what are the signs of an unhealthy one? There are many different symptoms that can indicate your canine companion isn't feeling great. If you don't yet know your dog, his habits, temperament and behaviour patterns, then spend some time getting acquainted with them.

What are his normal character and temperament? Lively or calm, playful or serious, a joker or an introvert, bold or nervous, happy to be left alone or loves to be with people, a keen appetite or a fussy eater? How often does he empty his bowels, does he ever vomit? (Dogs will often eat grass to make themselves sick, this is perfectly normal and a natural way of cleansing the digestive system).

You may think your Cavapoo can't talk, **but he can!** If you really know your dog, his character and habits, then he CAN tell you when he's not well. He does this by changing his patterns. Some symptoms are physical, some emotional and others are behavioural. It's important for you to be able to recognise these changes as soon as possible. Early treatment can be the key to keeping a simple problem from snowballing into something more serious.

If you think your dog is unwell, it is useful to keep an accurate and detailed account of his symptoms to give to the vet, perhaps even take a video on your mobile phone. This will help the vet to correctly diagnose and effectively treat your dog.

....

Four Vital Signs of Illness

1. **Temperature -** A new-born puppy has a temperature of 94-97°F. This reaches the normal adult body temperature of 101°F at about four weeks old. Anything between 100°F and 102.5°F is regarded as normal for an adult. The temperature is normally taken via the rectum. If you do this, be very careful. It's easier if you get someone to hold your dog while you do this. Digital thermometers are a good choice, but **only use one specifically made for rectal use,** as normal glass thermometers can easily break off in the rectum.

Ear thermometers are available *(pictured)* from Amazon and Walmart, among others, making the task much easier, although they can be expensive and don't suit all dogs' ears. Remember that exercise or excitement can cause the temperature to rise by 2°F to 3°F when your dog is actually in good health, so wait until he is relaxed before taking his temperature. If it is above or below the norms and he seems off-colour, give your vet a call.

2. **Respiratory Rate** - Another symptom of canine illness is a change in breathing patterns. This varies a lot depending on the size and weight of the dog. An adult dog will have a respiratory rate of 15-25 breaths per minute when resting. You can easily check this by counting your dog's breaths for a minute with a stopwatch handy. Don't do this if he is panting; it doesn't count.

3. **Heart Rate** - You can feel your dog's heartbeat by placing your hand on his lower ribcage – just behind the elbow. Don't be alarmed if the heartbeat seems irregular compared to that of a human; it IS irregular in some dogs. Your Cavapoo will probably love the attention, so it should be quite easy to check his heartbeat. Just lay him on his side and bend his left front leg at the elbow, bring the elbow in to his chest and place your fingers on this area and count the beats.

    * Tiny dogs have a heartbeat of up to 160 or 180 beats per minute

    * Small to medium dogs have a normal rate of 90 to 140 beats per minute. (A Cavapoo's heartbeat should be between 70 and 120 beats per minute)

    * Dogs weighing more than 30lb have a heart rate of 60 to 120 beats per minute; the larger the dog, the slower the normal heart rate

    * A young puppy has a heartbeat of around 220 beats per minute

    * An older dog has a slower heartbeat

4. **Behaviour Changes** - Classic symptoms of illness are any inexplicable behaviour changes. If there has NOT been a change in the household atmosphere, such as another new pet, a new baby, moving home, the absence of a family member or the loss of another dog, then the following symptoms may well be a sign that all is not well:

    * Depression

    * Anxiety and/or trembling

    * Falling or stumbling

    * Loss of appetite

    * Walking in circles

    * Being more vocal - grunting, whining and/or whimpering

    * Aggression

    * Tiredness - sleeping more than normal and/or not wanting to exercise

    * Abnormal posture

Your dog may normally show some of these signs, but if any of them appear for the first time or worse than usual, you need to keep him under close watch for a few hours or even days. Quite often he will return to normal of his own accord. Like humans, dogs have off-days too. If he is showing any of the above symptoms, then don't over-exercise him, and avoid stressful situations and hot or cold places. Make sure he has access to clean water. There are many other signals of ill health, but these are four of the most important. Keep a record for your vet, if your dog does need professional medical attention, most vets will want to know:

WHEN the symptoms first appeared in your dog

WHETHER they are getting better or worse, and

HOW FREQUENT the symptoms are. Are they intermittent, continuous or increasing?

....

Eyes

According to Cavalierhealth.org: "A 2008 study of Cavaliers conducted by the Canine Eye Registration Foundation showed that an average of 28% of all CKCSs evaluated had eye problems."

There is a range of eye conditions which can affect Cavaliers and Poodles - and therefore Cavapoos. Many of them can be carefully managed with medication and extra care from the owner. All breeding dogs should be examined annually by certified veterinary ophthalmologists. Ask to see the parents' up-to-date certificates if you are buying a Cavapoo puppy.

Progressive Retinal Atrophy (PRA)

PRA is the name for several progressive diseases that lead to blindness. First recognised at the beginning of the 20th century in Gordon Setters, this inherited condition has been documented in over 100 breeds, including both Cavaliers and Poodles, which is why PRA-testing of both Cavapoo parents is important.

PRA can develop any time from as early as one year old to middle age. PRA causes cells in the retina at the back of the eye to degenerate and die, even though the cells seem to develop normally early in life. A dog's rod cells operate in low light levels and are the first to lose normal function, and so the first sign of PRA is night blindness. Then the cone cells gradually lose their normal function in full light situations.

As yet there is no treatment and most affected dogs will eventually go blind. However, dogs do not rely on sight as much as humans. PRA develops slowly, allowing the dog to gradually adjust to life without sight, when the other senses, such as hearing and smell, will be heightened.

Our photo shows the healthy eyes of a young Cavapoo.

If your dog has PRA, you may first notice that he lacks confidence in low light; he is perhaps reluctant to go down stairs or along a dark hallway. If you look closely into his eyes, you may see the pupils dilating (becoming bigger) and/or the reflection of greenish light from the back of his eyes. As the condition worsens, he might then start bumping into things, first at night and then in the daytime too. The condition is not painful and the eyes often appear normal - without redness, tearing or squinting. The lenses may become opaque or cloudy in some dogs.

Retinal Dysplasia

This is an inherited disease which affects some Spaniels in which the cells and layer of retinal tissue at the back of the eye do not develop properly. One or both eyes may be affected. It can be detected by a vet using an ophthalmoscope when the puppy is six weeks old or even younger. Most cases of retinal dysplasia do get worse after puppyhood.

Retinal Dysplasia occurs when the two layers of the retina do not form together, causing folds. The disorder causes small blind spots which are probably not even noticed by the dog. However, the more serious geographic dysplasia may lead to large blanks in the visual field, and Cavapoos with retinal detachments are completely blind. Severely affected puppies may have symptoms such as a reluctance to walk into dark areas, bumping into things and obvious sight problems. There is sadly no treatment for the condition.

Juvenile Cataracts

The Cavalier King Charles Spaniel can develop one of two forms of hereditary cataracts. The most common is Juvenile Hereditary Cataract (JHC), sometimes also referred to as Early Onset Hereditary Cataract (EHC). It may be seen as early as eight weeks old or as late as six months old, when owners might notice small white flecks in their dog's eye or eyes - both eyes will develop the disease, but it may be at different rates.

The purpose of the transparent lens is to focus the rays of light to form an image on the retina. A cataract occurs when the lens becomes cloudy. Less light enters the eye, images become blurry and the dog's sight diminishes as the cataract becomes larger. The mutated gene has been identified by scientists as the HSF4, and the DNA test, called 'Juvenile Hereditary Cataract HC-HSF4' (HSF4 in the USA) is available both in the UK and USA. The gene is recessive, which means that both parents have to carry it for the puppy to inherit the disease.

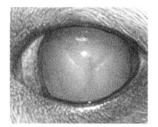 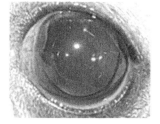

Left: eye with cataracts. Right: same eye with artificial lens

Unfortunately, most untreated dogs with JHC are completely blind by two to four years old. The good news is that surgery is often an (expensive) option in severe cases, often involving lens replacement, which is 90% successful. Eye drops have also been shown to be effective in improving vision in some cases.

Very occasionally, puppies born with congenital cataracts can sometimes improve as they mature. That's because the lens inside the puppy's eye grows along with the dog. When the area of cloudiness on the lens remains the same size, by the time the puppy becomes an adult, the affected portion of the lens is relatively small.

By adulthood, some dogs born with cataracts are able to compensate and see 'around' the cloudiness. The other type of hereditary cataracts affects dogs later in life, up to the age of around seven years.

Dry Eye (Keratoconjunctivitis sicca)

Keratoconjunctivitis sicca is the technical term for a fairly common condition known as Dry Eye which can affect any breed of dog. KCS is caused by not enough tears being produced. With insufficient tears, a dog's eyes can become irritated and the conjunctiva appears red. It's estimated that as many as one in five dogs can suffer from Dry Eye at one time or another in their lives.

NOTE: Dry Eye Curly Coat (congenital Keratoconjunctivitis sicca and Ichthyosiform Dermatosis) is a rarer but very much more severe syndrome affecting Cavaliers. It is a combination of extreme Dry Eye and a congenital skin condition called "Curly Coat" or "Rough Coat".

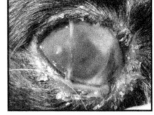

Dry Eye causes a dog to blink a lot, the eye or eyes typically develop a thick, yellowy discharge, *pictured,* and the cornea develops a film. Infections are common as tears also have anti-bacterial and cleansing properties, and inadequate lubrication allows dust, pollen and other debris to accumulate. The nerves of these glands may also become damaged.

The most common cause is an immune disease that damages the tear glands. Dry eye may also be caused by injuries to the tear glands, eye infections, disease such as distemper or reactions to drugs. Left untreated, the dog will suffer painful and chronic eye infections, and repeated irritation of the cornea results in severe scarring, and ulcers may develop which can lead to blindness.

Early treatment is essential to save the cornea and usually involves drugs: cyclosporine, ophthalmic ointment or drops. In some cases, another eye preparation – Tacrolimus - is also used and may be effective when cyclosporine is not. Sometimes artificial tear solutions are also prescribed.

Treating Dry Eye involves commitment from the owner. Gently cleaning the eyes several times a day with a warm, wet cloth helps a dog feel better and may also help stimulate tear production. In very severe and rare cases, an operation can be performed to transplant a salivary duct into the upper eyelid, causing saliva to drain into and lubricate the eye.

Eyelash Disorders

Distichiasis, trichiasis and **ectopic cilia** are canine eyelash disorders that can affect any breed. They are included here to help you recognise the signs. **Distichiasis** is an eyelash that grows from an abnormal spot on the eyelid, **trichiasis** is ingrowing eyelashes and **ectopic cilia** are single or multiple hairs that grow through the inside of the eyelid ('cilia' are eyelashes).

With distichiasis, *pictured below -* also called distichia, small eyelashes abnormally grow on the inner surface or the very edge of the eyelid, and both upper and lower eyelids may be affected. The affected eye becomes red, inflamed, and may develop a discharge. The dog will typically squint or blink a lot, just like a human with a hair or other foreign matter in the eye. The dog can make matters worse by rubbing the affected eye against furniture, other objects or the carpet. In severe cases, the cornea can become ulcerated and it looks blue. If left, the condition usually worsens and severe ulcerations and infections develop, which can lead to blindness.

Treatment usually involves electro- or cryo-epilation where a needle is inserted into the hair follicle emitting an ultra-fast electric current that produces heat to destroy the stem cells responsible for hair growth. This procedure may need to be repeated after several months because all of the abnormal hairs may not have developed at the time of the first treatment - although this is not common with dogs older than three years.

Sometimes surgery may be required and here the lid is split to remove the areas where the abnormal hairs grow. Both treatments require anaesthesia and usually result in a full recovery. After surgery, the eyelids are swollen for several days and the eyelid margins turn pink. Usually they return to their normal colour within four months. Antibiotic eye drops are often used following surgery to prevent infections. All three conditions are straightforward to diagnose.

Entropion

This is a condition in which the edge of the lower eyelid rolls inward, causing the dog's fur to rub the surface of the eyeball, or cornea. In rare cases the upper lid can also be affected, and one or both eyes may be involved. This painful condition is thought to be hereditary and is more commonly found in dog breeds with a wrinkled face, like the Bulldog.

The affected dog will scratch at the painful eye with his paws and this can lead to further injury. If your dog is to suffer from Entropion, he will usually show signs at or before his first birthday. You will notice that his eyes are red and inflamed and they will produce tears. He will probably squint. The tears typically start off clear and can progress to a thick yellow or green mucus.

If the Entropion causes Corneal Ulcers, you might also notice a milky-white colour develop. This is caused by increased fluid which affects the clarity of the cornea. For the poor dog, the irritation is constant. It's important to get your dog to the vet as soon as you suspect Entropion, before the cornea gets scratched. The condition can cause scarring around the eyes or other issues which can jeopardise a dog's vision if left untreated. A vet will make the diagnosis after a painless and relatively simple inspection, but they will have to rule out other issues, such as allergies, which might also be making your dog's eyes red and itchy.

In young dogs, some vets may delay surgery and treat the condition with medication until the dog's face is fully formed to avoid having to repeat the procedure at a later date. In mild cases, the vet may successfully prescribe eye drops, ointment or other medication. However, the most common treatment for more severe cases is a fairly straightforward surgical procedure to pin back the lower eyelid. Discuss the severity of the condition and all possible options with your vet before proceeding to surgery.

The Heart

Just as with humans, heart problems are fairly common among the canine population in general. However, **Mitral Valve Disease (MVD)** is the biggest killer of Cavalier King Charles Spaniels.

While MVD affects about 10% of older dogs of other breeds, it affects a big percentage of Cavaliers - and at an earlier age. One study suggests that half of all Cavaliers have a heart murmur (usually the first indication of MVD) by the age of five and nearly 100% have one by 10 years old. The Kennel Club says that it "affects more than 40% of the breed in the UK alone."

Of course, the best advice is to get a Cavapoo puppy whose Cavalier parent has tested Clear for heart issues. But if you already have your dog, don't worry, there is plenty you can do to prolong his or her life. A heart murmur does NOT mean that your dog will die of a heart attack – one of our

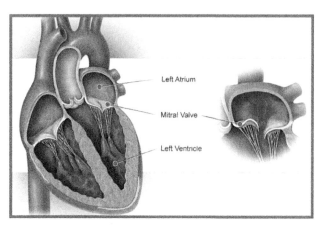

Left Atrium

Mitral Valve

Left Ventricle

dogs had a murmur for six or seven years and died of old age at 13. In fact, dogs don't have sudden heart attacks like humans, they experience a gradual onset of symptoms.

The heart muscle is a pump that moves blood through the four chambers using involuntary contractions. Blood is pumped around the body via a one-way system. The valves between the chambers form a tight seal that prevent the blood from flowing backwards into the chamber it has just come from; so the blood is always flowing forwards.

When the valves degenerate over time, they become thickened and deformed, losing their tight seal and causing some blood to seep backwards. When the valve between the left atrium and left ventricle – i.e. the mitral valve - no longer forms a tight seal, blood moves back into the left atrium. This means the heart has to work harder to pump the volume of blood the body needs for normal functions.

Symptoms

- Heart murmur
- Tiredness
- Decreased activity levels
- Restlessness, pacing around instead of settling down to sleep
- Intermittent coughing, especially during exertion or excitement. This tends to occur at night, sometimes about two hours after the dog goes to bed or when he wakes up. This coughing is an attempt to clear fluid in the lungs and is often the first clinical sign of MVD

If the condition worsens, other symptoms may appear:

- Shallow, rapid breathing
- Laboured, harsh-sounding breaths
- A panicky or unfocussed look as the dog struggles for breath
- Fainting (syncope)
- Abdominal swelling (due to fluid)
- Noticeable loss of weight
- Lack of appetite
- Paleness around the gums and eyes

If your dog has some of these symptoms, the vet may suspect a heart problem, so ask to be referred to a cardiologist. Further tests may include listening to the heart, chest X-rays, blood tests, electrocardiogram (a record of your dog's heartbeat) or an echocardiogram (ultrasound of the heart). A cardiologist will be familiar with the condition and the wide range of medications and other available options - and when and how to adjust them to best suit your dog.

Treatment

If the heart problem is due to valve disease or an enlarged heart (dilated cardiomyopathy - DCM), the condition cannot be reversed. However, the vast majority of affected dogs don't require any treatment at all until they show symptoms, and then they generally do well on medication. Only in very severe cases do dogs die from the disease. The only way to prevent the disease is to remove affected dogs from the breeding pool.

Treatment focuses on managing the symptoms with various medications. Diuretics may be prescribed to reduce fluid around the lungs and coughing – these will make your dog pee a lot. A special low salt diet may also be prescribed, as sodium (found in salt) determines the amount of water in the blood. The amount of exercise the dog has will have to be managed; it could be controlled exercise or complete rest. The treatment and medication may change as the condition develops. There is some evidence that vitamins and other supplements may be beneficial, discuss this with your vet or cardiologist. It is ESSENTIAL that the dog does not become overweight, as this places increased stress on the heart.

The prognosis (outlook) for dogs with heart problems depends on the cause and severity, as well as their response to treatment. Once diagnosed, many dogs can live a long, comfortable life with the right medication and regular check-ups.

The MDV Breeding Protocol is a set of guidelines introduced with the aim of eliminating, or greatly reducing, this hereditary disease. It was introduced following extensive studies by scientists in Europe and the USA. They concluded that the disease can be decreased and the age of onset

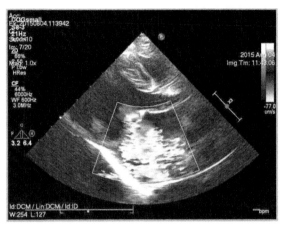

delayed by only breeding Cavapoos aged over 2.5 years, that have hearts free from MVD murmurs, and have parents whose hearts were MVD murmur-free at the age of five years. No Cavaliers which have murmurs before the age of five years should be bred. *Photo shows a Doppler scan.*

This Protocol is the gold standard for breeders and, while it is compulsory in Denmark, the uptake has been poor in the UK and North America - much to the scientists' disappointment. According to the UK Kennel Club: "The Danish scheme has seen a 73% reduction in risk of having Mitral Valve murmurs in dogs whose parents were on the breeding scheme."

A new Doppler (ultrasound-type) system of checking hearts is now being rolled out in the UK. It is a collaboration between the KC and Veterinary Cardiovascular Society (VCS) in consultation with Cavalier breed clubs. Compared with a vet or cardiologist simply listening to the heart through a stethoscope, a Doppler shows so much more and should be a guide for breeding for better hearts.

The dog has wired pads placed on different parts of his or her body and – this is the difficult part - has to lie very still for around 20 minutes. Dogs are given a Green, Amber or Red result, with Green being the best. Dogs with a Red test result should not be used for breeding, and only Ambers that are otherwise fit and have passed other health screens should be bred.

⋯⋯⋯

Heart Murmurs

Heart murmurs are not uncommon in dogs. When our dog was diagnosed with a Grade 1-2 murmur, my heart sank when the vet gave us the bad news. But once the shock is over, it's important to realise that there are several different severities of the condition and, at its mildest, it is no great cause for concern. The murmur did slightly develop, but never affected his quality of life; he remained fit and active.

Literally, a heart murmur is a specific sound heard through a stethoscope. It results from the blood flowing faster than normal within the heart itself or in one of the two major arteries. Instead of the normal 'lubb dupp' noise, an additional sound can be heard that can vary from a mild 'pshhh' to a loud 'whoosh'. Murmurs are caused by a number of factors, including MVD. Other reasons include hyperthyroidism, anaemia and heartworm. The different grades of heart murmurs are:

- ❖ **Grade I -** barely audible
- ❖ **Grade II -** soft, but easily heard with a stethoscope
- ❖ **Grade III** - intermediate loudness; most murmurs that are related to the mechanics of blood circulation are at least grade III
- ❖ **Grade IV** - loud murmur that radiates widely, often including opposite side of chest
- ❖ **Grades V and Grade VI** - very loud, audible with stethoscope barely touching the chest; the vibration is also strong enough to be felt through the animal's chest wall

In puppies, there are two major types of heart murmurs, and they will probably be detected by your vet at the first or second vaccinations. The most common type is called an innocent "flow murmur". This type of murmur is soft (typically Grade II or less) and is not caused by underlying heart disease. An innocent flow murmur typically disappears by four to five months of age.

However if a puppy has a loud murmur (Grade III or louder), or if the heart murmur is still easily heard with a stethoscope after four or five months of age, the likelihood of the puppy having an underlying congenital (from birth) heart problem becomes much higher. The thought of a puppy having lifelong heart disease is extremely worrying, but it is important to remember that the disease will not affect all puppies' life expectancy or quality of life.

A heart murmur can also develop suddenly in an adult dog with no prior history of the problem. This is typically due to heart disease that develops with age. In Toy and small breeds, a heart murmur may develop in middle-aged to older dogs due to an age-related thickening and degeneration of one of the valves in the heart, the mitral valve.

Luxating Patella

Luxating Patella, also called "floating kneecap", "loose knee" or "slipped stifle", can be a painful condition akin to a dislocated kneecap in humans; the most common cause is genetic and it affects some Miniature and Toy Poodles.

A groove in the end of the femur (thigh bone) allows the knee cap to glide up and down when the knee joint is bent, while keeping it in place at the same time. If this groove is too shallow, the knee cap may luxate – or dislocate. It can only return to its natural position when the quadriceps muscle relaxes and increases in length, which is why a dog may have to hold his leg up for some time after the dislocation.

The condition ranges from Grade 1 to Grade 4. In mild cases (Grade 1) the kneecap may pop back into its socket of its own accord, or be manipulated back into place by a vet. In severe cases the patella is permanently out of place and the dog has extreme difficulty extending the knees. He or she walks with bent knees virtually all the time - often with the whole leg angled and rotated out. Severe cases are usually dealt with by surgery. Sometimes the problem can be caused – and is

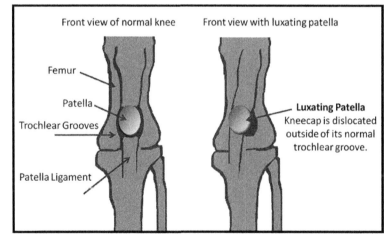

certainly worsened - by obesity, the excess weight putting too much strain on the joint – another good reason to keep your Cavapoo's weight in check.

Symptoms

A typical sign would be if your dog is running across the park when he suddenly pulls up short and yelps with pain. He might limp on three legs and then after a period of about 10 minutes, drop the affected leg and start to walk normally again. Another sign is that you might notice him stretching out a rear leg quite often or 'skipping' once in a while when walking or running. If the condition is severe, he may hold up the affected leg up for a few days.

Dogs that have a luxating patella on both hind legs may change their gait completely, dropping their hindquarters and holding the rear legs further out from the body as they walk. In the most extreme cases they might not even use their rear legs, but walk like a circus act by balancing on their front legs so their hindquarters don't touch the ground.

There is a DNA test that can tell if the parents are clear of the disease. It's run by the OFA in the USA and by qualified veterinary clinics in the UK. If you are in the USA, ask to see screening certificates for the parents.

Typically, many sufferers are middle-aged dogs with a history of intermittent lameness in the affected rear leg or legs, although the condition may appear as early as four to six months old.

Treatment

If moderate to severe cases are left untreated, the groove will become even shallower and the dog will become progressively lamer, with arthritis prematurely affecting the joint. This will cause a permanently swollen knee and reduce your dog's mobility. It is therefore important to get your dog in for a veterinary check-up ASAP if you suspect he or she may have a luxating patella.

Surgery is often required for Grade III and IV luxation. In these cases, known as a **trochlear modification**, the groove at the base of the femur is surgically deepened to better hold the knee cap in place. The good news is that dogs generally respond well, whatever the type of surgery, and are usually completely recovered within two months.

....

Chiari malformation/ Syringomyelia

Syringomyelia (SM) is an extremely serious hereditary disease affecting Cavaliers and is caused by the brain being too big for the skull or an abnormal skull shape. This restricts the normal flow of fluids between the brain and the spine, which are squeezed into cavities and eventually destroy the spinal cord. SM is a very painful disease, also known as "neck scratcher's disease", because one of the common signs is scratching the air near the neck.

The Cavalier Club in the US says: "The most common sign of this condition is shoulder/neck/ear scratching (with no evidence of skin or ear disease), especially when excited or walking on a lead – typically to one side only but may become bilateral. Affected dogs may also be sensitive around the head, neck and forelimbs and often cry/yelp/scream for apparently no reason. Pain may be related to head posture and some dogs prefer to sleep or eat with their heads up.

"Some severely affected young dogs develop a neck scoliosis, i.e. their neck is twisted. Some dogs may develop a wobbling hind limb gait and/or a forelimb weakness. Signs are usually recognised between six months and three years, however dogs of any age may begin showing symptoms. The only definite way to diagnose Syringomyelia and the associated skull malformation is by an MRI scan. Unfortunately, this expensive test, usually performed by a neurologist, is only available at specialist veterinary centers."

There is a hole at the base of the skull where the brain stem exits and becomes the spinal cord. Chiari-like Malformation (CM) occurs when this space is too small or there is some other malformation. The CM forces the brain and spine fluids to be squeezed into places they shouldn't go, causing Syringomyelia.

SM and CM are widespread among Cavaliers, and screening is recommended by the UK Kennel Club (KC). They say: "While some dogs show no or only mild symptoms, unfortunately, in some cases the condition progresses and deteriorates causing the dog pain and neurological problems.

Medical interventions can help to alleviate health problems, but very sadly in some cases this is not possible. Some show no symptoms at all; it all depends on the severity of the malformation. There is no cure and in severe cases, the dog is put to sleep.

....

von Willebrand's Disease

Von Willebrand's Disease is the most common inherited bleeding disorder in dogs and humans; it's similar to haemophilia in humans. In von Willebrand's Disease (vWD), the dog lacks a substance which helps to form blood clots. This substance ('von Willebrand's factor') normally forms clots and stabilises something called Factor VIII in the normal clotting process. Dogs that show symptoms of von Willebrand's Disease bleed excessively as their blood does not clot properly. However, many dogs diagnosed with vWD show no symptoms, or none until later life.

Certain breeds have a higher incidence of vWD than others - including Miniature and Standard Poodles. They can inherit Type 1 von Willebrand's, which is the least severe form of the disease. It is named after Erik Adolf von Willebrand (*pictured*), a Finnish doctor who documented and studied a rare bleeding disorder in an isolated group of people in 1924. He showed that the disease was inherited, rather than caught by infection.

A diagnosis is made through a test to check the levels of von Willebrand's factor in the blood. At one time it was thought that the faulty gene(s) was recessive, meaning BOTH parents had to have it for the puppy to be affected. Latest research shows that it may, in fact, be dominant, so it's possible that one affected parent can pass the disease on to a puppy. If you are buying a Miniature or Standard pup, check that both parents have been DNA-tested for vWD and ask to see the certificate giving them the all-clear.

Symptoms

The main symptom is excessive bleeding:

- Nosebleeds
- Blood in the faeces (black or bright red blood)
- Bloody urine
- Bleeding from the gums
- Females bleeding excessively from the vagina
- Bruising of skin
- Prolonged bleeding after surgery or trauma
- Blood loss anaemia if there is prolonged bleeding

If bleeding occurs in the stomach or intestine, you may notice something unusual in your dog's faeces; his stools may have blood in them or be black and tarry or bright red. Some dogs will have blood in their urine, while others may have bleeding in their joints. In this last case, the symptoms are similar to those of arthritis.

Sadly, as yet there is no cure for von Willebrand's Disease. The only way to stop the spread of the disease is to have dogs tested and to stop breeding from affected animals. Without treatment, an affected dog can bleed to death after surgery or what otherwise might normally be considered a less than life-threatening injury. The only proven way to treat vWD is with transfusions of blood collected from healthy dogs. Some dogs with von Willebrand's Disease are also **hypothyroid**, meaning they have lower than normal levels of thyroid hormone. These dogs benefit from thyroid hormone replacement therapy. A drug called DDAVP may help dogs with bleeding episodes. It can be administered into the nose to increase clotting, but opinion is still divided as to whether this treatment is effective.

....

Epilepsy

Cavapoos may statistically have a slightly higher chance of getting epilepsy than some other breeds, as are Cavaliers and Poodles. Epilepsy means repeated seizures (also called fits or convulsions) due to abnormal electrical activity in the brain. It can affect any breed of dog and in fact affects around four or five dogs in every 100.

A study carried out in Sweden (Heske et al. 2014), based on data on 35 breeds from insurance companies, found that the Boxer emerged as the breed most likely to be affected by epilepsy, with the Cavalier ranked third out of 35 and Miniature and Toy Poodles ranked fifth. The full results are at: www.instituteofcaninebiology.org/blog/epilepsy-incidence-and-mortality-in-35-dog-breeds The type of epilepsy affecting Cavaliers and Poodles is called *Idiopathic Epilepsy,* which means there is no detectable injury, disease or abnormality. Although yet to be proven, scientists believed that some forms of epilepsy are genetic and that the type that affects Cavaliers and small Poodles is **autosomal recessive** – i.e. both parents need a copy of the faulty gene(s) for the disease to be passed on.

The majority of epileptic dogs have their first seizure between one and five years old. Affected dogs behave normally between seizures. In some cases, the gap between seizures is relatively constant, in others it can be very irregular with several occurring over a short period of time, but with long intervals between 'clusters'. If they occur because of a problem somewhere else in the body, such as heart disease (which stops oxygen reaching the brain), this is not epilepsy.

Anyone who has witnessed their dog having a seizure knows how frightening it can be. Seizures are not uncommon, and many dogs only ever have one. If your dog has had more than one, it may be that he or she is epileptic. The good news is that, just as with people, there are medications to control epilepsy in dogs, allowing them to live relatively normal lives with normal lifespans.

Symptoms

Some dogs seem to know when they are about to have a seizure and may behave in a certain way. You will come to recognise these signs as meaning that an episode is likely. Often dogs just seek out their owner's company and come to sit beside them.

There are two main types of seizure: **Petit Mal**, also called a Focal or Partial Seizure, which is the lesser of the two as it only affects one half of the brain. This may involve facial twitching, staring into space with a fixed glaze and/or upward eye movement, walking as if drunk, snapping at imaginary flies, and/or running or hiding for no reason. Sometimes this is accompanied by urination and the dog is conscious throughout.

Grand Mal, or Generalised Seizure affects both hemispheres of the brain and is more often what we think of when we talk about a seizure. Most dogs become stiff, fall onto their side and make running movements with their legs. Sometimes they will cry out and may lose control of their bowels, bladder or both. The dog is unconscious once the seizure starts – he cannot hear or respond to you. While it is distressing to watch, **the dog is not in any pain** - even if howling. It's not uncommon for an episode to begin as a focal seizure, but progress into a generalized seizure. Sometimes, the progression is pretty clear - there may be twitching or jerking of one body part that gradually increases in intensity and progresses to include the entire body – other times the progression happens very fast.

Most seizures last between one and three minutes - it is worth making a note of the time the seizure starts and ends – or record it on your phone because it often seems that it goes on for a lot longer than it actually does. If you are not sure whether or not your dog has had a seizure, look on YouTube, where there are many videos of dogs having epileptic seizures. Afterwards dogs behave in different ways.

Some just get up and carry on with what they were doing, while others appear dazed and confused for up to 24 hours afterwards. Most commonly, dogs will be disorientated for only 10 to 15 minutes before returning to their old self. They often have a set pattern of behaviour that they follow - for example going for a drink of water or asking to go outside to the toilet. If your dog has had more than one seizure, you may well start to notice a pattern of behaviour which is typically repeated.

Most seizures occur while the dog is relaxed and resting quietly, often in the evening or at night; it rarely happens during exercise. In a few dogs, seizures seem to be triggered by particular events or stress. It is common for a pattern to develop and, should your dog suffer from epilepsy, you will gradually recognise this as specific to your dog.

The most important thing is to **stay calm**. Remember that your dog is unconscious during the seizure and is not in pain or distressed. It is likely to be more distressing for you than for him. Make sure that he is not in a position to injure himself, for example by falling down the stairs, but otherwise do not try to interfere with him. Never try to put your hand inside his mouth during a seizure or you are very likely to get bitten.

It is very rare for dogs to injure themselves during a seizure. Occasionally they may bite their tongue and there may appear to be a lot of blood, but it's unlikely to be serious; your dog will not swallow his tongue. If it goes on for a very long time (more than 10 minutes), his body temperature will rise, which can cause damage to other organs such as liver, kidneys and brain. In very extreme cases, some dogs may be left in a coma after severe seizures. Repeated seizures can cause cumulative brain damage, which can result in early senility (with loss of learned behaviour and housetraining, or behavioural changes).

When Should I Contact the Vet?

Generally, if your dog has a seizure lasting more than five minutes, or is having more than two or three a day, you should contact your vet. When your dog starts fitting, make a note of the time. If he comes out of it within five minutes, allow him time to recover quietly before contacting your vet.

It is far better for him to recover quietly at home rather than be bundled into the car and carted off to the vet right away. However, if your dog does not come out of the seizure within five minutes, or has repeated seizures close together, contact your vet immediately, as he or she will want to see your dog as soon as possible. If this is his first seizure, your vet may ask you to bring him in for a check-up and some routine blood tests. Always call the vet clinic before setting off to be sure that there is someone there who can help when you arrive.

There are many things other than epilepsy that cause seizures in dogs. When your vet first examines your dog, he or she will not know whether your dog has epilepsy or another illness. It's unlikely that the vet will see your dog during a seizure, so it is **vital** that you're able to describe in some detail just what happens. Your vet may need to run a range of tests to ensure that there is no other cause of the seizures. These may include blood tests, possibly X-rays, and maybe even an MRI scan of your dog's brain. If no other cause can be found, then a diagnosis of epilepsy may be made. If your Cavapoo already has epilepsy, remember these key points:

❖ Don't change or stop any medication without consulting your vet

❖ See your vet at least once a year for follow-up visits

❖ Be sceptical of 'magic cure' treatments

Treatment

It is not usually possible to remove the cause of the seizures, so your vet will use medication to control them. Treatment will not cure the disease, but it will manage the signs – in some cases even a well-controlled epileptic may have occasional seizures. As yet there is no cure for epilepsy, so don't be tempted with 'instant cures' from the internet.

There are many drugs used in the control of epilepsy in people, but very few of these are suitable for long-term use in a dog. Two of the most common are Phenobarbital and Potassium Bromide (some dogs can have negative results with Phenobarbital). There are also a number of holistic remedies advertised, but we have no experience of them or any idea if any are effective. Other factors that have proved useful in some cases are avoiding dog food containing preservatives, adding vitamins, minerals and/or enzymes to the diet and ensuring drinking water is free of fluoride.

Each epileptic dog is an individual and a treatment plan will be designed specifically for him. It will be based on the severity and frequency of the seizures and how he responds to different medications. Many epileptic dogs require a combination of one or more types of drug to achieve the most effective control of their seizures. You need patience when managing an epileptic pet. It is important that medication is given at the same time each day. Once your dog has been on treatment for a while, he will become dependent on the levels of drug in his blood at all times to control seizures. If you miss a dose of treatment, blood levels can drop and this may be enough to trigger a seizure.

Keep a record of events in your dog's life, note down dates and times of episodes and record when you have given medication. Each time you visit your vet, take this diary along with you so he or she can see how your dog has been since his last check-up. If seizures are becoming more frequent, it may be necessary to change the medication. The success or otherwise of treatment may depend on YOU keeping a close eye on your Cavapoo to see if there are any physical or behavioural changes.

It is not common for epileptic dogs to stop having seizures altogether. However, provided your dog is checked regularly by your vet to make sure that the drugs are not causing any side effects, **there is a good chance that he will live a full and happy life.**

Remember, live **with** epilepsy not **for** epilepsy. With the proper medical treatment, most epileptic dogs have far more good days than bad ones. Enjoy all those good days.

Thanks to www.canineepilepsy.co.uk for assistance with this article. If your Cavapoo has epilepsy, we recommend reading this website to gain a greater understanding of the illness.

....

Canine Diabetes

Diabetes can affect dogs of all breeds, sizes and both genders, as well as obese dogs. There are two types: **diabetes mellitus** and **diabetes insipidus. Diabetes insipidus** is caused by a lack of vasopressin, a hormone that controls the kidneys' absorption of water. **Diabetes mellitus** occurs when the dog's body does not produce enough insulin and cannot successfully process sugars.

Dogs, like us, get their energy by converting the food they eat into sugars, mainly glucose. This glucose travels in the dog's bloodstream and individual cells then remove some of that glucose from the blood to use for energy. The substance that allows the cells to take glucose from the blood is a protein called *insulin.*

Insulin is created by beta cells that are located in the pancreas, next to the stomach. Almost all diabetic dogs have Type 1 diabetes; their pancreas does not produce any insulin. Without it, the cells have no way to use the glucose that is in the bloodstream, so the cells 'starve' while the glucose level in the blood rises. Your vet will use blood samples and urine samples to check glucose concentrations in order to diagnose diabetes. Early treatment helps to prevent further complications developing.

Diabetes mellitus (sugar diabetes) is the most common form and, according to UFAW, affects one in 294 dogs in the UK. According to a study of 180,000 insured dogs, Miniature and Toy Poodles ranked 11th out of 46 breeds for the disorder, and Cavaliers were 18th, with the average age being 7.8 years when the condition was reported: https://onlinelibrary.wiley.com/doi/pdf/10.1111/j.1939-1676.2007.tb01940.x

Both males and females can develop it; unspayed females have a slightly higher risk. The typical canine diabetes sufferer is middle-aged, female and overweight, with unspayed females being at slightly higher risk, but there are also juvenile cases. The condition is now treatable and need not shorten a dog's lifespan or interfere greatly with his quality of life. Due to advances in veterinary science, diabetic dogs undergoing treatment now have the same life expectancy as non-diabetic dogs of the same age and gender.

Symptoms of Diabetes Mellitus

- Extreme thirst
- Excessive urination
- Weight loss
- Increased appetite
- Coat in poor condition
- Lethargy
- Vision problems due to cataracts

If left untreated, diabetes can lead to cataracts and even blindness, increasing weakness in the legs (neuropathy), other ailments and even death. Cataracts may develop due to high blood glucose levels causing water to build up in the eyes' lenses. This leads to swelling, rupture of the lens fibres and the development of cataracts.

In many cases, the cataracts can be surgically removed to bring sight back to the dog. However, some dogs may stay blind even after the cataracts are gone, and some cataracts simply cannot be removed. Blind dogs are often able to get around surprisingly well, particularly in a familiar home.

Treatment and Exercise

Treatment starts with the right diet. Your vet will prescribe meals low in fat and sugars. He or she will also recommend medication. Many cases of canine diabetes can be successfully treated with a combination of diet and medication, while more severe cases may require insulin injections. In the newly-diagnosed dog, insulin therapy begins at home.

Normally, after a week of treatment, you return to the vet for a series of blood sugar tests over a 12–14 hour period to see when the blood glucose peaks and when it hits its lows. Adjustments are then made to the dosage and timing of the injections. Your vet will explain how to prepare and inject the insulin. You may be asked to collect urine samples using a test strip of paper that indicates the glucose levels in urine.

If your dog is already having insulin injections, beware of a 'miracle cure' offered on some internet sites. It does not exist. There is no diet or vitamin supplement which can reduce your dog's

dependence on insulin injections, because vitamins and minerals cannot do what insulin does in the dog's body. If you think that your dog needs a supplement, discuss it with your vet first to make sure that it does not interfere with any other medication.

Managing your dog's diabetes also means managing his activity level. Exercise burns up blood glucose the same way that insulin does. If your dog is on insulin, any active exercise on top of the insulin might cause him to have a severe low blood glucose episode, called "hypoglycaemia". Keep your dog on a reasonably consistent exercise routine. Your usual insulin dose will take that amount of exercise into account. If you plan to take your dog out for some demanding exercise, such as running round with other dogs, you may need to reduce his usual insulin dose.

Tips

- ❧ You can usually buy specially formulated diabetes dog food from your vet
- ❧ You should feed the same type and amount of food at the same time every day
- ❧ Most vets recommend twice-a-day feeding for diabetic pets (it's OK if your dog prefers to eat more often). If you have other pets, they should also be on a twice-a-day feeding schedule, so that the diabetic dog cannot eat from their bowls
- ❧ Help your dog to achieve the best possible blood glucose control by not feeding table scraps or treats between meals
- ❧ Watch for signs that your dog is starting to drink more water than usual. Call the vet if you see this happening, as it may mean that the insulin dose needs adjusting

Remember these simple points:

Food raises blood glucose - Insulin and exercise lower blood glucose - Keep them in balance

For more information on canine diabetes visit **www.caninediabetes.org**

....

Canine Cancer

This is the biggest single killer and will claim the lives of one in four dogs, regardless of breed. It is the cause of nearly half the deaths of all dogs aged 10 years and older, according to the American Veterinary Medical Association. A study of more than 15,000 dogs of different breeds found that Miniature and Toys Poodles and Cavaliers are LESS likely than average to contract cancer - which is good news for the Cavapoo. Detailed cancer statistics by breed can be found at the NCBI (National Center for Biotechnology Information) website: www.ncbi.nlm.nih.gov/pmc/articles/PMC3658424

(Go to the top right of your screen in Google, click the three vertical dots, then click *Find* and type in *"Cavalier"* or *"Poodle"* - all the references will be highlighted in yellow).

Common Cancer Symptoms

Early detection is critical, and some things to look out for are:

- ❖ Swellings anywhere on the body or around the anus
- ❖ Lumps in a dog's armpit or under the jaw
- ❖ Sores that don't heal
- ❖ Weight loss
- ❖ Laboured breathing
- ❖ Changes in exercise or stamina level
- ❖ Change in bowel or bladder habits
- ❖ Increased drinking or urination
- ❖ Bad breath, which can be a sign of oral cancer
- ❖ Poor appetite, difficulty swallowing or excessive drooling
- ❖ Vomiting

If your dog has been spayed or neutered, there is evidence that the risk of certain cancers decreases. These cancers include uterine and breast/mammary cancer in females, and testicular cancer in males (if the dog was neutered before he was six months old). However, recent studies also show that some dogs may have a higher risk of certain cancers after early neutering. Spaying prevents mammary cancer in female dogs, which is fatal in about 50% of all cases.

Diagnosis and Treatment

Just because your dog has a skin growth doesn't mean that it's cancerous. Your vet will probably confirm the tumour using X-rays, blood tests or a biopsy. Often these are benign (harmless), but if you discover one you should get it checked out by a vet, as they can sometimes be malignant (cancerous). He or she will then decide whether it is **benign** (harmless) or **malignant** (harmful). Many older dogs develop fatty lumps, or *lipomas*, which are often benign, but still need checking out by a vet to make sure.

If your dog is diagnosed with cancer, there is hope. Advances in veterinary medicine and technology offer various treatment options, including chemotherapy, radiation and surgery. Unlike with humans, a dog's hair will not fall out with chemotherapy. Canine cancer is growing at an ever-increasing rate, and one of the difficulties is that your dog cannot tell you when a cancer is developing. However, if cancers can be detected early enough through a physical or behavioural change, dogs often respond well to treatment.

Over recent years, we have all become more aware of the risk factors for human cancer. Responding to these by changing our habits is having a significant impact on human health. Stopping smoking, protecting ourselves from over-exposure to strong sunlight and eating a healthy, balanced diet all help to reduce cancer rates. We know to keep a close eye on ourselves, go for regular health checks and report any lumps and bumps to our doctors as soon as they appear. **The same is true with your dog.**

Reducing the Risk

The success of treatment depends on the type of cancer, the treatment used and, importantly, how early the tumour is found. The sooner treatment begins, the greater the chances of success.

One of the best things you can do for your dog is to keep a close eye on him for any tell-tale signs. This shouldn't be too difficult and can be done as part of your regular handling and grooming sessions. If you notice any new bumps, for example, monitor them over a period of days to see if there is a change in their appearance or size. If there is, then make an appointment to see your vet as soon as possible. It might only be a cyst, but better to be safe than sorry.

While it is impossible to completely prevent cancer from occurring, the following points may help to reduce the risk:

- Feed a healthy diet with little or, preferably, no preservatives
- Consider adding a dietary supplement, such as antioxidants, Vitamins A, C, E, beta carotene, lycopene or selenium, or coconut oil – check compatibility with any other treatments
- Don't let your Cavapoo get overweight
- Give pure, filtered or bottled water (fluoride-free) for drinking
- Give your dog regular daily exercise
- Keep your dog away from chemicals, pesticides, cleaning products, etc. around the garden and home
- Avoid passive smoking
- Consider using natural flea remedies (check they are working) and avoid unnecessary vaccinations
- If your dog has light skin, don't leave him in the blazing sunshine for extended periods
- Check your dog regularly for lumps and bumps and any other physical or behavioural changes
- If you are buying a puppy, ask whether there is a history of cancer among the parents and grandparents

Research into earlier diagnosis and improved treatments is being conducted at veterinary schools and companies all over the world. Advances in biology are producing a steady flow of new tests and treatments that are now becoming available to improve survival rates and canine cancer care.

One of our dogs was diagnosed with T-cell lymphoma, a particularly aggressive form of cancer, when he was four years old. We had noticed a small lump on his anus, which grew to the size of a small grape within a couple of days. We rushed him down to the vet and he had surgery the following day. He died last year, aged 13, having lived a further nine very happy and energetic years.

If your dog is diagnosed with cancer, do not despair, there are many options and new, improved treatments are constantly being introduced.

....

Disclaimer: The author is not a vet. This chapter is intended to give owners an outline of some of the health issues and symptoms that may affect Cavapoos. If you want to know more about health issues that can specifically affect Cavalier King Charles Spaniels (and therefore possibly Cavapoos), there is an excellent website at: www.Cavalierhealth.org

If you have any concerns regarding your dog's health, our advice is always the same: consult a veterinarian.

12. Skin and Allergies

Allergies are a growing concern for owners of many dogs. Visit any busy veterinary clinic these days – especially in spring and summer – and it's likely that one or more of the dogs is there because of some type of sensitivity. And there is plenty of anecdotal evidence that some Cavapoos develop sensitive stomachs and food intolerances.

Any individual dog can have issues. Skin conditions, allergies and intolerances are on the increase in the canine world as well as the human world.

How many children did you hear of having asthma or a peanut allergy when you were at school? Not too many, I'll bet, yet allergies and adverse reactions are now relatively common – and it's the same with dogs. The reasons are not clear; it could be connected to breeding or feeding – or both, but as yet, there is no clear scientific evidence to back this up.

The skin is a complicated topic and a whole book could be written on this subject alone. While many dogs have no problems at all, some suffer from sensitive skin, dry or oily skin, hot spots, yeast infections or other skin disorders, causing them to scratch, bite or lick themselves excessively. Symptoms may vary from mild itchiness to a chronic reaction.

In common with other breeds with long, floppy ears, ear infections can also be a cause for concern with Cavapoos – more on these later.

Canine Skin

As with humans, the skin is the dog's largest organ. It acts as the protective barrier between your dog's internal organs and the outside world; it also regulates temperature and provides the sense of touch. Surprisingly, a dog's skin is actually thinner than ours, and it is made up of three layers:

1. **Epidermis** or outer layer, the one that bears the brunt of your dog's contact with the outside world.

2. **Dermis** is the extremely tough layer mostly made up of collagen, a strong and fibrous protein. This where blood vessels deliver nutrients and oxygen to the skin, and it also acts as your dog's thermostat by allowing his body to release or keep in heat, depending on the outside temperature and your dog's activity level.

3. **Subcutis** is a dense layer of fatty tissue that allows your dog's skin to move independently from the muscle layers below it, as well as providing insulation and support for the skin.

Human allergies often trigger a reaction within the respiratory system, causing us to wheeze or sneeze, whereas *allergies or hypersensitivities in a dog often cause a reaction in his or her skin.*

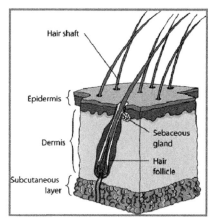

Skin can be affected from the **inside** by things that your dog eats or drinks.

Skin can be affected from the **outside** by fleas, parasites, inhaled or contact allergies triggered by grass, pollen, man-made chemicals, dust, mould, etc.

Like all dogs, Cavapoos can suffer from food allergies or intolerances as well as environmental allergies. Canine skin disorders are complicated. Some dogs can run through fields, digging holes and rolling around in the grass with no after-effects at all. Others may spend a lot of time indoors and have an excellent diet, but still experience severe itching and/or bald spots. Some dogs can eat almost anything and everything with no issues at all, while owners of others spend much of their time trying to find the magic bullet – the ideal food for their dog's sensitive stomach.

It's by no means possible to cover all of the issues and causes in this chapter. The aim here is to give a broad outline of some of the ailments most likely to affect your Cavapoo and how to deal with them. We have also included remedies tried with some success by ourselves (we had a dog with skin issues) and other owners of affected dogs, as well as advice from a holistic specialist. This information is not intended to take the place of professional help. We are not animal health experts and you should always contact your vet as soon as your dog appears physically unwell or uncomfortable. This is particularly true with skin conditions:

 If a vet can find the source of the problem early on, there is more chance of successfully treating it before it has chance to develop into a more serious condition with secondary issues and infections.

One of the difficulties with skin ailments is that the exact cause is often difficult to diagnose, as the symptoms may also be common to other issues. If environmental allergies are involved, some specific tests are available costing hundreds of pounds or dollars. You will have to take your vet's advice on this, as the tests are not always conclusive and if the answer is dust or pollen, it can be difficult to keep your lively dog away from the triggers while still having a normal life - unless you and your Cavapoo spend all your time in a hermetically sealed city apartment! If a skin issue is triggered by environmental factors, it is often a question of managing the condition, rather than curing it.

Another issue reported by some dog owners is food allergy or intolerance - there is a difference. There is anecdotal evidence that switching to a raw or home-cooked can significantly help some Cavapoos. See **Chapter 7. Feeding a Cavapoo** for more information on dealing with food intolerances and allergies.

Skin issues and allergies often develop in adolescence or early adulthood, which is often anything from a few months to two or three years old. Our affected dog was perfectly normal until he reached two when he began scratching, triggered by environmental allergies - most likely pollen. Over the years he was on various different remedies which all worked for a time. As his allergies were seasonal, he normally did not have any medication between October and March. But come spring and as sure as daffodils are daffodils, he started scratching again. Luckily, they were manageable and he lived a happy, active life until he passed away aged 13.

Allergies and their treatment can cause a lot of stress for dogs and owners alike. The number one piece of advice is that if you suspect your Cavapoo has an allergy or skin problem, try to **deal with it**

right away - either via your vet or natural remedies – before the all-too-familiar scenario kicks in and it develops into a chronic (long term) condition.

Whatever the cause, before a vet can diagnose the problem you have to be prepared to tell him or her all about your dog's diet, exercise regime, habits, medical history and local environment. The vet will then carry out a thorough physical examination, possibly followed by further (expensive) tests, before a course of treatment can be prescribed. You'll have to decide whether these tests are worth it and whether they are likely to discover the exact root of the problem.

Types of Allergies

'Canine dermatitis' means inflammation of a dog's skin and it can be triggered by numerous things, but the most common by far is allergies. Vets estimate that one in four dogs at their clinics is there because of some kind of allergy. Symptoms are:

- ❧ Chewing his or her feet
- ❧ Rubbing the face on the carpet
- ❧ Scratching the body
- ❧ Scratching or biting the anus
- ❧ Itchy ears, head shaking
- ❧ Hair loss
- ❧ Mutilated skin with sore or discoloured patches or hot spots

A Cavapoo who is allergic to something will show it through skin problems and itching; your vet may call this *'pruritus'*.

It may seem logical that if a dog is allergic to something inhaled, like certain pollen grains, his/her nose will run; if (s)he's allergic to something he eats, (s)he may vomit, or if allergic to an insect bite, (s)he may develop a swelling. But in practice this is seldom the case. **In dogs, the skin is the organ most affected by allergies,** often resulting in a mild to severe itching sensation over the body and possibly a chronic ear infection.

Dogs with allergies often chew their feet until they are sore and red. You may see yours rubbing his or her face on the carpet or couch or scratching the belly and flanks. Because the ear glands produce too much wax in response to the allergy, ear infections can occur - with bacteria and yeast (which is a fungus) often thriving in the excessive wax and debris. Cavapoos don't have to suffer from allergies to get an ear infection; the lack of air flow under the floppy hairy ears makes them prone to the condition.

Reddish coloured tear stains can also be a sign of a yeast infection.

Digestive health can play an important role. If your dog does develop a yeast infection and you switch to a grain-free diet, avoid those that are potato-based, as these contain high levels of starch.

Holistic vet Dr Jodie Gruenstern says: "It's estimated that up to 80% of the immune system resides within the gastrointestinal system; building a healthy gut supports a more appropriate immune response. The importance of choosing fresh proteins and healthy fats over processed, starchy diets (such as kibble) can't be overemphasized. Grains and other starches have a negative impact on gut health, creating insulin resistance and inflammation."

An allergic dog may cause skin lesions or 'hot spots' by constant chewing and scratching. Sometimes he or she will lose hair, which can be patchy, leaving a mottled appearance. The skin itself may be dry and crusty, reddened, swollen or oily, depending on the dog. It is very common to get secondary bacterial skin infections due to these self-inflicted wounds. An allergic dog's body is reacting to certain molecules called 'allergens.' These may come from:

- Trees
- Grass
- Pollens
- Foods and food additives, such as specific meats, grains or colourings
- Milk products
- Fabrics, such as wool or nylon
- Rubber and plastics
- House dust and dust mites
- Mould
- Flea bites
- Chemical products used around the house

Denise Knightley's F1 Carmen Rose (who doesn't have allergies) enjoys being out and about in the country among the grass and daffodils.

These allergens may be **inhaled** as the dog breathes, **ingested** as the dog eats, or caused by **contact** with the dog's body when (s)he walks or rolls. However they arrive, they all cause the immune system to produce a protein (IgE), which causes irritating chemicals like histamine to be released. In dogs these chemical reactions and cell types occur in sizeable amounts **only within the skin**, hence the scratching.

Inhalant Allergies (Atopy)

The most common allergies in dogs are inhalant and seasonal - at least at first; some allergies may develop and worsen. Substances that can cause an allergic reaction in dogs are similar to those causing problems for humans, and dogs of all breeds can suffer from them.

A clue to diagnosing these allergies is to look at the timing of the reaction. Does it happen all year round? If so, this may be mould, dust or some other trigger that is permanently in the environment. If the reaction is seasonal, then pollens may well be the culprit. A diagnosis can be made by one of three methods of **allergy testing.**

The most common is a blood test for antibodies caused by antigens in the dog's blood, and there are two standard tests: a RAST test (radioallergosorbent) and an ELISA test (enzyme-linked immunosorbent assay). According to the Veterinary and Aquatic Services Department of Drs. Foster and Smith, they are very similar, but many vets feel that the ELISA test gives more accurate results.

The other type of testing is intradermal skin testing where a small amount of antigen is injected into the skin of the animal and after a short period of time, the area around the injection site is inspected to see if the dog has had an allergic reaction. This method has been more widely used in the USA than the UK to date. Here is a link to an article written by the owner of a Boxer dog with severe inhalant allergies: www.allergydogcentral.com/2011/06/30/dog-allergy-testing-and-allergy-shots

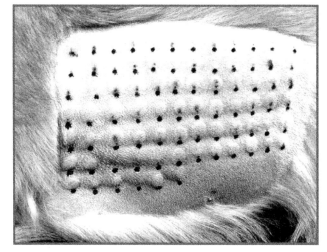

Our photo shows a Golden Retriever that has undergone intradermal skin testing. In this particular case, the dog has been tested for more than 70 different allergens, which is a lot. In all likelihood, your vet would test for fewer. The injections are in kits. If you consider this option, ask the vet or specialist how many allergens are in the kit.

Intradermal skin testing is regarded as 'the gold standard' of allergy testing for atopy. The dog is sedated and an area on the flank is shaved down to the skin. A small amount of antigen is injected into the skin on this shaved area. This is done in a specific pattern and order. After a short time, the shaved area is examined to detect which antigens, if any, have created a reaction. It may look pretty drastic, but reactions – the visible round bumps - are only temporary and the hair grows back.

Intradermal skin testing works best when done during the season when the allergies are at their worst. The good news is that it is not necessarily much more expensive than blood testing and after a while the dog is none the worse for the ordeal. The procedure is normally carried out by a veterinary dermatologist or a vet with some dermatological experience, and dogs need to be clear of steroids and antihistamines for around six weeks beforehand.

While allergy testing is not particularly expensive, the intradermal method usually requires your dog to be sedated. And there's also no point doing it if you are not going to go along with the recommended method of treatment afterwards - which is immunotherapy, or **'hyposensitisation'**, and this can be an expensive and lengthy process. It consists of a series of injections made specifically for your dog and administered over months (or even years) to make him or her more tolerant of specific allergens. Vets in the US claim that success rates can be as high as 75%.

But before you get to the stage of considering allergy testing, your vet will have had to rule out other potential causes, such as fleas or mites, fungal, yeast or bacterial infections and hypothyroidism. Due to the time and cost involved in skin testing, vets treat most mild cases of allergies with a combination of avoidance, fatty acids, tablets and sometimes steroid injections for flare-ups. Many owners of dogs with allergies also look at changing to an unprocessed diet (raw or cooked) and natural alternatives to long-term use of steroids, which can cause other health issues.

Environmental or Contact Irritations

These are a direct reaction to something the dog physically comes into contact with. It could be as simple as grass, trees, specific plants, dust or other animals. If the trigger is grass or other outdoor materials, the allergies are often seasonal. The dog may require treatment (often tablets, shampoo or localised cortisone spray) for spring and summer, but be perfectly fine with no medication for the other half of the year. This was the case with our dog.

Karen Howe has two red and white F1 Cavapoos, Rodney and Mabel and says: "Rodney's allergies, all started at around 18 months old. He began licking his paws a lot until he was making them sore.

The vet initially prescribed Piriton and diagnosed seasonal allergies but the Piriton didn't seem to have much effect. He was then prescribed steroids, which definitely stopped the licking, but as soon as he finished the course he was back licking again. During this time I did a lot of Google research and realised that I definitely didn't want him back on steroids again and I also wasn't happy about the next step the vet had suggested which was to go on Apoquel.

"This was when I decided to try him on a raw diet and although it hasn't completely cured him, it has definitely helped and made his paw licking more manageable. I feed raw completes from Naturaw which contain no vegetables. I also ensure that his treats are all grain free, as I do notice a flare up in his licking if he has had treats with grain in them. During the summer months he is definitely more itchy so I do believe he has seasonal allergies as well.

"He therefore has Piriton and an itchy dog supplement added to his dinner. I was never officially offered allergy tests for him, so I don't truly know exactly what he is allergic to, but feel that we are able to manage it well now without the use of drugs with long term side effects.

"I have noticed many benefits of switching them both to a raw diet, their coats are glossy and soft, their teeth are cleaner, they poo less and when they do poo it is solid and doesn't really smell. They also absolutely love it and clear every bowl. I definitely wouldn't switch back now."

Our photo, courtesy of Karen, shows Rodney full of beans on a day out at the seaside.

 If you suspect your Cavapoo may have outdoor contact allergies, here is one very good tip guaranteed to reduce scratching: get him or her to stand in a tray or large bowl of water on your return from a walk. Washing the feet and under the belly will get rid of some of the pollen and other allergens, which in turn will reduce the scratching and biting. This can help to reduce the allergens to a tolerable level.

Other possible triggers include dry carpet shampoos, caustic irritants, new carpets, cement dust, washing powders or fabric conditioners. If you wash your dog's bedding or if he sleeps on your bed, use a fragrance-free - if possible, hypoallergenic - laundry detergent and avoid fabric conditioner.

The irritation may be restricted to the part of the dog - such as the underneath of the paws or belly - which has touched the offending object. Symptoms are skin irritation - either a general problem or specific hotspots - itching (pruritus) and sometimes hair loss. Readers of our website sometimes report to us that their dog will incessantly lick one part of the body, often the paws, anus, belly or back.

Flea Bite Allergies

These are a very common canine allergy and affect dogs of all breeds. To compound the problem, many dogs with flea allergies also have inhalant allergies. Flea bite allergy is typically seasonal, worse during summer and autumn - peak time for fleas - and is worse in warmer climates where fleas are prevalent.

This type of allergy is not to the flea itself, but to proteins in flea saliva, which are deposited under the dog's skin when the insect feeds. Just one bite to an allergic Cavapoo will cause intense and long-lasting itching. If affected, the dog will try to bite at the base of his tail and scratch a lot. Most of the damage is done by the dog's scratching, rather than the flea bite, and can result in the hair falling out or skin abrasions. Some Cavapoos will develop hot spots. These can occur anywhere, but are often along the back and base of the tail. Flea bite allergies can only be totally prevented by keeping all fleas away from the dog. Various flea prevention treatments are available — see the section on **Parasites**. If you suspect your dog may be allergic to fleas, consult your vet for the proper diagnosis and medication.

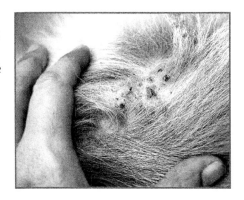

Diet and Food Allergies

Food is the third most common cause of allergies in dogs. Cheap dog foods bulked up with grains and other ingredients can cause problems. Some owners have reported their dogs having intolerance to wheat and other grains. If you feed your dog a dry commercial dog food, make sure that it is high quality, preferably hypoallergenic, and that the first ingredient listed on the sack is *meat or poultry,* not grain. Without the correct food, a dog's whole body - not just the skin and coat - will continuously be under stress and this manifests itself in a number of ways. The symptoms of food allergies are similar to those of most allergies:

- ❧ Itchy skin affecting primarily the face, feet, ears, forelegs, armpits and anus

- ❧ Excessive scratching

- ❧ Chronic or recurring ear infections

- ❧ Hair loss

- ❧ Hot spots

- ❧ Skin infections that clear up with antibiotics, but return after the antibiotics have finished

- ❧ Possible increased bowel movements, maybe twice as many as normal

The bodily process that occurs when an animal has a reaction to a particular food agent is not very well understood, but the veterinary profession does know how to diagnose and treat food allergies. As many other problems can cause similar symptoms (and also the fact that many sufferers also have other allergies), it is important that any other conditions are identified and treated before food allergies are diagnosed.

Owner of 15-month-old black F1 Winston, adds: "I think Winston is sensitive to grain, although nothing has been confirmed. Symptoms started at about seven months old and were itchiness and chewing his paws. We are eliminating grain and feeding Kefir (fermented goat's milk) daily and don't feed chicken or turkey. We are getting there; he doesn't seem to be as itchy now. He's not completely cured, but he's much better."

Atopy, flea bite allergies, intestinal parasite hypersensitivities, sarcoptic mange and yeast or bacterial infections can all cause similar symptoms. This can be an anxious time for owners as vets try one thing after another to get to the bottom of the allergy. The normal method for diagnosing a food allergy is elimination. Once all other causes have been ruled out or treated, then a food trial is the next step — and that's no picnic for owners either - see **Chapter 7. Feeding a Cavapoo** for more information.

In reality, most owners proceed with trial and error, researching online forums and other sources to find out what has worked for other Cavapoos. If this is the route you decide to take, look for a food that is completely natural - without preservatives - either raw or cooked. There are many pre-prepared frozen options available these days - most of which can be delivered to your home. They may not be the cheapest food, but will be worth it if your Cavapoo wolfs it down without any diarrhoea or skin issues.

As with other allergies, dogs may have short-term relief by taking fatty acids, antihistamines, and steroids, but removing the offending items from the diet is the only permanent solution.

Acute Moist Dermatitis (Hot Spots)

Acute moist dermatitis or 'hot spots' are not uncommon. A hot spot can appear suddenly and is a raw, inflamed and often bleeding area of skin. The area becomes moist and painful and begins spreading due to continual licking and chewing. They can become large, red, irritated lesions in a short pace of time. The cause is often a local reaction to an insect bite - fleas, ticks, biting flies or mosquitoes. Other causes of hot spots include:

- ❧ Allergies - inhalant allergies and food allergies
- ❧ Mites
- ❧ Ear infections
- ❧ Poor grooming
- ❧ Burs or plant awns
- ❧ Anal gland disease
- ❧ Hip dysplasia or other types of arthritis and degenerative joint disease

Once diagnosed and with the right treatment, hot spots disappear as soon as they appeared. The underlying cause should be identified and treated, if possible. Check with your vet before treating your Cavapoo for fleas and ticks at the same time as other medical treatment (such as anti-inflammatory medications and/or antibiotics), as he or she will probably advise you to wait.

Treatments may come in the form of injections, tablets or creams – or your dog might need a combination of them. Your vet will probably clip and clean the affected area to help the effectiveness of any spray or ointment and your poor Cavapoo might also have to wear an E-collar until the condition subsides, but usually this does not take long.

Interdigital Cysts

If your Cavapoo gets a fleshy red lump between the toes that looks like an ulcerated sore or a hairless bump, then there's a good chance it is an interdigital cyst - or *interdigital furuncle* to give the condition its correct medical term. This unpleasant condition can be very difficult to get rid of, since it is often not the primary issue, but a sign of some other problem. The 'Bully breeds' (Bulldogs, French Bulldogs, Pugs, etc.) are most susceptible, but Cavapoos can, like any dog, suffer from them – and often it's those dogs that suffer from other allergies.

Actually, they are not cysts, but the result of **furunculosis**, a condition of the skin which clogs hair follicles and creates chronic infection. They can be caused by a number of factors, including allergies, obesity, poor foot conformation, mites, yeast infections, ingrown hairs or other foreign bodies, and obesity.

These nasty-looking bumps are painful for your dog, will probably cause a limp and can be a nightmare to get rid of. Vets might recommend a whole range of treatments to get to the root cause of the problem. It can be extremely expensive if your dog is having a barrage of tests or biopsies, and even then you are not guaranteed to find the underlying cause. The first thing he or she will probably do is put your dog in an E-collar to stop him licking the affected area, which will never recover properly as long as it's constantly being licked. This again is stressful for your dog.

Cavapoos are sensitive dogs and some can be resistant to E-collars - they may slump down like you've hung a 10-ton weight on their neck or just become depressed by the whole thing. You might consider putting socks on the affected foot or feet, which will work well while your dog sleeps, but then you'll have to watch him or her like a hawk when awake to stop the affected areas being licked or bitten. Here are some remedies your vet may suggest:

- ❖ Antibiotics and/or steroids and/or mite killers
- ❖ Soaking the feet in Epsom salts twice daily to unclog the hair follicles
- ❖ Testing for allergies or thyroid problems
- ❖ Starting a food trial if food allergies are suspected
- ❖ Shampooing the feet
- ❖ Cleaning between the toes with medicated (benzoyl peroxide) wipes
- ❖ A referral to a veterinary dermatologist
- ❖ Surgery (this is a last-resort option)

If you suspect your Cavapoo has an interdigital cyst, get to the vet for a correct diagnosis and then discuss the various options. A course of antibiotics may be suggested initially, along with switching to a hypoallergenic diet if a food allergy is suspected. If the condition persists, many owners get discouraged, especially when treatment may go on for many weeks.

Be wary of going on to steroid injections or repeated courses of antibiotics, as this may mean that the underlying cause of the furuncle has not been diagnosed and will persist.

 Before you resort to any drastic action, first try soaking your Cavapoo's affected paw in Epsom salts for five or 10 minutes twice a day. After the soaking, clean the area with medicated wipes, which are antiseptic and control inflammation. In the US these are sold under the brand name Stridex pads in the skin care section of any grocery, or from the pharmacy.

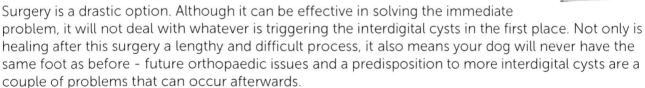

If you think the cause may be an environmental allergy, wash your dog's feet and under his belly when you return from a walk, as this will help to remove pollen and other allergens.

Surgery is a drastic option. Although it can be effective in solving the immediate problem, it will not deal with whatever is triggering the interdigital cysts in the first place. Not only is healing after this surgery a lengthy and difficult process, it also means your dog will never have the same foot as before - future orthopaedic issues and a predisposition to more interdigital cysts are a couple of problems that can occur afterwards.

All that said, your vet will understand that interdigital cysts aren't so simple to deal with, but they are always treatable. **Get the right diagnosis as soon as possible**, limit all offending factors and give medical treatment a good solid try before embarking on more drastic cures.

Parasites

Demodectic Mange

Demodectic Mange is also known as **Demodex,** *red mange, follicular mange* or *puppy mange.* It is caused by the tiny mite Demodex canis – *pictured* – which can only be seen through a microscope. The mites actually live inside the hair follicles on the bodies of virtually every adult dog, and most humans, without causing any harm or irritation. In humans, the mites are found in the skin, eyelids and the creases of the nose...try not to think about that!

The Demodex mite spends its entire life on the host dog. Eggs hatch and mature from larvae to nymphs to adults in 20 to 35 days and the mites are transferred directly from the mother to the puppies within the first week of life by direct physical contact. Demodectic mange is not a disease of poorly-kept or dirty kennels. It is generally a disease of young dogs with inadequate or poorly developed immune systems (or older dogs suffering from a suppressed immune system).

Vets currently believe that virtually every mother carries and transfers mites to her puppies, and most are immune to the mite's effects, but a few puppies are not and they develop full-blown mange. They may have a few (less than five) isolated lesions and this is known as localised mange – often around the head. This happens in around 90% of cases.

In the other 10% of cases, it develops into generalised mange that covers the entire body or region of the body. This is most likely to develop in puppies with parents that have suffered from mange. Most lesions in either form develop after four months of age. It can also develop around the time when females have their first season and may be due to a slight dip in the bitch's immune system.

Symptoms – Bald patches are usually the first sign, usually accompanied by crusty, red skin that sometimes appears greasy or wet. Usually hair loss begins around the muzzle, eyes and other areas on the head. The lesions may or may not itch. In localised mange, a few circular crusty areas appear, most frequently on the head and front legs of three to six-month-old puppies. Most will self-heal as the puppies become older and develop their own immunity, but a persistent problem needs treatment.

With generalised mange there are bald patches over the entire coat, including the head, neck, body, legs, and feet. The skin on the head, side and back is crusty, often inflamed and oozes a clear fluid. The skin itself will often be oily to touch and there is usually a secondary bacterial infection. Some puppies can become quite ill and can develop a fever, lose their appetites and become lethargic. If you suspect your puppy has generalised demodectic mange, get him to a vet straight away.

There is also a condition called pododermatitis, when the mange affects a puppy's paws. It can cause bacterial infections and be very uncomfortable, even painful. The symptoms of this mange include hair loss on the paws, swelling of the paws (especially around the nail beds) and red/hot/inflamed areas which are often infected. Treatment is always recommended, and it can take several rounds to clear it up.

Diagnosis and Treatment – The vet will normally diagnose demodectic mange after he or she has taken a skin scraping. As these mites are present on every dog, they do not necessarily mean the dog has mange. Only when the mite is coupled with lesions will the vet diagnose mange. Treatment usually involves topical (on the skin) medication and sometimes tablets. In 90% of cases localised demodectic mange resolves itself as the puppy grows. If the dog has just one or two lesions, these can usually be successfully treated using specific creams and spot treatments. There are also non-chemical treatments, such as the one pictured, to relieve symptoms.

With the more serious generalised demodectic mange, treatment can be lengthy and expensive. The vet might prescribe an anti-parasitic dip every two weeks. Owners should always wear rubber gloves when treating their dog, and it should be applied in an area with adequate ventilation.

Note that **some dogs – especially Toy breeds, which may include Cavapoos bred from Toy Poodles - can have a bad reaction to these dips,** so check with your vet as to whether it will be suitable for your dog. Most dogs with a severe issue need six to 14 dips every two weeks. After the first three or four dips, your vet will probably take another skin scraping to check the mites have gone. Dips continue for one month after the mites have disappeared, but dogs shouldn't be considered cured until a year after their last treatment.

Other options include the heartworm treatment Ivermectin. This isn't approved by the FDA for treating mange, but is often used to do so. It is usually given orally every one to two days, or by injection, and can be very effective. **Again, some dogs react badly to it.** Another drug is Interceptor (Milbemycin oxime), which can be expensive as it has to be given daily. However, it is effective on up to 80% of the dogs who did not respond to dips – but should be given with caution to pups under 21 weeks of age.

Dogs that have the generalised condition may have underlying skin infections, so antibiotics are often given for the first several weeks of treatment. Because the mite flourishes on dogs with suppressed immune systems, you should try to get to the root cause of immune system disease, especially if your Cavapoo is older when he or she develops demodectic mange.

Harvest Mite

Another parasitic mite that can affect dogs and other animals in late summer and autumn is the harvest mite, particularly if you walk your dog through long, grassy fields. The orange, six-legged mite is so small, it is barely visible to the human eye. It attacks warm blooded animals – and humans, as the larvae feed on tissue fluid and can cause considerable discomfort.

 The larvae congregate on small clods of earth or vegetation and are particularly active in dry, sunny weather. When a warm-blooded animal comes into contact with them, they swarm on and attach to the skin – especially thin-skinned areas with not much hair. Individual larva injects a fluid which breaks down skin cells. The mite then sucks on the same place for two or three days before dropping off the host, leaving a red swelling that can itch severely.

The itching usually develops within three to six hours, but can continue for several weeks. The fluid injected by the mite is very irritating, causing the dog to scratch, bite and lick, which can result in further self-inflicted injury. Harvest mite larvae are only active during the day, so if your regular walk is through long, grassy fields, consider going very early in the morning in warm weather, before the mites become active. And if you do have a problem, wash all clothes you were wearing when you think the mites first attacked.

There are sprays available from your vet that can help, but it is more important to thoroughly wash your dog with a good insecticidal shampoo. *Thornit* is a remedy used for ear mites that can also be used for harvest mites. Thornit is a powder based on Iodoform that can be lightly dusted on to the itchy areas, or in to itchy ears. Relief usually comes within two to five days. *Yumega Plus* for dogs can also help to relieve itching as it has a combination of Omega and Omega 6.

THORNIT
CANKER POWDER
For dogs, cats and rabbits
07596 740454
w.thornitearpowder.co

Cheyletiella (Rabbit Fur Mite)

"My dog appears to have dandruff, there's lots of white scurf in his coat," is a commonly-heard claim. Occasionally, scurf can be caused by a very dry skin or even by shampoo not being

thoroughly rinsed out of the coat after a bath, but in many cases, the parasitic Cheyletiella mite is to blame.

There are few symptoms, but a heavy infestation can cause itching, skin scaling and hair loss. The mites, their eggs and the scurf they produce have been called *"walking dandruff"*, which is most frequently seen on the back and sides of the dog. Skin scales are carried through the hair coat by the mites, so the dandruff appears to be moving along the back of the animal, hence the nickname.

The mite spends its entire life cycle on the dog. Eggs are laid glued to the hair shafts and go on to form larvae, then nymph and then adult mites. They are spread by direct contact with an infected individual or infested bedding. These mites are non-burrowing and feed on the keratin layer or epidermis. They most often inhabit the dorsal coat (along the backbone or spine). The mite's life cycle lasts around 21 days on the host, which gives it plenty of time to spread to other areas and animals or humans.

Most affected dogs respond quite well to treatment, although it can sometimes take a while to completely cure the infestation. Your vet may prescribe a pyrethrin-based shampoo. Frontline spray has also been proved to be effective in killing off the mites.

After bathing with an insecticidal shampoo, it can also be quite effective if the dog is rinsed in a benzyl benzoate mixture prescribed by the vet and diluted as per the recommendations. Great care should be taken to not allow this to go anywhere near your dog's face. Always consult your vet.

Your dog's bedding area should be treated and you should also be aware that these mites can temporarily infest humans, causing a mild skin irritation and some itching. In some severe cases, open lesions may occur.

Sarcoptic Mange (Scabies)

Also known as canine scabies, this is caused by the parasite *Sarcoptes scabiei*. This microscopic mite can cause a range of skin problems, the most common of which is hair loss and severe itching. The mites can infect other animals such as foxes, cats and even humans, but prefer to live their short lives on dogs. Fortunately, there are several good treatments for this type of mange and the disease can be easily controlled.

In cool, moist environments, the mites live for up to 22 days. At normal room temperature they live from two to six days, preferring to live on parts of the dog with less hair. These are the areas you may see him scratching, although it can spread throughout the body in severe cases. Diagnosing canine scabies can be somewhat difficult, and it is often mistaken for inhalant allergies.

Once diagnosed, there are a number of effective treatments, including selamectin (Revolution – again, some dogs can have a bad reaction to this), an on-the-skin solution applied once a month which also provides heartworm prevention, flea control and some tick protection. Various Frontline products are also effective – check with your vet for the correct ones. There are also holistic remedies for many skin conditions. Because your dog does not have to come into direct contact with an infected dog to catch scabies, it is difficult to completely protect him. Foxes and their environment can also transmit the mite so, if possible, keep your Cavapoo away from areas where you know foxes are present.

Fleas

When you see your dog scratching and biting, your first thought is probably: "He's got fleas!" and you may well be right. Fleas don't fly, but they do have very strong back legs and they will take any opportunity to jump from the ground or another animal into your Cavapoo's lovely warm coat. You can sometimes see the fleas if you part your dog's hair.

And for every flea that you see on your dog, there is the awful prospect of hundreds of eggs and larvae in your house or apartment. So, if your dog is unlucky enough to catch fleas, you'll have to treat your environment as well as your dog in order to completely get rid of them.

The best form of cure is prevention. Vets recommend giving dogs a preventative flea treatment every four to eight weeks. This may vary depending on your climate, the season - fleas do not breed as quickly in the cold - and how much time your dog spends outdoors. Once-a-month topical (applied to the skin) insecticides - like Frontline and Advantix - are the most commonly used flea prevention products on the market. You part the skin and apply drops of the liquid on to a small area on your dog's back, usually near the neck. Some kill fleas and ticks, and others just kill fleas - check the details.

It is worth spending the money on a quality treatment, as cheaper brands may not rid your Cavapoo completely of fleas, ticks and other parasites. Sprays, dips, shampoos and collars are other options, as are tablets and injections in certain cases, such as before your dog goes into boarding kennels or has surgery. Incidentally, a flea bite is different from a flea bite allergy.

One UK breeder said that many breeders are opposed to chemical flea treatments, such as Spot On or ones from the vet, as so many dogs have been reported as reacting to the area it's applied to on the skin - and in extreme cases some have been known to have seizures. She added that when she found a flea, she simply washed all of her dogs, one after the other, and then washed every last piece of bedding and hadn't seen them since. There are also holistic and natural remedies to chemical flea treatments, discussed later in this chapter.

NOTE: There is also anecdotal evidence from owners of various breeds that the US flea and worm tablet *Trifexis* may cause severe side effects in some dogs. You may wish to read some owners' comments at: www.max-the-schnauzer.com/trifexis-side-effects-in-schnauzers.html

Ticks

A tick is not an insect, but a member of the arachnid family, like the spider. There are over 850 types of them, divided into two types: hard shelled and soft shelled. Ticks don't have wings - they can't fly, they crawl. They have a sensor called Haller's organ that detects smell, heat and humidity to help them locate food, which in some cases is a Cavapoo. A tick's diet consists of one thing and one thing only – blood! They climb up onto tall grass and when they sense an animal is close, crawl on.

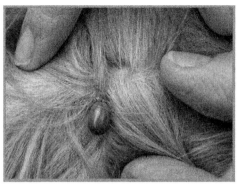

Ticks can pass on a number of diseases to animals and humans, the most well-known of which is **Lyme Disease**, a serious condition that causes lameness and other problems. Dogs that spend a lot of time outdoors in high risk areas, such as woods, can have a vaccination against Lime Disease.

One breeder added: " We get ticks from sand dunes sometimes and, if removed quickly, they're not harmful. We use a tick tool which has instructions in the packet. You put the forked end either side of the tick and twist it till it comes out."

If you do find a tick on your Cavapoo's coat and are not sure how to get it out, have it removed by a vet or other expert. Inexpertly pulling it out yourself and leaving a bit of the tick behind can be detrimental to your dog's health. Prevention treatment is similar to that for fleas. If your Cavapoo has sensitive skin, he or she might do better with a natural flea or tick remedy.

Heartworm

Heartworm is a serious and potentially fatal disease affecting pets in North America and many other parts of the world (but not the UK). It is caused by foot-long worms (heartworms) that live in the heart, lungs and associated blood vessels of affected pets, causing severe lung disease, heart failure and damage to other organs in the body.

The dog is a natural host for heartworms, which means that heartworms living inside the dog mature into adults, mate and produce offspring. If untreated, their numbers can increase; dogs have been known to harbour several hundred worms in their bodies. Heartworm disease causes lasting damage to the heart, lungs and arteries, and can affect the dog's health and quality of life long after the parasites are gone. For this reason, prevention is by far the best option and treatment - when needed - should be administered as early as possible.

The mosquito (*pictured*) plays an essential role in the heartworm life cycle. When a mosquito bites and takes a blood meal from an infected animal, it picks up baby worms that develop and mature into 'infective stage' larvae over a period of 10 to 14 days.

Then, when the infected mosquito bites another dog, cat or susceptible wild animal, the infective larvae are deposited onto the surface of the animal's skin and enter the new host through the mosquito's bite wound. Once inside a new host, it takes approximately six months for the larvae to develop into adult heartworms. Once mature, heartworms can live for five to seven years in a dog. In the early stages of the disease, many dogs show few or no symptoms. The longer the infection persists, the more likely symptoms will develop. These include:

- ❖ A mild persistent cough
- ❖ Reluctance to exercise
- ❖ Tiredness after moderate activity
- ❖ Decreased appetite
- ❖ Weight loss

As the disease progresses, dogs may develop heart failure and a swollen belly due to excess fluid in the abdomen. Dogs with large numbers of heartworms can develop sudden blockages of blood flow within the heart leading to the life-threatening caval syndrome. This is marked by a sudden onset of laboured breathing, pale gums and dark, bloody or coffee-coloured urine. Without prompt surgical removal of the heartworm blockage, few dogs survive.

Although more common in the south eastern US, heartworm disease has been diagnosed in all 50 states. And because infected mosquitoes can fly indoors, even dogs that spend much time inside the home are at risk. For that reason, the American Heartworm Society recommends that you get your dog tested every year and give your dog heartworm preventive treatment for 12 months of the year. If you live in a risk area, check that your tick and flea medication also prevents heartworm. In the UK, heartworm has only been found in imported dogs.

Thanks to the American Heartworm Society for assistance with the section.

Ringworm

This is not actually a worm, but a fungus and is most commonly seen in puppies and young dogs. It is highly infectious and often found on the face, ears, paws or tail. The ringworm fungus is most prevalent in hot, humid climates but, surprisingly, most cases occur in autumn and winter. Ringworm infections in dogs are not that common; in one study of dogs with active skin problems, less than 3% had ringworm.

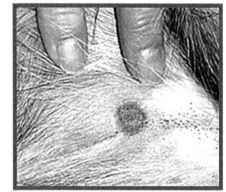

Ringworm is transmitted by spores in the soil and by contact with the infected hair of dogs and cats, which can be typically found on carpets, brushes, combs, toys and furniture. Spores from infected animals can be shed into the environment and live for over 18 months, but fortunately most healthy adult dogs have some resistance and never develop symptoms. The fungi live in dead skin, hairs and nails - and the head and legs are the most common areas affected.

Tell-tale signs are bald patches with a roughly circular shape (*pictured*). Ringworm is relatively easy to treat with fungicidal shampoos or antibiotics from a vet. Humans can catch ringworm from pets, and vice versa. Children are especially susceptible, as are adults with suppressed immune systems and those undergoing chemotherapy. Hygiene is extremely important.

If your dog has ringworm, wear gloves when handling him and wash your hands well afterwards. And if a member of your family catches ringworm, make sure they use separate towels from everyone else or the fungus may spread. (As a teenager I caught ringworm from horses at the stables where I worked at weekends - much to my mother's horror - and was treated like a leper by the rest of the family until it cleared up!).

Bacterial infection (Pyoderma)

Pyoderma literally means 'pus in the skin' (yuk!) and fortunately this condition is not contagious. Early signs of this bacterial infection are itchy red spots filled with yellow pus, similar to pimples or spots in humans. They can sometimes develop into red, ulcerated skin with dry and crusty patches.

Pyoderma is caused by several things: a broken skin surface, a skin wound due to chronic exposure to moisture, altered skin bacteria, or impaired blood flow to the skin. Dogs have a higher risk of developing an infection when they have a fungal infection or an endocrine (hormone gland) disease such as hyperthyroidism, or have allergies to fleas, food or parasites.

Pyoderma is often secondary to allergic dermatitis and develops in the sores on the skin that occur as a result of scratching. Puppies often develop 'puppy pyoderma' in thinly-haired areas such as the groin and underarms. Fleas, ticks, yeast or fungal skin infections, thyroid disease, hormonal imbalances, heredity and some medications can increase the risk. If you notice symptoms, get your dog to the vet quickly before the condition develops from **superficial pyoderma** into **severe pyoderma**, which is very unpleasant and takes a lot longer to treat.

Bacterial infection, no matter how bad it may look, usually responds well to medical treatment, which is generally done on an outpatient basis. Superficial pyoderma will usually be treated with a two to six-week course of antibiotic tablets or ointment. Severe or recurring pyoderma looks awful, causes your dog some distress and can take months of treatment to completely cure. Medicated shampoos and regular bathing, as instructed by your vet, are also part of the treatment. It's also important to ensure your dog has clean, dry, padded bedding.

Canine Acne

This is not that common and - just as with humans - generally affects teenagers, often between five and eight months of age with dogs. Acne occurs when oil glands become blocked causing bacterial infection and these glands are most active in teenagers. Acne is not a major health problem as most of it will clear up once the dog becomes an adult, but it can reoccur. Typical signs are pimples, blackheads or whiteheads around the muzzle, chest or groin. If the area is irritated, then there may be some bleeding or pus that can be expressed from these blemishes.

Hormonal Imbalances

These occur in dogs of all breeds. They are often difficult to diagnose and occur when a dog is producing either too much (hyper) or too little (hypo) of a particular hormone. One visual sign is often hair loss on both sides of the dog's body. The condition is not usually itchy. Hormone imbalances can be serious as they are often indicators that glands that affect the dog internally are not working properly. However, some types can be diagnosed by special blood tests and treated effectively.

....

Ear Infections

Cavapoos have long, floppy, hairy ears, which can make some dogs susceptible to ear infections. Infection of the external ear canal (outer ear infection) is called *otitis externa* and is one of the most

common types seen. One cause is moisture in the ear canal, which in turn allows bacteria to flourish there.

However, the fact that a dog has recurring ear infections does not necessarily mean that his ears are the source of the problem – although they might be. Some dogs with chronic or recurring ear infections have inhalant or food allergies or low thyroid function (hypothyroidism) Sometimes the ears are the first sign of allergy. The underlying problem must be treated or the dog will continue to have long term ear problems. Tell-tale signs include your dog shaking his head, scratching or rubbing his ears a lot, or an unpleasant smell coming from the ears.

If you look inside the ears, you may notice a reddy brown or yellow discharge, it may also be red and inflamed with a lot of wax. Sometimes a dog may appear depressed or irritable; ear infections are painful. In chronic cases, the inside of his ears may become crusty or thickened.

Causes of ear problems include:

- Allergies, such as environmental or food allergies
- Ear mites or other parasites
- Bacteria or yeast infections
- Injury, often due to excessive scratching
- Hormonal abnormalities, e.g. hypothyroidism
- The ear anatomy and environment, e.g. excess moisture
- Hereditary or immune conditions and tumours

In reality, many Cavapoos have ear infections due to the structure of the ear. The long, hairy ears often prevent sufficient air flow inside the ear. This can lead to bacterial or yeast infections - particularly if there is moisture inside. These warm, damp and dark areas under the ear flaps provide an ideal breeding ground for bacteria.

Treatment depends on the cause and what – if any - other conditions your dog may have. Antibiotics are used for bacterial infections and antifungals for yeast infections. Glucocorticoids, such as dexamethasone, are often included in these medications to reduce the inflammation in the ear. Your vet may also flush out and clean the ear with special drops, something you may have to do daily at home until the infection clears.

A dog's ear canal is L-shaped, which means it can be difficult to get medication into the lower (horizontal) part of the ear. The best method is to hold the dog's ear flap with one hand and put the ointment or drops in with the other, if possible tilting the dog's head away from you so the liquid flows downwards **with gravity**. Make sure you then hold the ear flap down and massage the medication into the horizontal canal before letting go of your dog, as the first thing he will do is shake his head – and if the ointment or drops aren't massaged in, they will fly out.

Nearly all ear infections can be successfully managed if properly diagnosed and treated. But if an underlying problem remains undiscovered, the outcome will be less favourable.

Deep ear infections can damage or rupture the eardrum, causing an internal ear infection and even permanent hearing loss. Closing of the ear canal (*hyperplasia* or *stenosis)* is another sign of severe infection. Most extreme cases of hyperplasia will eventually require surgery as a last resort; the most common procedure is called a 'lateral ear resection'.

Our dog with allergies had a lateral ear resection following years of recurring ear infections and the growth of scar tissue. It was surgery or deafness, the vet said. We opted for surgery and the dog has been free of ear infections ever since. However, it is an **extremely** painful procedure for the animal and should only be considered as a very last resort.

To avoid or alleviate recurring ear infections, check your dog's ears and clean them regularly. Hair should be regularly plucked from inside your Cavapoo's ears – either by you or a groomer, or both.

When cleaning or plucking your dog's ears, be very careful not to put anything too far down inside. Visit YouTube to see videos of how to correctly clean without damaging them. DO NOT use cotton buds inside the ear, they are too small and can cause injury. Some owners recommend regularly cleaning the inside of ears with cotton wool and a mixture of water and white vinegar once or twice a week.

If your Cavapoo is one of the many that enjoys swimming, great care should be taken to ensure the inside of the ear is thoroughly dry afterwards - and after bathing at home. There is more information in **Chapter 13. Grooming.**

 Consider buying elevated food and water bowls. They have higher, narrower tops than normal dog dishes and help to keep your dog's ears out of his or her food and water.

If your dog appears to be in pain, has smelly ears, or if his ear canals look inflamed, contact your vet straight away. If you can nip the first infection in the bud, there is a chance it will not return. If your dog has a ruptured or weakened eardrum, ear cleansers and medications could do more harm than good. Early treatment is the best way of preventing a recurrence.

Some Allergy Treatments

Treatments and success rates vary tremendously from dog to dog and from one allergy to another, which is why it is so important to consult a vet at the outset. Earlier diagnosis is more likely to lead to a successful treatment. Some owners whose dogs have recurring skin issues find that a course of antibiotics or steroids works wonders for their dog's sore skin and itching. However, the scratching starts all over again shortly after the treatment stops.

NOTE: While a single steroid injection is highly effective in calming down symptoms almost immediately, frequent or long-term steroid use is not a good option as it can lead to serious side effects. Read more at: https://vcahospitals.com/know-your-pet/steroid-treatment-long-term-effects-in-dogs

Food allergies require patience, a change or several changes of diet and maybe even a food trial, and the specific trigger is notoriously difficult to isolate – unless you are lucky and hit on the culprit straight away. With inhalant and contact allergies, blood and skin tests are available, followed by hypersensitisation treatment. However, these are expensive and often the specific trigger for many dogs remains unknown. So, the reality for many owners of Cavapoos with allergies is that they manage, rather than curing it completely.

Our Personal Experience

After corresponding with numerous other dog owners and consulting our vet, Graham, it seems that our experiences with allergies are not uncommon. This is borne out by the dozens of dog owners who have contacted our website about their pet's allergy or sensitivities. According to Graham, more and more dogs are appearing in his waiting room every spring with various types of allergies. Whether this is connected to how we breed our dogs remains to be seen.

Our dog was perfectly fine until he was about two years old when he began to scratch a lot. He scratched more in spring and summer, which meant that his allergies were almost certainly inhalant or contact-based and related to pollens, grasses or other outdoor triggers. One option was a barrage of tests to discover exactly what he was allergic to. We decided not to do this, not because of the cost, but because the vet said it was highly likely that he was allergic to pollens.

If we had confirmed an allergy to pollens, we were not going to stop taking him outside for walks, so the dog was treated on the basis of seasonal inhalant or contact allergies, probably related to pollen.

As mentioned, it's beneficial to have a shallow bath or hose outside and to rinse the dog's paws and underbelly after a walk in the countryside. This is something our vet does with his own dogs and has found that the scratching reduces as a result. Regarding medications, our dog was at first put on to a tiny dose of Piriton, an antihistamine for hay fever sufferers (human and canine) and for the first few springs and summers, this worked well.

Allergies can often change and the dog can also build up a tolerance to a treatment, which is why they can be so difficult to treat. This has been the case with us over the years. The symptoms changed from season to season, although the main ones remained and were: general scratching, paw biting and ear infections.

One year he bit the skin under his tail a lot (near the anus) and this was treated very effectively with a single steroid injection followed by spraying the area with cortisone once a day at home for a period. This type of spray can be very effective if the itchy area is small, but no good for spraying all over a dog's body.

Not every owner wants to treat his or her dog with chemicals, nor feed a diet which includes preservatives, which is why this book includes alternatives. Fifteen years ago, when we were starting out on the "Allergy Trail" there were far fewer options than there are now.

A few years ago he started nibbling his paws for the first time - a habit he persisted with - although not to the extent that they become red and raw. Over the years we tried a number of treatments, all of which worked for a while, before he came off the medication in autumn for six months when plants and grasses stop growing outdoors. He managed perfectly fine the rest of the year without any treatment at all.

We fed a high quality hypoallergenic dry food. If we were starting again from scratch, knowing what we know now, I would probably investigate earlier a raw or home-cooked diet (which is what he was fed towards the end of his life), if necessary in combination with holistic remedies. Max's allergies were manageable; he loved his food, was full of energy and otherwise healthy, and lived a happy life to the age of 13 years.

One season the vet put him on a short course of steroids. These worked very well for five months, but steroids are not a long-term solution. Another spring, we were prescribed Atopica, a non-steroid daily tablet sold in the UK only through vets. The active ingredient is **cyclosporine**, which suppresses the immune system. Some dogs can get side effects, although ours didn't, and holistic practitioners believe that it is harmful to the dog. This treatment was expensive, but initially extremely effective – so much so that we thought we had cured the problem completely. However, after a couple of seasons on cyclosporine he developed a tolerance to the drug and started scratching again.

A few years ago he went back on the antihistamine Piriton, a higher dose than when he was two years old, and this worked very well again. One advantage of this drug is that is it manufactured by the million for dogs and is therefore very inexpensive.

In 2013 the FDA approved **Apoquel** (oclacitinib) to control itching and inflammation in allergic dogs. In some quarters it was hailed a wonder drug for canine allergies. In fact it proved so popular in the UK and North

America that in the following two years there was a shortage of supply, with the manufacturers not being able to produce it fast enough. We tried Apoquel with excellent results. There was some tweaking at the beginning to get the daily dose right, but it really proved effective. The tablets are administered according to body weight and cost around £1 or $1.50 each. It's not cheap, but Apoquel can be a miracle worker for some dogs.

NOTE: This article from Dogs Naturally magazine recommends NOT giving Apoquel to your dog: www.dogsnaturallymagazine.com/wouldnt-give-dog-new-allergy-drug - make up your own mind what is best for your dog. Allergies are often complex and difficult to treat; you should weigh up the pros and cons in the best interests of your individual dog.

Vets often recommend adding fish oils (which contain Omega-3 fatty acids) to a daily feed to keep your dog's skin and coat healthy all year round – whether or not he has problems. We added a liquid supplement called Yumega Plus, which contains Omegas 3 and 6, to one of the two daily feeds all year round. When the scratching got particularly bad, we bathed our dog in an antiseborrheic shampoo (**called Malaseb, pictured**) twice a week for a limited time. This also helped, although was not necessary once on Apoquel.

The main point is that most allergies are manageable, although they may change throughout the life of the dog and you may have to alter the treatment. Here are some suggestions:

Bathing - bathing your dog using shampoos that break down the oils that plug the hair follicles. These shampoos contain antiseborrheic ingredients such as benzoyl peroxide, salicylic acid, sulphur or tar. One example is Sulfoxydex shampoo, which can be followed by a cream rinse such as Episoothe Rinse afterwards to prevent the skin from drying out.

Dabbing – Using an astringent such as witch hazel or alcohop on affected areas. We have heard of zinc oxide cream being used to some effect. In the human world, this is rubbed on to mild skin abrasions and acts as a protective coating. It can help the healing of chapped skin and nappy rash in babies. Zinc oxide works as a mild astringent and has some antiseptic properties and is safe to use on dogs, **as long as you do not allow the dog to lick it off**.

Daily supplements - Vitamin E, vitamin A, zinc and omega oils all help to make a dog's skin healthy. Feed a daily supplement that contains some of these, such as fish oil, which provides omega.

Here are some specific remedies from owners. We are not endorsing them; we're just passing on the information. Check with your vet before trying any new remedies. A medicated shampoo with natural tea tree oil has been suggested by one owner. Some have reported that switching to a fish-based diet has helped lessen scratching, while others have suggested home-cooked food is best, if you have the time to prepare the food.

Another reader said: "I have been putting a teaspoon of canola (rapeseed) oil in my dog's food every other day and it has helped with the itching. I have shampooed the new carpet in hopes of removing any of the chemicals that could be irritating her. And I have changed laundry detergent. After several loads of laundry everything has been washed."

And from another reader: "My eight-month-old dog also had a contact dermatitis around his neck and chest. I was surprised how extensive it was. The vet recommended twice-a-week baths with an oatmeal shampoo. I also applied organic coconut oil daily for a few weeks and this completely cured the dermatitis. I also put a capsule of fish oil with his food once a day and continue to give him twice-weekly baths. His skin is great now."

Many owners have tried coconut oil with some success. Here is a link to an article on the benefits of coconut oils and fish oils, check with your vet first: www.dogsnaturallymagazine.com/the-health-benefits-of-coconut-oil

If you suspect your dog has a skin problem, ear infection or allergy, bite the bullet and get her or him to the vet straight away. You can hopefully nip it in the bud before secondary infections develop – and save a lot of heartache and money in the long run.

The Holistic Approach

As canine allergies become increasingly common, more and more owners of dogs with allergies and sensitivities are looking towards natural foods and remedies to help deal with the issues. Others are finding that their dog does well for a time with injections or medication, but then the symptoms slowly start to reappear. A holistic practitioner looks at finding the root cause of the problem and treating that, rather than just treating the symptoms.

Dr Sara Skiwski is a holistic vet working in California. She writes here about canine environmental allergies: "Here in California, with our mild weather and no hard freeze in Winter, environmental allergens can build up and cause nearly year-round issues for our beloved pets. Also seasonal allergies, when left unaddressed, can lead to year-round allergies.

"Unlike humans, whose allergy symptoms seem to affect mostly the respiratory tract, seasonal allergies in dogs often take the form of skin irritation/inflammation.

"Allergic reactions are produced by the immune system. The way the immune system functions is a result of both genetics and the environment: Nature versus Nurture. Let's look at a typical case. A puppy starts showing mild seasonal allergy symptoms, for instance a red tummy and mild itching in Spring. Off to the vet!

"The treatment prescribed is symptomatic to provide relief, such as a topical spray. The next year when the weather warms up, the patient is back again - same symptoms but more severe this time. This time the dog has very itchy skin. Again, the treatment is symptomatic - antibiotics, topical spray (hopefully no steroids), until the symptoms resolve with the season change. Fast forward to another Spring...on the third year, the patient is back again but this time the symptoms last longer, (not just Spring but also through most of Summer and into Fall).

"By Year Five, all the symptoms are significantly worse and are occurring year round. This is what happens with seasonal environmental allergies. The more your pet is exposed to the allergens they are sensitive to, the more the immune system over-reacts and the more intense and long-lasting the allergic response becomes. What to do?

"In my practice, I like to address the potential root cause at the very first sign of an allergic response, which is normally seen between the ages of six to nine months old. I do this to circumvent the escalating response year after year. Since the allergen load your environmentally-sensitive dog is most susceptible to is much heavier outdoors, I recommend two essential steps in managing the condition. They are vigilance in foot care as well as hair care.

"What does this mean? A wipe down of feet and hair, especially the tummy, to remove any pollens or allergens is key. This can be done with a damp cloth, but my favorite method is to get a spray bottle filled with Witch Hazel and spray these areas. First, spray the feet then wipe them off with a cloth, and then spray and wipe down the tummy and sides. This is best done right after the pup has been outside playing or walking. This will help keep your pet from tracking the environmental allergens into the home and into their beds. If the feet end up still being itchy, I suggest adding foot soaks in Epsom salts."

Dr Sara also stresses the importance of keeping the immune system healthy by avoiding unnecessary vaccinations or drugs: "The vaccine stimulates the immune system, which is the last thing your pet with seasonal environmental allergies needs.

"I also will move the pet to an anti-inflammatory diet. Foods that create or worsen inflammation are high in carbohydrates. An allergic pet's diet should be very low in carbohydrates, especially grains. Research has shown that 'leaky gut,' or dysbiosis, is a root cause of immune system overreactions in both dog and cats (and some humans). Feed a diet that is not processed, or minimally processed; one that doesn't have grain and takes a little longer to get absorbed and assimilated through the gut. Slowing the assimilation assures that there are not large spikes of nutrients and proteins that come into the body all at once and overtax the pancreas and liver, creating inflammation.

"A lot of commercial diets are too high in grains and carbohydrates. These foods create inflammation which overtaxes the body and leads not just to skin inflammation, but also to other inflammatory conditions, such as colitis, pancreatitis, arthritis, inflammatory bowel disease and ear infections. Also, these diets are too low in protein, which is needed to make blood. This causes a decreased blood reserve in the body and in some of these animals this can lead to the skin not being properly nourished, starting a cycle of chronic skin infections which produce more itching."

After looking at diet, check that your dog is free from fleas and then these are some of Dr Sara's suggested supplements:

✓ **Raw (Unpasteurised) Local Honey** - an alkaline-forming food containing natural vitamins, enzymes, powerful antioxidants and other important natural nutrients, which are destroyed during the heating and pasteurisation processes. Raw honey has anti-viral, anti-bacterial and anti-fungal properties. It promotes body and digestive health, is a powerful antioxidant, strengthens the immune system, eliminates allergies, and is an excellent remedy for skin wounds and all types of infections. Bees collect pollen from local plants and their honey often acts as an immune booster for dogs living in the locality.

Dr Sara says: "It may seem odd that straight exposure to pollen often triggers allergies, but that exposure to pollen in the honey usually has the opposite effect. But this is typically what we see. In honey, the allergens are delivered in small, manageable doses and the effect over time is very much like that from undergoing a whole series of allergy immunology injections."

✓ **Mushrooms** - make sure you choose the non-poisonous ones! Dogs don't like the taste, so may have to mask it with another food. Medicinal mushrooms are used to treat and prevent a wide array of illnesses through their use as immune stimulants and modulators, and antioxidants. The most well-known and researched are reishi, maitake, cordyceps, blazei, split-gill, turkey tail and shiitake. The mushrooms stabilise mast cells in the body, which have the histamines attached to them. Histamine is what causes much of the inflammation, redness and irritation in allergies. By helping to control histamine production, the mushrooms can moderate the effects of inflammation and even help prevent allergies in the first place.

WARNING! Mushrooms can interact with some over-the-counter and prescription drugs, so do your research as well as checking with your vet first.

✓ **Stinging Nettles** - contain biologically active compounds that reduce inflammation. Nettles have the ability to reduce the amount of histamine the body produces in response to an allergen. Nettle tea or extract can help with itching. Nettles not only help directly to decrease the itch, but also work overtime to desensitise the body to allergens, helping to reprogramme the immune system.

✓ **Quercetin** – is an over-the-counter supplement with anti-inflammatory properties. It is a strong antioxidant and reduces the body's production of histamines.

✓ **Omega-3 Fatty Acids** - these help decrease inflammation throughout the body. Adding them into the diet of all pets - particularly those struggling with seasonal environmental allergies – is very beneficial. If your dog has more itching along the top of their back and on their sides, add in a fish oil supplement. Fish oil helps to decrease the itch and heal skin lesions. The best sources of Omega 3s are krill oil, salmon oil, tuna oil, anchovy oil and other fish body oils, as well as raw organic egg yolks. If using an oil alone, it is important to give a vitamin B complex supplement.

✓ **Coconut Oil** - contains lauric acid, which helps decrease the production of yeast, a common opportunistic infection. Using a fish body oil combined with coconut oil before inflammation flares up can help moderate or even suppress your dog's inflammatory response.

Dr Sara adds: "Above are but a few of the over-the-counter remedies I like. In non-responsive cases, Chinese herbs can be used to work with the body to help to decrease the allergy threshold even more than with diet and supplements alone. Most of the animals I work with are on a program of Chinese herbs, diet change and acupuncture.

"So, the next time Fido is showing symptoms of seasonal allergies, consider rethinking your strategy to treat the root cause instead of the symptom."

With thanks to Dr Sara Skiwski, of the Western Dragon Integrated Veterinary Services, San Jose, California, for her kind permission to use her writings as the basis for this section.

....

This chapter has only just touched on the complex subject of skin disorders. As you can see, no two dogs are the same and the causes and treatments are many and varied. One thing is true whatever the condition: if your Cavapoo has a skin issue, seek a professional diagnosis as soon as possible before attempting to treat it yourself and before it becomes entrenched.

Early diagnosis and treatment give the best chance of a full recovery.

Some skin conditions cannot be completely cured, but they can be successfully managed, allowing your dog to live a happy, pain-free life. Once you have your pup or adult dog, remember that these factors go a long way in preventing or managing skin problems and ear infections in Cavapoos:

🐾 Regular grooming

🐾 A high quality diet

🐾 Attention to ears and cleanliness

13. Grooming the Cavapoo

When dog lovers weigh up all the pros and cons of different breeds before finally deciding on a Cavapoo, one topic which often seems to slip under the radar is ...grooming. Many new owners are very surprised at just how high maintenance the Cavapoo coat is, and Cavapoo forums are full of posts on the subject - not to mention countless photos of shaggy dogs! This chapter gives owners a real insight into just what's involved, with excellent advice from US breeder Laura Koch, of Petit Jean Puppies, UK breeder Charlotte Purkiss, of Lotties Cavapoos, and several owners.

The Cavapoo Coat

The coat is one of the big attractions of the Cavapoo, with many inheriting the low-shedding properties of the Poodle. Although this type of coat is best for allergy sufferers and leaves little or no trace around the house, it comes at a price as maintenance is time-consuming as well as expensive - unless you learn to trim your dog yourself.

A Cavapoo that has inherited more of the characteristics of the long, silky coat of the Cavalier or the wiry-type coat will shed hair, but these coats are actually easier to look after. Regular brushing at home and the occasional bath are enough to keep the coat clean and shiny. Although the coat does not need overall trimming, some Cavalier King Charles Spaniel owners do take their dogs to the groomer's every few months for a bath, general tidy up, ear plucking, anal glad squeezing and nail trimming.

All Cavapoos are born with a soft, wavy puppy coat, which starts to change to an adult coat at around six to eight or nine months old, a process which can last several months. The texture of an adult coat can vary from soft to curly, wiry or silky, depending on genetics, although the wavy coat is the most common.

It is around this time of change that a Cavapoo puppy's coat can become matted if it hasn't been regularly brushed. After several months, the whole matted coat is so tangled that sometimes it has to be shaved off, which can ruin the coat.

There is no denying that Cavapoo puppies look extremely cute when left with a natural coat, as shown by this *photo of Dolly, aged six months, just before her first trip to the groomer's, by Laura Lambert*.

But if you ignore grooming for the first few months, your puppy will return traumatised from his or her first trip to the grooming parlour and you will then have a lifelong battle, as the initial experience was negative. This is why it is so important to get your puppy used to being handled and brushed from the very beginning - and there's plenty of advice on that later in this chapter.

Coat colour (covered in **Chapter 3**) is governed by genetics, and although breeders may breed for a certain colour, genetics are complicated and there is no guarantee that all puppies from the same litter will all turn out to be the same colour. Also, coat colour may change or fade between puppyhood and adulthood. It is unlikely that a mature Cavapoo will be exactly the same shade as he or she was when first seen as a pup. For example, blacks may fade, reds may fade to apricot, some cream puppies may grow up to be almost white, and apricot may lighten. The change often happens by the time the dog is two years old.

Coats also fade as a dog enters his or her senior years, while injury to the skin - caused by bites, clipper cuts, surgical procedures, etc. – can make the affected area darker. And, like any breed, the Cavapoo can have coat or skin-related health issues. These are covered in detail in **Chapter 11. Cavapoo Health** and **Chapter 12. Skin and Allergies.**

Maintenance

Grooming doesn't just mean giving your Cavapoo a quick tickle with a brush every couple of weeks. There are other facets that play a part in keeping your dog clean and skin-related issues at bay. Time spent grooming is also time spent bonding with your dog; this physical and emotional inter-reliance brings us closer to our pets. Routine grooming sessions also allow you to examine your dog's coat, skin, ears, teeth, eyes, paws and nails for signs of problems. And once they have got used to it, most Cavapoos enjoy the attention.

Tip Most Cavapoos require extensive clipping and grooming throughout their lives, so it's important to get a puppy used to being groomed from an early age; adults will not take kindly to being handled if they are not used to it. You can start gently brushing your Cavapoo puppy a few days after you bring him or her home, and book an introductory trip to the groomer's as soon as it's safe to do so after vaccinations.

Puppy hair is soft and mats easily, so regular grooming early on, i.e. a few times a week, is essential. Don't risk permanently destroying some of the coat qualities by neglecting the task. A slicker or pin brush *(pictured)* is the best tool for brushing your puppy and getting the tangles out. Be careful not to damage the skin. Other benefits of regular brushing are that it removes dead hair and skin, stimulates blood circulation and spreads natural oils throughout the coat, helping to keep it in good condition.

If your adult Cavapoo has a wiry or straight coat, brushing once or twice a week is enough, but the more common wavy, soft coat requires more time and effort on the part of the owner. Cavapoos with low-shedding coats need to be trimmed regularly, which could be anything from every six to 12 weeks. Over the course of a year, this adds up to many hundreds of pounds or dollars, which is why many Cavapoo owners invest in a training course and a set of grooming tools. Over the course of your dog's life, you will save the cost of the investment many times over.

If you are considering full grooming at home, here are some things to consider buying:

- Electric clippers –the quality and price varies; cheap ones blunt quicker
- Brush - a slicker brush and/or pin brush
- Steel comb and possibly a de-matting comb
- Pet scissors with rounded ends
- Shampoo formulated for dogs
- Nail clippers or grinder
- Styptic powder to stop bleeding from the quick (nail)
- Eye wipes
- Canine toothbrush and toothpaste
- Ear powder to aid ear hair plucking if your Cavapoo has hairy ears

Tip If your Cavapoo is resisting your grooming efforts, place him on a table or bench - make sure he can't jump off or fasten him on. You'd be surprised what a difference this can make once out of his normal environment - i.e. floor level - and at your level.

A few things to look out for when grooming are:

Acne - Little red pimples on a dog's face and chin means he has got acne. A dog can get acne at any age, not just as an adolescent. Plastic bowls can also trigger the condition, which is why stainless steel ones are often better. Daily washing followed by an application of an antibiotic cream is usually enough to get rid of the problem; if it persists it will mean a visit to your vet.

Dry skin - A dog's skin can dry out, especially with artificial heat in the winter months. If you spot any dry patches, for example on the inner thighs or armpits, or a cracked nose, massage a little petroleum jelly or baby oil on to the dry patch.

Eyes - These should be clean and clear. Cloudy eyes, particularly in an older dog, could be early signs of cataracts. Red or swollen tissue in the corner of the eye could be a symptom of cherry eye, which can affect dogs of all breeds. Ingrowing eyelashes is another issue which causes red, watery eyes. If your dog has an issue, you can start by gently bathing the eye(s) with warm water and cotton wool - but never use anything sharp; a dog can suddenly jump forwards or backwards, causing injury. If the eye is red or watering for a few days or more, get it checked out by a vet.

Tear Stain – This is more noticeable in Cavapoos with light-coloured coats, as it is often reddy-brown. It is usually caused by excessive tear production, but can also be a sign of a yeast infection or an underlying eye problem. There are several widely available products – including natural remedies - which can help the condition. NOTE: The US's FDA has sent a letter of warning to three manufacturers of tear stain removal products, including Angels' Eyes, Angels' Glow and Pets' Spark, as they contain the antibiotic tylosin tartrate, which has not been approved for use in dogs or cats.

Bathing Your Cavapoo

Even if your Cavapoo has regular trips to the grooming parlour, he may still need a bath in between visits, especially if he enjoys running through fields and swimming in muddy water. If your dog regularly gets covered in mud, hose him down before allowing him back into the house. This is perfectly acceptable; a Cavapoo's coat is designed to cope with water. A bath will also be necessary if your dog has rolled in something smelly and unmentionable, like fox or cow poo(p) – both of which are irresistible to many dogs.

A canine's skin has a different pH to that of a human, and human shampoos irritate your dog's skin. Use a shampoo specially medicated for dogs, they may be expensive, but last a long time. There is also a wide range of shampoos containing natural and organic ingredients.

If your dog is low-shedding, this website suggests five shampoos for Poodle-type coats: https://dogstruggles.com/best-shampoos-poodles/

Leaving a Cavapoo with dirty skin and coat can cause irritation, skin issues, scratching and/or excessive shedding.

Ear Cleaning

It is not uncommon for some Cavapoos to suffer from ear infections. Breeds with pricked-up ears like the German Shepherd Dog suffer far fewer ear infections than those with long, floppy ears. This is because an upright ear allows air to circulate inside, whereas covered inner ears are generally warm, dark and moist, making them a haven for bacteria and yeast. This can lead to recurring infections and, in severe cases, the dog going deaf or even needing a surgical operation.

Whether or not your Cavapoo needs the hair plucking out of his ears to allow better air flow depends on:
- How hairy the inside of the ear is
- How big the ear canal is, and
- Whether he or she sheds naturally

Many Cavapoos love swimming, and this can also cause ear infections if the area under the ear flap remains wet for long periods. The wetness, combined with the warmth of an enclosed space, is an ideal breeding ground for bacteria. A good habit to get into is to towel dry under the ear flaps after your dog has been swimming. Keep an eye out for redness or inflammation of the ear flap or inner ear, or a build-up of dark wax. Also, wash or hose your dog down after swimming in the sea to keep the coat free from salt – don't forget to dry the ears afterwards.

Some owners with susceptible dogs bathe the inner ear with cotton wool and warm water or a veterinary ear cleaner as part of their regular grooming routine. Whether or not your dog has issues, it is good practice to check his or her ears and eyes regularly.

Photo of Carmen Rose (left) enjoying a dip with Truffles courtesy of Denise Knightley.

Denise says: "Poodles were bred to retrieve ducks from water originally. Their big bouffant 'lion' cut with pompom legs was created to keep them warm and buoyant in the water. I didn't know this before and just associated Poodles with the Parisian-chic stereotype of a fashion accessory dog.

"Hence I was surprised and quite worried when Carmen Rose first dived into the local canal! I had visions of having to strip off to rescue her, but she swam like a pro and jumps in at any chance. Domino is not so keen, but she will paddle and go a bit deeper if her ball falls in. They both enjoy a day out at the seaside."

Typical signs of an ear infection are: your dog shaking his head a lot, scratching his ears, rubbing his ears on the carpet or ground, and/or an unpleasant smell coming from the ears, which is a sign of a yeast infection. If your dog exhibits any of these signs, consult your vet ASAP, as simple routine cleaning won't solve the problem, and *ear infections are notoriously difficult to get rid of* once your dog's had one.

The best way of avoiding ear infections is to keep your dog's ears clean, dry and free from too much hair right from puppyhood.

One method is to get a good quality ear cleaning solution from your vet's or local pet/grooming supply shop. Then squeeze the cleaner into your Cavapoo's ear canal and rub the ear at the base next to the skull. Allow your dog to shake his or her head and use a cotton ball to gently wipe out any dirt and waxy build up inside the ear canal. Method Two is to use a baby wipe and gently wipe away any dirt and waxy build up. In both cases it is important to only clean as far down the ear canal as you can see to avoid damaging the eardrum.

The first method is preferred if you are also bathing your dog, as it will remove any unwanted water that may have got down into the ears during the bath. See **Chapter 12. Skin and Allergies** for more information on ear infections.

Never put anything sharp or narrow - like a cotton bud – inside your dog's ears, as you can cause injury.

Nail Trimming

If your Cavapoo is regularly exercised on grass or other soft surfaces, the nails may not be getting worn down sufficiently, so they may have to be clipped or filed. Nails should be kept short for the paws to remain healthy. Long nails can interfere with a dog's gait, making walking awkward or painful and they can also break easily, usually at the base of the nail where blood vessels and nerves are located.

Get your dog used to having his paws inspected from puppyhood; it's also a good opportunity to check for other problems, such as cracked pads or interdigital cysts (swellings between the toes, often due to a bacterial infection). Be warned; many dogs dislike having their nails trimmed, so it requires patience and persistence on your part.

To trim your dog's nails, use a specially designed clipper. Most have safety guards to prevent you cutting the nails too short. Do it before they get too long; if you can hear the nails clicking on the

floor, they're too long. You want to trim only the ends, before 'the quick', (hence the expression "cut to the quick"), which is a blood vessel inside the nail. You can see where the quick ends on a white nail, but not on a dark nail.

Clip only the hook-like part of the nail that turns down. Start trimming gently, a nail or two at a time, and your dog will learn that you're not going to hurt him. If you accidentally cut the quick, stop the bleeding with styptic powder.

Another option is to file your dog's nails with a nail grinder tool. Some dogs may have tough nails that are hard to trim and this may be less stressful for your dog, with less chance of pain or bleeding. The grinder is like an electric nail file and only removes a small amount of nail at a time.

Some owners prefer to use one as it is harder to cut the quick, and many dogs prefer them to a clipper. However, you have to introduce your Cavapoo gradually to the grinder - they often don't like the noise or vibration at first. If you find it impossible to clip your dog's nails, or you are at all worried about doing it, take him to a vet or a groomer - ask her to squeeze your dog's anal sacs while he's there!

And while we're discussing the less appealing end of your Cavapoo, let's dive straight in and talk about anal sacs. Sometimes called scent glands, these are a pair of glands located inside your dog's anus that give off a scent. Dogs explore the world with their noses, which is why you often see dogs that meet for the first time sniffing each other's rear ends.

You won't want to hear this, but problems with impacted anal glands are not uncommon! When a dog passes firm stools, the glands normally empty themselves, but soft poo(p) can mean that not enough pressure is exerted to empty the glands, causing discomfort. If they become infected, this results in swelling and pain. In extreme cases one or both anal glands can be removed. A dog can live perfectly well with one anal gland.

If your dog drags himself along on his rear end - 'scooting' - or tries to lick or scratch his anus, he could well have impacted anal glands that need squeezing - also called expressing - either by you if you know how to do it, your vet or a groomer. He might also have worms. Either way, it pays to keep an eye on both ends of your dog!

....

Keeping Teeth Healthy

Veterinary studies show that by the age of three, 80% of dogs show signs of gum or dental disease. The Cavapoo, like the Poodle, can be affected by dental problems. Symptoms include yellow and brown build-up of tartar along the gum line, red inflamed gums and persistent bad breath (halitosis).

It is important to make the time to take care of your Cavapoo's teeth – regular dental care greatly reduces the onset of gum/tooth decay and infection. If left, problems can escalate very quickly. Without brushing, plaque coats the teeth and within three to five days this starts to harden into tartar, often turning into gingivitis (inflammation of the gums). Gingivitis is regularly accompanied by periodontal disease (infections around the teeth). This can be serious as it can in extreme cases lead to infections of the vital organs, such as heart, liver and kidneys.

Even if the infection doesn't spread beyond the mouth, bad teeth are very unpleasant for a dog, just as with a human, causing painful toothache and difficulty chewing. You can give your dog a daily dental treat, such as Dentastix or Nylabone, or regularly give him a large raw bone to help with dental hygiene, but you should also brush your Cavapoo's teeth regularly. There are also various tools owners can buy to control plaque, such as dental picks and scrapers.

Our photo shows Cookie trying to decide whether or not she wants to have her teeth cleaned, courtesy of Kit Lam.

Some owners book their dog in for a teeth clean at the local veterinary clinic every few months. However, if your dog needs a deep clean, remedial work or teeth removing, he or she will have to be anaesthetised, a procedure which is to be avoided unless it is absolutely necessary. (If your dog has to be anaesthetised for another procedure, ask the vet to clean the teeth while he or she is under). Prevention is better than cure.

Start getting your pup used to teeth cleaning as soon as they have settled in. Take things slowly in the beginning and give lots of praise. Cavapoos love your attention (and food) and many will start looking forward to tooth brushing sessions - especially if they like the flavour of the toothpaste. Use a pet toothpaste; dogs don't rinse and spit and the human variety can upset a canine's stomach.

In the beginning, get your dog used to the toothpaste by letting him lick some off your finger. If he doesn't like the flavour, try a different one. Continue until he looks forward to licking the paste - it might be instant or take days. Put a small amount on your finger and gently rub it on one of the big canine teeth at the front of his mouth. Over the next one to two weeks, rub your finger with the toothpaste all over his teeth.

Then get either a finger brush or the right size of three-sided brush for your Cavapoo's mouth and put the toothpaste in between the bristles (rather than on top) so more of it actually gets on to the teeth and gums. Allow him to get used to the toothbrush being in his mouth several times - praise him when he licks it — before you start proper brushing.

Lift his upper lip gently and place the brush at a 45° angle to the gum line. Gently move the brush backwards and forwards. Start just with his front teeth and then gradually do a few more. You don't need to brush the inside of his teeth as the tongue keeps them relatively free of plaque. Do the top ones first. Regular brushing shouldn't take more than five minutes - well worth the time and effort when it spares your Cavapoo the pain and misery of periodontal disease.

Getting to Grips with Grooming

In this section, Cavapoo breeders and owners give their top tips to owners, beginning with Laura Koch, of Petit Jean Puppies, Arkansas, USA, who gives detailed and comprehensive advice: "Regular grooming is very important with Cavapoos for health and happiness. As a puppy, it's fairly easy, but if you don't brush every few days and get them used to this, it will be hard later to get them accustomed to the brushing.

"It also helps to use a surface such as the kitchen counter rather than your lap or in a chair; they just always cooperate better if elevated. Secure a grooming noose or leash for safety, and a rubber mat or a rug helps keep them from slipping around. Home grooming is an important part of dog ownership and very doable for the novice until around four to five months old. Watch some

YouTube instructional dog grooming videos and research techniques and puppy trims. A soft slicker brush and a wire comb are a great start, and a flea comb is another must-have to get those little dried eye debris.

"Things to keep short: potty trail, bottom of feet and inside corners under the eye, and bangs/visor area. Always be conservative at first and be very careful with scissors or clippers! It's a good idea to just get the pup used to the vibration of clippers and just play around before you actually do any trimming. Before bathing, always get matts out of the coat because bathing and drying will tighten the matts even more.

Photo of F1 Petit Jean Puppy Luis by Heather Darnell.

"Also, make sure to use a quality conditioner after shampooing to help with brushing and to help keep the skin from drying out. Blowing dry with a dog dryer is a must, as just letting them air dry can make their coat matt easy. Forced blow drying gets them dry quickly and lifts the coat away from the skin, giving it body and keeping them smelling fresh longer.

"I would recommend a trip to the professionals around the time they are done with the puppy vaccinations (usually around 12 to 16 weeks); take them to a local small groomer shop to meet the staff and then again just for a quick bath while you wait. Maybe mention to the groomer to use the clippers on the bottom of the feet for a good clean-up and to expose them to the clippers so they don't fear them the next trip. These couple of visits will pay off when they are left there for their first long day. Send one of their blankets and toys to remind them of home. Also, don't feed that morning just in case of car sickness.

"As the Cavapoo gets their adult coat around six to seven months, you will need to graduate to a firm and longer slicker brush to get all the way to the skin. A comb and a rake are also very helpful. Some use a soft brush on their adults, but this will only skim the surface of the coat and can leave matts to get worse. We like to keep the undercarriage shorter for easy maintenance, under the arms, belly and potty trail. De-matting sprays are good to have, but a spray bottle with diluted conditioner is about the same thing!

"To avoid ear infections we also keep the underneath of the ear flap super short to aerate the area so moisture can escape. Make sure after baths to use ear cleaner to help evaporate any water. This can cause yeast to grow if left with moisture. Some Cavapoos will have a few ear hairs that will need to be pulled, but most F1 don't have any or have just a few.F1b Cavapoos will have more hair in the ear canal and this must be kept clean and free of hair and wax to avoid yeast infections of the ear. Clean ears mean less scratching and less odor.

"To clean ears, we use dog ear wipes and cotton balls. You can go in with your finger and see if the ear is clean with a wipe. If you smell a musky foul odor or see a brown dirty-looking wax, you need to see the vet for some ear drops for yeast infection. It won't go away on its own.

"For home grooming you can buy some ear powder to help you easily pluck the hairs from the ear canal. The powder gives you amazing grab power; do a few hairs at a time and start out small, don't remove them all in one day. It can be painful to begin with, but they all get used to this and it really makes for a nice, clean-smelling ear. If your Cavapoo has really heavy, thick and hairy ear leathers or thick tails that are hard to keep matts down, you can keep them shorter or thin them out with thinning shears. We prefer the shorter ears to keep the puppy look.

"Most of a Cavapoo's odor comes from their ears or mouth. So brushing of the teeth is an important part of daily care. Most Cavapoos lose their puppy teeth around four months old and within a few weeks they will start to come back with beautiful sparkly white adult teeth. If you don't brush daily, then be prepared for an annual dental cleaning at the vet. Your dog's health is directly related to their dental care.

"Dental treats or chews are important and can knock off tartar with aggressive chewing, but beware these can cause odor on the hair around the face and may need a quick face washing. Another part of a professional groom is expressing the anal glands. If your pup is scooting their bottom on the floor, that is a sign of full anal glands. This needs to be done by the vet or a trained professional. Dogs have scent glands just inside their rectum that need to be expressed about every other month."

Charlotte Purkiss, of Lotties Cavapoos, Hampshire, UK, adds: "Grooming a Cavapoo should start as early as four weeks old when the breeder introduces combing of the coat, so the puppy is already used to being brushed and grooming will become a normal routine for them when settling into a new home environment. I recommend a small soft brush to start with and I include one in my Going Home Puppy Packs.

"Adult Cavapoos should not be bathed too often as this can strip the natural oils from their skin and coat. However, I do recommend to my families that it's good to start introducing bathing once the puppy has settled in, so around the 12-week mark. Just pop a little lukewarm water in the bath and let puppy paddle around with a couple of toys, so they're gently introduced by play. At this stage, you're not getting them wet all over; that can be done when they start to feel happy in the bath. Use this strategy regularly, then start to turn on the shower hose for 30 seconds each time too.

"When you go to the next phase of washing the puppy all over with shampoo, only do it maximum once a month for a few months. There are so many grooming shampoos on the market these days. I recommend an organic one which has as many natural ingredients as possible so it's super gentle on your puppy's skin and coat. Once you start taking your puppy to a professional groomer every three months, they will wash them as part of the grooming session and your dog will be used to it. Check with your groomer when they like to first see a puppy, as you will have introductory sessions to get your puppy used to the groomer and surroundings.

"When drying a Cavapoo, I think it's best to use a microfibre towel as this is really good at absorbing water. I also put a hairdryer on every few days for a couple of minutes from four weeks old so they are familiar with the noise. Then at six weeks I use the hairdryer on the coat for around a minute every few days until they leave me. Only use a hairdryer on a very low heat setting and speed.

"A Cavapoo does need to be seen by a groomer regularly due to the coat becoming long in certain areas, like the face and ears, which need to be kept short to prevent smelly ears and eye infection. They also get their nails trimmed/clipped, so I always suggest that you handle each paw and touch each claw gently each day so puppy gets used to it. I know some owners love the longer look on the main body, and that's OK as long as you brush thoroughly every day to prevent any knotting. A visit to a groomer is like you going to the hairdresser; you will have a posh, trimmed pooch that smells divine!"

Denise Knightley, who now owns two Cavapoos, agreed to take her daughter's Cavapoo Carmen Rose after the dog developed a severe medical issue, Grade 4+ Patella Luxation, at just five months old. Afterwards Denise was unable to regularly groom her, as Carmen Rose required a long period of convalescence confined to a crate.

She says: "I am a qualified dog groomer and thought it would be interesting to show what happens when the coat is too matted to brush or comb out. The kindest thing is to clip the dog almost back to the skin and then try to keep it brushed and matt-free as it grows back," *(pictured, it also shows why this type of coat is called a fleece).*

"Sadly, Carmen Rose got very matted after her surgery, as she has a very thick, curly Poodle-type coat and I wasn't able to keep up the daily brushing whilst she was recuperating. Domino has more of a wavy and silky Cavalier King Charles Spaniel coat, so she needs much less regular grooming.

"Both dogs are brushed daily using a metal greyhound comb and a slicker brush. Their paws are washed after every walk. We use 'Equafleece full dog suits – they look like onesies - which keep their bodies clean and dry in all weathers and reduce the amount of grooming."

Laura Lambert, owner of Dolly, and founder of Facebook group All AboutPoos: "We weren't aware of how high maintenance the Cavapoo coat was before we got Dolly. We thought it would be a case of just brushing her, but it quickly became apparent that this wasn't enough, especially once the puppy coat grew out. I didn't like the results I was getting from the groomer, so I've now home-groomed for the last 12 months. Every three weeks we clip Dolly's body quite short and leave her legs longer. We clip her bottom area short otherwise it gets mucky. I trim her ears with scissors and brush them through.

"I bath Dolly with shampoo about every three weeks and, if we've been somewhere muddy, rinse her off with water in the bath. I try not to use too much shampoo as it can remove the oils from the fur. I don't pluck her ears; they're not hairy inside, although the vet suggested I start doing it with my fingers every few months.

"The worst thing about grooming is the matts; I hate dealing with matts - it's a constant battle to keep them at bay! My tips are to snip any out as soon as they start to form. You can't notice where you've cut them out when they're little and it saves having to take the fur really short when the matt has grown too big to manage. Also, learn to groom your dog yourself, it saves a fortune and I personally think I get a better result! Now I'm home-grooming it doesn't really cost anything, just shampoo. The clippers cost about £20 ($26) and are perfectly adequate."

Kit Lam, owner of Cookie: "Grooming was one of our considerations before we got Cookie. I took her for her puppy groom within weeks of her final vaccination, just so that she could get used to it. She goes to Eda her groomer every five weeks, and possibly four in the summer. It costs £32 a time, which equates to an average of £374 ($486) per annum.

"I have considered grooming her myself, but I'm not sure that I can do her face, pluck the hair in her ears or trim her nails, which is what is included at the professional groomer's. I do bath her once a week (sometimes more depending how mucky she gets) and comb her twice a week. She's not keen on her front legs being combed, nor having her face and chin washed and blow dried, though she does tolerate it."

Claire Cornes: "I brush and comb Bob and Boris daily, and have done since Day One. You must start when they are young to get them used to a routine. Bob hates being brushed, but it must be done regularly to stop matting, I would be mortified if they had to be shaved. They have baths quite often, as they enjoy getting mucky on walks. When we get home and I open the bathroom door, they will jump straight in the bath! They have both loved a bath from eight weeks old and are happy to sit or stand in it whilst they are groomed."

Our photo shows Bob and Boris sporting their smart Equafleece outfits and keeping nice and clean on this walk, courtesy of Claire.

"I groom Bob and Boris myself as I couldn't find a groomer locally that trimmed them how I wanted, plus it was £80 ($104) a time! I have paid out for decent clippers, scissors and a one-day Groom Your Own Dog course. I keep my two short as they seem to like rolling in anything they can find!"

Five-year-old Ethel's owner, Trevor Nott: "Ethel has a thick coat, the under layer is almost the texture of cotton wool. Initially, we tried to let the coat grow with her and groomed her twice a day for about half an hour, but this still didn't prevent some matting. As we went into summer, it was clear the coat was too much, so we found a groomer that came to our home.

"We have a look that we like for Ethel so she has a full groom every six weeks and a facial in between. Cavapoos can be high maintenance in this area - both in terms of grooming by the owner and by a professional. Ethel costs more than my wife for hairdos and that's not cheap!!"

Val Boshart: "We comb Millie out fully about once every couple days. I started doing it very early, so she's now quite used to being combed and really enjoys it. I also wait until she's in a sleepy mood, which makes her more tolerant of being repositioned. We take her to a professional groomer every six to eight weeks and trim her ourselves in between as needed (e.g. if she can't see) and we wash her at home every two to three weeks. After walks we also usually wash off her feet in the tub if it's muddy or raining, which helps keep her white feet clean. We use Burts Bees products and have found that they work well with her coat."

Lindsey McDonald and Alex Kostiw: "Winston really doesn't like being groomed, so we don't spend long. We also keep him quite short so that he doesn't matt easily. I probably give him a good brush once a week and try to do little bits every few days. He goes to the groomer every five to six weeks in summer and seven to eight weeks in winter."

Hilary Morphy: "I brush Teddy every evening whilst I'm watching TV and he's on my knee; possibly for about 20 minutes every night."

June Hicks, owner of Archie: "You do need to groom daily. I do it for about 15 minutes, especially the ears and tail. Archie is regularly groomed at dog groomer's every six to eight weeks."

Karen Howe: "I brush Rodney and Mabel every evening for roughly 15 to 20 minutes each and have done since they were pups. You have to keep on top of the brushing as their coats can matt so easily. If you do it regularly from the start, they will get used to it and it will make life so much easier in the future.

....

As you can see, grooming isn't just about brushing once a week. Cavapoos definitely do require extra care when it comes to grooming... it's all part of the bargain when you decide that this stunning dog is the one for you.

*Photo, left to right: Lindsey McDonald's Winston, Warren Photographic, StockPhotoSecrets, Petit Jean Puppy Dennis by Heather **Darnell**, Lotties Cavapoo Phoebe by Nivien Speith.*

14. The Birds and the Bees

Judging by the number of questions our website receives from owners who ask about the canine reproductive cycle and breeding their dogs, there is a lot of confusion about the doggy facts of life out there. Some owners want to know whether they should breed their dog, while others ask if and at what age they should have their dog neutered – this term can refer to both the spaying of females and the castration of males.

Owners of females often ask when she will come on heat, how long this will last and how often it will occur. Sometimes they want to know how you can tell if a female is pregnant or how long a pregnancy lasts. So here, in a nutshell, is a chapter on The Facts of Life as far as Cavapoos are concerned.

....

Females and Heat

Just like all other female mammals, including humans, a female Cavapoo has a menstrual cycle - or to be more accurate, an oestrus cycle *(estrus* in the US). This is the period of time when she is ready (and willing!) for mating and is more commonly called *heat* or being *on heat*, *in heat* or *in season*.

A Cavapoo female has her first cycle at six to nine months old, although there are no hard and fast rules; some may not have their first heat until later. Females may follow the pattern of their mother, so if you are getting a female puppy, it may be worth asking your breeder at what age the dam (mother) first came on heat.

She will then come on heat roughly every six months. There is no season of the year which corresponds to a breeding season, so it could be winter and summer or spring and autumn (fall), etc.

When a young female comes on heat, it is normal for her cycles to be somewhat irregular, and can take up to two years for regular cycles to develop. The timescale also becomes more erratic with old, unspayed females. Unlike women, female dogs do not stop menstruating when they reach middle age, although the heat becomes shorter and lighter. A litter for an older female (over seven years old) is not advisable as it can result in complications – for both mother and pups.

On average, the heat cycle will last around 21 days, but can be anything from seven to 10 days up to four weeks. Within this period there will be several days in the middle of the cycle that will be the optimum time for her to get pregnant. This is the phase called the *oestrus.*

The third phase, called *dioestrus*, begins immediately afterwards. During this time, her body will produce hormones whether or not she is pregnant. Her body thinks and acts like she is pregnant. All the hormones are present; only the puppies are missing. This can sometimes lead to what is known as a 'false pregnancy'.

The first visual sign of heat that you may notice is that your dog's vulva (external sex organ, or pink bit under her tail) becomes swollen, which she will lick to keep herself clean. If you're not sure, hold a tissue against her vulva – does it turn pink or red? She will then bleed; this is sometimes called spotting. It will be a light red or brown at the beginning of the heat cycle, turning more watery after a week or so. Some females can bleed quite heavily; however, this is not usual with Cavapoos. If you have any concerns, contact your vet to be on the safe side.

Females on heat often urinate more frequently than normal, or may 'mark' various objects on a walk or even in the home by doing a small pee on them! She may also start to 'mate' with your leg, other

dogs or objects. These are all normal signs. The good news is that both Cavaliers and Poodles generally want to keep themselves clean by licking their rear end when on heat – and this is usually true of Cavapoos too.

If your girl does leaves an unwanted trail around the house, cover anything you don't want stained. You might consider using doggy diapers/nappies, also called heat pants, (*pictured on a Cavalier*). Some are disposable, others have washable linings and they are all widely available online.

Owners have reported a variety of behavioural changes when their female has her first heat cycle. Some go off their food or start shedding hair. Others may become more clingy - or ignore you and sulk in their beds.

While a female is on heat, she produces hormones that attract male dogs. Because dogs have a sense of smell thousands of times stronger than ours, your girl on heat is a magnet for all the neighbourhood males. It is believed that they can detect the scent of a female on heat up to two miles away! They may congregate around your house or follow you around the park (if you are brave or foolish enough to venture out there while she is in season), waiting for their chance to prove their manhood – or mutthood in their case.

Don't expect your precious little Cavapoo princess to be fussy. Her hormones are raging when she is on heat and, during her most fertile days (Day 9-10 of heat for five or more days) she is ready, able and ... VERY willing! As she approaches the optimum time for mating, you may notice her tail bending slightly to one side. She will also start to urinate more frequently. This is her signal to all those virile male dogs out there that she is ready for mating.

Although breeding requires specialised knowledge on the part of the owner, it does not stop a female on heat from being extremely interested in attention from any old mutt. To avoid an unwanted pregnancy you must keep a close eye on your female on heat and not allow her to freely wander where she may come into contact with other dogs - and that includes the garden, unless it is 100% dog proof.

It is amazing the lengths some uncastrated (also called intact or entire) males will go to impregnate a female on heat. Travelling great distances to follow her scent, jumping over barriers, digging under fences, chewing through doors or walls and sneaking through hedges are just some of the tactics employed by canine Casanovas on the loose. Some dogs living in the same house as a female in season have even been known to mate with her through the bars of a crate!

If you do have an intact male, you need to physically keep him in a separate place, perhaps with a friend, separate kennel or even boarding kennels. The desire to mate is all-consuming and can be accompanied by howling or 'marking' (urinating) indoors from a frustrated Romeo.

Avoid taking your female out in public places while she is in season, and certainly don't let her run free anywhere where you might come across other dogs. The instinct to mate may trump all of her training. Wrst case scenario is your precious and expensive little pooch suddenly becomes deaf to your increasingly panicky calls as she gallops off into the distance with a gleam in her eye and the scruffy mutt from down the road!

During her heat period you can compensate for these restrictions by playing more indoor or garden games to keep her mentally and physically active. You can buy a spray which masks the natural oestrus scent of your female. Marketed under such attractive names as *"Female Spray"*, these will lessen the scent, but not eliminate it. They might be useful for reducing the amount of unwanted attention, but are not a complete deterrent. There is, however, no canine contraceptive and the only sure-fire way of preventing your female from becoming pregnant is spaying.

There is a "morning after pill" – actually a series of oestrogen tablets or an injection - which some vets may administer after an unwanted coupling, but reported side effects are severe, including Pyometra (a potentially life-threatening infection of the womb which can affect up to one in four middle-aged females), bone marrow suppression and infertility. Unlike women, female dogs don't go through the menopause and can give birth even when they are quite old – but it is not good for their health.

Good Breeding

Normally, responsible breeders wait until a female is fully health tested, has had one or two heat cycles and is at least 18 months to two years old before mating. Females should not be used for breeding too early; pregnancy draws on the calcium reserves needed for their own growing bones. If bred too soon, they may break down structurally and have health issues in later life.

However, with Cavapoos, there is a further consideration on the Cavalier side, and it's called the **MVD Breeding Protocol.** Many Cavalier King Charles Spaniels suffer from a heart condition called *early-onset Mitral Valve Disease* (MVD), and the MVD Protocol is a set of (non-compulsory) guidelines introduced with the aim of greatly reducing this hereditary disease. A major recommendation is that Cavaliers less than two-and-a-half years' old are not used for breeding, as it is not always possible to tell if a Cavalier younger than this will go on to suffer from a heart issue. The age of the Cavalier parent is another question to ask your breeder if you haven't got your Cavapoo yet. There is more information on this in **Chapter 11. Cavapoo Health.**

Good breeders also limit the number of litters from each female, as breeding can take a lot out of them. To protect females from overbreeding, the UK's Kennel Club has introduced Breeding Restrictions. These do not apply to crossbreeds, as they cannot be registered with the Kennel Clubs, but should be adhered to by all responsible breeders of crossbreeds and pure breeds. Now the Kennel Club will not register a litter from any female:

1. That has already had four litters.
2. If she is less than one year old at the time of mating.
3. If she is eight years or older when she whelps (gives birth).

4. If the litter is the result of any mating between father and daughter, mother and son or brother and sister.

5. If she has already had two C-Sections (Caesarean Sections).

6. In the UK, the dam has to be resident at a UK address at the date of whelping – this is to try and discourage people buying from foreign puppy farms.

All national breed clubs recognised by the Kennel Clubs have a Code of Ethics for their breeders. One of the issues with Cavapoos is that there is no overarching association governing Cavapoo breeders anywhere, which is why it has become a bit of a free-for-all. Here are some of the major points adapted from the Code of Ethics of various breed clubs – if you have not got your Cavapoo yet, look for a breeder that meets these standards:

1. **The health and welfare of the Cavapoo is of paramount importance. It supersedes any other commitment, whether that is personal or financial.**

2. **The purpose of breeding Cavapoos is to attempt to bring their natural qualities to the fore. There is a constant danger that ignorant or disreputable breeders may, by improper practices, produce physically, mentally or temperamentally unsound specimens to the detriment of the crossbreed.**

3. **If I decide to breed a litter, I will be selective with respect to the health, conformation, physical wellbeing, and temperament of the pair to be mated.**

4. **I will breed only after a careful study of the two dogs involved.**

5. **I will provide all my Cavapoos with proper veterinary and home care, which includes:**
   i. The elimination of parasites, internal or external
   ii. The necessary inoculations as determined by a veterinarian
   iii. A properly balanced nutritional diet

6. **I will do my best to evaluate my breeding dogs objectively and to use for breeding only those that are excellent examples.**

7. **I will to the very best of my ability screen all prospective new owners to determine their suitability and their motives for acquiring a Cavapoo. Special attention will be given to the necessary commitment to financial responsibility for proper care and adequate physical facilities.**

8. **I will not allow any puppy to leave for its new home before the age of eight weeks.**

Neutering - Pros and Cons

Once a straightforward subject, this is currently a hot potato in the dog world. Dogs which are kept purely as pets – i.e. not for showing, breeding or working – are often spayed or neutered. There is also the very real life-threatening risk of **Pyometra** in unspayed middle-aged females. While early spay/neuter has been traditionally recommended, there is some scientific evidence that, for some breeds, it may be better to wait until the dog is through puberty. (The procedure of removing ovaries or testicles is also known as a gonadectomy).

Armed with the facts, it is for each individual owner to decide what is best for their dog – unless there was a Spay/Neuter clause in your Puppy Contract. A major argument for neutering of both sexes is that there is already too much indiscriminate breeding of dogs in the world. As you will read in **Chapter 15. Cavapoo Rescue**, it is estimated that 1,000 dogs are put to sleep **every hour** in the USA alone. It is for this reason that rescue organisations in North America, the UK and Australia neuter all dogs that they rehome. Some areas in the United States, e.g. LA, have even adopted a compulsory sterilisation policy: www.avma.org/Advocacy/StateAndLocal/Pages/sr-spay-neuter-laws.aspx aimed at "reducing and eventually eliminating the thousands of euthanizations conducted in Los Angeles' animal shelters every year."

The RSPCA, along with most UK vets, also promotes the benefits of neutering: www.rspca.org.uk/adviceandwelfare/pets/general/neutering. It is estimated that more than half of all dogs in the UK are spayed or castrated. Another point is that you may not have a choice. Some Puppy Contracts from breeders may stipulate that, except in special circumstances, you agree to neuter your Cavapoo as a Condition of Sale. Others may state that you need the breeder's permission to breed your dog.

The other side of the coin is that there is recent scientific evidence that neutering – and especially early neutering - can have a detrimental effect on the health of some dogs, especially larger, fast-growing breeds. In 2013, the University of California, Davis School of Veterinary Medicine published a study revealing that neutered Golden Retrievers and Labradors appear to be at a higher risk of joint disorders and cancers compared with sexually intact dogs of the same breed: http://www.aaha.org/blog/NewStat/post/2014/07/17/785809/UC-Davis-study-neutering-Golden-retrievers-Labradors.aspx

A follow-up study involving both males and females (with around a 5% incidence of joint disorders in intact dogs) found that Retrievers that had been neutered before six months of age were four or five times more likely to have joint problems. The same study looked at cancer. Intact females had a 3% rate of cancer, while females spayed up to eight years old were three to four times more likely to get cancer. Neutering males had "relatively minor effects." The full report is at: http://journals.plos.org/plosone/article?id=10.1371/journal.pone.0102241 A 2018 article, published in The IAABC Journal (International Association of Animal Behavior Consultants), highlights the pros and cons of neutering. Written by a vet, it's a bit technical, but worth a read: https://fall2018.iaabcjournal.org/2018/10/31/spay-and-neuter-surgery-effects-on-dogs The table at the end of the article summarises the pros and cons.

As yet, there are no studies on neutering smaller dogs such as Cavaliers, Miniature or Toy Poodles or Cavapoos. There is also the very real threat of unspayed females contracting the serious illness Pyometra in middle age.

Spaying

Spaying is the term traditionally used to describe the sterilisation of a female dog so that she cannot become pregnant. This is normally done by a procedure called an *'ovariohysterectomy'* and involves the removal of the ovaries and uterus (womb). Although this is a routine operation, it is major abdominal surgery and she has to be anaesthetised.

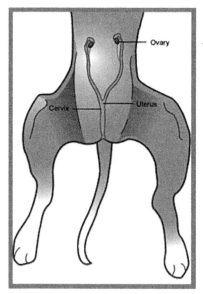

One less invasive option offered by some vets is an *'ovariectomy'*, which removes the ovaries, but leaves the womb intact. It requires only a small incision and can even be carried out by laparoscopy (keyhole surgery). The dog is anaesthetised for a shorter time and there is less risk of infection or excess bleeding during surgery. NOTE: One breeder said that her vet had advised against getting very small dogs spayed by keyhole surgery, as it is very "fiddly". Check with your vet.

One major reason often given for not opting for an ovariectomy is that the female still runs the risk of Pyometra later in life. However, there is currently little or no scientific evidence of females that have undergone an ovariectomy contracting Pyometra afterwards.

If a female is spayed before her first heat cycle, she will have an almost zero risk of mammary cancer (the equivalent of breast cancer in women). Even after the first heat, spaying reduces the risk of this cancer by 92%. Some vets claim that the risk of mammary cancer in unspayed female dogs can be as high as one in four. There is, however, emerging evidence (with Retrievers) that is it better to wait until a female is four years old.

Spaying is a much more serious operation for females than neutering is for males. It involves an internal abdominal operation, whereas the neutering procedure is carried out on the male's testicles, which are outside his abdomen. As with any major procedure, there are pros and cons.

For:

❧ Spaying prevents infections, cancer and other diseases of the uterus and ovaries. A spayed female will have a greatly reduced risk of mammary cancer

❧ Spaying eliminates the risk of Pyometra, which results from hormonal changes in the female's reproductive tract. It also reduces hormonal changes that can interfere with the treatment of diseases like diabetes or epilepsy

❧ You no longer have to cope with any potential mess caused by bleeding inside the house during heat cycles

❧ You don't have to guard your female against unwanted attention from males as she will no longer have heat cycles

❧ Spaying can reduce behaviour problems, such as roaming, aggression towards other dogs, anxiety or fear (not all canine experts agree)

❧ A spayed dog does not contribute to the pet overpopulation problem

Against:

❧ Complications can occur, including an abnormal reaction to the anaesthetic, bleeding, stitches breaking and infections; **these are not common**

❧ Occasionally there can be long-term effects connected to hormonal changes. These include weight gain or less stamina, which can occur years after spaying

- Older females may suffer some urinary incontinence, but it only affects a few spayed females. NOTE: Some younger dogs can also suffer from urinary incontinence after spaying - discuss with your vet.

- Cost. This can range from £100 to £250 in the UK, more for keyhole spaying, and approximately $150-$500 at a vet's clinic in the USA, or from around $50 at a low cost clinic, for those that qualify

- There is early evidence that spaying some Retrievers before six months of age can increase the chance of joint problems developing.

Neutering

Neutering male dogs involves castration (the removal of the testicles). This can be a difficult decision for some owners, as it causes a drop in the pet's testosterone levels, which some humans – men in particular! - feel affects the quality of their dog's life. Fortunately, dogs do not think like people and male dogs do not miss their testicles or the loss of sex.

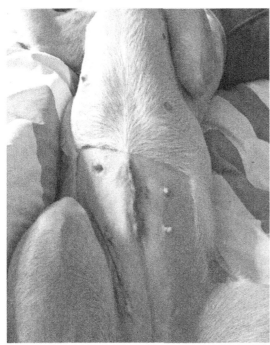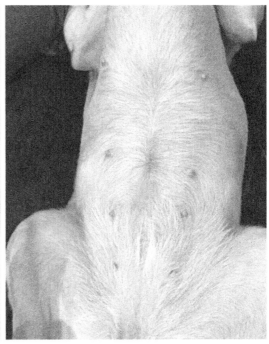

These photographs are reproduced courtesy of Guy Bunce and Chloe Spencer, of Dizzywaltz Labrador Retrievers, Berkshire, England. The one on the left shows four-year-old Disney shortly after a full spay (ovariohysterectomy). The one on the right shows Disney a few weeks later.

Neutering is recommended by animal rescue organisations and vets. Dogs working in service or for charities are routinely neutered and this does not impair their ability to perform their duties. There are countless unwanted puppies, many of which are destroyed. There is also the huge problem of a lack of knowledge from the owners of some dogs, resulting in the production of poor puppies with congenital health or temperament problems.

Technically, neutering can be carried out at any age over eight weeks, provided both testicles have descended. However, recent research is definitely coming down on the side of waiting until the dog is at least one year old. Surgery is relatively straightforward, and much less of a major operation for a male than spaying is for a female. Complications are less common and less severe than with spaying.

Although he will feel tender afterwards, your dog should return to his normal self within a couple of days.

Dogs neutered before puberty tend to grow a little larger than dogs done later. This is because testosterone is involved in the process that stops growth, so the bones grow for longer without testosterone. When a dog comes out of surgery, his scrotum (the sacs that held the testicles) will be swollen and it may look like nothing has been done. But it is normal for these to shrink slowly in the days following surgery. Here are the main pros and cons:

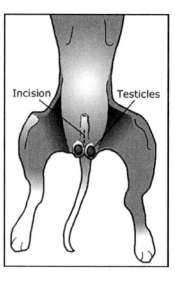

For:

❧ Castration is a simple procedure, and dogs usually make a swift recovery afterwards

❧ Behaviour problems such as aggression and wandering off are reduced (some experts disagree with this)

❧ Unwanted sexual behaviour, such as mounting people or objects, is usually reduced or eliminated

❧ Testicular problems such as infections, cancer and torsion (painful rotation of the testicle) are eradicated

❧ Prostate disease, common in older male dogs, is less likely to occur

❧ A submissive un-neutered male dog may be targeted by other dogs. After he has been neutered, he will no longer produce testosterone and so will not be regarded as much of a threat by the other males, so he is less likely to be bullied

❧ A neutered dog is not fathering unwanted puppies

Against:

❧ A major scientific study focussed on Retrievers seems to show that some dogs neutered before six months of age are four to five times more likely to have joint problems

❧ As with any surgery, there can be bleeding afterwards; you should keep an eye on him for any blood loss after the operation. Infections can also occur, generally caused by the dog licking the wound, so try and prevent him doing this. If he persists, use an Elizabethan collar (E-collar). In the **vast majority** of cases, these problems do not occur

❧ Some dogs' coats may be affected (this also applies to spaying); supplementing the diet with fish oil can compensate for this

❧ Cost - this starts at around £80 in the UK. In the USA this might cost upwards from $100 at a private veterinary clinic, or from $50 at a low cost or Humane Society clinic

Two other phrases you may hear when discussing neutering of males and females are 'tubal ligation' or 'vasectomy'. Many veterinary papers have been written on these topics, but as yet, not many vets offer them as options, possibly because they have not been trained to carry out these procedures at vet school.

The first is the tying of a female's Fallopian tubes and the second is the clamping shut of the sperm ducts from the male's testicles. In both procedures, the dog continues to produce hormones (unlike with spaying and neutering), but is unable to get pregnant or father puppies. With further data on the positive effects of hormones, these operations could become more common in the future – although more vets will first have to learn these new techniques.

A new non-surgical procedure to sterilise male dogs called *Zeutering* has been developed. It involved injecting zinc gluconate into the dog's testicles. Dogs are lightly sedated but not anaesthetised. It's inexpensive, there's little recovery time and no stitches. However, studies show that Zeutering is only 99% effective, and its long-term effects are still being researched. A downside is that, while it makes dogs sterile, they still retain some of their testosterone. Therefore habits which usually disappear with traditional castration, such as marking, roaming, following females on heat and aggression towards other males, remain. Zeutering isn't for every dog, but worth discussing with your vet. Here are some common myths about neutering and spaying:

Neutering or spaying will spoil the dog's character - There is no evidence that any of the positive characteristics of your dog will be altered. He or she will be just as loving, playful and loyal. Neutering may reduce aggression or roaming, especially in male dogs, because they are no longer competing to mate with a female.

A female needs to have at least one litter - There is no proven physical or mental benefit to a female having a litter.

Mating is natural and necessary - We tend to ascribe human emotions to our dogs, but they do not think emotionally about sex or having and raising a family. Unlike humans, their desire to mate or breed is entirely physical, triggered by the chemicals called hormones within their body. Without these hormones – i.e. after neutering or spaying – the desire disappears or is greatly reduced.

Male dogs will behave better if they can mate - This is simply not true; sex does not make a dog behave better. In fact, it can have the opposite effect. Having mated once, a male may show an increased interest in females. He may also consider his status elevated, which may make him harder to control or call back.

 If you, like most dogs owners, are considering having your dog spayed or neutered, discuss the optimum age for the procedure with your breeder and vet.

Pregnancy

Regardless of how big or small the dog is, a canine pregnancy lasts for 58 to 65 days; 63 days is average. This is true of all breeds of dog. Sometimes pregnancy is referred to as the *"gestation period"*. It is recommended to take a female for a pre-natal check-up after mating when the vet should
answer any questions about type of food, supplements and extra care needed, as well as informing the owner about any physical changes likely to occur in your female.

There is a blood test available that measures levels of **relaxin**. This is a hormone produced by the ovary and the developing placenta, and pregnancy can be detected by monitoring relaxin levels as early as 22 to 27 days after mating. The levels are high throughout pregnancy and then decline rapidly after the female has given birth.

A vet can usually see the puppies (but not how many) using Ultrasound from around the same time. X-rays carried out 45 days into the pregnancy show the puppies' skeletons and give the breeder a good idea of the number of puppies. They can also help to give the vet more information, which is particularly useful if the female has had previous whelping problems.

Here are some of the signs of pregnancy:

❧ After mating, many females become more affectionate. (However, others may become uncharacteristically irritable and maybe even a little aggressive)

- The female may produce a slight clear discharge from her vagina about one month after mating

- Three or four weeks after mating, a few females experience morning sickness – if this is the case, feed little and often. She may seem more tired than usual

- She may seem slightly depressed and/or show a drop in appetite. These signs can also mean there are other problems, so you should consult your vet

- Her teats (nipples) will become more prominent, pink and erect 25 to 30 days into the pregnancy. Later on, you may notice a fluid coming from them

- After about 35 days, or seven weeks, her body weight will noticeably increase

- Many pregnant females' appetite will increase in the second half of pregnancy

- Her abdomen will become noticeably larger from around day 40, although first-time mums and females carrying few puppies may not show as much

- Her nesting instincts will kick in as the delivery date approaches. She may seem restless or scratch her bed or the floor

- During the last week of pregnancy, females often start to look for a safe place for whelping. Some seem to become confused, wanting to be with their owners and at the same time wanting to prepare their nest. Even if the female is having a C-section, she should still be allowed to nest in a whelping box with layers of newspaper, which she will scratch and dig as the time approaches

If your female becomes pregnant – either by design or accident - your first step should be to consult a vet.

Litter Size

Generally, the larger the dog, the bigger the litter; Cavaliers, Miniature and Toys Poodles are small or very small dogs and not known for having large litters. Typical litter sizes are two to six pups. However, the number of pups can vary, affected by such factors as the age of the dam and sire (mother and father), size of the gene pool and even the dam's diet. Younger and older females tend to have smaller litters.

False Pregnancies

As many as 50% or more of intact (unspayed) females may display signs of a false pregnancy. In the wild it was common for female dogs to have false pregnancies and to lactate (produce milk). This female would then nourish puppies if their own mother died.

False pregnancies occur 60 to 80 days after the female was in heat - about the time she would have given birth – and are generally nothing to worry about for an owner. The exact cause is unknown; however, hormonal imbalances are thought to play an important role. Some dogs have shown symptoms within three to four days of spaying; these include:

- Making a nest

- Mothering or adopting toys and other objects

- Producing milk (lactating)

- Appetite fluctuations

- Barking or whining a lot

- Restlessness, depression or anxiety

- Swollen abdomen

- She might even appear to go into labour

Try not to touch your dog's nipples, as touch will stimulate further milk production. If she is licking herself repeatedly, she may need an E-collar to minimise stimulation. To help reduce and eliminate milk production, you can apply cool compresses to the nipples

Under no circumstances should you restrict your Cavapoo's water supply to try and prevent her from producing milk. This is dangerous as she can become dehydrated.

Some unspayed females may have a false pregnancy with each heat cycle. Spaying during a false pregnancy may actually prolong the condition, so better to wait until it is over to have her spayed. False pregnancy is not a disease, but an exaggerated response to normal hormonal changes. Owners should be reassured that, even if left untreated, the condition almost always resolves itself.

However, if your dog appears physically ill or the behavioural changes are severe enough to worry you, visit your vet. He or she may prescribe Galastop, which very effectively stops milk production and quickly returns the hormones to normal. In rare cases, hormone treatment may be necessary. Generally, dogs experiencing false pregnancies do not have serious long-term problems, as the behaviour disappears when the hormones return to their normal levels in two to three weeks.

One exception is **Pyometra**, a serious and potentially deadly infection of the womb, caused by a hormonal abnormality. It normally follows a heat cycle in which fertilisation did not occur and the dog typically starts showing symptoms within two to four months. Commonly referred to as 'pyo', there are 'open' and 'closed' forms of the disease. Open pyo is usually easy to identify with a smelly discharge, so prompt treatment is easy. Closed pyo is often harder to identify and you may not even notice anything until your girl becomes feverish and lethargic. When this happens, it is very serious and time is of the essence. Typically, vets will recommend immediate spaying in an effort to save her life.

Signs of Pyometra are excessive drinking and urination, with the female trying to lick a white discharge from her vagina. She may also have a slight temperature. If the condition becomes severe, her back legs will become weak, possibly to the point where she can no longer get up without help. Pyometra is serious if bacteria take a hold, and in extreme cases it can be fatal. It is also relatively common and needs to be dealt with promptly by a vet, who will give the dog intravenous fluids and antibiotics for several days. In most cases this is followed by spaying.

Should I Breed From My Cavapoo?

The short and simple answer is: **NO, leave it to the experts.** The rising cost of puppies and increasing number of dog owners are tempting more people to consider breeding their dogs. Producing healthy, happy Cavapoos with good temperaments doesn't just happen; it is a learned skill.

Due to several genetic diseases which can and do affect this hybrid, any responsible person who is considering breeding Cavapoos needs an extensive knowledge of genetic disorders affecting Cavaliers and Poodles and the relevant health tests prior to breeding. The suitability of a mate with regards to health and temperament then has to be fully researched.

Any good breeder also has to be prepared to part with a four-figure sum before a single pup is born. Good care, health screening and stud fees come at a cost and, although Cavapoos are expensive, they arrive in small litters. Don't enter into this thinking you will make a lot of money. If you do it properly, you won't.

You can't just put any two dogs together and expect perfect, healthy puppies; ethical and successful breeding is much more scientific and time-consuming than that. Inexperience can result in tragic health consequences, poor specimens of the breed, the loss of pups - or even the mother. Sometimes a C-section (Caesarean section) may be necessary. These are carried out when the mother is unable to birth the pups naturally – and timing is critical. Too early and the pups may be underdeveloped or the mother can bleed to death; too late and the pups can die.

Breeding healthy Cavapoos to type is a complex, expensive and time-consuming business when all the fees, DNA and health tests, care, nutrition and medical expenses have been taken into account.

Breeding Costs

Here's a list of considerations to do it properly:

- Annual heart tests on the Cavalier parent
- Eye tests – both Cavalier and Poodle
- MRI scan for Chiari Malformation/Syringomyelia (CM/SM) – recommended for breeding Cavaliers in in UK
- Testing the Cavalier for Episodic Falling (EF) – UK
- Testing the Cavalier for Curly Coat Dry Eye (CC/DE) – UK
- Patella Luxation – Toy Poodles, also Cavaliers in the US
- Hip Dysplasia – Cavaliers and Miniature Poodles
- Stud fees
- Pregnancy – ultrasound scan, worming, extra food and supplements for the mother
- Equipment – whelping box, vet bed, thermometer, feeding bottles, heat mat, hibiscrub, etc.
- Birth – vet's fees
- Puppies – vaccinations and worming, puppy food, coloured collars

And these are just the basics! These four-figure costs are considerable and swallow up a large chunk of any profit you thought you might make. And if there is a problem with the mother, birth or puppies and you rack up vet's bills, you can actually make a loss on a litter!

Ask Yourself This...

1. Did I get my potential breeding dog from a good, ethical breeder? Dogs sold in pet stores and on general sales websites are seldom good specimens and can be unhealthy.

2. Are my dog and his or her close relatives free from health issues? Heart, eye and joint issues are just some of the illnesses Cavapoo pups can inherit. Are you 100% sure your breeding dog – Cavapoo, Cavalier or Poodle - is free from them all? Also, an unhealthy female is also more likely to have trouble with pregnancy and whelping.

3. Do not breed from a dog that is not an excellent specimen, hoping that somehow the puppies will turn out better. They won't. Talk with experienced breeders and ask them for an honest assessment of your dog.

4. Is my female at least in her second heat cycle? The Cavalier MVD Breeding Protocol goes further than that and recommends breeders wait until a Cavalier is at least two-and-a-half years old. A female should be physically mature, able to carry a litter to term and robust enough to whelp and care for a litter. Even then, not all females are suitable. Some are simply poor mothers who don't care for their puppies; others don't produce enough milk - which means you have to do it.

5. Does my potential breeding dog have a good temperament? Does she or he socialise well with people and other animals? Dogs with poor temperaments should not be bred, regardless of how good they look.

6. Am I financially able to provide good veterinary care for the mother and puppies, particularly if complications occur? If you are not prepared to make a significant financial commitment to a litter, then don't breed your dog. A single litter can cost several thousands of pounds or dollars - and what if you only get a couple of puppies?

7. Have I got the indoor space? Mother and pups will need their own space in your home which will become messy, as new-born pups do not come into this world housetrained (potty trained). It should also be warm and draught-free.

8. Can I cope with several puppies at once?

9. Can I devote the time to breeding? Caring for mother and young pups is a 24/7 job in the beginning and involves many sleepless nights. During the day, you cannot simply go off to work or leave the house with the mother and young pups unattended. Also, it is not uncommon for a dam to be unable or unwilling to provide milk for her puppies. In which case, you have to tube-feed the puppies every couple of hours throughout the day and night. Breeding is a huge tie.

10. Am I confident enough to offer a full Puppy Contract with a health warranty?

11. Will I be able to find good homes for all the pups and be prepared to take them back if necessary? Good Cavapoo breeders do not let their precious puppies go to any old home. They almost always have a waiting list before the litter is born.

UK breeder Charlotte Purkiss, of Lotties Cavapoos, Hampshire, added: "With the Cavapoo mix, breeding is a complex field and there are so many things to think about. It needs a lot of research and time spent planning ahead; it's not just a quick thought of mating two dogs as soon as possible.

"In my opinion, breeding is best left to professionals who have extensive knowledge of the breed, i.e. the parents' family trees and ancestors' DNA history. On the Cavalier side, there is the annual report from the cardiologist, plus the eye specialist too.

"I also think that every breeder should have a valid canine first aid certificate, as you need to know how to resuscitate a puppy if it's not breathing at birth and what to do if any complications occur with mum or puppies before they leave you."

Pictured is Charlotte's Cavapoo mother Rosella with one of her F1b puppies

"In the UK, you have to declare **any money** you receive from the sale of a litter with HMRC, which means you're a business - even if you want to breed just once. Also, puppy and health contracts need to be written and issued to the new puppy parents stating how you intend to support the puppies in the early days of settling and then for the rest of their lives. This is a big commitment and you have to be confident of your breeding programme.

"In the UK, strict new laws came into place at the end of 2018, including: 'A breeding licence will be required for anyone breeding three or more litters and **selling at least one puppy in a 12-month period**,' and 'Anyone in the business of selling dogs (even one or two litters in a 12 month period) may require a licence'. You have to check with your local council to see if you need a licence, as it varies, depending on where you live.

"A professional breeder will search and have made sure all of the above is in place before mating and have copies of everything to give to the puppy's new owner.

"Once the homework and careful planning have been done, now ask yourself if you have the dedicated time 24/7 to look after mum and puppies. This means you cannot leave them to pop out unless someone else is canine first aid-trained to replace you, as myself and my husband are. When we have a litter, we share the care, so they are never left alone - and we even take turns on night shifts to be downstairs on the sofa."

··

You may have the most wonderful Cavapoo in the world, but don't enter the world of canine breeding without the motivation and knowledge. Don't do it for the money or the cute factor – or to show the kids 'The Miracle of Birth!' Breeding poor examples only brings heartache in the long run when health or temperament issues develop.

Having said all of that, good breeders are made, not born. Like any expert, they learn over time. If you're serious, spend time researching Cavaliers, Poodles and Cavapoos and their genetics and make sure you are going into it for the right reasons and not just for the money - ask yourself how you intend to improve the Cavapoo.

One useful resource is **Book of the Bitch** by J. M. Evans and Kay White. Another good way of learning more about breeding is to find a mentor, someone who is already successfully breeding. By 'successful' we mean somebody who is producing healthy, handsome Cavapoos with good temperaments, not someone who is making lots of money from churning out puppies.

While there is no universal Cavapoo club, there are some reputable organisations covering popular crossbreeds. In the USA there is GANA, the Goldendoodle Association of North America www.goldendoodleassociation.com and in the UK there is The Cockapoo Owners Club www.cockapooowners-club.org.uk - both of which have a Code of Ethics on their websites; good breeders meet these standards. But before you take a look, read *Why NOT To Breed* by the Doodle Trust at www.doodletrust.com/education/why-not-to-breed

Committed Cavapoo breeders aren't in it for the cash. They use their skills and knowledge to produce healthy, attractive, structurally sound pups with good temperaments that ultimately improve this crossbreed.

15. Cavapoo Rescue

Not everybody who is thinking of getting a Cavapoo gets one as a puppy from a breeder. Some people prefer to adopt a dog from a rescue organisation. What could be kinder and more rewarding than giving a poor, abandoned dog a happy and loving home for the rest of his or her life?

Not much really; adoption saves lives and gives unfortunate dogs a second chance of happiness. The problem of homeless dogs is truly depressing. It's a big issue in Britain, but even worse in the US, where the sheer numbers in kill shelters are hard to comprehend. Randy Grim states in "Don't Dump The Dog" that 1,000 dogs are being put to sleep every hour in the US.

According to Jo-Anne Cousins, Executive Director at IDOG Rescue, who has spent many years involved in US canine rescue, the situations leading to a dog ending up in rescue can often be summed up in one phrase: "Unrealistic expectations."

Jo-Anne said: "In many situations, dog ownership was something that the family went into without fully understanding the time, money and commitment to exercise and training that it takes to raise a dog. While they may have spent hours on the internet pouring over cute puppy photos, they probably didn't read any puppy training books or look into actual costs of regular vet care, training and boarding."

That lack of thought was highlighted in a story that appeared in the Press in my Yorkshire home town. A woman went shopping on Christmas Eve in a local retail centre. She returned home £700 ($910) poorer with a puppy she had bought on impulse. The pup was in a rescue centre two days later.

Common reasons for a dog being put into rescue include:

* A change in family circumstance, such as divorce or a new baby
* A change in work patterns
* Moving home
* An elderly owner has died or moved to a care home
* The dog develops health issues

Often, the "unrealistic expectations" come home to roost and the dog is given up because:

* He has too much energy, needs too much exercise, knocks the kids over and/or jumps on people - young dogs are often boisterous and sometimes lack co-ordination
* He is growling and/or nipping. All puppies bite, it is their way of exploring the world; they have to be trained not to bite the things (such as humans) that they are not supposed to bite
* He needs a lot more exercise/grooming/attention than the owner is able or prepared to give. Cavapoos are "Velcro" dogs and require a lot of attention from the owner

❖ He chews or eats things he shouldn't

❖ He makes a mess in the house - housetraining requires time and patience from the owner

❖ He costs too much to keep - the cost of feeding, vets' bills, grooming (unless you do it yourself), etc. are not insignificant

There is, however, a ray of sunshine for some of these dogs. Every year many thousands of people in the UK, North America and countries all around the world adopt a rescue dog and the story often has a happy ending.

··

The Dog's Point of View...

If you are serious about adoption, then you should do so with the right motives and with your eyes wide open. If you're expecting a perfect dog, you could be in for a shock. Rescue dogs can and do become wonderful companions, but a lot of it depends on you.

Cavapoos are sensitive, people-loving dogs. Sometimes those that have ended up in rescue centres are traumatised. Some may have health or behaviour problems. They don't understand why they have been abandoned, neglected or badly treated by their beloved owners and may arrive at your home with 'baggage' of their own until they adjust to being part of a loving family again. This may take time.

Time and patience are the keys to help the dog to adjust to his or her new surroundings and family and to learn to love and trust again. Ask yourself a few questions before you take the plunge and fill in the adoption forms:

❖ Are you prepared to accept and deal with any problems - such as bad behaviour, chewing, timidity, aggression, jumping up or peeing/pooing in the house - which a rescue dog may initially display when arriving in your home?

❖ How much time are you willing to spend with your new dog to help him or her integrate back into normal family life?

❖ Can you take time off work to be at home and help the dog settle in at the beginning?

❖ Are you prepared to take on a new addition to your family that may live for another decade?

❖ Are you prepared to stick with the dog even if he or she develops health issues later?

Think about the implications before rescuing a dog - try and look at it from the dog's point of view...What could be worse for the unlucky dog than to be abandoned again if things don't work out between you?

Other Considerations

Cavapoos that have been badly treated or have had difficult lives need plenty of time to rehabilitate. Some may have initial problems with potty training, others may need socialisation with people and/or other dogs. And if you are serious about adoption, you may have to wait a while until a suitable dog comes up.

In the UK, the Doodle Trust rescues and rehome Doodles – i.e. Labradoodles, Goldendoodles, Cockapoos, Cavapoos and other Poodle crosses. They have a long list of "Things to Consider BEFORE Getting a Doodle," including:

❖ If you are just not a Poodle person, DON'T GET A DOODLE. All doodles have Poodle in them and if the word Poodle makes you cringe, then do not get a Doodle

- If you are allergic to dogs, DON'T GET A DOODLE. Doodles go through coat changes and even if you are not allergic to your Doodle's puppy coat, you may be allergic to his adult coat. Doodles are often deemed hypoallergenic by the media, but for most, this is not the case

- If you want a clean dog, DON'T GET A DOODLE. Many doodles love water, mud and rolling in smelly things. Their coats can be like Velcro and will collect twigs, dirt, burrs, leaves etc.

- If you want a low-energy dog, DON'T GET A DOODLE. Most Doodles require at least 30-60 minutes of real exercise a day. Simply letting your Doodle out in the backyard is not exercise. There are plenty of low-energy dog breeds that would be a better fit if you aren't overly active

- If you can't devote time and money into training, DON'T GET A DOODLE. Doodles are intelligent and want to please you, but they are not born with manners

- If you want an independent dog, DON'T GET A DOODLE. Doodles thrive on human companionship and most are Velcro dogs. They need your attention and will demand it

- If you want the perfect dog, DON'T GET A DOODLE. There is no such thing as a perfect dog, and just like other breeds, Doodles can have a wide variety of temperaments and health issues

- If you want a low-maintenance dog, DON'T GET A DOODLE. The look that attracts so many would-be Doodle owners requires a lot of time and money; there is major grooming involved

- If you want a dog 'for the kids', DON'T GET A DOODLE. Doodles need lots of time on a daily basis, keeping their minds stimulated and reinforcing their behaviours. Kids won't keep that commitment

To combat some unrealistic expectations, The Doodle Trust adds a more realistic version of events: "Doodles are lively, enthusiastic and sometimes boisterous dogs that require a lot of time and attention. If you are out at work for much of the time or lead a busy life, a Doodle is NOT the right breed for you. These are people dogs and they demand human companionship, they thrive as a much-loved family member. If left to their own devices for long periods, they will find their own amusement and could become destructive.

"Most Doodles love water and can be mud magnets, bringing in an enormous amount of dirt into your home. They are certainly not a breed for the house-proud. Some coat types require grooming on a daily basis in order to keep them matt-free, whilst Doodles with a shorter coat will require less brushing. Many Doodles also need professional grooming on a regular basis in order to keep the coat manageable and this can be expensive. You should therefore consider grooming costs on top of food, insurance, toys, vaccinations, worming, etc. It all mounts up!

"Doodles are not necessarily compatible with small children and, in any case, it is unwise to leave any dog with small children. When considering a rescue Doodle, please also give some thought as to how this may affect any other pets you might own. Some cats for example may not take kindly to a big bouncy dog, and if you already own another dog, how will the new addition impact on them?

"Most Doodles coming into rescue are large boys so there may be a considerable waiting period before we can match you with the right dog. Waiting times are further increased if you specify a certain colour and coat type and our dogs will always be matched to families by their suitability, rather than looks."

Adopting a rescue dog is a big commitment for all involved. It is not a cheap way of getting a Cavapoo and shouldn't be viewed as such. It could cost you several hundred pounds - or dollars. You'll have adoption fees to pay and often vaccination and veterinary bills as well as worm and flea medication and spaying or neutering. Make sure you're aware of the full cost before committing.

One way of finding out if you, your family and home are suitable is to volunteer to become a foster home for one of the rescue centres. Fosters offer temporary homes until a forever home becomes available. It's a shorter-term arrangement, but still requires commitment and patience.

Despite the fact that so many dogs need rehoming, it's not just the dogs that are screened - you'll also have to be vetted too. You might even have to provide references. Rescue groups and shelters have to make sure that prospective adopters are suitable and they have thought through everything very carefully before making such a big decision.

They also want to match you with the right dog - putting a young Cavapoo with an elderly couple might not be the perfect match, for example. Or putting any Cavapoo with somebody who is out at work all day would also be unsuitable. Most rescue groups will ask a raft of personal questions - some of which may seem intrusive. If you are serious about adopting, you will have to answer them. Here are some of the details required on a typical adoption form:

* Name, address and details, including ages, of all people living in your home
* Extensive details of any other pets
* Your work hours and amount of time you spend away from the home each day
* Type of property you live in
* Size of your garden (if you have one) and height of the fence around it
* Whether you have any previous experience with dogs
* Your reasons for wanting to adopt a Cavapoo
* If you have ever previously given up a dog for adoption
* Whether you have any experience dealing with canine behaviour or health issues
* Details of your vet
* If you are prepared for destructive behaviour/chewing/fear/aggression/timidity/soiling inside the house/medical issues
* Whether you agree to insure your dog
* Whether you are prepared for the financial costs of dog ownership
* Whether you are willing to housetrain and obedience train the dog
* Your views on dog training methods classes
* Where your dog will sleep at night

After you've filled in the adoption form, a chat with a representative from the charity usually follows. There will also be an inspection visit to your home - and your vet may even be vetted! If you work away from the home, it is useful to know that as a general rule of thumb, UK rescue organisations will not place dogs in homes where they will be left alone for more than about four hours at a time. If all goes well, you will be approved to adopt and it's then just a question of waiting for the right match to come along. When he or she does, a meeting will be arranged with the dog for all family members. You will then pay the adoption fee and become the proud new owner of a Cavapoo. It might seem like a lot of red tape, but the rescue groups have to be as sure as they can that you will provide a loving, forever home for the unfortunate dog. It would be terrible if the dog had to be placed back in rescue again.

All rescue organisations will neuter the dog or, if he or she is too young, specify in the adoption contract that the dog must be neutered and may not be used for breeding. Many rescue organisations have a lifetime rescue back-up policy, which means that if things don't work out, the dog must be returned to them.

....

Rebecca and Max

One person who has rescued a dog through the Doodle Trust is experienced dog owner Rebecca Seabrook, who adopted nine-month-old Cavapoo Max, *pictured,* a year ago. As is not uncommon with rescue dogs, Max arrived with issues.

Rebecca is patiently working with him and professionals to help Max overcome his anxieties. It would have been far less complicated for her to have bought a puppy from a breeder instead. But, like many people, Rebecca wanted to give an unfortunate dog the chance of a new life - and now she wouldn't swap Max for the world.

Rebecca says: "After having to have our Bichon Frise put to sleep, we were looking for a new addition to the family and another mate for our other dog, Amble, who was grieving. We wanted a rescue dog and were introduced to Billie, a Cockapoo, who came to see us as we board dogs, and Dad and I both said we would like one like her...

"We filled out a Doodle Trust form and they got straight back to say they had the perfect dog for us, a nine-month-old Cavapoo who was being fostered and needed a forever home. The lady who was fostering Max sent us photos and lots of messages, keeping us up to date on him as he was neutered. We arranged to go and see him about a week later and by this time our house-check had been done. When we met Max, we fell in love with him and Amble liked him, so we brought him home.

"Max is such a loving dog and has a great temperament around the house, but because he was kept in a house for his first nine months without being taken out and socialised with other dogs, animals or people, he has issues. When he goes out and meets other dogs, or a car goes by, or sometimes a human, he can turn extremely aggressive. Most of it is fear and he gets himself so worked up, he doesn't know what to do so gets angry.

"We first went to the vet when he started biting us when he got into his rages on walks. They referred us to a neurologist to have him checked to make sure it was not a medical problem, and this was all ruled out. They then referred us to a specialist Veterinary Behaviourist in Lincoln, as it is felt that he is suffering from a dog version of agoraphobia, and we are currently waiting to see him.

"Max was mostly housetrained when he arrived; he had a few accidents but that is because we had not picked up the signs for when he wanted to go out. He is great with other dogs who come into the house and can be very caring, and he is very easy to train as is motivated by treats. We have taken him to one-on-one training.

"While we are waiting to see the behaviour specialist, we have stopped taking Max out for walks, but have increased taking him out in the car and into social situations, where he is getting much better. We even tried taking him into the nursing home to see my Gran and he was so gentle and calm it was amazing. It has surprised us how loving he is.

"We will keep on working with Max until he no longer has his insecurity issues. He has settled into our family life so well and Amble and Max are now the best of friends and spend a lot of time playing together. Max has healed Amble and brought laughter back into our house. So thank you Max and thank you Doodle Trust."

Rescue Organisations

There are only a few rescue groups specialising in Poodle crosses. In the UK, there is **The Doodle Trust** at www.doodletrust.com and Many Tears Rescue sometimes has Cavapoos www.manytearsrescue.org There are also online Cavapoo forums where people sometimes post information about a dog that needs a new home, e.g. www.facebook.com/Cavapooclub

In the USA there is **Oodles of Doodles** at http://www.doodlerescuecollective.com and **The Doodle Rescue Collective** at http://doodlerescueinc.ning.com There are general websites, such as www.petfinder.com, www.aspca.org/adopt-pet and www.adoptapet.com

You can also go to Facebook and type "CAVAPOO" into the search bar and details of Cavapoo Facebook groups will appear.

If you visit these websites and social media pages, you cannot presume that the descriptions are 100% accurate. They are given in good faith, but ideas of what constitutes a 'lively' dog may vary. Some Cavapoos advertised may have other breeds in their genetic make-up. It does not mean that these are necessarily worse dogs, but if you are attracted to the Cavapoo for its temperament and appearance, make sure you are looking at a Cavapoo.

DON'T get a dog from eBay, Craig's List, Gumtree or any of the other general advertising websites that sell golf clubs, jewellery, old cars, washing machines, etc.

If you can't spare the time to adopt - and adoption means forever - you might want to consider other ways of helping. You can become a foster home, a home checker or a fundraiser, you can help with transport or donate money. Many canine rescues have online shops with all profits going back into the charity. However you decide to get involved, **Good Luck!**

If you haven't been put off with all of the above...
Congratulations, you may be just the family or person that poor homeless Cavapoo is looking for!

Saving one dog will not change the world,
But it will change the world for one dog.

16. Caring for Senior Cavapoos

If your Cavapoo has been well looked after and had no serious illnesses, he or she could live for as long as 15 years. Lifespan is influenced by genetics and also by owners; how you feed, exercise and generally look after your dog will all have an impact on his or her life.

Although the Cavalier/Poodle is a relatively new cross and there are not lots of elderly Cavapoos around yet, initial feedback is that they can stay relatively fit and youthful right into their senior years.

Approaching Old Age

However fit your ageing Cavapoo is, at some point, he or she will start to feel the effects of ageing. After having got up at the crack of dawn when your dog was a puppy, you may find that they now like to sleep in longer in the morning. They may be less keen to go out in the rain and snow.

Physically, joints will probably become stiffer and organs - such as heart, liver and kidneys - may not function as effectively. And on the mental side - just as with humans - your dog's memory, ability to learn and awareness will start to dim.

Your faithful companion might become a bit stubborn, grumpier or a little less tolerant of lively dogs and children. She may start waking up or wandering about the house in the middle of the night, taking forever to sniff a blade of grass, or seeking out your company more often. She might even have the odd "accident" inside the house. *Our photo shows a nine-year-old Cavapoo*

You may also notice that she doesn't see or hear as well as she used to. On the other hand, your old friend might not be hard of hearing at all. She might have developed that affliction common to many older dogs - ours included - of "selective hearing." Our 12-year-old Max had bionic hearing when it came to the word "Biscuit" whispered from 20 yards, yet was strangely unable to hear the commands "Stay" or "Here" when we were right in front of him!

You can help ease your mature dog gracefully into old age by keeping an eye on him or her, noticing the changes and taking action to help as much as possible. This might involve a visit to the vet for supplements and/or medications, modifying your dog's environment, changing his or her diet and slowly reducing the amount of daily exercise.

Much depends on the individual dog. Just as with humans, a Cavapoo of ideal weight that has been physically and mentally active all of her life is likely to age slower than an overweight, under-stimulated couch potato.

Keeping some older dogs at that optimum weight can be challenging as they age, especially if they are greedy. Some become more food-orientated, even though they are getting less exercise. Also, their metabolisms slow down, making it easier to put on the pounds unless their daily calories are reduced. At the same time, extra weight places additional, unwanted stress on joints and organs, making them have to work harder than they should.

We normally talk about dogs being old when they reach the last third of their lives. This varies greatly from dog to dog and bloodline to bloodline. Some Cavapoos may remain active with little signs of ageing until the day they die, others may start to show signs of ageing at seven or eight years old. A dog is classed as a 'Veteran' at seven years old in the show ring.

Physical and Mental Signs of Ageing

If your Cavapoo is in or approaching the last third of her life, here are some signs that her body is feeling its age:

❧ She has generally slowed down and no longer seems as keen to go out on her walks – or if she does want to go, she doesn't want to go as far. She is happy pottering and sniffing - and often takes forever to inspect a single clump of grass! Some are less keen to go outside in bad weather

❧ She gets up from lying down more slowly and goes up and down stairs more slowly. She can no longer jump on to the couch or bed. These are all signs that joints are stiffening, often due to arthritis

❧ Grey hairs are appearing, particularly around the muzzle (it's harder to tell on dogs with lighter coats)

❧ She has put on a bit of weight

❧ She may have the occasional "accident" (incontinence) inside the house

❧ She urinates more frequently

❧ She drinks more water

❧ She has bouts of constipation or diarrhoea

❧ The foot pads thicken and nails may become more brittle

❧ One or more lumps or fatty deposits (lipomas) develop on the body. Our dog developed two small bumps on top of his head aged 10 and we took him straight to the vet, who performed minor surgery to remove them. They were benign (harmless), but always get them checked out ASAP in case they are an early form of cancer - they can also grow quite rapidly, even if benign They often appear on the chest, flanks or armpit

❧ She can't regulate body temperature as she used to and so feels the cold and heat more

❧ Hearing deteriorates

❧ Eyesight may also deteriorate – if her eyes appear cloudy she may be developing cataracts, so see your vet as soon as you notice the signs. Just as with humans, most older dogs live quite well with failing eyesight

❧ Your dog has bad breath (halitosis), which could be a sign of dental or gum disease. Brush the teeth regularly and if the bad breath persists, get her checked out by a vet

❧ If inactive she may develop callouses on the elbows, especially if she lies on hard surfaces – this is more common with large dogs than small ones

It's not just your dog's body that deteriorates; her mind does too. It's often part of the normal ageing process. Your dog may display some, all or none of these signs of *Canine Cognitive Dysfunction:*

* Sleep patterns change; an older dog may be more restless at night and sleepy during the day. He may start wandering around the house at odd times, causing you sleepless nights

* She barks more, sometimes at nothing or open spaces

* She stares at objects, such as walls *(like the Cavalier in this photo)*, or wanders aimlessly around the house or garden

* Your dog shows increased anxiety, separation anxiety or aggression; although aggression is not common in older Cavapoos

* She forgets or ignores commands or habits she once knew well, such as the recall and sometimes toilet training

* Some dogs may become more clingy and dependent, often resulting in separation anxiety. She may seek reassurance that you are near as faculties fade and she becomes a bit less confident and independent. Others may become a bit disengaged and less interested in human contact

Understanding the changes happening to your dog and acting on them compassionately and effectively will help ease your dog's passage through his or her senior years. Your dog has given you so much pleasure over the years, now he or she needs you to give that bit of extra care for a happy, healthy old age. You can also help your Cavapoo to stay mentally active by playing gentle games and getting new toys to stimulate interest.

Helping Your Dog Age Gracefully

There are many things you can do to ease your dog's passage into his declining years.

As dogs age they need fewer calories and less protein, so many owners switch to a food specially formulated for older dogs. These are labelled *Senior, Ageing* or *Mature.* Check the labelling; some

are specifically for dogs aged over eight, others may be for 10 or 12-year-olds. If you are not sure if a senior diet is necessary for your Cavapoo, talk to your vet the next time you are there. Remember, if you do change brand, switch the food gradually over a week or so. Unlike with humans, a dog's digestive system cannot cope with sudden changes of diet.

UK breeder Charlotte Purkiss says: "Old age shows when your Cavapoo starts to slow down but it's a very gradual process and this may not be until around 10 years old if a senior diet has been given since around seven years old. But every dog is different and I'm basing this on a fully healthy problem-free Cavapoo, which is why purchasing a health-tested Cavapoo puppy is a wise choice.

"I strongly advise that an older Cavapoo should have a specific diet to meet the needs of his/her changing body. Cavapoos can be prone to putting on weight in the senior years. Always feed a high end diet and be careful of giving too many treats. I suggest feeding a quality, low fat Senior food, which will include more vitamins and omega oils and less calories than an Adult feed, and the nutritional balance will be right too. Supplements aren't particularly necessary if you are feeding a high end diet as this should be sufficient and any supplements could be a potential overload."

Years of eating the same food, coupled with less sensitive taste buds can result in some dogs going off their food as they age. If you feed a dry food, try mixing a bit of gravy with it; this has worked well for us, as has feeding two different feeds: a morning one of kibble with gravy and the second tea-time feed of home-cooked rice and fish or chicken. Rice, white fish and chicken − all cooked − can be particularly good if your old dog has a sensitive stomach.

If you are considering a daily supplement, Omega-3 fatty acids are good for the brain and coat and glucosamine and various other supplements are available to help joints. Our dog gets a squirt of Yumega Omega 3 and half a small scoop of Joint Aid in one of his daily feeds.

We had one dog that became very sensitive to loud noises as he got older and the lead up to Bonfire Night was a nightmare. (This is November 5th in the UK, a cause for celebration, but a worry if you have animals as there are countless firework displays and loud bangs). Some dogs also become more stressed by trips to the groomer's as they get older. There are medications and homeopathic remedies, such as melatonin which has natural sedative properties, to help relieve such anxieties. Check with your vet before introducing any new medicines.

One of the most important things you can do for your Cavapoo is regular tooth brushing throughout his life. Cavapoos can be prone to tooth and gum decay. Not only is toothache painful and unpleasant, it can be traumatic for dogs to have teeth removed under anaesthetic or when they start to lose weight due to being unable to eat properly.

If your old friend has started to ignore your verbal commands when out on a walk − either through 'switching off' or deafness - you can try a whistle to attract his or her attention and then use an exaggerated hand signal for the recall. Once your dog is looking at you, hold your arm out, palm down, at 90 degrees to your body and bring it down, keeping your arm straight, until your fingers point to your toes.

This worked very effectively with our Max. He looked, understood and then decided if he was going to come or not - but at least he knew what he should be doing! More often than not he did come back, especially if the arm signal was repeated while he was still making up his mind.

Weight - no matter how old your Cavapoo is, he still needs a waist! Maintaining a healthy weight with a balanced diet and regular, gentler exercise are two of the most important things you can do for your dog.

Environment - Make sure your dog has a nice soft place to rest his old bones, which may mean adding an extra blanket to his bed. This should be in a place that is not too hot or cold, as he may not be able to regulate his body temperature as well as when he was younger. He needs plenty of undisturbed sleep and should not be pestered and/or bullied by younger dogs, other animals or young children. If his eyesight is failing, move obstacles out of his way, and/or use pet barriers to reduce the chance of injuries.

Jumping on and off furniture or in or out of the car is high impact for his old joints and bones. He will need a helping hand on to and off the couch or your bed, if he's allowed up there, or even a little ramp to get in and out of the car. We bought an expensive plastic ramp for one old dog as she became hesitant to jump in or out of the car. However, this proved to be a complete waste of money, as she didn't like the feel of the non-slip surface on her paws and after a couple of tentative attempts, steadfastly refused to set a paw on it. We ended up lifting the dog in and out of the car and donating the ramp to a canine charity!

Exercise - Take the lead from your dog, if he doesn't want to walk as far, then don't. But if your dog doesn't want to go out at all, you will have to coax him out. ALL old dogs need exercise, not only to keep their joints moving, but also to keep their heart, lungs and joints exercised and to help keep their minds engaged with different places, scents, etc.

Charlotte added: "Ear problems occur in older Cavapoos if a grooming regime has not been kept up throughout its entire life starting as a puppy. Cavapoos need to see a groomer regularly to keep on top of all the little things - and ears is a crucial one. Some can become deaf due to recurrent ear infections over time.

"As well as visits to the groomer's, owners can help by using (cooled down) boiled water with a clean cotton pad to gently wipe the ear of any debris that is visible. This is especially important when your Cavapoo reaches its senior years, as they seem to produce more debris in this area."

Time to Get Checked Out

If your dog is showing any of these signs, get him to the vet for a full check over:

- Excessive increased urination or drinking can be a sign of something amiss, such as reduced liver or kidney function, Cushing's disease or diabetes

- Constipation or not urinating regularly could be a sign of something not functioning properly with the digestive system or organs

- Incontinence, which could be a sign of a mental or physical problem

- Cloudy eyes, which could be cataracts

- Decreased appetite – often one of the first signs of an underlying problem

- Lumps or bumps on the body - often benign, but can occasionally be malignant (cancerous)

- Excessive sleeping or a lack of interest in you and his or her surroundings

- Diarrhoea or vomiting

- A darkening and dryness of skin that never seems to get any better - this can be a sign of hypothyroidism

- Any other out-of-the-ordinary behaviour for your dog. A change in patterns or behaviour is often your dog's way of telling you that all is not well

The Last Lap

Huge advances in veterinary science have meant that there are countless procedures and medications that can prolong the life of your dog, and this is a good thing. But there comes a time when you do have to let go.

If your dog is showing all the signs of ageing, has an ongoing medical condition from which he or she cannot recover, is showing signs of pain, mental anxiety or distress and there is no hope of improvement, then the dreaded time has come to say goodbye. You owe it to him or her.

There is no point keeping an old dog alive if all the dog has ahead is pain and death. We have their lives in our hands and we can give them the gift of passing away peacefully and humanely at the end when the time is right.

Losing our beloved companion, our best friend, a member of the family, is truly heart-breaking. But one of the things we realise at the back of our minds when we got that gorgeous, lively little puppy that bounded up to meet us like we were the best person in the whole wide world is the pain that comes with it. We know that we will live longer than them and that we'll probably have to make this most painful of decisions at some time in the future.

It's the worst thing about being a dog owner.

If your Cavapoo has had a long and happy life, then you could not have done any more. You were a great owner and your dog was lucky to have you. Remember all the good times you had together. And try not to rush out and buy another dog straight away; wait a while to grieve for your Cavapoo.

Assess your current life and lifestyle and, if your situation is right, only then consider getting another dog and all that that entails in terms of time, commitment and expense.

A Cavapoo coming into a happy, stable household will get off to a better start in life than a dog entering a home full of grief.

Whatever you decide to do, put the dog first.

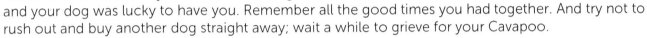

List of Contributors

Laura Koch, of Petit Jean Puppies, Arkansas, USA www.petitjeanpuppies.com

Charlotte Purkiss, of Lotties Cavapoos, Hampshire, UK www.lottiescavapoos.co.uk

Brent and Windie, of Calla Lily Cavapoo, Oklahoma, USA www.callalilycavapoo.com

Dr Sara Skiwski, holistic vet and proprietor, The Western Dragon Integrated Veterinary Solutions, California, USA www.thewesterndragon.com

Pets As Therapy (UK) https://petsastherapy.org

The Doodle Trust (UK) www.doodletrust.com

Val Boshart, Trevor and Tracey Nott, Rebecca Seabrook, Lindsey McDonald and Alex Kostiw, Kit Lam, Karen Rowe, June Hicks, Hilary Morphy, Gina Desmond, Denise Knightley, Dayna Rosindale, Claire Cornes, Beverley Burlison, and Laura Lambert, founder of All About Poos Facebook Group.

....

Useful Contacts

Association of Pet Dog Trainers USA - www.apdt.com

Association of Pet Dog Trainers UK - www.apdt.co.uk

Dog foods - Useful information on grain-free and hypoallergenic food: www.dogfoodadvisor.com UK dog food advice: www.allaboutdogfood.co.uk

Help finding **lost or stolen dogs,** register your dog's microchip (USA) - www.akcreunite.org

Checking the health of a puppy's parents or a mate (USA) - www.k9data.com

Internet forums and **Facebook groups** are a good source of information from other owners, including: www.thecavapooclub.co.uk

Facebook Groups: Cavapoos www.facebook.com/Cavapoos-146786258690741

All About Poos www.facebook.com/groups/342817333136642

Disclaimer

This book has been written to provide helpful information on Cavapoos. It is not meant to be used, nor should it be used, to diagnose or treat any medical condition. For diagnosis or treatment of any animal medical problem, consult a qualified veterinarian.

The author is not responsible for any specific health or allergy conditions that may require medical supervision and is not liable for any damages or negative consequences from any treatment, action, application or preparation, to any animal or to any person reading or following the information in this book.

The views expressed by contributors to this book are solely personal and do not necessarily represent those of the author. References are provided for informational purposes only and do not constitute endorsement of any websites or other sources.

Author's Notes:

I have alternated between the masculine pronoun 'he' and feminine pronoun 'she' in an effort to make this book as relevant as possible for all new and prospective owners.

The Cavapoo Handbook uses UK English, except where Americans have been quoted, when the original US English has been preserved.

Printed in Great Britain
by Amazon

81541935R00147